SOCIAL APPLICATIONS AND ISSUES IN PSYCHOLOGY

Proceedings of the XXIV International Congress of Psychology
of the
International Union of Psychological Science (I.U.Psy.S.)
Sydney, Australia, August 28–September 2, 1988

Selected/Revised Papers

Volume 8
(For further volumes see back of the cover)

Published for the
International Union of Psychological Science (I.U.Psy.S.)

Social Applications and Issues in Psychology

Edited by

Ronald C. KING

Department of Learning Studies
Wollongong University
Australia

and

John K. COLLINS

School of Behavioural Sciences
Macquarie University
Australia

1989

NORTH-HOLLAND
AMSTERDAM · NEW YORK · OXFORD · TOKYO

NORTH-HOLLAND
ELSEVIER SCIENCE PUBLISHERS B.V.
Sara Burgerhartstraat 25
P.O. Box 211, 1000 AE Amsterdam, The Netherlands

Distributors for the United States and Canada:
ELSEVIER SCIENCE PUBLISHING COMPANY INC.
655 Avenue of the Americas

```
         Library of Congress Cataloging-in-Publication Data
International Congress of Psychology (24th : 1988 : Sydney, N.S.W.)
   Social applications and issues in psychology / edited by Ronald C.
King and John K. Collins.
      p.   cm. -- (Proceedings of the XXIV International Congress of
Psychology of the International Union of Psychological Science
(I.U.Psy.C.), Sydney, Australia, August 28-September 2, 1988 ; v. 8)
   "Published for the International Union of Psychological Science
(I.U.Psy.S)"--Ser. t.p.
   "Australian Psychological Society (A.P.S.)"--Cover.
   Includes bibliographical references.
   ISBN 0-444-88526-9 (U.S.)
   1. Psychology, Applied--Congresses.  2. Psychology--Social
aspects--Congresses.   I. King, Ronald C.  II. Collins, John K.
III. International Union of Psychological Science.  IV. Australian
Psychological Society.  V. Title.  VI. Series: International
Congress of Psychology (24th : 1988 : Sydney, N.S.W.).  Proceedings
of the XXIV International Congress of Psychology of the
International Union of Psychological Science (I.U.Psy.S.), Sydney,
Australia, August 28-September 2, 1988 ; v. 8.
BF20.I614  1988 vol. 8
[BF636]
150 s--dc20
[158]                                                       89-25514
                                                               CIP
```

ISBN: 0 444 88526 9
ISBN set: 0 444 88509 9

Printed in The Netherlands

FOREWORD

The XXIV International Congress of Psychology was held in Sydney, Australia in August/September 1988, as an official activity of Australia's Bicentennial Year.

In undertaking the task of organising the Congress on behalf of the International Union of Psychological Science (I.U.Psy.S.), the Australian Psychological Society (A.P.S.) was acutely aware of the responsibilities it was assuming. In particular, the Society recognised that to be judged a success, the Congress must serve as a milestone in the development of psychology as a discipline, and in the recognition of the I.U.Psy.S. as the international body of psychology.

The response of the international community of psychologists to the invitation to participate in the scientific program was most gratifying. In all, the program included a total of 2,500 individual and symposium contributions covering all the major areas of psychology. Authors from over 50 countries contributed.

The present volume of Proceedings is one of nine volumes containing selections of written versions of Congress presentations. The task of selecting papers to appear in the Proceedings was an unenviable one, as it was impossible to include all worthy papers. The principal selection criterion was quality, i.e., judged contribution to the body of scientific psychological knowledge.

Secondary, but important, criteria were balance and represent-ativeness. We sought to achieve both a reasonable balance across the major areas of psychology, and adequate representation of authors from the various participating countries.

An important decision taken by the Editorial Committee was to ask Volume Editors to provide laser printed copies of their volumes. In order to achieve this goal, Volume Editors requested authors to submit their papers on disk. If authors were unable to accede to this request, it was necessary for Volume Editors to key the papers into a word-processor.

Given the present state of the art of desk top publishing, Volume Editors were required to expend enormous effort and overcome countless technical problems. We trust the final form of the volumes is sufficient recompense for their efforts.

In each of the centres where the work of compiling the volumes was undertaken, the required facilities were made available, and unpaid work on a grand scale was undertaken.

We wish to record our grateful thanks to the Psychology Departments in the following universities: University of Adelaide, Flinders University, La Trobe University, University of Newcastle, Macquarie University, University of Melbourne (Institute of Education), University of New South Wales, and Wollongong University Department of Learning Studies. It is impossible to thank individually all those persons whose contributions were crucial to the enterprise. I must, however, make one exception and record thanks to Louise Kahabka of the School of Psychology, University of New South Wales.

S. H. Lovibond
Sydney, 1989

PREFACE

This volume on social applications and issues in psychology is intended to provide a snapshot of the current contributions of psychologists to matters of public importance. By its very nature, such a volume ranges over much more territory than any of the other volumes in the series. The section headings should be taken only as a guide because many of the papers cross boundaries.

The common element in all of the papers is that they serve as indicators of the kinds of contribution that psychologists can make in areas where public policy decisions are at stake. In some cases, for example Lipsitt et al., the work is highly specific. In others, for example Sedgwick, a broad ethical issue is tackled at the level of policy and the law.

Many of the papers suggest the opening up of relatively new fields for psychologists. Syme and Williams on water policy and Pieters on cost conceptions in economic behaviour may offer surprises for some readers who have not yet become used to psychologists making serious (or any) contributions in these areas. Less surprising will be the contributions, increasingly well-organised and more frequent, about environmental matters and the human condition. Larsen et al., Rigby et al., Ardila and Bretherton are representative of a growing movement among psychologists whose passionate concerns about the future of the planet and the equitable treatment of its people are more and more reflected in their day-to-day scientific and professional work.

In the papers that refer to humans and computer technology and to television as a medium of persuasion, the issues *per se* may not be surprising in any collective sense. What is especially interesting, however, is that each represents a very different way of creating a window for helping us to examine our relationship with the technologies that we utilise or have thrust upon us. Underwood, Jackson et al., Kunkel and Ida can be seen as tackling different features of what is essentially this same overarching issue.

The delivery of health services at the level of systems and at the personal level is now analysed more closely in most countries than ever before. Psychologists not only contribute in the delivery processes, for example Holtzman, Duncan and Backenroth, but in tracking the effectiveness and re-development of those processes, for example Driscoll on a changing health system and Knight and Hay on quit-smoking advice from medical practitioners.

Pithers et al., on relapse prevention in sexual aggressors, Teichman, on marital violence and Knight and Hatty, on domestic violence, sharpen the focus on the continuing responsibilities that psychologists have in helping communities to deal with the more pathological behaviour of their citizens. While understanding of the causes of much of this pathological behaviour has improved in recent years, we see demonstrated in these pages the need for more rapid progress in treatment, control and rehabilitation.

Personnel studies, including those that emphasise selection processes and the determination of characteristics that will predict subsequent performance more adequately, are not new, but as the papers by Trost, Robertson and Farnill and Swartz et al. perhaps indicate, matching role requirements to individual life stages, personal attributes and the often chronic features of large human systems remains as perplexing a task as it was a generation earlier.

In collating material for this volume, 110 papers were considered. The selection eventually published here shows clearly that the concern of psychologists with social applications and issues is world-wide. Many of the papers that could not be included will be published elsewhere in many different forums in due course.

Finally, it must be said that when we conceived the notion of a volume dedicated to showing the variety, extent and level of commitment of psychological research and practice in social issues, we were taking a considerable risk. Both from the viewpoint of the volume editors and that of the series editor it seems to have been a worthwhile risk. It may be that such a volume, published every four years following the International Congress of Psychology, will serve to generate or consolidate work at those growing edges of psychology concerned with events in the public domain.

Ronald C. King
John K. Collins
Editors

An Acknowledgment

Editors rarely do their work in isolation from staff who help in word-processing, preparation of manuscripts and the myriad secretarial tasks that accompany papers gathered from around the world. Our thanks to Birgitt Baader for her contribution to this volume are profound and without qualification.

R.C.K.
J.K.C.

CONTENTS

Section 3

PEOPLE AND THE TECHNOLOGICAL ENVIRONMENT

Section 4

COMMUNITY ISSUES

Section 5

SOCIAL PATHOLOGY AND WELL-BEING

Section 1

PEOPLE AND GLOBAL ISSUES

Social Applications and Issues in Psychology
R.C. King and J.K. Collins (editors)
©Elsevier Science Publishers B.V. (North-Holland), 1989

RESEARCH ON THE PSYCHOLOGY OF PEACE:
A GLOBAL PERSPECTIVE

Ruben Ardila

National University of Colombia

Psychology has contributed to a better understanding of the problems
associated with aggression, war, peace and so forth. However, no
systematic integration has been attempted of the psychology of war and
peace. A large amount of data is available at the present time that can be
integrated into a cohesive framework. This paper presents a review of the
most recent investigations on psychology of peace, carried out in different
countries. Special emphasis is given to the cross-cultural nature of the data.
Given the importance of this topic, it is very likely that psychologists will
continue working in this area, in association with political scientists,
economists, historians, and philosophers.

The statement that humanity is facing three important perils – the destruction of
natural resources, overpopulation and nuclear war – continues to be valid. The
first two problems have received a great deal of attention and, little by little, we
have begun finding solutions for them. On the other hand, the threat of nuclear
war continues without any realistic solution.

Our times are characterized by violence and terrorism: political violence and
family violence; left-wing violence and right-wing violence; in the streets of Beirut
and in the streets of New York; violence of parents against children and of children
against parents.

Terrorism is one of the horrors of our days. It is absurd and without
justification. The majority of the victims of terrorism are persons not involved in
the struggle that the terrorists are fighting (against the government, against
capitalism, against communism, against the wealthy, against the poor, against the
Church, in favour of a given ideology, against another ideology) . The victims are
innocent people, generally common persons who have nothing to do with the
terrorists. They are the victims of the bombs, of the kidnapping, sometimes even
of the tortures. They receive the "punishment" and the cruelty without knowing
why are they being victims of the violence.

On the other hand, terrorism and violence have increased in the last few years
and do not give any signal of diminishing. The problem is becoming worse. Once
it was terrorism in the Middle East, for political and religious reasons. Then

followed terrorism in Europe because of conflicting ideologies. At the present time it exists almost universally.

Attempts to understand and to modify such a chaotic situation require the contributions from the scientific disciplines that have as their core the study of human behaviour: psychology, anthropology, economics, political science and sociology.

Psychologists have a great deal of information about violence, terrorism, aggression, war and peace because they have worked in these areas for a number of decades. We have theories, hypotheses, facts and scientific explanations. We have adequate ways to modify the behaviour of individuals and groups. An approach based on social psychology and another based on psychobiology are the main trends. As everyone knows, Freud was the first psychologist to state that war was "inevitable" because it was based on the "death instinct." Much later Lorenz, when referring to aggression, insisted that it had a biological foundation, and that it was part of human nature and of the nature of other animal species. This biological approach to aggression and violence continues having a certain importance in our time, in spite of the many arguments and facts against it.

The contrary point of view is based on social learning. Violence is learned. Aggression, terrorism and war are not inevitable, but they are consequences of frictions among groups or among individuals. We could have lasting peace, if humanity really wants it. In this sense we have the "Statement on Violence" of the Seville group, to which we will refer later on.

Social psychologists have a lot to offer in this respect. The social learning approach is very promising, much more than the psychobiological approach. Osgood (1962) was the main pioneer in this respect and his work still has great relevance. We can mention other social psychological research on stereotypes, prejudices, errors of communication and the phenomenon of the "image of the enemy". There is no doubt that wars begin in the minds of people, follow in the offices of the generals where the most effective strategies are planned and continue on the battlefields.

Our generation possesses a destructive power like no other before it. In comparison with the possibility of a nuclear war, the wars of Dario of Persia, of Alexander the Great, of Atila, even of Hitler, seems to be just children's games. We have never before had in our hands the possibility of destroying humanity as a whole, or at least all civilization, the survivors of which would be left to return to the era of the caverns.

THE INTERNATIONAL CONTEXT

Research on the problems associated with peace is an international endeavour. It is carried out in the United States, the USSR, Poland, Czechoslovakia, the U.K., France, Sweden and Third World countries. In this sense, the field of investigation goes beyond national and cultural barriers. The First Congress of European Psychologists for Peace took place in Helsinki (Finland), from August 8 to 10, 1986. That year was designated by the United Nations as the International Year of Peace.

The International Union of Psychological Science (I.U.Psy.S.) has a committee named "Psychologists for Peace and Against Nuclear War," coordinated by A. Kossakoswki, of the German Democratic Republic. It publishes a newsletter called *Psychologists for Peace.* The Interamerican Society of Psychology (SIP) has a task force on conflict resolution. It focuses on the problems of peace and is coordinated by Tana Dineen (from Canada), with the collaboration of Abelardo Brenes (Costa Rica) and Carmi Harari (USA).

The group of Seville (Spain) that published the "Statement on Violence" (1986) and the book *Essays on Violence* (Martin-Ramírez, Hinde and Groebel, 1987) includes people from many nations and many scientific disciplines. It is clear that the problems of peace and war have to be studied by persons with different ideologies, who live in different cultures and have different political viewpoints. Only in this way we can have a balanced and objective understanding of these complex problems.

Here, we are going to analyze the role that psychology plays in investigations concerning peace, the role played by the experimental analysis of behaviour, as a part of psychology and ways of educating children and youth to live in peace. We will conclude by discussing the inadequacy of the belief that war is inevitable and then present the Statement on Violence (Seville).

THE ROLE OF PSYCHOLOGY

Among the German psychologists who emigrated to the United States, Kurt Lewin was one of those most interested in peace and its problems. The Society for the Psychological Study of Social Issues (SPSSI) grants annually the Kurt Lewin Award. In 1986 it was given to M. Brewster Smith whose lecture centred on the topic of war and peace. He discussed the role of psychologists for the prevention of the nuclear holocaust. He insisted that the main contribution of psychology for the cause of peace consists in framing issues related to Soviet-American relations differently from what has become conventional: asking different questions more than drawing different conclusions based on prejudices and stereotypes.

In the Soviet Union, Shorokhova (1985) maintained that it is the psychologists' civic and professional duty to help preserve peace. She suggested that this task might be fulfilled more efficiently if psychologists unite in the form of an organization of world psychologists against nuclear war.

In the United States, Kimmel (1985), who has worked for many years on important social issues, proposed the foundation of an Institute for Peace. He stated that there are two approaches to preventing nuclear war: peace-through-strength (PTS) and peace-through-cooperation (PTC).   A curriculum was presented based on the second alternative, that tries to change the emphasis on PTS throughout current education. Supportive data were given. The idea of a USA Institute for Peace was discussed. The author maintained that psychologists can help in many ways, including real-world studies and mediation of conflicts.

In the Federal Republic of Germany, Nolting (1984) asked why there is so little research in psychology on problems of war and peace. The issues that should be investigated were presented. The difficulties and possibilities of using psychological knowledge in public political argumentation and the international work of peace groups were examined.

Czechoslovakia is one of the countries with a more complex history of war and peace. Linhart (1985) contrasted in that country the ideological and psychological struggles for peace and discussed strategies of human development. Principles of Western psychoanalysis and its "contributions" were criticized.

Hoffmann (1986) contrasted two approaches to the psychology of strategic and diplomatic behaviour. One of these was traditional and the other radical. They differed over what it is possible to accomplish in international affairs. One approach is analytic and derived from the specific logic of international politics. The other approach – the radical – is therapeutic, critical and often derived from individual psychology and pathology. The weaknesses of the radical approach were emphasized and agenda for research and action on which both groups could cooperate was suggested.

Our investigations on the psychological impact of the nuclear war threat (Ardila, 1986 a, 1986 b, 1987) indicate the way in which the threat of a nuclear war is perceived by children and youth from Colombia, from both high and low socio-economic levels. We found that the possibility of a nuclear war is a very real threat for these people, in spite of living in a country without nuclear arms.

THE EXPERIMENTAL ANALYSIS OF BEHAVIOUR

Behaviour analysts have always been very interested in social problems and their solution. The causes of war and peace are not an exception. In the last few years important investigations have been carried out, concerning the way in which behavioural psychology can throw light on understanding and solving the issues of war, aggression and peace, mainly in the context of the nuclear threat.

Skinner (1985) discussed the way in which psychology and scholars can contribute to the establishment of world peace. Building a better way of life apart from governments, religion or capital (business and industry) by learning to treat each other well and by finding alternatives to punishment, was considered.

Nevin (1985) insisted that the experimental analysis of behaviour can teach peaceful behaviours to human beings. Behavioural perspectives on the nuclear arms race and the concept of deterrence were presented. Implications for political action were also examined in terms of the view that peace activism is an operant behaviour.

Murphy (1986) defended the idea that an active public, strongly opposed to the nuclear arms race, may offer the best hope to prevent the escalation of weapons and thereby decrease the risk of nuclear war. The peace movement is considered necessary and potentially powerful in creating social change. Possible applications of behavioural psychology to the peace movement include self-control, response allocations and the promotion of novelty in responding. At the same time, efforts to create social change provide a proving ground for behavioural principles.

TEACHING PEACE

In this section we will review the investigations that centred on the role that psychology plays in teaching peace. There are international works, from many nations, but with a higher proportion of investigations carried out in the Scandinavian countries. However, there are also works carried out in the USA and in other nations.

Barnet (1982) considered at the beginning of the 1980s that the teaching profession had failed to prepare young people to live in the nuclear age and that there were no courses that explain the most important fact in this era: This is the first generation in human history with the theoretical capability to end human history. Therefore, the collective madness of war must be addressed at the social-organization and also at the individual levels. A nation cannot feel secure until its citizens feel secure.

In Finland, Washlstrom (1984) investigated the psychological antecedents of warfare and the obstacles to it, along with the benefits of disarmament education. Psychological effects of living under the threat of nuclear war and the relation between fear conceptions of war and the self-esteem of youth, were considered.

In another work, (Washlstrom, 1985) examined the attitudes of 375 Finnish youngsters on questions about war and peace and studied the subjects' answers in relation to their self-concept and moral development. Results show that girls apparently value peace more and participate in peace-saving activities more than boys. For both sexes, moral development correlates with a positive attitude toward peace: the higher the moral stage, the more favourable the attitudes. It is interesting to note that a disbelief in the effectiveness of peace work was expressed by those who considered that warfare was a "natural" component of human behaviour.

Hass (1986) reviewed research on views of school age children on war and peace. In children from the United States, the concept of war was seen to develop with age. Parental viewpoints have been found to be the most important factor in a child's acceptance of war. In international studies, adolescents were not able to define peace, but all knew what was not peace. The tendency was to reject war at a young age, but to accept it increasingly in the teenage years. Peace was never viewed as an international movement but rather as the absence of war. Reference was made to the theory of cognitive development and its extension to the moral thoughts of children and their views of good and evil. Great importance was given to the theory of moral development proposed by Kohlberg. It stands to reason that we have to understand much better the role that teaching (formal and informal) plays on the concepts of war and peace.

Peace education has been a common aim of many investigators. Bjerstedt (1986) presents an overview of the situation of peace education in various countries of the world. It is pointed out that the task of schools is to prepare pupils for the future. Education for peace can be accomplished through the psychological study of preparedness for nonviolence, world citizen responsibility, equality attitudes and the search for alternatives. A list of 12 subgoals for peace education is also presented.

IS WAR INEVITABLE?

Apparently war has been an extended phenomenon in human societies. But this does not mean that war is inevitable. It can be compared with the prevalence of certain diseases – that can be avoided with the advancements of medicine – and also with the prevalence of many social problems – that can be avoided with adequate social policies. If something has existed for centuries, it does not follow that it belongs to human nature and that it is inevitable.

People who consider that war is "inevitable" centre their beliefs in biological justifications. See, however, Valzelli (1981) for a treatment of the psychobiology of aggression and Sandler (1979) for the psychopharmacology of aggression. The scientific treatment of this problem does not support the belief that war is inevitable. On the other hand, psychoanalysts have followed Freud and his pessimistic concepts on the inevitability of war (see Botstein, 1984). Even people who do not accept psychoanalysis as a therapeutic method, nor as a theory of human nature, agree with Freud's ideas on war and its inevitability. However, the truth is very different. Violent, aggressive behaviour is learned (see Stuart, 1981). We can learn to be violent or to be peace-loving. On this topic, probably the Statement on Violence (Seville, Spain, May 16, 1986) is the most scientific document that we have. It has been accepted by major learned societies at the world level, including societies of psychologists, biologists, anthropologists and sociologists. Among the psychological associations that have done so, are the American Psychological Association (APA) and the International Society for Comparative Psychology (ISCP). The "Statement on Violence" was signed by many of the world's most distinguished experts on war and peace, including Federico Mayor-Zaragoza, present day Secretary of UNESCO.

The text of the Declaration follows.

STATEMENT ON VIOLENCE

Believing that it is our responsibility to address from our particular disciplines the most dangerous and destructive activities of our species, violence and war; recognizing that science is a human cultural product which cannot be definitive or all-encompassing; and gratefully acknowledging the support of the authorities of Seville and representatives of the Spanish UNESCO; we, the undersigned scholars from around the world and from relevant sciences, have met and arrived at the following Statement on Violence. In it, we challenge a number of alleged biological findings that have been used, even by some in our disciplines, to justify violence and war. Because the alleged findings have contributed to the atmosphere of pessimism in our time, we submit that the open, considered rejection of these mis-statements can contribute significantly to the International Year of Peace.

Misuse of scientific theories and data to justify violence and war is not new but has been made since the advent of modern science. For example, the theory of evolution has been used to justify not only war, but also genocide, colonialism and suppression of the weak.

We state our position in the form of the five propositions. We are aware that there are many others issues about violence and war that could be fruitfully addressed from the standpoint of our disciplines, but we restrict ourselves here to what we consider a most important first step.

IT IS SCIENTIFICALLY INCORRECT to say that we have inherited a tendency to make war from our animal ancestors. Although fighting occurs widely throughout animal species, only a few cases of destructive intra-species fighting between organized groups have ever been reported among naturally living species and none of these involve the use of tools designed to be weapons. Normal predatory feeding upon other species cannot be equated with intra-species violence. Warfare is a peculiarly human phenomenon and does not occur in other animals.

That fact that warfare has changed so radically over time indicates that it is a product of culture. Its biological connection is primarily through language which makes possible the coordination of groups, the transmission of technology and the use of tools. War is biologically possible, but it is not inevitable, as evidenced by its variation in occurrence and nature over time and space. There are cultures which have not engaged in war for centuries and there are cultures which have engaged in war frequently at some times and not at others.

IT IS SCIENTIFICALLY INCORRECT to say that war or any other violent behaviour is genetically programmed into our human nature. While genes are involved at all levels of nervous system function, they provide a developmental potential that can be actualized only in conjunction with the ecological and social environment. While individuals vary in their predispositions to be affected by their experience, it is the interaction between their genetic endowment and conditions of nurturance that determines their personalities. Except for rare pathologies, the genes do not produce individuals necessarily predisposed to violence. Neither do they determine the opposite. While genes are co-involved in establishing our behavioural capacities, they do not by themselves specify the outcome.

IT IS SCIENTIFICALLY INCORRECT to say that in the course of human evolution there has been a selection for aggressive behaviour more than for other kinds of behaviour. In all well-studied species, status within the group is achieved by the ability to cooperate and to fulfil social functions relevant to the structure of that group. "Dominance" involves social functions and affiliations; it is not simply a matter of the possession and use of superior physical power, although it does involve aggressive behaviour. Where genetic selection for aggressive behaviour has been artificially instituted in animals, it has rapidly succeeded in producing hyper-aggressive individuals; this indicates that aggression was not maximally selected under natural conditions. When such experimentally-created hyper-aggressive animals are present in a social group, they either disrupt its social structure or are driven out. Violence is neither in our evolutionary legacy nor in our genes.

IT IS SCIENTIFICALLY INCORRECT to say that humans have a "violent brain". While we do have the neural apparatus to act violently, it is not automatically activated by internal or external stimuli. Like higher primates and unlike other animals, our higher neural processes filter such stimuli before they can be acted upon. How we act is shaped by how we have been conditioned and socialized. There is nothing in our neurophysiology that compels us to react violently.

IT IS SCIENTIFICALLY INCORRECT to say that war is caused by "instinct" or any single motivation. The emergence of modern warfare has been a journey from the primacy of emotional and motivational factors. Modern war involves institutional use of personal characteristics such as obedience, suggestibility, and idealism, social skills such as language, and rational considerations such as cost-calculation, planning, and information processing. The technology of modern war has exaggerated traits associated with violence both in the training of actual combatants and the preparation of support for war in the general population. As a result of this exaggeration, such traits are often mistaken to be the causes rather than the consequences of the process.

We conclude that biology does not condemn humanity to war and that humanity can be freed from the bondage of biological pessimism and empowered with confidence to undertake the transformative tasks needed in this International Year of Peace and in the years to come. Although these tasks are mainly institutional and collective, they also rest upon the consciousness of individual participants for whom pessimism and optimism are crucial factors. Just as "war begins in the minds of men", peace also begins in our minds. The same species who invented war is capable of inventing peace. The responsibility lies with each of us.

Seville, May 16, 1986

David Adams, Psychology, Wesleyan University, Middletown (CT) USA.

S.A. Barnett, Ethology, The Australian National University, Canberra, Australia.

N.P. Bechtereva, Neurophysiology, Institute for Experimental Medicine of the Academy of Medical Sciences of USSR, Leningrad, USSR.

Bonnie Frank Carter, Psychology, Albert Einstein Medical Center, Philadelphia (PA) USA.

José M. Rodríguez Delgado, Neurophysiology, Centro de Estudios Neurobiológicos, Madrid, Spain.

José Luis Díaz, Ethology, Instituto Mexicano de Psiquiatría, México, D.F., México

Andrzej Eliasz, Individual Differences Psychology, Polish Academy of Sciences, Warsaw, Poland.

Santiago Genovés, Biological Anthropology, Instituto de Estudios Antropológicos, México D.F., México.

Benson E. Ginsburg, Behaviour Genetics, University of Connecticut, Storrs (CT) USA.

Jo Groebel, Social Psychology, Erziehungswissenschaftliche Hochschule, Landau, Federal Republic of Germany.

Samir-Kumar Ghosh, Sociology, Indian Institute of Human Sciences, Calcutta, India.

Robert Hinde, Animal Behaviour, Cambridge University, UK.

Richard E. Leakey, Physical Anthropology, National Museums of Kenya, Nairobi, Kenya.

12   *Ardila*

Diana López Mendoza, Ethology, Universidad de Sevilla, Spain.
Taha H. Malasi, Psychiatry, Kuwait University, Kuwait.
J. Martín Ramírez, Psychobiology, Universidad de Sevilla, Spain
Federico Mayor Zaragoza, Biochemistry, Universidad Autónoma, Madrid, Spain.
Ashis Nandy, Political Psychology, Center for the Study of Developing Societies,
     Delhi, India.
John Paul Scott, Animal Behaviour, Bowing Gren State University, Bowling
     Green (OH) USA.
Riita Wahlstrom, Psychology, University of Jyvaskyla, Finland.

REFERENCES

Ardila, R. (1986 a). *Impacto psicológico de la guerra nuclear.* Bogotá: Editorial Catálogo
     Científico.
Ardila R. (1986 b). The psychological impact of the nuclear threat on the Third World:
     The case of Colombia. *International Journal of Mental Health, 15* , 162-171.
Ardila, R. (1987). La amenaza de una guerra nuclear y sus consecuencias psicológicas. In J.
     Mendoza -Vega (Ed.).   *Ante la guerra nuclear. Médicos Colombianos para la
     Prevención de la Guerra Nuclear* (pp. 115-129). Bogotá: Academia Nacional de
     Medicina.
Barnet, R. J. (1982). Teaching peace. *Teachers College Record, 84,* 30-37.
Bjerstedt, A. (1986).   Peace education today and tomorrow: Some glimpses from an
     ongoing international survey and some reflections on the specifications of
     educational objectives. *Educational and Psychological Interactions,85,* 22.
Botstein, L. (1984).   Freud on war and death: Thoughts from a nuclear perspective.
     Psychoanalysis and Contemporary Thought, 7, 291-338.
Haas, M. E. (1986). War and peace: The students views. *Journal of Research and
     Development in Education, 19* (3), 84-89.
Hoffmann, S. (1986).   On the political psychology of peace and war. A critique and an
     agenda.   *Political Psychology, 7,* 1-21.
Kimmel, P. R. (1985).   Learning about peace: Choices and the U.S. Institute of Peace an
     seen from two different perspectives.   *American Psychologist, 40,* 536-541.
Linhart, J. (1985).   Psychologicke vedy a   nektere soucasne globalni problemy lidstva.
     Ceskoslovenska Psychologie, 29 (6), 475-480.
Martin Ramírez, J., Hinde, R. A., & Groebel, J. (1987).   *Essays on violence.* Seville,
     Spain: University of Seville Press.
Murphy, C. M. (1986).   Contingencies to prevent catastrophe: Behavioural psychology
     and the anti-nuclear arms movement.   *Behaviour Analysis and Social   Action, 5,*
     30-35.
Nevin, J. A. (1985). Behaviour analysis, the nuclear arms race, and the peace movement.
     Applied Social Psychology Annual, 6, 27-44;
Nolting, H. P. (1984).   Frieden ist auch ein psychologisches Problem – doch nutzt uns die
     Psychologie? *Gruppendynamik, 15,* 333-341.
Osgood, C. L. (1962).   *An alternative to war and surrender.* Urbana, Illinois: University
     of Illinois Press.
Sandler, M. (Ed.). (1979). *Psychopharmacology of aggression.* New York: Raven Press.
Shorokhova, E. V.   (1985)   Psychologists in   the   fight   against   nuclear
     war.*Psikologischeskii Zhurnal, 6,* 3-8 (In Russian).
Skinner, B. F. (1985).   Toward the cause of peace: What can   psychology   contribute?
     Applied Social Psychology Annual, 6, 21-25.

Smith, M. B. (1986).   Kurt Lewin Memorial Address, 1986: War, peace, and psychology. *Journal of Social Issues, 42*, 2 3 - 3 8.

Stuart, R. B.   (Ed.).   (1981).   *Violent behaviour: Social learning approaches to prediction, management, and treatment.* New York: Brunner/Mazel.

Valzelli, L (1981).   *Psychobiology of aggression and violence.* New York: Raven Press.

Washlstrom, R.   (1984).   Sodan psykologisista edellytysista ja kasvatus rauhaan. *Psykologia, 19 ,* 408-413.

Washlstrom, R. (1985). De ungas uppfattningar om kring och fred. *Nordisk Psykologi, 37* (4), 298-309.

Social Applications and Issues in Psychology
R.C. King and J.K. Collins (editors)
©Elsevier Science Publishers B.V. (North-Holland), 1989

ATTITUDES TOWARD NUCLEAR DISARMAMENT: INTERNATIONAL COMPARISONS OF UNIVERSITY STUDENTS AND ACTIVISTS

Knud S. Larsen, Oregon State University
Goyrgy Csepeli, University of Budapest
Hanns-Dietrich Dann, Friedrich-Alexander University
Howard Giles, University of Bristol
Reidar Ommundsen, University of Oslo
Robert Elder, Oregon State University
Ed Long, University of Illinois

This article summarizes responses from an international study of attitudes toward nuclear disarmament based on 712 participants from five countries. Results show highly significant Pearson-product moment correlations between nuclear disarmament attitudes and attitudes toward patriotism (-.79, $p < .001$), the Soviet Union (.69, $p < .001$), authoritarianism (-.53, $p < .001$) and peace demonstrations (.48, $p < .001$). Smaller correlations were produced for anomy (-.22, $p < .001$), machiavellianism (-.21, $p < .001$) and religious orthodoxy (.20, $p < .001$). Further discussion reports on a regression analysis, correlations within national samples and differences between national participants.

Neither depth psychology nor crisis process psychology (e.g., Blight 1987, Rusk, 1983) evaluate the relevance of public attitudes. Both positions assume that armaments decisions are made in a social vacuum. Yet, public opinion reflects not only ideological mobilization, but effectively delimits the disarmament process. As Deutsch (1983) has noted about U.S.-U.S.S.R. relations, "the conditions for social order or mutual trust do not exist" (p. 5). In other words the problem is ideology and resulting attitudes.

Larsen (1986) points to the role of ritualized ideology used by national decision makers to maintain the moral mobilization of their societies. Beliefs, attitudes and values often serve "to bolster the arms race through ingrained dogmatic and ritualistic thinking" (p. 396). One of the functions of ritualized ideology is to move the nuclear disarmament issue from the level of rational discussion to that of moral absolutism. Cold war rhetoric often reflects inane polarization that precludes a rational settlement. Thus, attitudes toward nuclear disarmament are partly an outcome of the ritualized ideology produced by the cold war and also a reinforcer of the armaments race. It is a matter of some importance, therefore, to study the socio-personality factors that contribute to negative attitudes toward nuclear disarmament. Larsen (1984) developed a Likert type scale of attitudes toward nuclear disarmament. The study yielded in three phases a scale with high part-whole correlations, internal reliability, promising known group and construct validity. In particular, the scale differentiated effectively between groups favouring nuclear disarmament and a reserve officer training corps group. Further, attitudes toward nuclear disarmament are in particular related to chauvinism and stereotypical views of the Soviet Union. Patriotic attitudes reflect a primary concern with the superiority of one's own nation state at the cost of hostility toward other countries. Christiansen's (1967) scale in particular sought to reflect tendencies to see one's own nation as superior to humanity as a whole. Thus patriotism measures a superordinate loyalty to one's own country as related to other countries or reference groups. One can therefore expect patriotic attitudes to be related to negative attitudes toward nuclear disarmament.

Since the founding of the Soviet state, relations with western countries have been marked by mutual suspicion and a history of unbridled hostility. Attitudes toward the Soviet Union are therefore likely to be at the centre of a person's attitudes toward nuclear disarmament. Smith (1946) developed a measure designed to scale a person's relative trust and acceptance of the Soviet Union, its leadership and form of government. Evidence of known group validity was reported as well as concurrent validity (Helfant, 1952). It is expected, therefore, that those with negative attitudes toward the Soviet Union would also display negative attitudes toward nuclear disarmament. Undoubtedly, attitudes toward international issues are linked to underlying personality dispositions. Research into authoritarianism shows consistently that high authoritarians adhere to a rigid and dogmatic ideology and discriminate against outgroups (Adorno, Frenkel-Brunswik, Levinson and Sanford, 1950). These fascist proclivities are also more likely to cause a person to adhere to extreme rightist political programs including continual confrontation with the Soviet Union. A major component of the authoritarian mind is ethnocentrism wherein the esteem of one's own nation or group is achieved by the low ranking of or hostility toward other groups. This ideological outlook is central to the idea of ritualized ideology and would predispose an individual toward negative attitudes to nuclear disarmament.

Anomy refers to a sense of normlessness which is assumed to derive from social conditions and have behavioural consequences (McClosky and Schaar, 1965). This variable was moderately related to pessimism, political impotence and cynicism. This position may be reflected in a sense of hopelessness in achieving disarmament. Anomy thus reflects a negativistic and despairing outlook not only regarding one's own life, but that of the larger community as well. An alienated person is less likely to become involved and to see purpose or meaning in disarmament and would be more likely to distrust the outcome of any negotiations. Ever since Machiavelli wrote "The Prince and Discourses", the cynical manipulation of others in international affairs has often been a norm as well as an attitude. Since this variable especially reflects a sense of distrust, (Christie, 1973) it is expected to generalize to attitudes toward nuclear disarmament. In particular, it is expected that high scores on the machiavellianism scale will correspond to more negative attitudes on nuclear disarmament.

In recent years, the religious right-wing has made significant gains in the U.S. and is well represented elsewhere. In ideology the various groups and churches combine fundamentalist Christian beliefs (Putney and Middleton, 1961) with virulent anti-communism (and, in the case of the identity churches, racism as well). It is therefore predicted that such an orthodox and fundamentalist outlook is also reflected in uncompromising attitudes toward the Soviet Union and the disarmament process.

The purpose of the current study was to investigate student attitudes toward nuclear disarmament in several countries. The countries bridged two continents (Europe and North America); socialist (Hungary) and capitalist (United States, Federal Republic of Germany, Great Britain and Norway) states.

The first objective was to evaluate the relationship of the survey variables in the overall international sample to test the aforementioned hypotheses. Further, the pattern of predictions was examined within the separate national samples. Finally, mean differences between the national samples, analyzing for differences on nuclear disarmament and other survey variables, were examined.

METHOD

Respondents

Respondents (712) completed the survey as follows: 166 from Hungary; 125 from the United States; 105 from the Federal Republic of Germany, 111 from Great Britain; 180 from Norway and 25 peace activists from Norway. The survey was administered in large psychology undergraduate classes held at the University of Budapest, Oregon State University, University of Constance, University of Bristol and the Universities of Oslo and Bergen during academic year 1986. In addition, several peace organizations were approached in Norway and 25 peace activists responded to this appeal for participation. In the overall sample, 57.8% were female and the average age was 24.98 years.

Survey

The survey included 67 items composed of a three item patriotism scale (Christiansen, 1967); a three item attitudes toward the Soviet Union scale (Smith, 1946); a four item F scale (Lane, 1955); a survey item measuring participation in demonstrations (Have you ever participated in a peace demonstration? - never, sometimes, at every opportunity); a nine item anomy scale (McClosky & Schaar, 1963); a twenty item machiavellianism scale (Christie, 1973); a six item religious orthodoxy scale (Putney & Middleton, 1961) and the twenty-one item attitudes toward nuclear disarmament scale (Larsen, 1984). Sample items for each of the scales follows: patriotism (no duties are more important than duties towards one's country); attitudes toward the Soviet Union (I feel friendly toward the Soviet Union); F scale (A few strong leaders could make this country better than all the laws and talk); anomy (the trouble with the world today is that most people really don't believe in anything); machiavellianism scale (never tell anyone the real reason you did something unless it is useful to do so); religious orthodoxy (I believe that there is a physical hell where men are punished after death for the sins of their lives); and nuclear disarmament scale (nuclear disarmament is the only way to prevent a nuclear disaster in the future). Although some researchers may question the reliability of short inventories, actual research supports both their reliability and validity. For example, the four-item F scale (Lane, 1955) was found to be a better measure of authoritarianism than the larger balanced version used by Campbell, Converse, Miller and Stokes (1960). Further, there is evidence of construct validity in several findings reported by Lane. The scales were all Likert type with the usual five point response categories from agree strongly to disagree strongly. In addition, the survey also contained age and sex identification questions.

RESULTS AND DISCUSSION

Attitudes toward nuclear disarmament

Results of Pearson-product moment correlations between the survey variables and attitudes toward nuclear disarmament show that the survey variables can be broadly placed in three major categories according to the strength of the correlations. In the first category, patriotism (-.70, $p < .001$), negative attitudes toward the Soviet Union (.69, $p < .001$), authoritarianism (-.53, $p < .001$) and lack of participation in peace demonstrations (.48, $p < .001$) all relate strongly to negative attitudes toward disarmament. Considering the diversity of nationality, language and culture, these are impressive correlations. These results suggest again the key role played by chauvinism, combined with hostility toward the Soviet Union - as well as more basic authoritarian or fascist proclivities. The content of these dimensions describe a world outlook of continued hostility between the two world camps; identity with the nation state and right-wing political content, on the part of those hostile to disarmament.

The second set of variables [anomy (-.22, $p < .001$), machiavellianism (-.21, $p < .001$) and orthodoxy (-.20, $p < .001$)] are significantly correlated, but account for relatively smaller amounts of the variance. Nevertheless, an outlook of alienation, the cynical manipulation of others and religious orthodoxy content contribute to negative attitudes. This perspective perhaps contributes mostly to an acceptance of the inevitability of superpower conflict, indifference to the consequences and fuelling anti-Sovietism.

Finally, females appear to be slightly more in favour of disarmament (-.17, $p < .001$), a result quite consistent with the literature on female compassion. Age is also a small factor (.16, $p < .001$), i.e., older respondents, having lived longer with the nuclear threat, are perhaps more aware and concerned.

Regression analysis lends support to this three-level examination. The regression analysis reveals the order in which the variables contribute to attitudes. The pattern is generally that revealed by the correlational analysis. Patriotism, peace demonstration, authoritarianism and attitudes toward the Soviet Union account for most of the variance, with anomy, orthodoxy and machiavellianism together accounting for only about 4% of the variance.

Correlations within national samples

Table 1 summarizes the results of Pearson product-moment correlations between survey variables and attitudes toward nuclear disarmament.

TABLE 1

Pearson Product-Moment Correlations* Between Attitudes Toward Nuclear
Disarmament and Survey Variables by Country and Peace Activists

Survey scales and indexes	Norway	U.S.	Great Britain	Germany	Hungary	Peace Activists
Patriotism	.57*	.24*	.64*	.44*	.01	.58*
Soviet Union	.19*	.15*	.47*	.52*		.32
F Scale	-.51*	-.12	-.35*	-.45*	.14*	-.22
Peace demonstration	.46*	.15*	.37*	.45		.30
Anomy	.05	.20*	.13	-.07	.17*	-.26
Machiavellianism	-.28*	-.04	-.27*	-.42*	.12	-.44*
Religious orthodoxy	.35*	-.18*	-.16*	-.22*	-.17*	-.14

* Significant at .05 level or better.

The results yield a consistent pattern across the several samples. In general, high levels of patriotism, anti-Soviet attitudes and authoritarianism and low levels of peace activity (demonstration) correlate moderately with negative attitudes toward nuclear disarmament. For the remaining three variables, results show significant but low correlations between anomy, machiavellianism, religious orthodoxy and disarmament attitudes. These attitudes appear to be consistent within the western group (Norway, U.S., Great Britain and Germany) and the results for the peace activists are very similar. Peace activists in Norway are essentially similar in socio-personality predictors to the more general student samples in the western group. Hungary, however, is a separate case as the correlations of survey variables are all small. In the case of authoritarianism, results yielded a significant correlation in the opposite direction from the western samples, i.e., low authoritarians are opposed to disarmament. The reason for this finding may be found in the relation of low authoritarians to their government. Perhaps low authoritarians rebel against a government which favours nuclear disarmament. Additionally, perhaps nuclear polarization is seen as a protection of a pluralistic world and is therefore favoured by low authoritarians. In the case of the Hungarian sample, attitudes toward nuclear disarmament are undoubtedly also related to attitudes toward the Soviet Union.

Differences between national samples on nuclear disarmament

Do the national samples differ in regard to attitudes toward nuclear disarmament? Table 2 shows the results of a multiple range test between countries.

TABLE 2

Multiple Range Test Between Countries on Attitudes Toward Nuclear Disarmament

Source	D.F.	Sum of Squares	Mean Squares	F Ratio
Between nations	5	101546.66	20309.33	168.08*
Within nations	705	85185.75	120.83	
Total	710	186732.41		

* < .001

	x	Hungary	U.S.	G.B.	Norway	Germany
Hungary	44.67					
U.S.	60.92	*				
Great Britain	67.41	*	*			
Norway	73.16	*	*	*		
Germany	75.54	*	*	*		
Peace Activists	82.24	*	*	*	*	*

(*) Denotes pairs of national samples significantly different at the .05 level.

The F ratio is highly significant and mean differences are very high between Hungary (with the least positive attitudes) and the other samples. The mean differences between all possible pairs of national samples are all significant except between Norway and Germany. The high score of the peace activists might be considered further support for the known group validity of the attitudes toward nuclear disarmament scale.

These means differences suggest several possible interpretations. The low score of the Hungarian sample might be explained by the configuration of the socio-personality variables in the Hungarian sample. The Hungarian sample scored high on patriotism, authoritarianism, machiavellianism and anomy as compared to other national samples. Thus students in the Hungarian sample possessed many of the traits linked to negative attitudes. (No measure on attitudes toward the Soviet Union was available for the Hungarian sample.)

The explanation for the similarly low ranking of the U.S. sample is probably found in the polarization and distrust caused by the cold war. Within this framework the Soviet Union is perceived as an "evil empire" that cannot be trusted to keep disarmament agreements. Great Britain and Norway have experienced intermediate violence during the Second World War, reflected in part by their moderate attitudes toward nuclear disarmament. The peace activists should, by nature of their commitment, be most positive, as shown in Table 2.

Differences between national samples on survey variables

Are there significant differences between the national samples on the survey variables? A multiple range of F ratios and significant mean differences across the several samples was completed. As noted, Hungary scored highest or high on all variables correlated with negative attitudes toward nuclear disarmament. The U.S. sample is also high on patriotism, negative toward the Soviet Union and high on authoritarianism, machiavellianism and religious orthodoxy. Religious orthodoxy, . of course, plays a unique role on the American political scene. Great Britain and Norway score more moderately on patriotism and authoritarianism, reflecting their intermediate position on attitudes toward nuclear disarmament. Finally, it is worth observing that both the German and peace activist samples score very low on patriotism (i.e., score in the humanitarian direction) and relatively positive toward the Soviet Union, consistent with their positive scores on attitudes toward nuclear disarmament.

1. All statistical tables are available by writing to Dr. Knud S. Larsen, Oregon State University, Corvallis, Oregon, USA, 97331-5303.

REFERENCES

Adorno, T.W., Frenkel-Brunswik, E., Levinson, D.J. and Sanford, R.N. (1950). *The authoritarian personality*. New York: Harper.

Blight, J.G. (1987). Toward a policy-relevant psychology of avoiding nuclear war: lessons for psychologists from the Cuban Missile crisis. *American Psychologist, 42,* 12-29.

Campbell, A., Converse, P.E., Miller, W.E. & Stoker, D.E. (1960). *The American Voter*. New York: Wiley.

Christiansen, B. (1967). Attitudes toward foreign affairs as a function of personality. In Shaw, M.E. & Wright, J.M., *Scales for the measurement of attitudes*. New York: McGraw-Hill, 206-207.

Christie, R. (1973). Machiavellianism Scale. In J.P. Robinson & P.R. Shaver (Eds.), *Measures of social psychological attitudes*. Ann Arbor: University of Michigan Press.

Deutsch, M. (1983). The prevention of world war III: A psychological perspective: *Political Psychology, 4*, 3-31.

Helfant, R. (1952). Parents attitude vs. adolescent hostility in the determination of adolescent socio-political attitudes. *Psychological Monographs, 66*, 1-23.

Holt, R.R. (1984). Can psychology meet Einstein's challenge? *Political Psychology, 24*, 55-64.

Lane, R. (1955). Four-item F scale in "political personality and electoral choice." *American Political Science Review, 49*, 173-190.

Larsen, K.S. (1986). Social psychological factors in military technology and strategy. *Journal of Peace Research, 23*, 391-298.

Larsen, K.S. (1984). Attitudes toward nuclear disarmament and their correlates. *The Journal of Social Psychology, 125*, 17-21.

Mack, J.E. (1985). Toward a collective psychopathology of the nuclear arms competition. *Political Psychology, 6*, 291-321.

McClosky, H. & Schaar, J.H. (1965). Psychological dimensions of anomy. *American Sociological Review, 30*, 14-40.

Putney, S. & Middleton, R. (1961). Dimensions of religious ideology. *Social Forces, 39*, 285-290.

Rogers, L. (1982). Nuclear war: A personal perspective. *APA Monitor*, August, 6-7.

Rusk, D. (Speaker), & Singer, A. (Producer). (1983). *Maximum Peril*. Videotape, June 27, New York: Alfred P. Sloan Foundation.

Smith, G.H. (1946). Attitude toward Soviet Russia: The standardization of a scale and some distribution of scores. *Journal of Social Psychology, 23*, 3-16.

White, R.K. (1984). *Fearful warriors: A psychological profile of U.S.-Soviet relations*. New York: Free Press.

Social Applications and Issues in Psychology
R.C. King and J.K. Collins (editors)
©Elsevier Science Publishers B.V. (North-Holland), 1989

A CROSS-CULTURAL STUDY OF FACTORS PREDISPOSING INDIVIDUALS TO SUPPORT NUCLEAR DISARMAMENT

K. Rigby, J.C. Metzer, B. Dietz

South Australian Institute of Technology, Australia.

A cross-cultural study of factors predisposing individuals to support nuclear disarmament was conducted during 1986 concurrently in Australia, West Germany, the Netherlands and the United States of America. Community samples (N >160) of residents in each of the countries completed questionnaires containing measures of worldmindedness, attitude toward institutional authority and stress engendered by the prospect of nuclear war ("nuclear stress"), as well as questions tapping support (both attitudinal and behavioural) for nuclear disarmament. Degree of support for nuclear disarmament varied widely between countries, with respondents in the European countries being most supportive and those in the United States being least supportive. Despite the variations, results for multiple regression analyses showed that comparatively high degrees of worldmindedness and nuclear stress, along with relatively unfavourable attitudes toward institutional authority, were each independently and significantly associated with support for nuclear disarmament in each of the four countries. It is concluded that although local conditions may determine the degree of support for the peace movement, predisposing factors operate similarly across national boundaries.

At the 16th Annual Australian Social Psychology Conference in Canberra, various factors thought to influence support for nuclear disarmament in Australia were examined (Rigby, 1987). A survey of South Australians revealed that the supporters of nuclear disarmament differed significantly from others on three psychological dimensions. Firstly, they were relatively "worldminded"; secondly, they were less positive than others in their attitudes toward institutional authority; and thirdly, they were comparatively anxious about the prospect of nuclear war.

The first two results especially were of interest to educators and political activists of different persuasions, suggesting, as they do, how support for the Peace Movement can be influenced. If we are prepared to make the assumption that attitudes influence behaviour - and in recent years more and more psychologists have questioned the "old" orthodoxy that they don't, in favour of the common sense view that quite often they *do* (see Ajzen and Fishbein,1977) -

then an education that encourages students to question institutional authority and to adopt a world-minded view of history and the future of the human race, might indeed have a powerful effect upon support for a policy of nuclear disarmament.

However, before any research bases for such a position could be seriously entertained, it was obvious that results were needed extending well beyond Australia. Though large in size, Australia is, of course, quite small in population and distant from the Western World. Indeed, with the exception of New Zealand, it is perhaps the land furthest removed from the geopolitical centre of the earth. Inevitably, there arises the question of whether the earlier findings were idiosyncratic and anomolous.

There were some grounds for supposing that the Australian results would have wider generality. A large cross-cultural study conducted with students in USA, England and Australia (Zweigenshaft, Jennings, Rubenstein and Van Hoon, 1986) concluded with the claim that belief in "peace through co-operation" as opposed to "peace through strength" may be a more relevant factor in determining attitude to nuclear disarmament than the amount of factual knowledge one may have about nuclear weapons and their effects. This notion of "peace through co-operation" is closely related to the concept of "world-mindedness" employed in the earlier Australian study.

Worldmindedness is a concept first proposed and operationalised by Sampson and Smith (1957). It was intended to designate a value orientation according to which one's primary reference group is mankind rather than that of a particular nationality. A highly worldminded person would favour a world-view of the problems of humanity, emphasising the need for international cooperation.

As against such positive motivation suggested by the concept of worldmindedness, a popular view of the policy of nuclear disarmament has been that it is essentially a protest against the Establishment. A strong exponent of this position has been the Swedish historian, Kim Saloman (1986). He has argued that the contemporary Peace Movement (centering upon nuclear disarmament) is driven by a sub-culture that is permamently pitted against establishment norms. "It is this environment of critical attitudes", he asserts, "rather than a quest for peace or an opposition against (sic) nuclear weapons, which induces people to involve themselves in the peace movement". (p 115).

For evidence, Saloman pointed to the affiliations of peace activists with the political parties of the left: the Green Party in Germany; the Socialist Party in Denmark; the Social Democrats in the Netherlands; and the Labour Party in Britain. These parties are described by Salomon as containing large groups which ostentatiously display anti-establishment attitudes (p.123).

The "Establishment" is more of a slogan than a readily definable concept. It is commonly viewed as the means by which the power structure of a community is maintained. Its power is largely expressed through formal or institutional authority in the sense identified by Weber (1961). Now it has become clear from work extending over the last ten years, in various countries, that the concept of attitude toward institutional authority can be satisfactorily operationalised. It has both generality and predictive validity (see Rigby, 1982; Rigby,1986; Rump, Rigby & Waters,1985). If Saloman was right in ascribing a determining role to anti-establishment sentiment, a negative correlation between attitude to institutional authority and support for nuclear disarmament would be expected, more especially perhaps in European countries, where Saloman's political analyses had been developed.

A final variable upon which the earlier study had focussed was anxiety about the possibility of nuclear war. Previous studies had left no doubt that among *some* people there are high levels of anxiety or stress associated with the possible use of nuclear weapons. Although it does *not* follow that such people must support nuclear disarmament, a study conducted in the Netherlands (reported by Van Dommelen, 1985) suggested that stress associated with the threat of nuclear war was positively correlated with support for nuclear disarmament, just as it was in the Australian study.

There appeared, then, to be good reasons to expect that the Australian results would replicate cross-culturally and that each of the factors - worldmindedness, attitude to authority and anxiety about nuclear war (or nuclear stress) - would each have a significant and independent effect upon support for nuclear disarmament. Furthermore, it appeared desirable to take into account two demographic factors, namely age and sex, because survey results in Australia (Clark et al, 1985) and in the United States (see Fiske, 1987) have shown a tendency, albeit slight, for younger people and females to be more supportive of nuclear disarmament.

The replication studies were carried out in the U.S.A. and in two European countries, namely, the Netherlands and Germany. The American and European samples were expected to differ in social attitudes, particularly so because in 1986 when the data were collected, in both of the selected European countries a strong movement had been mounted to oppose nuclear weapons and demonstrations had become commonplace. It was to be expected therefore that wide differences in attitudes and opinions about nuclear weapons would be found between the European and American samples. A study carried out in contrasting social milieux was expected to provide a rigorous test of the generality of the proposition which had thus far received support only in Australia.

MEASURES

Worldmindedness. In three of the countries, Australia, the Netherlands and the U.S.A., worldmindedness was assessed using a nineteen item scale selected from a 58-item measure developed by Der Kerabetian (1984), based upon earlier work from Sampson and Smith (1957) and Silvernail (1979). A different version of the worldmindedness scale, comprising 16 items, was selected for the West German study. This variation in scale content enabled us to extend the generality of the findings, but prevented strict comparability between the results for the West German sample and those of others. Items tapping "worldmindedness" related to a variety of areas, namely, race, religion, immigration, government, economics, education and ecology. Examples are : "The rich nations should share their wealth with less fortunate people of the world" (pro-worldmindedess) and "Immigrants should not be permitted to come to our country if they compete with our workers" (anti-worldmindedness). The scale is approximately balanced; six response categories are employed, ranging from "strongly agree" to "strongly disagree". After appropriate reverse scoring, high scores indicate a highly world-minded view.

Attitude to Institutional Authority. This was measured in each of the four countries using nineteen items from a General Attitude toward Institutional Authority Scale developed by Rigby (Rigby, 1982). The authorities included in the test are the police, the law, the army, medical practitioners and teachers. Previous studies had shown that attitudes towards these authorities were significantly and positively intercorrelated. An example of a pro-authority item is "The Police in this country are pretty trustworthy"; an anti-authority item is: "A person should obey only those laws that seem reasonable." Five response categories are provided, ranging from "agree strongly" to "disagree strongly". High scores reflect favourable attitudes to institutional authority.

Nuclear Stress. This was inferred from answers to a single question: "How anxious are you concerning the possibility of nuclear war ?" There were 7 response categories, ranging from "not at all anxious" to "extremely anxious".

Attitude to nuclear disarmament. Respondents were asked whether they thought there should be nuclear weapons in their country. [Response categories were "Yes" (coded 1), "unsure" (coded 2) and "No" (coded 3)]

Action tendency to support nuclear disarmament. This was inferred from answers to the question: "Have you been part of any mass political action (donation, letter writing, or demonstration) concerning the danger of nuclear war?"

In addition to these main measures, respondents were asked (1) whether nuclear weapons in their own country and elsewhere in the world increased or decreased the likelihood of war, (2) how likely a nuclear war was in the next 10 years and (3) to give their estimations of their chances of personal survival in a nuclear war. Data were also collected on the age and sex of the respondents. Questionnaires were translated into Dutch (by Dr. Jacques Metzer) and into German (by Biruta and Christian Dietz), prior to adminstration in the Netherlands and West Germany.

DATA COLLECTION

Data were collected from community samples in Adelaide, South Australia and Central Texas, USA, by means of a door-knock carried out by students assisting in the work. In Nijmegen, Netherlands the sample was obtained by a a mail survey (40% return rate) and in West Germany (West Berlin and Freiberg) by nominated collectors who obtained quota samples of respondents from their neighbourhood. Hence, the groups were *convenience* samples only. The composition of the samples was as follows: Australia, 340 males and 338 females, mean age 36.81, SD= 14.66; U.S.A.,154 males, 162 females, mean age, 35.53, yrs, SD=12.49; the Netherlands, 220 males, 118 females, mean age, 41.41 yrs, SD=15.96; West Germany, 89 males, 80 females. mean age, 41.22 yrs, SD=13.53.

RESULTS

Attitudes to nuclear disarmament as indicated by responses to the question whether there should be nuclear weapons in one's country are given in Table 1.

TABLE 1
Percentages of responses in three categories for four national samples to the question:
" Do you think there should be nuclear weapons in your country?"

	Sample			
	Australia	U.S.A.	Netherlands	W. Germany
Yes	18.0	61.1	27.5	22.5
Unsure	12.8	10.8	10.9	2.4
No	69.2	28.2	61.5	75.1

The results show that the sample from the USA is exceptional, with only 28% of the sample adopting what may be called the nuclear disarmament position, compared with percentages ranging from 62% (Netherlands) to 75% (West Germany) and Australia (69%) occupying an intermediate position.

Whether nuclear weapons in one's country was seen as increasing the likelihood of war varied between national samples. West German respondents were the most pessimistic with 56.8% indicating that nuclear weapons in their countries made war more likely. The corresponding percentages for the other samples were: Australia, 49.7%; U.S.A., 33.2%; and Netherlands 29.3 On the broader question of whether the existence of nuclear weapons *in the world* increased the likelihood of war, there was more agreement between samples. Between 50% and 70% of respondents in each sample thought that under such conditions war was likely. So much for any general acceptance of the notion that the existence of nuclear weapons on a world scale acts as a deterrent to war!

Asked how likely it is that there would be a nuclear war in the next 10 years, the percentage of people thinking it was *more likely than not* ranged from 19% in the Netherlands to 50.3% in Australia, with intermediate estimates being given by the West Germans (45.5%) and the Americans (46.9%). The figure for the American sample is slightly in excess of the 40% estimate provided by Gallup in a U.S.A. survey reported in 1983. (See Fiske, 1987). The mean likelihood of *survival* in a nuclear war was seen as quite low: 8% in West Germany; 10% in the Netherlands; 24% in the United States and 29% in Australia.

The percentages of people in the four national samples who reported that they had taken *some political action* in relation to nuclear danger, by actions such as demonstrating, are given in Table 2.

TABLE 2

Percentages reporting some participation in political action concerning nuclear disarmament in four countries

Participation:	Aust	U.S.A.	Neths	W.Germany
Yes	14.5	5.1	43.2	43.2
No	85.5	94.9	56.8	56.8

Here there is a marked contrast between the European samples and the American sample, with 43% reporting taking action in both West Germany and in the Netherlands, but *only 5%* in the U.S.A. sample. The Australian sample provided intermediate results, with 15% having taken some action. With these figures in mind, it is interesting to quote an authoritative judgement from Fiske (1987) in a recent paper in the *American Psychologist.* "For most people," she writes, "for most of the time, nuclear war is not a salient concern. But for a tiny fraction of the population it is". This nicely illustrates an ethnocentric approach to the problem. A tiny fraction for the US sample perhaps; 43%, however, in the European samples is not exactly a tiny fraction.

The measures of Worldmindedness and Attitude to Institutional Authority were found to be reliable in each of the countries where they were administered, with satisfactory alpha coefficients ranging from .79 to .90. Several aspects of these results may be noted briefly. Among the three sets of respondents completing *the same* worldmindedness scale, the Dutch sample scored highest (mean = 85.62) and the U.S.A. the lowest (mean = 70.28). Perhaps it is no accident that the International Court of Justice is at The Hague. The U.S.A. sample was the most pro-authority of the four national samples (mean = 65.37); the German the least (mean = 50.82). So much for the prototypical authoritarianism of the German people! On the measure of nuclear stress, the positions were reversed: the Germans were most anxious (mean = 4.78) and the Americans least anxious (mean = 3.06).

The relationship between the predictor and dependent variables was examined in two ways: first by Pearson product-moment correlations and secondly by means of either multiple regression analyses or discriminant analyses, as appropriate, in which all 5 variables, worldmindedness, attitude to authority, nuclear stress, age and sex were entered in the equation. In the table that follows zero order correlations are given, together with beta coefficients (or standardised discriminant coefficient functions) to provide estimates of the relative importance of the different contributions. In Table 3 attitudinal support for nuclear disarmament is the dependent variable.

TABLE 3
Relationships between 5 independent variables and rejection of nuclear weapons in ones's own country for four national samples

	Sample							
	AUST		U.S.A.		NETHS		W GER	
	r	beta	r	beta	r	beta	r	beta
Independent Vars:								
Worldmindedness	.40	.30	.30	.25	.40	.19	.48	.26
Att. to Authority	-.28	-.10	-.26	-.24	-.44	-.24	-. 51	-.32
Nuclear Stress	.25	.15	.16.	07	.30	.19	.30	.06
Age (years)	-.23.	-12.	-.12	-.04	- 28	-16	-.03	.03
Sex (m=1; f=2)	.10	.03	.16	.19	.10	.01	.18	.10
Multiple r	.46		.43		.53		.57	

Note: All correlations and beta coefficients are significant at the .05 level (two-tail test), except for those underlined.

The results were generally as predicted. Across each one of the national samples, Worldmindedness and Nuclear Stress were positively related to support for nuclear disarmament; whilst attitude to authority was related negatively. All the correlations for these variables were significant at the .05 level, as were the beta coefficients. The relationship with attitude to authority was somewhat stronger in the European samples. Age and sex were of minor importance, with a slight, but inconsistent tendency for younger people and females to favour nuclear disarmament. As indicated by the multiple correlations, the amount of variance accounted for ranged from 18% (U.S.A) to 32% (West Germany).

A similar pattern of results was found with perceived negative consequences of the existence of nuclear weapons. To obtain the dependent variable in this analysis, results for the effects attributed to weapons in one's own country and for the world, were combined, providing a 10-point scale, with high scores indicating *greater* likelihood of war. The obtained relationships are given in Table 4.

TABLE 4
Relationships between 5 independent variables and perceived negative consequences of the existence of nuclear weapons for four national samples

	Samples							
	AUST		U.S.A.		NETHS		W. GERMANY	
Independent Vars	r	beta	r	beta	r	beta	r	beta
Worldmindedness	.34	.20	.25	.17	.44	.20	.50	.18
Att to Authority	-.26	-.08	-.30	-.26	-.46	-.21	-.58	-.33
Nuclear Stress	.37	.28	.26	.17	.44	.34	.51	.30
Age (in years)	-.26	-.17	-.22	-.13	-.25	-.14	-.15	-.09
sex (m=1; f=2)	.20	.13	.17	.21	.16	.06	.20	.07
Multiple r	.51		.48		.62		.68	

Note: All correlations and beta coefficients are significant at the .05 level (two-tail test), except for those underlined.

Again the results were replicated across samples: respondents who were relatively worldminded and anxious about nuclear weapons viewed the possession of nuclear weapons more negatively than others, as in general did those who were relatively distrustful of institutional authority, young and female. Again the main relationships tended to be stronger in the samples of European respondents.

Finally, with taking *some political action* scored as 1 and none as zero, point bi-serial correlations were computed, then followed by a discriminant analysis, to assess the relative contribution of each factor.

Again, a similar pattern was found for each country, with the more worldminded, those who were anxious about nuclear weapons and those opposed to institutional authority more likely to have taken action to promote nuclear disarmament than others. Again stronger relationships were found in the results for the European samples. Notably, however, gender did not play a significant role in any of the national samples.

TABLE 5
Relationships between 5 independent variables and reported political action on the dangers of nuclear war for four national samples

	AUSTRALIA		U.S.A.		NETHS		W. GERMANY	
	r	dfc	r	dfc	r	dfc	r	dfc
Independent vars								
Worldmindedness	.35	.49	.26	.64	.45	.52	.40	.29
Att to Authority	−.39	−.63	−.23	−.58	−.46	−.52	−.51	−.68
Nuclear Stress	.22	.28	.17	.34	.26	.27	.28	.22
Age (in years)	−.16	.07	−.07	.03	−.24	−.18	−.22	−.33
Sex (m =1; f=2)	.02	.08	−.01	.05	.09	.03	.01	.20
Multiple r	.46		.35		.54		.56	

Note: Point biserial correlations were used to compute zero order correlations (r)
To estimate the relative importance of the contribution of the independent variables a discriminant analysis was used to provide discriminant function coefficients (dfcs)
All correlations are significant at the .05 level (two-tail test),except for those underlined.

CONCLUSIONS

We have seen that the Australian results were replicated cross-culturally. Despite marked variations in the degree of support for nuclear disarmament - with the European samples showing strongest support, the U.S.A. sample least and the Australian sample occupying an intermediate position - for each of the samples *stronger* support for nuclear disarmament was found among people who were comparatively worldminded, more negatively disposed towards institutional authorities and relatively anxious about the prospects of nuclear war. Compared with these qualities, the characteristics of age and gender were relatively unimportant. Individual psychological or attitudinal predispositions clearly *do* matter, even among groups of people who are comparatively conservative and ethnocentric.

It seems that Saloman was right in asserting that the Peace Movement is, to some extent, an expression of anti-authority feeling. But it is also true that the attitude of worldmindedness is at least an equally important factor. And it is one which educators and politicians can seek to develop with fewer misgivings. Peace, let it be said, is more likely to be promoted by the concept of "one world" than of "One Australia"- or one of any other country.

CORRESPONDENCE

K Rigby, J.C. Metzer, B. Dietz, School of Social Studies, South Australian Institute of Technology, North Terrace, Adelaide, S.A., Australia.

REFERENCES

Ajzen, I. & Fishbein, M. Attitude-behavior relations: a theoretical review of empirical research. *Psychological Bulletin, 84,* 888-918.

Clark, A.W., Trehair, R.C., Powell, R.J. & Walker R. M. (1985). Australians' attitudes to nuclear disarmament. Unpublished paper, Dept. of Sociology, La Trobe University, Australia.

Der Kerabetian, A. (1984) A questionnaire to assess worldmindedness. Unpublished paper. University of La Verne, California, U.S.A

Fiske, S. T. (1987). People's reactions to nuclear war: Implications for psychologists, *American Psychologist, 42,* 207-217.

Rigby, K. (1982). A concise scale for the assessment of attitudes towards institutional authority. *Australian Journal of Psychology, 34,* 469-487.

Rigby, K (1986). Orientation to authority: attitudes and behaviour. *Australian Journal of Psychology, 38,* 153-160.

Rigby, K. (1987). Factors influencing support for nuclear disarmament in Australia. Paper delivered at the 16th Annual Social Psychology Conference, Australian National University, Canberra, Australia.

Rump, E.E., Rigby, K. & Waters, L. K. (1985) The generality of attitudes to authority: cross-cultural comparisons. *Journal of Social Psychology, 52,* 307-312.

Saloman, K. (1986). The Peace Movement: An anti-establishment movement. *Journal of Peace Research, 37,* 115-127.

Sampson, D. L. & Smith, H. P. (1957) A scale to assess world-minded attitudes. *Journal of Social Psychology, 45,* 99-106.

Silvernail, D.L. (1979). The assessment of teachers' future world perspective values. *The Journal of Environmental Education, 10,* 7-11.

Van Dommelen, J.J.C.M. (1986). The relationship between anxiety and opinions about nuclear arms in a Dutch sample. Paper presented at the Ninth Annual Scientific Meeting of the International Society of Political Psychology, Amsterdam, Holland.

Weber, M. (1961). "The types of authority". In T. Parsons et al. (Ed.). *Theories of Society,* .New York, Free Press.

Zweigenhaft, R.L., Jennings, P., Rubinstein, S. C. & Van Hoorn, J. (1985) Nuclear knowledge and nuclear anxiety: a cross-cultural investigation. *Journal of Social Psychology, 125,* 473-484.

Social Applications and Issues in Psychology
R.C. King and J.K. Collins (editors)
©Elsevier Science Publishers B.V. (North-Holland), 1989

THEORY, POLITICS AND STRATEGIES IN SOLVING INTERNATIONAL CONFLICTS

Toshio Iritani

Department of Mass Communication, Tokai University, Japan

This paper discusses the relative indifference of psychologists toward such great issues as international conflicts (war) and peace, at present as well as in the past. The reason for such indifference is explored and the little communication among psychologists, political scientists and politicians is noted. After a brief review of the above two issues, the paper offers a change of the direction in the attitudes of psychologists in order to fill the gap.

THE DEFINITION OF CONCEPTS

A conflict (sometimes called struggle) is understood to mean the state or the process in which more than two persons, or a group of persons, attempt to interfere with each other's purpose or with the interest of others, or to hurt and break each other down.

Often competition and conflict are used to explain the forms of opposing forces in human society. However, in the case of the former, the intention of the opponent is directed unconsciously toward material or spiritual objects, and it eventually terminates; in the case of the latter, the intention is directed toward an individual or a group and the opposition, which is expressed emotionally and consciously and occurs intermittently. In many cases, the behaviour is mutually interrelated and when a competition reaches a grave state, it often extends to the level of a conflict.

In the historical development of human society, competitions or conflicts have been repeated in a lesser or a greater degree. It has often been claimed that the emergence of conflict is essential for, or intrinsic to, man's struggle in life. Because the human species is composed of many types and their motives and directions differ and often change in the course of time, it is often stated that an occurrence of a certain level of conflict is more or less normal and assimilation to the other, or escape from it, is rather uncommon. As a matter of fact, human conflict occurs in many dimensions of life. More than twenty-five years ago, German sociologist, Ralf Dahrendorf (1962) proposed a useful taxonomy for studying conflicts that occur at different levels. For the details of his taxonomy, we can look at Angell's (1965) article, the Sociology of Human Conflict.

In Dahrendorf's (1962) taxonomy one pole has five dimensions: (A) roles, (B) groups, (C) sectors, (D) societies and (E) supra-societal relations. The other pole has three dimensions: (1) equal against equal, (2) superordinate against subordinate and (3) whole against part. The cross-tabulation of these fifteen cells leads to the following six types: 1) role conflicts (e.g., family roles versus occupational role, A_1, occupational role versus labor union role A_2,); 2) competition (e.g., boys versus girls in school class, B_1, air-force and army, C_1); 3) class conflicts (e.g., father and children, B_2, free men versus slaves D_2); 4) minority conflict and deviation (e.g., family versus prodigal son B_3, the state versus criminal gang, D_3); 5) proportion struggle (e.g., protestants versus catholics, D_1); and 6) international relations (Soviet Bloc versus Western bloc E_1, common market versus France, E_3).

In accordance with these criteria, Angell (1965) has set up the following seven questions that contribute to the study of conflict. (1) What set of basic concepts are necessary for the study of conflict? (2) What types of conflict need to be discriminated? (3) What casual process leads to the conflict situation? (4) What are the main processes (or developmental stages) of conflict itself? (5) What are the effects of the conflict process on the conflicting units and on the context of their conflict? (6) What sort of external factors exacerbate conflict, and what sorts tend to modify or resolve it? (7) What are the alternative forms of termination of conflict, and how can they be reached?

As this paper focuses on the solution of international conflicts, emphasis will be on the supra-societal relations in Dahrendorf's sense and, keeping in mind the above seven questions set up by Angell, will involve some of the recent issues in international conflicts relevant to Angell's questions. When one has to deal with the phenomenon of international conflicts, it is especially important to specify the socio-political and socio-psychological dimensions of the context. A nation is always in association with political power, or the power of national leaders who tackle this national interest, for the maintenance of sovereignity, i.e., the state's and the people's existence.

When the maintenance of national power is not in harmony with the course for neighbouring countries or the rest of the world, the likelihood of growing conflict becomes great (in terms of the arms race, racial and ethnic antagonism or trade and economic conflicts). If a political leader, when performing political actions, does not take into account the attitudes of neighbouring countries or the regional and global context, then the tension or conflict within the country or regional conflicts among the countries with which the country is tied up will grow larger and the final outcome is likely to be war. (meaning not only physical wars, (meaning not only physical wars, but also trade wars, economic sanctions, retaliations or embargoes).

HOW TO COPE WITH THE UPHEAVAL OF CONFLICTS

In discussing various facets of international conflicts, Katz (1965) proposed six strategies for dealing with conflict resolution. They are: 1) the use of force, threats, counterthreats, and deterrence; 2) conflict denial; 3) conflict restriction and containment; 4) nonviolence and ideological conversion; 5) bargaining and compromise; and 6) problem -solving and creative integration. Strategies 1) and 6) are the most extreme cases, the former being the most primitive and the latter the most moderate. The solutions from 2) to 5) are intermediate. Katz has applied each of the six cases to the resolution of various international conflicts that have occurred in contemporary world society.

Among these, solution 5, bargaining and compromise, is most frequently observed nowadays, especially in resolving economic conflicts among advanced industrial countries. Consequently, I will take up the discussion starting from the recent conflict resolution of economic friction between Japan and the United States and explore how strategy 5 proposed by Katz has been applied to the recent resolution of the U.S.-Japan economic conflict.

The so-called U.S.-Japan Economic Friction has a rather long history. It started around 1962. No complete solution has yet been found. Friction has been continuing under the guise of various trading items between the U.S. and the Japanese governments. It started first with the textile trade conflicts in 1962, then developed to steel trade (1966-78), television (1966-77), manufacturing machines (1978-87) and, most recently, the trade conflict concerning agricultural products (1987-88). In each of the above cases, negotiators at the government level on both sides have succeeded in restricting import and export materials (thus achieving a compromise solution) or have succeeded in taking retaliatory action by imposing special tariffs, as seen in the recent conflict over semiconductor materials. At the present stage of conflict on agricultural products, the U.S. Government has taken the measure of legislation on the incorporative trade law, which is aimed at the protection of the U.S. agricultural products, while demanding that the Japanese block the protectionist measures advocated by Japanese farmers. This dispute has been running between the U.S. and Japanese government almost over a year.

The Coping Patterns in the U.S. - Japan Economic Conflict

Confronted with such a conflict, what Japan has to cope with has been much discussed by economic specialists. Some of the arguments are as follows:

(i)   One must seek the counsel of many people in consultation with GATT, i.e., General Agreement on Tariffs and Trade and work toward the establishment of a new framework for an international economic order which harmonizes with a balance of restriction and free trade.

(ii)   One must aid the revival of the effete American economy through improving Japanese economic policies, which have always depended on exports to the U.S. and through expanding domestic needs in Japan and other countries in such a way as to diminish the deficit of American trade. (Comments by one economic specialist, cited in Asahi Shimbun, April 28, 1988.)

However, the above two solutions are more or less idealistic and bear a close relationship to the ideological conversion and the use of non-violence methods, the fourth solution proposed by Katz (1965). For example, because the idea that the U.S. has taken over the world economic leadership has firmly been established since the end of the World War II, it would be extremely difficult to effect such a conversion, i.e., to change the national consciousness without hurting the sense of national pride and dignity of the American nation. On the other hand, the Japanese people and Government, even though they have a high sense of economic superiority in terms of production skills and efficiency, have become accustomed to a sense of dependency upon large nations with superior military power. Once such a dependency has been established as it has during the forty years since the end of the war, it is extremely difficult to convert it into a sense of independence and to foster a global consciousness with regard to the world economy. Furthermore, the Japanese sense of national pride would be hurt if economic sanctions were to be imposed by multinational agreement, a matter which is said to be under consideration in such organizations as GATT, OPEC and OECD.

As can be seen in this example, conversion at the ideological level is not an easy, practical solution for the reduction of economic conflicts. Needless to say, the implantation of high technological skill and collective organization to promote the production, efficiency and circulation of goods from Japan to other countries would be almost impossible since the ideologies, behaviour, mentalities and social and political systems differ so much from one country to another.

As seen here, the actual means used for solving economic conflicts is far from ideal. Negotiations at the governmental level are directed toward a narrow arrangement, i.e., agreement on certain items which does not go beyond the level of negotiation and bargaining, thus remaining at level 5 of Katz's proposal. Such a bilateral negotiation is often hampered if the agreements on certain items do not succeed. A vicious circle of action and reaction (sanction and retaliation) is likely to emerge, often escalating to more extreme dimensions, as past history has shown. The additional disadvantage of the bilateral negotiation is that the general public pays attention to the outcome of the negotiations and they often get emotional when the negotiations reach a deadlock. Because of this, the economic sanctions often become a basis for fostering antagonistic attitudes towards the other nation. Some people fear that the current U.S.-Japan negotiations recall the events surrounding the Pacific War, which broke out just after the breakdown of economic negotiations between the United States and Japan.[1]

When we compare the arguments made by both governments in the past and present, there are certainly similarities and differences in these arguments. In the former pre-war case, the U.S. government insisted that the invasion of the Japanese army into Mainland China and the French zone of Indo-china at that time was a violation of international law (Kellog-Brian Anti-war Pact in 1928 and the Treaties among Nine Countries made during 1921-22). At the same time, the Japanese government insisted that the occupation of the Japanese Army in foreign territories was not a violation of international law because the occupation was carried out for the purpose of maintaining international peace.

In the present U.S.-Japan economic friction, the U.S. government is insisting that the degree of import control imposed by the Japanese government is against GATT, (the General Agreement of Tariffs and Trade), while the Japanese government insists the amount of the penalty tax on imported goods is not against the principle of GATT. The basic difference in both arguments is that the former (the U.S. government) focused on the *basic principles* for maintaining peace through occupation or economic trade, while the latter (the Japanese government) concentrated on proposing *a concrete solution* just to suit the immediate situation in both the pre-war and present negotiations. It is clear that the basic differences in philosophy concerning the solution of conflicts by governments are manifested in the negotiations of today as well as in those of the past.

Thus, because of the perception gap between the two countries, their agreement often hangs in the balance and the argument is brought onto the international scene to obtain a consensus of both nations. The bilateral conflict solution will lead to a successful resolution without hurting either nation. However, if the consensus is forced on a particular country through the pressure of multinational agreements, then it will result in injury to the sentiments of that country. Some retaliatory action will be likely to occur and inter-governmental tensions will grow stronger.

In this context, the tension in the recent conflict between the U.S. and Japan concerning the trade of beef and citrus was relaxed as of June 19, 1988, just before the Toronto Summit Meeting took place. The initiative was taken by the United States Government in order to save the face of the Japanese Government. Namely, the U.S. decided to allow a three year moratorium on import controls on the Japanese side after the Japanese liberalized the import-export trade of beef (which had been the most important issue). They agreed to re-discuss the matter at a later date with a new round of multifaceted negotiations on trade problems.

Such a pattern of conflict resolution can be regarded as a combination of strategy 5, bargaining and compromise and strategy 6, problem-solving and creative integration, as proposed by Daniel Katz.

A Comparison of Public Consciousness and Government Policy

Due to the wide-spread diffusion and development of the mass media, particularly television, people are well informed about what government leaders say and how they react to trade conflicts and sanctions. However, the general public is less worried about the trade conflicts between the U.S.-Japan nations than are specialists, i.e., business people in trade or agriculture. For example, the American Time magazine reported on April 13, 1987 that, based upon their telephone survey of 1,014 American adults on February 17 and 18, 1987, American people expressed moderate opinions. Namely, 51-23% said that the Japanese people work harder than Americans and 53-25% thought that Japanese corporations are better managed than U.S. companies. On the other hand, answers to questions about Japan's invasion of the American market were more or less mixed. Fifty per cent of those surveyed thought that U.S. products were superior in quality to Japanese goods, but only 29% believed Japanese merchandise to be better.

However, respondents were divided just about evenly on which products offer the best value for the price. Forty-two per cent nominated American products, 41% Japanese. When they were asked about imposing a tariff that would make Japanese products more expensive, only 48% were in favour and 44% were opposed. The conclusion of the survey is that American citizens express a complete absence of the fiery anti-Japanese rhetoric that is currently fashionable in Washington.

The finding that the public is less worried than was thought about Japanese competition proves that they do not believe the competition is so unfair that the U.S. government should consider some limited retaliation. However, the congressmen, congresswomen and administrators are impressed by the cries of the protectionist lobbyists and justifiably annoyed by the frustrating experience of negotiating with the Japanese government.

One can criticize the governments by saying that they sometimes serve merely as power maintaining organs, acting as intermediaries between national demands and foreign pressures. As we saw in both the case of the American and of the Japanese governments, government itself is playing a see-saw game with international conflicts one after the other when it proposes new compromises without seeking an internal reform or solution to alleviate further conflicts. Such governmental conservativeness can be seen in other countries as well to a great extent.

CONCLUSION: THE ROLE OF PSYCHOLOGISTS IN THE FUTURE

Looking in retrospect at the above-mentioned theoretical discussions and cited examples, which were drawn from the recent case study concerning the economic conflict between the U.S. and Japan, why do we need new psychological theories and research work in the future? I think that the past theories devised and research performed by psychologists show promise for making worthwhile contributions to present and future international conflicts that are intricately tied up with given economic, ethnic-racial, socio-cultural, religious, and political backgrounds. The so-called experimental or laboratory-oriented research on conflict solution (e.g., game theory) has not contributed much to the actual problem solving of international conflicts. Also, one-sided hypotheses on aggressive or non-aggressive arguments in human nature are also a side-step approach to solving many conflicts with which the different dimensions have dealt. What is needed is a new psychological theory that is a complex multi-faceted and integrative theory to be applied to the different dimensions of conflicts. It must relate to the multidimensional and interdisciplinary theories and also to the intrinsic and meticulous theories, based on careful case study.

In this context, what we psychologists must do is to take the role of reconciliator, or intermediary, between the people who have anxieties, uncertainties, discontent and complaints about their civic life and those governments who are busy maintaining their powers and have no vision or long range plan for dealing with economic conflicts. Psychologists should persuade their governments with their research data and theories and then encourage them to take the first move in developing strategies for the solution of international conflicts.

The role of psychologists may differ from country to country, but it is the duty of psychologists to take such a job of social responsibility. By so doing, psychologists in the future, perhaps at the beginning of the 21st century, will be able to establish a firmer position and be recognized by the public and politicians with respect not only within the domain of social sciences, but also as valued citizens in national and international community as well.

NOTE

1. It has often been argued that there is a similarity in the negotiating patterns practised between the U.S. and Japan in the present situation and just before the outbreak of the Pacific War. However, the pre-war U.S.-Japanese conflict concerned the escalation of the Japanese armed forces in Asian territories, especially in mainland China and the French-occupied zone of Indo-china. The present U.S.-Japan conflict concerns the

escalation of the unlimited export of Japanese products into the U.S. and European countries.

REFERENCES

Dahrendorf, R. (1962). *Gesellschaft und Freiheit,* München: R. Piper und Co. Verlag.

Angell, R. C. (1965). The Sociology of Human Conflict In E. B. McNeil (Ed.) *The Nature of Human Conflict* , 91-115 Englewood Cliff, N.J.: Prentice-Hall.

Katz, D. (1965). Nationalism and Strategies of International Conflict Resolution. In H. C. Kelman (Ed.). *International Behavior,* 336-390. New York: Holt, Rinehart and Winston.

Pruitt, D. G. (1965). Definition of the Situation as a Determinant of International Action. In H. C. Kelman (Ed.) *International Behavior,* 393-432. New York: Holt, Rinehart and Winston.

Comments by Prof. Jun Nishikawa (1988, April 28). *Asahi Shimbun,* Evening Edition, p. 3.

Trade Wars (1987, April 13). *Time Magazine, Special Issue,* 4-14.

Osgood, C. E. (1962). *An Alternative to War or Surrender,* Urbana, Ill.: Univ. of Illinois Press.

Shepard, H. A. (1961). Responses to Situations of Competition and Conflict. In E. Boulding (Ed.) *Conflict Management in Organizations,* 33-41. Ann Arbor, Michigan: Foundation for Research on Human Behavior.

Wright, Q. Evan, W. M., & Deutsch, M. (Eds.). (1962). *Preventing World War III,* New York: Simon and Schuster.

Social Applications and Issues in Psychology
R.C. King and J.K. Collins (editors)
©*Elsevier Science Publishers B.V. (North-Holland), 1989*

AN ECOLOGY OF EMPOWERMENT

Di Bretherton

University of Melbourne Institute of Education, Australia

An ecological approach to human development, such as that described by Bronfenbrenner, provides a synthesis of individual psychology and sociological structures. If the dimension of consciousness is added to this model, the writings of many theorists such as Freud, Jung, Bion, Bateson and Fromm can be integrated into the schema. This gives a view of human ecology that is personal and political, conscious and unconscious, but still describes the dynamics of masculine dominance. Changing the ecology involves changing not only our personal behaviour and political structures but also our mentality. This is not simply at the conscious level where different cognitive strategies are called for, but also, as Mary Daly suggests, in our unconscious and symbolic levels of functioning there are no simple panaceas. Forms that can liberate, such as assertion training for women, can also reinforce the values of the patriarchy. But women can weave a new fabric. Her vision of the process of empowerment is the exuberant gyn-ecology.

This paper sketches a blueprint for developing a theoretical framework for the practice of empowering women. The aim is to give psychological substance to the feminist tenet that the personal is political. May (1976) points out that the word for power comes from the Latin posse meaning "to be able". He argues that, "As soon as powerlessness is referred to by its more personal name, helplessness or weakness, many people will sense that they are heavily burdened by it" (p. 21).

Walker and Browne (1985) suggest that sex role training that encourages girls to be passive creates a sense of helplessness. Seligman (1975) showed that animals who experienced helplessness early in life were vulnerable to helplessness later in life and hypothesised that the same principle might apply to humans. Walker and Browne (1985) conclude that:

> if women are to escape violent relationships, they must overcome their tendency to helplessness by, for instance, becoming angry rather than depressed, active rather than passive and more realistic about the likelihood of the relationship continuing on its aversive course rather than improving.In doing so, they must also overcome the sex role socialisation they have been taught from early childhood (p. 192).

Schmied and Lawler (1986) studied a number of factors and found that of these, only the powerlessness scale was related to illness in women. It is clear from feminist critiques that psychological ideas have been used to oppress women. Hysteria for example, was labelled a woman's disease, due to the wandering of the womb. Bowlby (1965) promised mothers (not fathers) that deviation from maternal duties would lead to children becoming psychopathic or even dwarved. Friedan (1963) documented the use of the psychiatric label of neurosis to keep women in place, at home in the suburbs. Chesler (1972) notes the use of psychiatric treatment as an instrument of male power.

However, it is also true that many of the ideas of psychology are liberating and empowering to women. For example, Jung's idea that crisis is also opportunity can rob the psychiatric label of its potential to disempower and Kelly's (1955) idea that the construction of reality is personal extends the power of thought to liberate. Personal growth groups, with their emphasis on sharing, expression of feeling, and intimacy, oppose those habits of secrecy which support violence in private.

The challenge is to sort through and select hypotheses that help in the task of empowering women and to put these together in a framework that is integrated and coherent, rather than pragmatic and ecclectic. A further challenge is that, as Spender (1980) points out, the very language that must be used to do this invalidates women. Like Jung, I have accepted the position that individual and collective liberation are not in opposition, that individual liberation is not possible in an oppressive culture, and that as we free ourselves, we free our culture. This is similar to Gorbochev's (1987) concept of perestroika. Social, political and economic reform are expressions of reforming our consciousness. This is basic to feminist philosophy which links personal consciousness to political action. The usefulness of the concept of empowerment in women is the bridge it forms between a feeling of positive self-esteem and ability and the vision of being active in the external world. Political oppression rests on personal invalidation. Psychology can help women reclaim their own experience and act to create a world which gives that experience expression in social, economic and political forms that are just.

THE ECOLOGICAL MODEL

Bronfenbrenner (1977), working from the topological theories of Lewin (1951) proposes a:

> broader approach to human development that focuses on the progressive accommodation, throughout the life span, between the growing human organism and the changing environments in which it actually lives and grows. The latter include not only the immediate settings containing the developing person, but also the larger social

contexts, both formal and informal, in which these settings are embedded (p. 513).

The environment is conceived as a nested arrangement of structures: the immediate settings or microsystems sit within the overarching institutional patterns of the culture. The developing individual belongs to a number of microsystems, such as the family, school and peer group, whose interrelations are termed the mesosystem. These are embedded in a locality or neighbourhood which is termed the exosystem. The exosystem includes the majority institutions of society as they operate at a concrete local level: transport, communication, government agencies. The micro, meso and exosystems are concrete manifestations of the economic, social, educational, legal and political systems which are the macrosystem. Bronfenbrenner contends that much current research lacks ecological validity and reflects the specific properties of the particular laboratory setting, rather than invariant processes. He argues that the researcher should move from the traditional model to an approach that invites consideration of the interactions between settings and extends to the examination of the larger context. He suggests that there is a place for the innovative restructuring of ecological systems in ways that depart from existing institutional ideologies and structures.

The feminist precept that the personal is political can usefully be mapped onto Bronfenbrenner's research paradigm. As individuals, children learn gender roles from the cradle. The microsystems reflect the sexual inequalities, for example in the speech patterns between men and women. The exosystems manifest sexism as discriminatory practices which reflect the broader patriarchal structures of the macrosystems.

Feminism argues that existing social arrangements are unjust, that change is both possible and necessary. This is contrary to the traditional research model which tends to posit a fixed order, to which individuals adjust. The ecological approach sees change as the source of our knowledge of human development, be it individual change through transition from one environment to another, or change due to transformation of an environment. Hence, it is more congruent with a feminist approach than is the traditional research paradigm.

Interestingly, Bronfenbrenner cites work by Sherif, Harvey, Hoyt, Hood and Sherif (1961) on male aggression as the best example of a transforming ecological experiment. By altering the structure of social organisations, they evoked high levels of aggression and then transformed the same boys back into cooperative, altruistic group members. Given that social arrangements that support male aggression are the crux of feminist concern, this seems to be the seed from which to begin research which is both empirically rigorous and speaks to the female condition.

THE INDIVIDUAL

Elizabeth Wilson calls her novel published in 1986 about women's struggle for freedom "Prisons of Glass" because glass is invisible yet impermeable. Invisible and impermeable walls are recurrent themes in feminist writings. Empowerment for women involves seeing the barriers,convincing others that the invisible barriers exist and making the barriers more permeable.

Lykes (1985) argues that notions of the self dominant in Western culture emphasise the self as autonomous and individual. A more collective view of the self as being in relationship is articulated by women. Consciousness itself, she suggests, is formed by the infant mother connection which is inseparable from a dynamic ecological system that shapes both mother and child. A dialectical understanding of individuality and social relationships tends to be grounded in the experience of being less powerful. Women and minority groups, she says, maintain this concept of self as being in relationship.

Early in life, children are discriminated by their clothing and name. A baby dressed in pink and called Jane elicits different behaviour from caregivers than the same baby dressed in blue and called Tim. This is illustrated in the film "The Fight to be Male". Boys are discouraged from expressing vulnerability while girls are constantly reminded of their dependence. Fastening on clothing for children is more often at the front for boys, to encourage autonomy, at the back for girls, assuming the need for assistance.

As the child grows, the behavioural differences that have been cultivated are reinforced by toys, television, books and games. Dolls for girls, active games and war toys for boys. The toys we give our children both express our mentality and reinforce its emergence in them. For example, Americans and Australians in Vietnam during the war built playgrounds for the Vietnamese children with helicopters, planes, tanks and the like. There remain, in a country where rotting tanks and bombed bridges attest to the past, rusting playgrounds which replicate the conflict in miniature.

A number of practitioners believe that positive comment will build self-esteem and empower the child. While there is doubtless value in adopting a supportive attitude and introducing cooperative, personally validating activities, empowerment is not such simple fare. The classic study of self-esteem by Coopersmith (1967) used boys as subjects and then these results were generalised to girls. Other scales of self-esteem follow his example. Reflection on experience of counselling men and women suggests that male self-esteem is often contingent on achievement while women may maintain a sense of self dignity despite social denigration. If a woman's self-esteem depends on the social recognition of her ability, then she is doomed to devalue herself in the current social order. However, girls use different constructs than do boys to define themselves (Jones,

1988) and choose their network of friends for different reasons. Girls' construction of self maintains the dialectic that Lykes (1985) describes containing the awareness of how I appear to another, as well as, or even at the expense of, how I am in myself. Boys, not surprisingly, emphasise doing. The dominant concept of self as autonomous and independent, self as active ego, is then more male, while girls have a more decentered concept in the Piagetian sense, self-in-relationship.

Bronfenbrenner describes individual growth as a series of successive accommodation to environments. The opportunities for women to move into other environments are likely to be much more limited. There is a piece of graffiti that says "I wanted to change the world but I could not find a babysitter". The idea that women are contained in private life is commonplace in sociology. A glass barrier to women's individual development then, is the restriction to small systems. The self is defined dialectically in relation to mother, home, school and work (i.e., individual, micro and mesosystems), but lack of opportunity to participate in the larger systems blocks further growth of the self.

THE MICROSYSTEM

The microsystem that has been most studied by psychologists is the family. Freud believed our nuclear family arrangements reflect our biological heritage. Psychoanalysis attributed women with a yielding personality and a maternal instinct that naturally suits them for their role of child bearers. Greater freedom and opportunity for boys followed from their natural asset, the penis, which girls envy. Horney (1967) suggested that any envy of the male might stem from the better social opportunity open to them rather than an envy of their biology. Contemporary research tends to back Horney. Children develop socially condoned gender behaviour before they acquire speech. (Smart & Smart, 1973). That is, masculine or feminine patterning of behaviour precedes acquisition of the knowledge that one is actually a boy or a girl and occurs long before a child has knowledge of the function of sex organs. For women, family pressure is to be a good daughter, then a good wife and a good mother. The role of the woman as supporter and nurturer is a difficult one in an exploiting society. While it is important to nurture and create a more nurturant society, an individual woman may be consumed by other people's emotional and physical needs.

Therapy, or the therapeutic group, is another microsystem which has been systematically explored. Psychoanalysis assumes a transfer of the family relationships onto the therapeutic interaction such that changes in therapy will transfer back to the family system. The group movement of the 60s, the consciousness raising groups of the women's movement, set up alternative microsystems with altered rules. Women were encouraged to support one another, to express their feelings and to gain a sense of self-worth through sharing. The outcome was not necessarily happiness. Rogers (1978) described the growing realisation of the gap between what is, and what could be, as "higher order discontent". Women felt deprived and acutely aware of the lack of depth, honesty and intimacy in interpersonal relationships. Given that Hite's (1988) respondents are daughters of this tradition, her results are not implausible. Wallen (1965) describes the conditions of personal change as being "a moderate degree of discomfort within an atmosphere of trust". Group support may allow consciousness of discontent to surface.

An important element in women's groups is the teaching of assertion. Spender argues against this on the grounds that assertion teaches women to speak like men. Her concern echoes another piece of graffiti which says "women who want to be like men lack ambition". However, it is not true that women are unequivocally less assertive than men. Hollandsworth and Wall (1977) and Crassini, Law and Wilson (1979) find that assertion needs are sexually differentiated. Men are more assertive in relation to work superiors, stating opinions and expressing disagreement. Women are more assertive in the expression of feeling. That is, women are allowed freedom within the devalued realm of feeling and relationship.

In relation to teaching assertion, I think Spender's position is incorrect. Assertion training involves thinking about the rights of others and the inhibition of one's own aggression which is not compatible with male dominance. However, assertion is by no means a panacea. Studies of violence suggests that the occasion which triggers an attack may well be a woman's expression of autonomy. Teaching assertion to women, without a full sense of the dangers inherent in challenging the masters of the universe, is unfair, as documented in the film "No Myth". Teaching assertion may also end up as more of the same. While its intent is to allow the individual to be more assertive, a woman can easily hear this as another emotional responsibility added on to the rest. When relationships break down, the woman is blamed for being insufficiently assertive. The old mysogeny gains modern dress.

Spender (1982) points out that power is maintained by men in a human relations group by their not disclosing vulnerability, refusing to talk on someone else's topic and withholding personal information. The men discuss sexism in abstract terms, but will silence a woman wanting to talk about her experience of sexism.

Bateson (1973) argues that sending double-messages is schizophrenogenic. May (1976) echoes this proposition contending that the origin of schizophrenia is outward powerlessness (and inner violence). All women are presented with a fundamental double-message, that the qualities put forward as being female endow one with less than full being as a person, or that the qualities of being a well-developed person make one unfeminine. It is not then surprising to find that Laing and Esterson (1964) describe schizophrenic daughters, or that many women do not trust the evidence of their own experience.

THE MESOSYSTEM

The interaction between microsystems has been less studied by psychologists. As the effect of refusal to conform to sex role stereotype can trigger repressive behaviour in others (Chesler, 1972), this seems to be an area of further research. Lips (1981) points out that women, like other non-dominant groups, avoid confrontation and exert power indirectly. Membership of a micro-system which encourages greater autonomy and directness in communication will be both liberating and risky. The natural ecological experiment, via Bronfenbrenner, may prove useful. Studying effects of the teaching of exertion of power in one system to the human repercussions of behaviour change in another, would be an example.

THE EXOSYSTEM

The difficulty in bringing about change in the status of women rests in the interlocking nature of the systems such that each reinforces the other. Friedan (1963) pointed out that the discontented housewife went to a therapist who reinforced the idea that women ought to be happy with their condition.

The patterns of the exosystem express and reinforce gender roles. Hotchin (1986) studied children's maps of their play space in high rise buildings on a Melbourne housing estate and found that girls tend to be restricted to the veranda, especially in certain ethnic groups, while boys establish extensive neighbourhood territories. Edgar and McPhee (1974) documented images of women in the media which maintain stereotyped ideas of gender. Behavioural psychology finds that vicarious reinforcement alters patterns of action and that children replicate those behaviours which are rewarded (Bandura, 1970). This seems to apply to behaviours of the dominant group, such that girls could be expected to incorporate the standards of male behaviour and yet be punished for acting according to them.

THE MACROSYSTEM

The feminist critique argues that society devalues women and that this inequality permeates the diverse contexts in which the child grows (Boulding, 1976). Daly (1973) argues that men not only own the external world but have also commandeered the unconscious. Christ (1978) suggests that religions centred on the worship of a male God keep women in a state of dependence on male authority and legitimate the authority of fathers and sons. Daly sees the denigration of female power as an historical phenomenon. The Malleus Maleficum stated that all witchcraft stems from carnal lust which in women is insatiable. The powerful women were tortured and killed. Goody (1987) examines witchcraft in various societies and concludes that the crime is not to be a witch, but to be female. The female. The same mystical aggressive powers used by men are proof of political authority. When the powers are used by women they are frightening and dangerous. Sometimes their use leads to the execution of the female witch by sadistic methods. This dark streak in the collective unconscious tends to undermine conscious advances. For example, in professions where women make gains, the status of the profession backslides.

IMPLICATIONS FOR CHANGE

> The Feminist Therapy Support Group (1983) writes:
> what feminists entering therapy saw was that a much higher percentage of women than men were in psychotherapy, that most of the therapists were men, and that the majority of training institutions were sexist to the core in their teaching of female psychology (p. 23).

In traditional therapy, that which is personal and individual stays personal and individual, but the feminist therapist includes political action as a possible outcome. Jung felt that the task of individuation involves men accommodating to the feminine and women coming to terms with the masculine within them. The feminist perspective might be to focus on men accommodating to the feminine within, while women move outwards to learn about the male dominated public realm. That is, given that socialisation leads girls and boys along different paths, their needs as adults in therapy might be expected to differ. The devalued female might need encouragement to reach out more actively, to think about the social, political, technological and economic realities, to trust her own perceptions, to accept her own anger. The male who already strives may find better balance in getting in touch with his feelings of vulnerability, learning empathy, reflecting in a more passive mode. That is, traditional therapy modes which encourage the exploration of intimacy seem to match better the needs of men, but are largely consumed by women.

The ecological model is useful in synthesising human development and social context and offers some interesting points for change. First, it is noticeable that most measures are introduced in a single location with insufficient consideration to the flow-on effects; that is, for therapy (microsystem) or legislation (macrosystem). Wilson (1988) quotes an effective campaign to prevent crime in France. In this scheme, local (exosystem) initiatives are supported by national (macrosystem) resources and prestige. That is, the successful scheme crosses the barriers of the systems and makes them more permeable.

In my work with women students, I begin with the individual in relationship to the group. Students keep journals which express feelings, clarify and validate experience. They are encouraged to explore issues that are raised in class and follow these through to wider contexts such as the workplace, the home, society. The group is encouraged to work collectively and cooperatively in the mode described by Miller (1976). Because the students are professionally linked, the group becomes the core of a network which persists beyond the course. Students are strongly encouraged to participate in course committees and professional bodies to help shape their own study and work environments. They are also encouraged to communicate their findings and ideas through newsletters, suburban newspapers and community radio, not just academic journals. The curriculum includes proactive strategies such as cooperative learning and negotiation skills, not just therapy. The ecological model is used as a basis for viewing human problems from an individual through to a broad societal perspective.

PRACTICAL APPLICATION

To use the ecological model in practice, I draw it up as a topological diagram and ask people to fill in their own data. For example, a group of evening students had a great deal of trouble with their research projects and many felt disempowered and discouraged. One student even had her idea stolen by a work superior who obtained a grant to carry it out. We drew out the topological figures on the floor and put into them our own characteristics. It became clear that what was happening was that the idea of doing research upset hierarchical relationships in the workplaces. Women at the bottom of the rung just don't do research; research is the province of the medical practitioners, not the nurses or patients. The picture that emerged was one in which the expectations of the college caused behaviour that stepped outside the work roles. The result was abuse and humiliation, which each student had privatised. Talking over the experience together, it became apparent that about a third of the students in the group had experienced a serious disruption in their work relationships, unique in the experience of each. They came to the conclusion that the good relationships they experienced in the past were based on a hidden premise about keeping in place. Asserting themselves by undertaking a research role became an attempt to cross a glass barrier previously invisible but all too tangible. Setting a research project, to be carried out in the workplace, became an ecological experiment about gender relations in their workplaces. Feeling battered and bruised, we nonetheless concluded that we had learnt a great deal from inadvertently running into a glass wall.

From the discussion of the ecology of human development some quite specific guide lines for the feminist therapist can be listed in the form of objectives. These may give a focus for psychologists whose practical aim is the empowerment of women.

OBJECTIVES FOR THE FEMINIST THERAPIST

(i) To begin with the idea that we create, as we are created by, our environment. That is, the paradigm is transformational.

(ii) To be aware of the socialisation process that teaches boys to dominate and girls to submit.

(iii) To understand the importance of concrete things in expressing and reinforcing passivity in women and activity in men; e.g., clothing, toys, television images.

(iv) To foster participation in non-hierarchical structures, e.g., co-operative learning, codes of behaviour rather than discipline policies in schools.

(v) To foster active, dynamic learning strategies that decentre consciousness; e.g., role plays that explore other perspectives, science fiction that empathises with the alien, conflict resolution techniques.

(vi) To encourage women to accept and love their own bodies; e.g., explore slang words that illustrate the association between female reproductive organs and abuse, read matriarchical myths such as the "Daughters of Copperwoman" by Cameron (1984).

(vii) To participate as a psychologist in the public realm; e.g., inform politicians about Fromm's (1956, 1968) ideas on the humanisation of technology, publicise the dangers of nihilistic images of the future in young people, campaign against war and victim toys. That is, be spokespeople about the psychological needs of human kind.

(viii) To address the underdeveloped areas in female consciousness; e.g., learning about and participating in the public realm, becoming conscious of the broader implications, learning more active modes, accepting one's power and strength.

(ix) To address the underdeveloped areas in male consciousness; e.g., accepting one's own vulnerability and emotions, exploring mental processes, learning how body language can assume dominance, learning to listen and to be able to be passive.

(x) To build female solidarity; e.g., run support groups, take care in criticising other women, write letters of support to women in public life, foster the use of non-sexist language and non-discriminatory employment practices.

(xi) To reclaim the feminine tradition, both to celebrate the past and to apply the lessons of history; e.g., see the Judy Chicago exhibition, read Dale Spender's work or visit the women's museum in Ho Chi Minh City.

(xii) To explore the meso and exosystems as mediating influences between the personal and the political; e.g., greater participation by women in local government, residents' groups, the community media.

Feminist therapy is not health for women at the expense of men. Bacon (1986) expresses the convergence beyond power relations of the needs of both women and men. She writes

Feminism is a call for authentic spiritual development, based on the authority of one's own experience of the light. It is a rejection of hierarchy (which has generally meant male authority) and an embracing of community. It is a dream of a future based on preservation, not exploitation; cooperation not competition; the weaving of a web of networks, not their destruction by conflict. It is a vision of the divine spirit that nurtures and supports each individual ... and gives to humans the wonderful gift of personal affirmation and creativity. (p. 7).

REFERENCES

Bacon, M. H. (1986). Quaker women today. *Friends journal.* November, 4-7.

Bandura, A. (1970). The role of modelling processes in personality development. In Foley, J.M., Lockhart, R.A., & Messick, D.M. *Contemporary readings in psychology.* New York: Harper & Row. 328-331.

Bateson, G. (1973). *Steps to an ecology of mind.* London: Paladin.

Boulding, E. (1976). *The underside of history: a view of women through time.* Colorado: Westview Press.

Bowlby, J. (1965). *Child care and the growth of love.* Harmonsworth : Penguin.

Bronfenbrenner, V. (1977). Toward an experimental ecology of human development. *American Psychologist.* July, 513-531.

Cameron, A. (1984). *Daughters of copperwoman.* London: Womens Press.

Chesler, P. (1972). *Women and madness.* Garden City, NY: Doubleday.

Chicago, J. (1979). *The dinner party - a symbol of our heritage.* New York: Anchor Press/Double Day.

Christ, C. (1978). Why women need the goddess. *Heresies.* Spring, 8-13.

Coopersmith, S. (1967). *The antecedents of self-esteem.* San Francisco: W.H. Freeman.

Crassini, B., Law, H., & Wilson, E. (1979). Sex differences in assertive behaviour. *Australian Journal of Psychology. 31,* 15-19.

Daly, M. (1973). *Beyond God the father.* Boston: Beacon Press.

Edgar, P., & McPhee, H. (1974). *Media she.* Melbourne: Heineman.

Feminist Therapy Support Group (1983). Feminist therapy. *Journal of cooperation.* March, 21-27.

Fight to be male. (1979). Motion picture. U.K.: British Broadcasting Commission. 16mm. 54 minutes.

Friedan, B., (1963). *The feminine mystique.* Harmondsworth: Penguin.

Fromm, E. (1956). *The art of loving.* New York: Bantam.

Fromm, E. (1968). *The revolution of hope: toward a humanised technology.* New York: Harper & Row.

Gordy, E. (1987). Why must might be right? Observations on the sexual herrschaft. *Quarterly newsletter of the laboratory of comparative human cognition. 9,* 55-77.

Gorbachev, M. (1987). *Perestroika.* London: Collins.

Hite, S. (1988). *Women and love: the new Hite report.* New York: Viking.

Hollandsworth, J.G. & Wall, K.E. (1977). Sex differences in assertive behaviour: an empirical investigation. *Journal of counselling psychology. 24,* 217-222.

Horney, K. (1967). *Feminine psychology.* New York: Norton.

Hotchin, L. (1985). Children's attitudes toward living on the North Richmond Ministry of Housing Estate. Unpublished project, Melbourne College of Advanced Education.

Jones, A. (1988). Gender and the personal construction of self. Unpublished project, Melbourne College of Advanced Education.

Kelly, G. (1955). *The psychology of personal constructs.* New York: Norton.

Laing, R.D. & Esterson, A. (1964). *Sanity, madness and the family.* London: Tavistock Publications.

Lewin, K. (1951). *Field theory in social science.* New York: Harper.

.NP Lips, H. (1981). *Women, Men and the psychology of power.* Englewood Cliffs: Prentice Hall.

Lykes, M. (1985). Gender and individualistic vs. collectivist bases for notions about the self. *Journal of personality, 53,* 356-383.

May, R. (1976).*Power and innocence.* Great Britain: Fontana/Collins.

Miller, J.B. (1976).*Toward a new psychology of women.* Boston: Beacon Press.

No Myth. (1986). Video tape. Australia: Open Channel. VHS. 26 minutes.

Rogers, C. (1978). *Carl Rogers on personal power.* London: Constable.

Schmied, L., & Lawler, K. (1986). Hardiness, type A behaviour and stress-illness in working women. *Journal of personality and social psychology. 51,* 1218-1223.

Seligman, M. (1975). *Helplessness: on depression,development and death.* San Francisco: Freeman Press.

Sherif, M., Harvey, O.J., Hoyt, B.J., Hood, W.R. & Sherif, C.W. (1961). *Intergroup conflict and cooperation: the robbers cave experiment.* Norman: University of Oklahoma   Book Exchange.

Smart, M., & Smart, R. (1973). *Infants: development and relationships.* New York: Macmillan.

Spender, D. (1982). *Women of ideas (and what men have done to them).* London: Ark Paperbacks.

Walker, L.E., & Browne, A. (1985). Gender and victimization   by intimates. *Journal of personality. 53,* 179-195.

Wallen, J. (1965). *Mimes.* Portland, Oregon: Northwest Laboratory Handouts.

Wilson, E. (1986), *Prisons of glass.* Methuen.

Wilson, P. (1988). *The roots of violence.* Canberra: National Women's Consultative Council and Australian Institute of Criminology Forum on Violence.

Section 2

PROFESSIONAL ISSUES

Social Applications and Issues in Psychology
R.C. King and J.K. Collins (editors)
©Elsevier Science Publishers B.V. (North-Holland), 1989

PREDICTION OF DANGEROUSNESS:
THE PSYCHOLOGIST'S DUTY TO WARN

Rae Sedgwick

Bonner Springs, Kansas, U.S.A.

This paper examines the prediction of dangerousness and the psychologist's duty to warn. Three areas are discussed: (a) the complexities associated with defining and predicting future dangerousness, (b) legal issues associated with predictions of dangerousness and the psychologist's responsibility to others, and (c) the issue of confidentiality and the duty to warn. The author discusses these issues in light of the Tarasoff doctrine, other courts expansion of the doctrine, and the implications for psychologists.

"...once a therapist does in fact determine, or under applicable professional standards reasonably should have determined, that a patient poses a serious danger of violence to others, he bears a duty to exercise reasonable care to protect the foreseeable victim of that danger. (Tarasoff v. Regents of University of California, 1976, p. 345)

The 1976 California Supreme Court ruled in the Tarasoff case that (a) psychologists have the duty to warn, and (b) psychologists have the duty to protect third parties from a threat of serious danger posed by a patient under the psychologist's care. This author will examine that holding and discuss its implications for psychologists.

"...Once a Therapist..."

In the Tarasoff case, Poddar sought psychiatric treatment at the student health facility at Berkeley. He was evaluated by a psychiatrist who referred Poddar to a psychologist for psychotherapy. During the course of treatment, the psychologist determined that Poddar was dangerous. Poddar communicated his intent to harm his girlfriend, readily identifiable as Tatiana, when she returned from spending the summer abroad. The psychologist, along with the psychiatrist who initially evaluated Poddar and the assistant to the director of the department of psychiatry decided that Poddar should be committed for observation in a mental hospital. The treating psychologist telephoned the campus police requesting commitment and wrote a letter to the Chief of Police requesting his assistance in Poddar's commitment.

Officers took Poddar into custody, but based on their assessment of him, determined that he was rational and subsequently released him. Poddar gave the police assurance that he would stay away from Tatiana. Poddar did not return for outpatient psychotherapy. Sixty-seven days later, Poddar killed Tatiana. No warning had been given Tatiana. While police were given statutory immunity, the psychologist and psychiatrists were not.

The therapist in this case was a psychologist. In its holding, however, the court made it clear that the ruling applied to the psychiatrists as well. Their liability extended to Tatiana, even though she was not a patient of any of the professionals. She was an unrelated third party, for whom the courts held the therapist liable.

Although the therapist in this case was the psychologist and/or psychiatrist, there is no reason to believe that liability would not be extended to other mental health professionals as well, including nurses, social workers, and counsellors (Jensen v. Conrad, 1983; Peck v. Counseling Service, 1985; Prins, 1981). Similarly, while this case involved a psychologist treating a voluntary outpatient, there is reason to believe that evaluation alone, without treatment, may establish a basis for liability (Note, 1980).

"...Determines...or Should Have Determined..."

In the Tarasoff case, the psychologist did determine, based on an actual threat, that Poddar was dangerous. The psychologist in this case did, in a sense, know of inherent danger. The court did not limit itself to situations where the therapist determines, through a patient's actual threat, for example, that there is a threat of serious danger and takes no action but extended its holding to situations where the therapist "should have determined" that the patient might present a serious threat of danger to another person (p. 345).

Courts in other jurisdictions have expanded the duty to warn and duty to protect in a variety of ways. In Lipari v. Sears (1980), the court concluded that a psychotherapist has a duty to warn and a duty to protect unknown victims, as well as those readily identifiable. In Lipari, a former psychiatric patient of a Veterans' Hospital entered a nightclub with a shotgun. The patient shot and injured the plaintiff and killed her husband. The United States District Court for the District of Nebraska, imposed on the therapist a duty to protect the public at large from the patient's foreseeable dangerous actions. In Lipari, however, no specific threats of harm were made to any particular person. The court, however, concluded that the psychiatrists could be held liable for failing to protect nightclub patrons from the patient's violent behavior, even where the victims were not known by the patient or the psychiatrist.

In Peterson v. State (1983), the Washington Supreme Court extended psychiatric liability. There, a state hospital was held liable when one of its psychiatrists failed to confine a drug-addicted mental patient who unintentionally injured another while under the influence of drugs. In Petersen , five days after release from a state hospital where he was being treated for drug addiction and mental problems, a patient drove through a red traffic light and injured another person in the resulting automobile accident. Petersen was the first case to hold a therapist liable for a patient's unintentional negligent act. In Lipari, it will be recalled, the act was intentional.

Some courts have held, in the absence of a specific threat against an identifiable victim, that the psychotherapist has no legal duty to warn or protect third persons (Brady v. Hopper, 1984; Perrerira v. State of Colorado, 1986). Other courts have imposed a duty on the psychotherapist to take reasonable measures to protect potential victims even though no actual threats were made against a particular individual (Jablonski v.United States, 1983; Hedlund v.Superior Court of Orange County 1983).

"...Patient Poses a Serious Danger..."
"...of Violence to Others..."

In Jablonski v. United States (1983), Jablonski was being treated as an outpatient in a Veterans' Administration Hospital by a psychiatrist. When the psychiatrist recommended that Jablonski, who had been diagnosed as an "anti-social personality" and as "potentially dangerous," voluntarily hospitalize himself, he refused. The psychiatrist and the psychiatrist's supervisor determined that this situation, though an emergency, was not a sufficient basis for involuntary commitment. Jablonski subsequently attacked and killed his girlfriend.

During the course of outpatient therapy, Jablonski's girlfriend had communicated her fear of Jablonski to the psychiartist. On both occasions, each psychiatrist recommended that she stay away from Jablonski. It was believed that she would not heed further warnings because of her stated love for Jablonski.

Jablonski had not made threats to any specific individuals. However, the court concluded that had the psychiatrist obtained the patient's prior medical records, in which Jablonski's history of violence toward women was documented, he would have been able to determine that the patient was dangerous. The court determined that the records contained information sufficient about Jablonski's past history of violence toward his wife and other women close to him, to make it possible for the psychiatrist to determine that the deceased would be a foreseeable victim. Failure to obtain past medical records, documenting the past history of the patient's violence, became the basis of liability. Although the predictors of future dangerousness are many and varied, the single most reliable indicator is previous acts of violence (Kozol, 1982; Note, 1983).

In <u>Hedlund</u> v. <u>Superior Court of Orange County</u> (1983), the Supreme Court of California determined that it was reasonable to recognize the plaintiff's son as a foreseeable bystander. In <u>Hedlund,</u> Wilson had communicated to his therapist his intent to harm the mother of the boy. The psychologist who knew of the threats did not warn the potential victim of the threat. Subsequently, Wilson injured the plaintiff. At the time of the injury, the child was present and the mother threw herself over the child to protect him from the shotgun blasts. The child did not sustain apparent physical injury; but the mother sustained severe injuries. It was alleged that the child suffered psychological and emotional trauma.

The Court in <u>Hedlund</u> held that failure to warn an identifiable victim was professional negligence; that it was foreseeable that the threats, if carried out against the mother, posed a risk of harm to bystanders and those in close relationship as well; and that the therapist's duty to warn extended to the child. The court noted further that diagnosis and the appropriate steps necessary to protect the victim are not separate or severable but taken together constitute a duty giving rise to a cause of action for failure to warn (<u>Hedlund</u>, 1983, p. 41).

"...Duty to Exercise Reasonable Care to Protect..."

The <u>Tarasoff</u> court imposed upon the therapist a duty without clear guidelines as to how to carry out that duty. The discharge of the duty may require that the therapist warn the victim or others likely to apprise the victim, notify the police, or take other steps reasonably necessary under the circumstances (<u>Tarasoff</u>, 1976, p. 340).

Under common law, a person had no duty to prevent a third party from causing physical injury to another. American courts have, however, carved out an exception to the general rule. Under this exception , a person has a duty to control the conduct of a third person and thereby prevent physical harm to another if:

> (a) a special relationship exists between the actor and the third person which imposes a duty upon the actor to control the third person's conduct, or (b) a special relationship exists between the actor and the other which gives to the other a right to protection. (Restatement (Second) of Torts ss 315, 1965).

Under the Restatement approach, the psychotherapy relationship has been found to be a sufficient basis for imposing an affirmative duty on the therapist for the benefit of third persons. The <u>Tarasoff</u> court adopted the special relationship analysis of the Restatement (Second) of Torts 315. Other courts have found the duty to protect inherent in the obligation to warn third parties of infectious or contagious diseases (McIntosh v. Milano, 1979, p. 512).

In McIntosh, New Jersey became the second jurisdiction to impose upon a psychiatrist the duty to warn a third person of a patient's dangerous propensities. The psychiatrist in that case treated, on a weekly basis, a patient who confided his fantasies, previous sexual experiences and his jealousies of the deceased. The patient, Morgenstein, was known by the psychiatrist to be in the possession of a knife and to have previously fired a BB gun at the victim's house and car. In July of 1975, Morgenstein, having been a patient of Milan's for nearly two years, fatally shot the deceased.

The court in McIntosh, like the court in Tarasoff, did not hold the therapist to a perfect standard of performance, but rather to a standard for a therapist in "the particular field in the particular community" (McIntosh, 1979, p. 508). Prediction of dangerousness was recognized to be a complex matter, but in this case Morgenstein demonstrated his dangerousness by (a) firing a weapon at the victim's car, (b) exhibiting a knife to the therapist, (c) forging a prescription, and (d) verbalizing threats. Dangerousness in this case was considered by the courts, not as an opinion of the therapist, but rather as a known fact (McIntosh, 1979, p. 506).

Despite the complexities associated with the prediction of dangerousness, it is clear that the courts consider the therapist's assessment of dangerousness to be a reasonable and necessary step in the protection of third parties. The courts have not faulted therapists for failure to predict dangerousness so much as for the failure to gather sufficient background material and past medical records regarding violent behavior (Jablonski v. United States, 1980), for the failure to conduct thorough investigations when the situation warrants, as for example in reported child abuse (Jensen v. Conrad, 1983), or for the failure to take appropriate measures when it is apparent that dangerous propensities exist (McIntosh v. Milano 1979).

Measures to be taken include warning the victim or others likely to apprise the victim of the danger, to notify the police (Tarasoff, 1976), warning close family members (Hedlund, 1983), extending therapy to include the victim or family members (Wexler 1979), or initiating voluntary or invountary hospitalization (Petersen, 1983). There is some concern that therapists' difficulty in predicting dangerousness may result in overcommitment of mental patients (Taig v. State, 1963).

The nature of the measures taken will vary from case to case depending upon the specific circumstances. It does seem clear, however, that for a warning to be adequate, it must be more than mere notification, and that reasonable steps taken may require some direct action on the part of the therapist, including the initiating of hospitalization.

Although evidence has been presented about the difficulties of accurate predictions of dangerousness (Diamond, 1975; Steadman, 1980; Dix, 1980),the capacity of clinicians to predict dangerousness (Stone, 1976; Gurevitz, 1977) and about lack of specificity of whom and how to warn adequately, the courts continue to hold therapists liable where it is determined that they knew or should have known of the patient's potential for violence. This is in spite of the concerns raised about the need to protect the confidential nature of the therapist-patient relationship and the potentially disruptive effects of the duty to warn-duty to protect.

Confidentiality is recognized as essential to the therapy process and as important to the therapist-patient relationship. In some jurisdictions, it is a privilege analogous to that of the attorney-client privilege. However, like the attorney-client privilege, the therapist-patient privilege is not absolute (Plaut, 1974; McIntosh, 1979; Peck, 1985). In Tarasoff, the court reasoned as follows:

> Open and confidential character of the psychotherapeutic dialogue encourages patients to express threats...that therapists should not be routinely encouraged to reveal such threats ... and that the therapist's obligations to his patient require that he not disclose a confidence ... unless necessary to avert danger to others...even then discretely and in a fashion to preserve the privacy of the patient to the fullest extent compatible with the prevention of the threatened danger. (Tarasoff, 1976, p. 347).

There is, then, no general duty to warn of each threat. However, when the therapist determines or should determine that the patient poses a serious threat, reasonable care must be taken to protect the foreseeable victim. While public policy favors the protection of confidentiality, disclosure is deemed warranted to protect the welfare of others. According to the Tarasoff court, "the protective privilege ends where public peril begins" (Tarasoff, 1976, p. 347). Other courts, while recognizing the physician-patient privilege, have advocated waiver of the privilege in the interest of public policy (Peck v. Counseling, 1985, p. 423). Some therapists may consider the legally imposed duty to warn to be in conflict with the right of privacy of clients. In exercising due care in carrying out the duty to warn, therapists must balance the duty to protect third parties against what might become a breach of confidentiality with the patient. Whether or not a breach occurs depends upon each jurisdiction's position on the therapist's duty not to disclose confidential information. Five states have developed statutes addressing the need to balance effective confidential psychotherapy and a safe society (Cal. Civ. Code, 1987; Ky. Rev. Stat. Ann., 1986; Kan. Stat. Ann., 1986; Minn. Stat. Ann, 1987; N.H. Rev. Stat.Ann., 1986). There will be those therapists, who either because of a state law prohibiting disclosure of privileged information except in cases of abuse or dangerousness or because of their ethical position, will elect some other measure, such as hospitalization, as the appropriate manifestation of their duty to warn (Roth & Meisel, 1977).

Determining what are reasonable measures must itself be carried out with due care on the part of the therapist. To warn adequately, to proceed cautiously but thoroughly and to limit personal liability are all part of this process. Due care must be exercised in determining the identity of foreseeable victims, as the courts have issued a variety of ruling since Tarasoff.

"...Foreseeable Victim..."

In Tarasoff, foreseeability was considered one of the more important considerations in establishing the duty to use reasonable care to avert harm to third parties (Tarasoff, 1976, p. 342). Mavroudis v. Superior Court of San Mateo (1980), was the first decision to state clearly that the victim be "readily identifiable" (p. 277). Prior to Jablonski, the California Supreme Court refused to extend the duty to warn in Thompson v. County of Alameda (1980), where the patient had made generalized threats toward a segment of the population. In Thompson, a juvenile offender, with a propensity for sexual assault of young children, was confined to a county institution. After discharge into his mother's custody, the offender murdered a neighbor's son. The court ruled that the victim need not be specifically named but must be "readily identifiable". The court concluded that the county owed no duty to warn the community of the offender's release as no specific threats were directed toward any specific victims (Thompson v. County of Alameda, 1980, p. 76).

In Jablonski, there were no specific threats made to a particular person. The psychiatrist was, however, held liable because had he searched past medical records, the court held, he should have been able to determine that the potential victim was in danger and that her identity was foreseeable had he taken appropriate steps. In Hedlund, the court held the psychologist liable for failure to warn and protect the son of a potential victim, thereby recognizing the "foreseeable bystander" (p. 46).

A more recent case, to expand the Tarasoff doctrine, was Peck v. Counseling Service of Addison Conty, Inc. (1985). In Peck, John Peck sought counselling following a fight with his father. He discussed with the therapist his anger with his father, his desire to "get back at his dad", and his plan to retaliate by burning down his father's barn. The therapist exacted a promise from Peck that he would not carry out his threat. Believing that Peck would keep his promise, the therapist did not warn Peck's father of the threat. Six days later, John Peck burned down his father's barn.

The Supreme Court of Vermont held that a mental health professional had a duty to take reasonable steps to protect a third party from threats of physical harm posed by the patient (Peck v. Counseling Service, 1985, p. 423). Where previous decisions found therapists liable for harm to third parties, the Peck case expanded the liability to include harm to property of third parties as well.

In light of the expansion of the Tarasoff doctrine, it seems apparent that even in those jurisidictions not having considered Tarasoff, the prudent clinician should proceed under the assumption that, given the opportunity, the courts will find a basis of liability for failure to warn-protect (Applebaum, 1985). In order to limit liability in the light of that duty the clinician may consider a number of options: (a) advising clients of the limits imposed on confidentiality because of the psychologist's duty to society (Fleming & Maximov, 1974), (b) conducting a thorough evaluation to include a thorough history regarding violent or otherwise dangerous behavior, (c) obtaining past medical and psychological records, (d) seeking opinions of colleagues or supervisors where one's own expertise is limited or the findings questionable, (e) designing treatment plans specific to the needs of the volatile patient, (f) involving the patient and members of the patient's family in the diagnostic as well as the treatment process, and (g) hospitalizing or initiating the hospitalization of the difficult to treat, potentially volatile outpatient.

Finally, courts are not persuaded by the argument that dangerousness is difficult or impossible to predict. The prudent clinician will become familiar with those factors most predictive of behavior likely to cause harm to others and will undertake appropriate measures to avert that harm (Monahan, 1981; Givelber, Bowers, & Blitch, 1984).

CONCLUSION

The Tarasoff court in 1976 created for the psychotherapist a duty to warn-duty to protect third parties from potential harm caused by their patients. This duty arises out of a special relationship between the therapist and patient, and extends to third parties through the courts' belief that the psychotherapist has the expertise to foresee harm to a potential victim. This is an exception to the general rule holding no duty to third parties.

At the outset, the duty to protect involved third parties who were readily identifiable, potential victims. The duty has been expanded to include the public at large, foreseeable bystanders, unintentional negligent acts of drug-addicted patients, and property of third persons.

Inherent in the duty to protect is the therapist's responsibility to assess and predict dangerousness of patients. Courts have held that this may require the therapist to obtain past medical records, investigate reports fully, and take appropriate action where dangerous propensities are determined or should have been determined to exist. It may include an assessment of environmental stress factors, family history, and job factors. The therapist must make an adequate assessment and must make decisions based on that assessment as well, including taking apppropriate action necessary to avert harm to others.

The duty to exercise reasonable care to protect may include: (a) the duty to warn the victim or other persons, (b) to notify the police, (c) to medicate, (d) to initiate or intensify therapy to include the potential victim, or (e) to hospitalize. It may require a breach of confidentialty in the interest of protecting the welfare of the community at large. While public policy favors the protection of confidentiality, disclosure is deemed warranted to protect the welfare of others. Courts have held that the privacy inherent in the therapist-patient relationship is not absolute and may be waived in the interest of protecting the welfare of others.

Courts have not expected the therapist to give a perfect performance in carrying out the duty to warn-duty to protect but rather have expected the therapist to adhere to a standard of performance for a practitioner in a particular field in a particular community. In carrying out the duty, it is expected that the clinician will proceed with due care.

The clinician will need to proceed with due care, conduct thorough assessments, seek the counsel of colleagues, provide adequate warnings and take appropriate steps necessary to avert harm and protect others. Courts have noted that diagnosis and appropriate measures to be taken are not separate or severable but taken together constitute a duty giving rise to a cause of action for failure to warn.

REFERENCES

Applebaum, P. (1985). Tarasoff and the clinician: Problems in fulfilling the duty to protect. *American Journal of Psychiatry, 142* (4), 425-429.

Brady v. Hopper, 570 F.Supp. 1333 (D.Colo.1983) aff'd,751 F.2d 239 (10th Cir. 1984).

Cal. Civ. Code ss 43.92 (West Supp. 1987).

Diamond, B. (1974). The psychiatric prediction of dangerousness. *U. Pa. Law Review, 123,* 439-452.

Dix, G. (1980). Clinical evaluation of the "dangerousness" of "normal" criminal defendants. *Virginia Law Review, 66,* 523-581.

Fleming, J. & Maximov, . (1974). The patient or his victim: The therapist's dilemma. *California Law Review, 62,* 1025.

Givelber, D., Bowers, W. & Blitch, C. (1984). Tarasoff, myth and reality: An empirical study. *Wisconsin Law Review,* pp. 443-497.

Gurevitz, H. (1977). Tarasoff: Protective privilege versus public peril. *American Journal of Psychiatry, 134,* 289-292.

Hedlund v. Superior Court of Orange County, 34 Cal.3d 695,669 P.2d 41, 194 Cal. Rptr. 805, (1983).

Jablonski by Pahls v. United States 712 F.2d 391 (9th Cir. 1983).

Jensen v. Conrad, 570 F.Supp. 114 (D.S.C. 1983).

Kan. Stat. Ann. ss 65-5603 (6) (Supp.1986).

Kozol, H.L. (1982). Dangerousness in society and law. *U. Toledo Law Review, 13,* 241.

Ky. Rev. Stat. Ann. ss 202A, 400 (1986).

Lipari v. Sears, Roebuck & Co., 497 F.Supp.185 (D.Neb.1980).

Mavroudis v. Superior Court, 102 Cal.App. 3d 594 162 Ca. Rptr. 724 (1980).

McIntosh v. Milano, 168 N.J. Super.466, 403 A.2d 500 (Law Div.1979).

Minn. Stat. Ann. ss 148.975 (2) (West Supp.1987).

Monahan, J. (1981). *The clinical prediction of violent behavior.* Rockville, MD: National Institute of Mental Health.

N.H. Rev. Stat. Ann. ss 330-A:22 (Supp.1986).

Note. (1980). The application of the Tarasoff duty to forensic psychiatry. *Virginia Law Review, 66,* 715-726.

Note. (1983). Clinical prediction of dangerousness: Two year follow-up of 408 pre-trial forensic cases. *Am. Acad. Psychl. & L. Bull., 11,* 171.

Peck v. Counseling Service of Addison County, Inc., 499 A.2d 422 (Vt. 1985).

Perreira v. State of Colorado, 15 Colo.Law.2245 (Dec.1,1986) (App. No. 84CA0402, annc'd, 10/9/86).

Petersen v. State, 100 Wash.2d 421,761 P.2d 230 (Wash.1983) (en banc).

Plaut, E. (1974). A perspective on confidentiality, *American Journal of Psychology, 131,* 1021.

Prins, H. (1981). Dangerous people or dangerous situations? Some implications for assessment and management. *Med. Sci. Law, 21* (2), 125-132.

Restatement (Second) of Torts ss 325 (1965).

Roth, L. & Meisel, A. (1977). Dangerousness, confidentiality, and the duty to warn. *American Journal of Psychiatry, 134,* 508-511.

Steadman, H.J. (1980). The right not to be a false positive: Problems in the application of the dangerousness standard. *Psychiatric Quarterly, 52,* 84.

Stone, A. (1976). The Tarasoff decisions: Suing psychotherapists to safeguard society. *Harvard Law Review, 90,* 358-378.

Taig v. State, 19 A.D.2d 182, 241 N.Y.S. 495 (1963).

Tarasoff v. Regents of University of California, 131 Cal.Rptr. 14, 551 P.2d 334 (Cal. Sup. Ct. 1976).

Thompson v. Alameda, 27 Cal. 3d 741, 614 P .2d 728, 167 Cal. Rptr. 70 (1980).

Wexler, D. (1979). Patients, therapists, and third parties: The victimological virtue of Tarasoff. *International Journal of Law and Psychiatry, 2,* 1-28.

Social Applications and Issues in Psychology
R.C. King and J.K. Collins (editors)
©Elsevier Science Publishers B.V. (North-Holland), 1989

FAIR TESTING PRACTICES: ISSUES AND RESOLUTIONS
THE WORK OF THE JOINT COMMITTEE ON TESTING PRACTICES

Esther E. Diamond

Educational and Psychological Consultant, Illinois , USA.

This paper deals with the organization of the Joint Committee on Testing Practices and in particular its development of the Code of Fair Testing Practices in Education; the critical issues in testing for both test users and test takers; and the qualifications of those who give tests and interpret the results. The possible applications for other countries and cultures will be mentioned, and future plans for developing other Codes –for example, for industrial-organizational and clinical psychologists – will be discussed.

With the latest revision of the Standards for Educational and Psychological Testing (American Educational Research Association {AERA}, American Psychological Association , & National Council on Measurement in Education {NCME}, 1985) close to completion, came the realization that concern for and work on the Standards could not be ignored until the next revision. Ongoing implementation and extension of the fair testing practices implicit in the Standards, in a way that is meaningful to the testing community and the general public, seemed to be urgently needed, especially in the light of ongoing criticsm of tests and their use. Resnick and Resnick (1982), for example, reviewed changing testing practices in the United States resulting from societal pressures that led to testing legislation and court decisions regarding test use in the schools and in job selection and placement. They concluded that test use must be adapted to fit a different social context from that to which tests were originally applied.

FORMATION OF THE JCTP

A conference in 1984 with representatives of 23 test publishers, AERA, APA, and NCME, as well as the Canadian Psychological Association (Fremer, 1988) resulted in the formation of the Joint Committee on Testing Practices (JCTP). One of the principal purposes of the conference was to formulate a system for productive collaboration between test professionals and test publishers. Two working groups were formed: The Code of Fair Testing Practices in Education Work Group, which produced a document that will be discussed in detail here; and the Test User Qualifications Work Group, which empirically developed two suggested forms to be used by publishers for screening the qualifications of test purchasers. Sponsors now include, in addition to AERA, APA, and NCME, the American Association for Counseling and Development (AACD) and the American Speech-Language-Hearing Association (ASHA). A second test publishers conference in 1987 was attended by representatives of 35 testing companies and 22 representatives of other professional associations with some involvement in testing. In March 1988 an invitational forum, "Working Together to Improve Testing Practices," drew 55 representatives of interested associations and organizations. Included were clinicians, industrial-organizational psychologists, occupational therapists, mental health counsellors, marriage counsellors, nurses, teachers, curriculum specialists, the National Parent-Teacher Association, and many others. The spectrum of concerns they represented was very broad and very diverse. They included a common core of concerns that would be expressed in the Code of Fair Testing and, at the same time, a number of unique concerns not specified in the Code, which deals with fair testing practices in education.

PURPOSES AND CONTENT OF THE CODE OF FAIR TESTING PRACTICES

While a number of critical issues in testing have dealt with problems intrinsic to the test itself—such as not matching the curriculum, containing biased items, and not measuring special abilities such as leadership and creativity—most criticsms of testing have been directed toward the misuse of tests. Linn (1986), for example, pointed out that despite scientific and technical advances in testing, many issues of appropriate test interpretation and use remain unresolved. The Institute for Research on Teaching (1980) defined the issue as not so much one of making better tests as one of making better use of tests; making them a more effective means of diagnosis and translating that diagnosis into educational intervention, remediation and competency efforts. The Institute's report was particularly critical of the inadequate training of educational personnel in the use of tests and the understanding of various kinds of test scores. A major issue in test use is whether the content of the test and the resulting norms reflect the dominant culture and are insensitive to differences in experiences, language and the test-taker's cognitive style. The charge is made that comparisons of cultural minorities with mainstream populations are used to label minority students erroneously, limiting their options with reference to both education and career. This is apparently a worldwide issue, as will be documented later in this paper.

Another issue in test use is the need for appropriately modified forms of tests or test administration procedures, when feasible, for test takers with handicapping conditions. Willingham (1988) and his team studied the use of nonstandard versions of tests of admission to higher education for examinees with handicapping conditions. He compared their performance with the performance of students without disabilities on the standard versions. The tasks posed to both kinds of students were generally comparable, except that the nonstandard versions had more lenient time limits. Timing appeared to be the critical issue, and Willingham concluded that empirically based comparable time limits are needed.

Eyde (1988) identified seven tentative factors of test misuse among eight clusters comprising a total of 50 tests. These were derived through a factor analysis based on 487 ratings of 86 generic subelements of good testing practices by an interdisciplinary panel of experts. The factors were: comprehensive assessment, proper test use, psychometric knowledge, integrity of test results, scoring accuracy, appropriate use of norms and interpretive feedback. The most comprehensive requirements fell under two empirically derived elements— knowledge of the test and its limitations, and acceptance of responsibility for competent use of the test. It was obvious, from this and other studies, that (1) an improved system was needed that would help test publishers assess the qualifications of test purchasers; and (2) a Code of Fair Testing Practices was needed to specify major obligations to test takers on the part of professionals who develop tests and those who use them.

The first effort of the Code of Fair Testing Work Group was to develop such a code for the use of tests in education. After a series of iterations, this effort was completed in August 1988 and is in the process of receiving endorsements or obtaining other forms of consideration from various interested professional associations and organizations. Endorsement implies a commitment to safeguarding the rights of test takers by following the principles listed.

The Code is not meant to add new principles over and above those in the Standards or to change the meaning of the Standards. It is intended to be consistent with the relevant sections of the Standards, but differs from them in both audience and purpose. It is meant to be understood by the general public and focuses primarily on those issues that affect the proper use of tests in education— admissions, educational assessment and diagnosis, and student placement. Nor is the Code designed to cover employment testing, licensure or certification testing, or other types of testing such as clinical assessment. Although relevant to many types of educational tests, it is directed primarily to professionally developed tests such as those sold by commercial test publishers or used in formally administered testing programs. It does not apply to teacher-made classroom tests.

The Code addresses the roles of test developers and test users separately, but side by side. Test developers are defined as those who actually construct tests as well as those who set policies for particular testing programs. Test users are defined as those who select tests, commission test development services, interpret test results to test takers, or make decisions on the basis of test scores. As the Code points out, these two roles may overlap—as when a state education agency commissions test development services, sets policies that control the test development process and makes decisions on the basis of the test scores.

Responsibilities of test developers and users are presented in four major areas, in parallel columns:

A. Developing/Selecting Appropriate Tests
       Includes the responsibilities of test developers for providing the information test users need in order to select appropriate tests and of test users for selecting tests that meet the purpose for which they are to be used and that are appropriate for the test-taking populations.

B. Interpreting Scores
       Includes the responsibilities of test developers for helping users interpret scores correctly and of users for the correct interpretation of scores.

C. Striving for Fairness
       Deals with the responsiblities of test developers for trying to make tests that are as fair as possible for test takers of different races, gender, ethnic backgrounds or handicapping conditions. Test users are considered responsible for selecting tests that have been developed to make them as fair as possible for these groups.

D. Informing Test Takers

       Whichever group—test developers or test users—has direct communication with test takers is considered responsible for providing information to help test takers (or their parents or guardians) to decide whether an optional test or an available alternative should be taken. Responsibilities also include providing information about what the test covers, types of questions and formats, directions and so on.

       A responsibility of whichever group has direct control of tests and test scores is to provide test takers (or parents or guardians) with information about rights of test takers to obtain copies of tests and completed answer sheets, to retake tests, have test rescored or cancel scores. Responsibilities also include providing information about how long scores will be kept on file; to whom and under what circumstances test scores will be released; and how to register complaints and have problems resolved.

FUTURE PLANS

With the completion of the Code of Fair Testing Practices in Education and the competency-based Test Purchaser Qualification forms, the JCTP is considering a number of possible future projects (Fremer, 1988). The ideas that have received the greatest support so far are: developing additional Codes—e.g., psychological (clinical) assessment, testing in health areas, industrial-organizational testing; training of test users; increasing the public's understanding of testing; and clarifying controversial issues in testing, such as item bias.

Possible Applications in Other Countries and Cultures

A survey of the literature indicates that other countries have many testing issues in common with those in the United States of America. Moreover, since a number of foreign countries rely on tests developed in the West and reflecting Western cultures and values, the potential for test misuse is greatly increased.

Lonner (1981) suggested the need for research toward establishment of a common reference point for norms developed independently in two or more countries. Poortinga (1982), reporting on testing in Western Europe, observed that "the so-called anti-test movement has had a clear impact on the image (if not the actual use) of tests in most countries with a strong testing tradition" (p. 1) and that "sooner or later instruments and testing practices will have to be adapted to new psychological insights and to new demands from the society at large" (p.2).

In the Netherlands, a new rating system for test quality was introduced in 1982 (Evers, 1984). Evaluations of 278 tests by the Dutch Committee on Testing (COTAN) are given as "Insufficient," "Sufficient," or "Good" in five main categories: (1) Theoretical background of the construction of the test; (2) Quality and completeness of the test material and manual; (3) Norms; (4) Reliability; and (5) Validity. Each category addresses a number of questions about the test derived from the Dutch edition of Standards for Educational and Psychological Tests and Manuals. Category 1, for example, checks whether the test purpose is adequately stated; Category 2 checks on standardization details; Category 3 checks whether norms are available, whether they are representative for the target groups as described and whether the processing of the norms has been carried out correctly.

In Zimbabwe, a Psychological Practices Act led to training in psychometric techniques in psychology and associated professions (Jordan, 1986). The Department of Psychology at Zimbabwe University developed an extensive curriculum in test construction and the problems of using foreign tests, as well as training in modern test techniques. The Schools Psychological Services have developed tests for a wide range of purposes and occupational psychologists have adapted tests for local use, restandardized foreign tests and assessed the effects of education, gender and other psycho-social variables on performance. However, Jordan noted, there is a need for synthesizing and integrating the results of adapting foreign tests from both a practitioner and a theoretical perspective.

Prinsloo (1984) described test practices and the legal control of tests in South Africa, where the test developer faces the difficult problem of standardizing tests in eleven different languages, with populations from diverse educational and cultural backgrounds and no common language. The distribution and use of psychological tests are controlled by the Medical, Dental, and Supplementary Health Service Professions Act. The ethical standards of the American Psychological Association, however, are always used as guidelines. The Test Commission of the Republic of South Africa (TCRSA), maintains and promotes the professional development of standardized tests and questionnaires and promotes practices to prevent their misuse. By law, only a psychologist may control a test, but the law does not define the terms "control" and "use"; the TCRSA has formulated clarifying definitions, with "use" of a test limited to administration, scoring, and reading of norms and implementing cut-off points. A psychologist may not use a test that he or she has not been trained to use.

Zeidner (1987), studied scholastic aptitude test scores of Jewish and Arab students in Israel and found little evidence for differential predictive validity by gender. Meaningful sex group performance differences on the Information and Mathematical Reasoning tests, however, suggested the need for bias review of the information items. He surmised that the test specificiations are overweighted toward science areas and do not sample as representatively as for other domains. The math differences, furthermore, might be due to the item context in the word problems. Overall, though, Zeidner concluded, the findings upheld the use of psychometric aptitude tests in Israel for college selection.

Witzlack (1982), reporting on a revival of psychological assessment in Eastern Europe, cited a need for a process approach—a moving away from structuralistic conceptions and rigid test administration. In New Zealand, the Tests and Standards Committee of the New Zealand Psychological Society conducted a survey regarding course content in the psychological and educational measurement programs and inservice test training opportunities among major test users in business and industry. Among other results, the survey found a need for upgrading the statistical components of test and measurement courses and for better coverage of the legal and ethical aspects of test use (Reid and St. George, 1982). Pieters and Zaal (1985), found that major factors that influenced performance on the Dutch Police Intelligence Test were level of education and place of schooling and that, where these were equivalent, minority groups did not obtain lower scores.

It appears obvious that there is a common core of testing problems around the world, as well as among different specialties within the profession of psychology. Differences between countries and cultures, however, might make a uniform Code of Fair Testing Practices highly unrealistic. The Code can, nevertheless, serve as a model for other countries and for various interest groups within psychology, just as the Standards for Educational and Psychological Testing has done.

CORRESPONDENCE
Esther E. Diamond, Educational and Psychological Consultant, 721 Brown Avenue, Evanston, Illinois 60202, USA

REFERENCES

American Educational Research Association, American Psychological Association, & National Council on Measurement in Education (1985). *Standards for educational and psychological testing.* Washington, D.C.: American Psychological Association.

Evers, A. (1984). A new rating system for testquality in the Netherlands. *Bulletin of the International Test Commission and of the Division of Psychological Assessment of the IAAP, 20,* 25-37.

Eyde, L.D. (1988, August). Professional responsibilities of test authors, publishers, and test users. Paper presented at a meeting of the American Psychological Association, Atlanta, Georgia.

Fremer, J.F. (1988, April). Report of the Joint Committee on Testing Practices: Notes for presentation at annual meeting of the National Council on Measurement in Education, New Orleans.

Institute for Research on Teaching. (1980). *Integrating assessment with instruction: A review. (Research series No. 75).* Michigan State University: Author.

Jordan, J. (1986). Psychometric testing in Zimbabwe. *Bulletin of the International Test Commission, 22,* 3-6.

Linn, R.L. (1986). Educational testing and assessment: Research needs and policy issues. *American Psychologist, 41,* 1153-1160.

Lonner, W.J. (1981). Psychological tests and intercultural counseling. In P.P. Pedersen, J.G. Draguns, W.J. Lonner, & J.E. Trimble (Eds.), *Counseling across cultures (Rev. ed.),* 275-303. Honolulu: The University Press of Hawaii.

Pieters, J.P.M., & Zaal, J.N. (1985, June). Investigating cultural bias in the Dutch police intelligence test. Paper presented at Malmo Conference, The Netherlands.

Poortinga, Y.H. (1982). Introduction. In Y.H. Poortinga (Ed.). The status of psychological tests in Western Europe (Special issue). *International Review of Applied Psychology, 31,* 1.

Prinsloo, R.J. (1984). Test practices and the legal control of psychological tests in the Republic of South Africa. *Bulletin of the International Test Commission and of the Division of Psychological Assessment of the IAAP, 20,* 39-53.

Reid, N.A., & St. George, R. (1982). Psychological and educational test training in New Zealand. *Newsletter of the International Test Commission, 16,* 17-21.

Resnick, L.B., & Resnick, D.P. (1982). Testing in America: The current challenge. *International Review of Applied Psychology, 31,* 75-90.

Willingham, W.W. (1988, January). Standard testing conditions and standard score meaning for handicapped examinees. *The Score, 10,* 4-6.

Zeidner, M. (1987). A cross-cultural test of sex bias in the predictive validity of scholastic aptitude examinations: Some Israeli findings. *Evaluation and Program Planning, 10,* 289-295.

Social Applications and Issues in Psychology
R.C. King and J.K. Collins (editors)
©Elsevier Science Publishers B.V. (North-Holland), 1989

THE ROLE OF THE PSYCHOLOGIST IN MODERN SOCIETY

John Raven

Edinburgh, Scotland

In this paper it will be argued that we now live in a managed world economy that is managed on the basis of explicit information and not by the "invisible hand òf the marketplace". This managed economy has come into being for the best of reasons. However, while it has conferred untold benefits on mankind, it has serious weaknesses. Psychologists have a crucial role to play in carrying out the studies and developing the tools required to enable the managed economy to function effectively. It is necessary to give teeth to the information generated by social R&D units. To do this we need new staff appraisal systems to give public servants credit for seeking more comprehensive information and acting on it in an innovative manner to promote the long term public interest. And we need a new supervisory structure to ensure that public servants act in the public interest. In other words, we need new concepts of democracy and bureaucracy. Psychologists have a crucial role to play in helping to make explicit the new organisational structures and develop the new accounting tools which are needed.

However, if we, as psychologists, are to contribute the new studies, understandings, and tools which are required, we will need to: (i) present the case for our involvement in this kind of work much more forcefully, (ii) press for changed concepts of the nature of science, and (iii) press for the establishment of an appropriate institutional framework within which to carry out the necessary research.

In writing the best case for social research that has ever been published, Rothschild (1982) argued that social scientists had not laid claim to the major role which they should be playing in modern societies. He argued that modern societies could not function effectively without a considerable volume of social research, but that social scientists had failed to perceive the need for studies of the type and scale actually required. They tended to mount studies which were too academic and too individualistic. Undergraduate training in psychology tended to lead researchers to avoid messy, policy-relevant studies, the results of which would not be beyond dispute and argument. It also led them to avoid the political activities involved in pressing for action on the basis of such studies as were carried out. They were also too inclined to criticise each other's work in ways that made it difficult to convince those who control funding that more money should be channelled into social research.

The fact is that, over the past 40 years, dramatic changes have occurred in the way in which society is organised. We live in what is essentially a managed world economy (Raven, 1977, 1984, 1987, 1988). The national economies of which it is composed, trans-national corporations and international trade are managed on the basis of explicit information. Decisions are made by "men" and not by the invisible hand of the economic marketplace. The role of money has been overturned; instead of providing a mechanism whereby people can vote with their pennies to determine the direction in which things develop, the control of cash flows is now used to achieve goals which have been established through the (information-based) politico-bureaucratic process. Customers are typically no longer individuals, but corporate giants purchasing on behalf of thousands of people - for health services, local authorities, national governments and alliances of countries. The citizen has the utmost difficulty in influencing the way in which the two thirds of income handed over as taxes is ultimately spent.

These changes have occurred for the best of reasons. An economy managed by the invisible hand of the marketplace gave us little control over the quality of the urban environment, crime, the distribution of income, plague and disease, environmental despoilation and pollution, or even continued economic development itself. The immense social and ecological costs of dealing with the by-products of an industrial civilisation and providing the education, highway, and regulatory infrastructure required for its effective operation, were not subject to market forces. Only an extension of explicit management will give us control over international forces until now uncontrollable. Only an increase in world management will enable us to improve further or even maintain the quality of life - the wealth - of modern society.

To underline the importance and nature of the social research that is required and in order to begin to discern something of the structures and expectations needed if that research is to be carried out effectively, the results of two programmes of research will be briefly summarised.

In the course of one of these (Raven, 1967), we showed that high-rise family housing was unacceptable to the tenants (Raven, 1988), was more costly to build than equivalent two-story housing, was more costly to maintain than two story housing, and accommodated fewer people per acre than two story housing.

Despite the impeccable quality of this research, no action was taken. Building high rise family housing continued into the nineteen eighties. The disastrous nature of the policy is now recognised, and these expensive blocks are being demolished. The lesson to be drawn from this example is not that the policies in force were misguided but that it is vital to evolve mechanisms that will enable us to ensure that public servants take appropriate action on the basis of good information.

Another, in many ways even more disturbing, set of examples of the failure of public servants to act on information in the best interests of their clients, comes from education. Education was one of the first sectors of the economy to be socialised. There were two main reasons for this: first, education is intended to benefit everyone and not just those who are passing through the system; second, the poor cannot pay for the education of their children and this is both unfair on the children concerned and is likely to deprive society of their talents.

Good though the reasons for socialising education are, research conducted between 1965 and 1972 (Raven, 1977) showed that some two thirds of the money spent on secondary education is wasted so far as the development of human resources is concerned. Secondary schools do little to foster the qualities that most parents, teachers, employers and ex-pupils think they should foster and which other research shows it is, indeed, important for them to foster. The qualities required include initiative, the ability to work with others, and the ability to understand and influence society.

There are many reasons why schools tend to neglect these goals. Most of these reasons were not obvious until the relevant research had been undertaken. Prior to that, Her Majesty's Inspectors of Schools and the Department of Education and Science in the United Kingdom tended to assume that exhortation was all that was necessary: if teachers did not follow their prescriptions it was assumed that the solution involved better teacher training or stronger management. But the problems actually stem from (among other things) value conflicts, inappropriate beliefs about the way the public sector should operate, and the absence of the tools needed to manage individualised, competency-oriented, educational programmes. A great deal more research and development activity - some of a fundamental nature - is required if they are to be overcome (Raven, 1977, 1983, 1984, 1987, 1988; Raven, Johnstone & Varley, 1985).

The conclusions to which our data point were not anticipated when the studies were initiated and are not unarguable. They involve going well beyond the data to draw sociological conclusions from psychological data and require us to ask what psychological tools could be invented to enable schools to harness sociological forces in such a way that they would push schools in the direction most people desire.

Another, equally important set of points, has to do with the further evidence – much of which has been available for 20 years – of misuse of public money. There is a need to provide variety within public provision and to hold public servants accountable against different criteria.

It is the growing awareness of deficiencies like those we have described in housing and education which has led many to embrace privatisation as a solution to the problems of public provision. Direct evidence for this assertion comes from our quality of life surveys (Raven, 1980). These show that people *are* dissatisfied with their washing machines and cars. They are more dissatisfied with the quality of the environments in which they live. They are still more dissatisfied with social, welfare, health and educational provision. But they are most dissatisfied with their relationship with public servants and politicians.

In this context, it is important to note that the above problems of the educational system cannot be solved by "returning" education to the marketplace. There are several reasons for this which include: (a) the fact that, if our society is to develop, many attitudes and skills - which it is the responsibility of the educational system to identify and foster - need to be widely shared in society and not just possessed by an elite; (b) the main benefits of education are not going to accrue to people *as individuals* but to them as members of a society which has developed *as a whole:* everyone is going to benefit, so everyone should pay; and (c) people would be most likely to pay, as individuals, for those "educational" programmes that would lead to credentials likely to secure entry to protected occupations (Raven, 1987, 1988). But those credentials would not testify to the development of important competencies. As a result, making clients pay for courses leading to such credentials would not encourage suppliers to focus on the development of the competencies that are really needed.

THE WAY FORWARD

It seems to me that, instead of encouraging privatisation, we need to recognise that the real problem is to find ways of making managed economies work. There is ample evidence (e.g., in the writings of Robertson (1985), Ekins (1986), Thurow (1983) and George (1988)) that the economic marketplace does not work in the public interest and that we have built our standard of living on economic processes which are not sustainable. We *must* develop a form of managed economy that works. If that is the case, what we have to do is to find out why public servants and politicians often do not act in the public interest on the basis of available information and ensure that they do so more frequently in the future. Since this involves organisational structures and social accounting and staff appraisal systems, it is surely a task for psychologists (Ferguson, 1980; Raven, 1984, 1988).

More specifically, we need to develop new expectations of public servants, new criteria against which to judge their performance (e.g., it is important for public servants to take innovative action in the public interest), new appraisal tools to assess their performance against these criteria, new concepts of bureaucracy and its functioning, new ways of thinking about the relationship between bureaucracy and government, new forms of democracy that enable us to ensure that politicians and public servants are more inclined to act in the public interest, new concepts of citizenship, and new concepts of wealth and wealth-creation (Raven, 1983, 1984, 1988).

IMPLICATIONS FOR PSYCHOLOGISTS

My objectives thus far have been to show that modern society needs psychologists:
(1) to carry out evaluations of a wide variety of public policies, to identify barriers to their effective operation and to contribute to the invention of better policies,
(2) to examine the workings of the public sector *as an organisation,*
(3) to develop the tools required to administer variety in public provision, provide feedback from each group of clients and ensure that each of the options is of high quality instead of forming a hierarchy from high quality to low, thus leading to pressures for equality and uniformity,
(4) to develop the tools required to take stock of organisational functioning in the public service and for use in staff appraisal and staff guidance, placement and development, so that: (i) it is possible to ensure that public servants pay attention to and take action on the information provided under (3); (ii) public servants can get credit for exercising high level competencies; and (iii) the public service can make the best use of the available talent in energetic, innovative activity.
(5) to contribute to the evolution of new concepts of democracy, the public service, the role of the public servant, wealth, wealth-creation, work, and citizenship.

These observations have major implications for the kind of research we see ourselves undertaking, the criteria we apply to research proposals and the products of research, the institutions we seek to establish to carry out that research, the relationships we seek to establish between researchers, policy makers and the public and the beliefs, expectations and attitudes we foster in the course of undergraduate education. The concluding sections of this paper address some of these issues.

THE CONCEPT OF RESEARCH

We will now discuss separately the kinds of research that are needed to evaluate and improve specific policies and those required to develop the more general concepts and tools required to run modern society effectively.

Evaluation of Public Policies

Accuracy and unarguability are widely believed to be the hallmarks of science. This view dominates the thinking of the US *Joint Committee on Standards for the Evaluation of Educational Policies and Programmes.* However, I will argue that, although this view may well be appropriate in academic research, it is not so in policy and evaluation research.

To take one example: There is little point in demonstrating that an innovative educational programme, weakly implemented and without other supporting changes, does not have a dramatic effect. Yet most pilot programmes *are* weak in this way. Among the other problems that commonly plague them, which I discuss more fully elsewhere (Raven, 1985), the teachers involved have typically only a limited grasp of what is to be achieved and how it is to be achieved. Crucial equipment has not arrived. There are no tools to enable the teachers concerned - or even the programme evaluators - to find out whether target goals are being achieved. Teachers in other classrooms - with whom the pupils may be spending much of their time - may have changed neither their teaching practices nor their expectations of pupils. The pupils will almost certainly be being assessed for certification and placement purposes against traditional criteria which are in conflict with the new goals. Under such circumstances, what is required is an evaluation that (a) uses the available evidence to infer what the effects of properly developed inputs, implemented in a supportive context, would be likely to be, (b) identifies the barriers preventing the programme being more effective, and (c) attempts to evaluate outcomes which it would require a considerable investment in fundamental research to index properly (Eisner, 1985; Hamilton, 1977; Raven, 1984, 1985).

An evaluation which does not endeavour to comment on (i) *all* important outcomes of an educational process (including both positive and negative outcomes), (ii) *all* important barriers to the effective implementation of the programme - whether from resources, psychological and pedagogic understanding, or sociological processes, and (iii) the crucial steps needed for progress, is hard to justify. Evaluators who fail to cover the ground because important variables are "intangible and hard to measure" commit crimes against mankind - because this will mean that significant programme benefits and failures, and real barriers to diffusion and dissemination, are overlooked in all subsequent discussion of, and decisions about, the activity.

It emerges that, while the hallmark of good academic research may well be accuracy, that of good evaluation is comprehensiveness. A good policy study is one that yields new understandings and insights and points the way forward.

In such a context, it is inappropriate to judge the work of an individual researcher against the criterion of "proof beyond reasonable doubt". What is needed is a contribution to a public debate that advances understanding. It is the *process* of science that leads to accurate and complete understanding, not the work of an individual scientist. We therefore need to encourage those who control the funding of policy-relevant research to fund research into important issues - even when neither we nor they know how it is to be done and when it is clear from the beginning that the conclusions will be open to argument.

Although many people will find what has been said disturbing, it is important to share another insight that has emerged in the course of 30 years of policy research. It is that such work regularly points to the need for studies of, and public debate about, fundamental social values, political beliefs, and beliefs about the operation of the public service. For example, some studies of educational policy have pointed to the conclusion that a major reason why much of the money spent on secondary schools is wasted so far as the development of human resources is concerned is that our preoccupation with equality prevents us respecting and fostering a wide variety of value-based competencies. To handle the problem we need (i) to legitimise the provision of variety in the public sector, (ii) to respect individual pupils' right to opt out of uncongenial programmes, and (iii) to introduce quality control mechanisms to ensure that all options are of high quality (Raven, 1980, 1988). Similarly, studies of values, attitudes and institutional structures associated with economic and social development have pointed to the conclusion that understandings of how society does and should work, along with the role of the citizen within it, are crucial. It has emerged that we need new understandings of terms like "management", "participation", "democracy" and "wealth" (Raven, 1984).

Not only are these conclusions debatable, typically they upset those who control funding. Even though in retrospect our sponsors were, in both cases, inclined to agree with our conclusions, they felt unable to support the research that would have been necessary to substantiate them (Raven, 1984). Closer to home, such results disturb psychologists who referee grant applications. As Rothschild noted, we do indeed need to put our own house in order before we complain about the low priority that public servants and politicians accord to research in our discipline.

If we are to encourage public servants and others to commission more useful evaluation studies we must:
(1) change our beliefs about the outcomes that it is appropriate to expect in research from "facts" to "insights",
(2) change our beliefs about what it is appropriate for researchers to study (so as to legitimise the study of important but messy problems),
(3) change our beliefs about the *research process* (so that it comes to be seen as appropriate for researchers to follow up unexpected observations and so that further research to pursue unexpected re-orientations can be funded),
(4) do more to protect researchers who stumble into new areas and find themselves in conflict with the assumptions of those who control funding, and, most importantly,
(5) emphasise that effective applied research almost always involves a considerable amount of fundamental research, the need for which academics who no have contact with applied problems would be unlikely to see. (Put the other way round, this means that the universities are far from ideal from the point of view

of pursuing their most important goals - namely stimulating new lines of fundamental research and paradigm shifts).

Relationships Between Researchers and Policy Makers and the Institutional Framework Required to Carry out Research

It will be clear by now that useful policy-relevant research is different in nature from what has in the past commonly been assumed to be the case. The structures required for its effective execution and the framework of expectations within which it is carried out are also different. Classical, but still highly relevant, discussions of these issues have been contributed by Cherns (1970), Donnison (1972) and Freeman (1973, 1974). However, I have myself discussed the issues more fully in papers which have been published elsewhere (Raven, 1975, 1985, 1987, 1988).

Beliefs, expectations, and understandings to be fostered in undergraduate education

The very different beliefs we need to develop about what constitutes science, psychology, good research and, especially, the role and nature of policy research and evaluation have already been briefly mentioned. It remains to emphasise how important it is for the universities to encourage students to develop more appropriate expectations.

Perhaps the most important message for the universities to disseminate is that what society urgently needs is not a new set of specific policies in health, housing, incomes, pricing, management, labour relations or third-world trade, but more policy development *units,* especially units to develop new concepts of bureaucracy and democracy and the tools required to run them more effectively. Psychologists have a major role to play in these units. We know more than anyone else about organisations, institutions and tools of policy appraisal and performance assessment.

These may sound like grandiose claims, but it must again be emphasised that we are living in an economy quite unlike that which most of us take it to be. Our claim as psychologists must therefore be, not that we can help to introduce some Utopia, but that we can help society to do better than it is already doing.

The question will arise of how all this is to be paid for. The answer is to be found in the fact that some two thirds of the cost of any article is spent on distribution and marketing - that is, on making the economic marketplace work. An effective, managed, economy in which most of the necessary information was contributed by psychologists – and not by financiers or "economists" – could hardly cost more to administer. Furthermore, in pressing our case, reference can be made to the fact that evidence that activity designed to enhance the quality of life through public management constitutes genuine wealth-creating work is abundantly available: people from other countries are prepared to pay considerable sums to move into societies which have more effective management structures.

REFERENCES

Cherns, A.B. (1970). Relations between research institutions and users of research. *International Social Science Journal*, XXII, 226-42.

Donnison, D. (1972). Research for Policy.*Minerva*, X, 519-37.

Eisner, E.W. (1985). *The Art of Educational Evaluation*. Lewes: The Falmer Press.

Ekins, P. (Ed.) (1986). *The Living Economy: A New Economics in the Making*. London: Routledge and Kegan Paul.

Ferguson, M. (1980). *The Aquarian Conspiracy: Personal and Social Transformation in the 1980s*. London: Paladin.

Freeman, F.C. (1973). A study of success and failure in industrial innovation. In B.R. Williams (Ed.), *Science and Technology in Economic Growth*. London: MacMillan.

Freeman, C. (1974). *The Economics of Industrial Innovation*. London: Penguin Books.

George, S. (1988). *A Fate Worse Than Debt*. London: Penguin Books.

Hamilton, D. (Ed.). (1977). *Beyond the Numbers Game* London: MacMillan Education.

Raven, J. (1967). Sociological evidence on housing, I: Space in the home and II: The home in its setting. *Architectural Review*, *142*, 68f and *143*, 236-239.

Raven, J. (1975). Social research in modern society: I: The role of social research. II: The institutional structures and management styles required to execute policy-relevant social research. *Administration*, *23*, 225-246 and 247-268.

Raven, J. (1977). *Education, Values and Society: The Objectives of Education and the Nature and Development of Competence*. London: H K Lewis.

Raven, J. (1977). Government policy and social psychologists. *Bulletin of the British Psychological Society*, *30*, 33-39.

Raven, J. (1979). Psychological assessment in modern society. *Newsletter of the International Test Commission, No. 11*, 31-35. Also published in the 52nd Annual Report of the Scottish Council for Research in Education, p52-56.

Raven, J. (1980). *Parents, Teachers and Children*. Edinburgh: The Scottish Council for Research in Education.

Raven, J. (1983). Towards new concepts and institutions in modern society. *Universities Quarterly*, *37*, 100-118.

Raven, J. (Ed.) (1983). The Relationship Between Educational Institutions and Society paying special Attention to the Role of Assessment. *International Review of Applied Psychology*, *32* Whole Issue.

Raven J. (1984). The role of the psychologist in formulating, administering and evaluating policies associated with economic and social development in western society. *Journal of Economic Psychology*, *5*, 1-16.

Raven, J. (1984). *Competence in Modern Society: Its Identification, Development and Release*. London: H.K.Lewis.

Raven, J. (1984). Some barriers to educational innovation from outside the school system. *Teachers College Record*, *85*, 431-443.

Raven, J. (1984). Some limitations of the *Standards. Evaluation and Program Planning,* - *7*, 363-370.

Raven, J. (1984). A Public Servant's Dilemma. In W.B. Dockrell (Ed.) *An Attitude of Mind*. pp. 127-136. Edinburgh: The Scottish Council for Research in Education.

Raven, J. (1985). The Institutional Framework Required for, and Process of, Educational Evaluation: Some Lessons from Three Case Studies. in B. Searle (Ed.) *Evaluation in World Bank Education Projects: Lessons from Three Case Studies.* Washington, DC: The World Bank, Education and Training Dept. Report EDT5, 141-170.

Raven, J. (1987). Values, diversity and cognitive development. *Teachers College Record, -89*, 21-38.

Raven, J. (1987). The role of the psychologist in the modern economy. *Proceedings of the ESRC/BPS Conference on the Future of the Psychological Sciences,* 122-140. Leicester, England: The British Psychological Society.

Raven, J. (1987). The crisis in education. *The New Era, 68,* 38-44.

Raven, J. (1988). Choice in a modern economy: New concepts of democracy and bureaucracy. In   S. Maital (Ed.) *Applied Behavioural Economics.* pp. 812-824.Brighton, England: Wheatsheaf.

Raven, J. and Dolphin, T. (1978). *The Consequences of Behaving: The Ability of Irish Organisations to Tap Know-How, Initiative, Leadership and Goodwill.* Edinburgh: The Competency Motivation Project.

Raven, J., Johnstone, J. and Varley, T. (1985). *Opening the Primary Classroom.* Edinburgh: The Scottish Council for Research in Education.

Robertson, J. (1985). *Future Work: Jobs, Self-Employment and Leisure after the Industrial Age.* Aldershot: Gower/ Maurice Temple Smith.

Rose, R. (1980). Ordinary people in extraordinary economic circumstances. In   R. Rose (Ed.) *Challenge to Governance.* London: Sage.

Rothschild, Lord (1971).   *A Framework for Research and Development.* London: HMSO.

Rothschild, Lord. (1982) *An Enquiry into the Social Science Research Council.* London: HMSO.

Thurow, L.C. (1983). *Dangerous Currents: The State of Economics.* New York: Randon House.

CORRESPONDENCE:

John Raven, Consultant,, 30 Great King St.,, Edinburgh EH3 6QH,, Scotland., Telephone: Country: 44; City: 31; No: 556 2912

Social Applications and Issues in Psychology
R.C. King and J.K. Collins (editors)
©Elsevier Science Publishers B.V. (North-Holland), 1989

PRIVATE INITIATIVES IN SUPPORT OF MENTAL HEALTH PROGRAMS

Wayne H. Holtzman

Hogg Foundation for Mental Health, The University of Texas, U.S.A.

Private initiatives in support of community mental health programs are of five kinds: (1) individual gifts of money or material goods, (2) individually volunteered time and energy, (3) voluntary nonprofit organizations dedicated to the cause, i.e., the National Association for Mental Health, (4) corporate gifts by businesses and industries, and (5) private philanthropy by foundations. Unique among private foundations is the Hogg Foundation for Mental Health which supports community mental health programs throughout the state of Texas. Although the Foundation is an integral part of The University of Texas, it makes grants and provides technical assistance for a wide range of mental health projects in every major community of the state. New experimental programs for the chronically mentally ill to encourage self-support are described to illustrate the manner in which the Foundation works with community groups.

Americans are widely noted for their extraordinary impulse to form voluntary groups and to devise nongovernmental institutions for serving public purposes. An amazing variety of American institutions has flourished under private auspices. Ranging from mutual aid societies to great universities, from 4-H Clubs to religious groups, these organizations number in the millions. These causes, and the private giving which supports them, are a vitally important part of American life. Together with its democratic form of government and its free enterprise system, the non-profit sector of voluntary giving and private initiative is distinctive and is one of the fundamental characteristics of the American way of life. This non-profit sector of American society is often referred to as the third sector or the independent sector.

What does this independent sector look like at the moment? Most private initiatives can be classified into one of five major categories: (1) individual gifts of money or material goods, either current donations or future bequests; (2) corporate gifts by business and industry; (3) private philanthropy by foundations; (4) individually volunteered time and energy; and (5) voluntary non-profit organizations dedicated to a cause, such as the American Red Cross or the Mental Health Association.

The greatest amount of private giving, by far, has always been gifts from individuals. In 1986, eighty-two percent of all private giving was accounted for by individual donations of charitable dollars. Individual bequests amounted to another $5.8 billion, a sizeable increase of over twelve percent from the year before. Most individual gifts go to religious organizations. But many religious organizations then use some of this money to support mental health programs. The amount of individual donations directly for support of community mental health programs is small but still significant.

Corporate contributions from business and industry amounted to $4.5 billion in 1986. Many corporations now give about one percent of their net income to charitable organizations, and a significant amount of this giving is earmarked for community mental health programs. When corporate in-kind contributions are added to actual monetary grants, the support of non-profit activities by business corporations more than doubles. Factoring in additional contributions of advertising, marketing, equipment, loaned executives, public-related investments and other aspects of corporate public responsibility yields a total figure well above $10 billion.

The third major source of private giving is money from private foundations. Although most people are familiar with the grant-in-aids programs of large foundations, such as Ford, Rockefeller, or the W. K. Kellogg Foundations, many are unaware that there are nearly 25,000 active grant-making private foundations in the United States. The great majority of these are small trust funds which are active only in local areas. Of the $5.2 billion granted by foundations in 1986, nearly half the money was provided by 142 large foundations with assets of $100 million or more.

The number of private foundations devoted specifically and exclusively to mental health is very small, the Hogg Foundation for Mental Health being the best example. More will be said about this statewide Texas foundation later. A broader definition of community mental health to include a wider range of health and human service activities would draw in a much larger number of private foundations. In addition, many foundations support community mental health activities as part of a much broader spectrum of other health, human service, and educational programs. In Texas alone at least 64 foundations have recently supported mental health projects. Total private giving by individuals, corporations, and foundations for health and human services combined was over $21 billion in 1986.

The fourth major area of private giving takes the form of personal service by millions of individuals throughout the country who volunteer time and energy in support of community efforts and the public good without any thought for financial compensation. Detailed information about voluntary service was obtained in a Gallup Poll in 1981 and again in 1985. Both surveys indicated that over half of all Americans have given some time to voluntary service during the past year. Regular volunteer activity is defined as devoting an average of at least two hours per week to volunteer work over the previous three months. Twenty percent of these volunteers give eight or more hours per week of service. It is estimated that a total of over sixteen billion hours of voluntary service were rendered in 1985, service that was worth at least $110 billion. A major portion of this service was rendered in the fields of health and human services including community mental health work. The most popular forms of voluntary service were assisting the elderly, the handicapped, and the poor.

The fifth and last area of private initiatives for public good consists of the voluntary non-profit organizations devoted to a specific cause. The oldest such organization in community mental health is the Mental Health Association with its national, state, and local chapters. More recently, the National Association for the Mentally Ill and the American Mental Health Fund have been organized. The first of these organizations has both state and local chapters comprised mainly of family members of the mentally ill and other social activists who advocate better community treatment and residential care for mentally ill persons. The American Mental Health Fund is a new organization founded by Jack Hinckley and other mental health leaders in the country following the near fatal shooting of President Reagan by Hinckley's schizophrenic son. Together with other citizens' groups, these three organizations are rapidly becoming an effective coalition to lobby for better community treatment of the mentally ill in America. As fund raisers for a specific cause, however, they have a long way to go before they catch up with the American Cancer Society or the American Heart Association.

Taken together, these private initiatives, ranging from voluntary service to corporate and foundation giving, constitute a very powerful source of support for mental health reform and improved community mental health services. An example drawn from my experience as president of a private foundation in Texas, the Hogg Foundation for Mental Health, will illustrate how these various kinds of private initiatives can be blended together with public sources of support to bring into being new programs of community mental health. But first, let me describe briefly the Hogg Foundation for Mental Health, since it represents a unique institution in this field.

Unlike any other private foundations, the Hogg Foundation for Mental Health is an integral part of a major state university supported largely with public funds. As an administrative component of The University of Texas System, the Foundation is directly under the Board of Regents as its trustees. The Foundation's program of activities is supported entirely by a major endowment given the University by the children of Governor James Hogg. Since 1940, it has carried out a mandate to initiate and support mental health programs to benefit all the people of Texas.

Most of the Foundation's $3 million annual budget is used to provide grants to non-profit organizations throughout Texas. Proposals are reviewed continuously by a staff of seven highly qualified professionals, all of whom also spend a great deal of time providing technical assistance to grant recipients and other agencies. A small number of mental health projects are developed and directed by Foundation officers themselves.

Most of the external grants in recent years have been made to community and state agencies, both public and private, with a focus upon community mental health. Major funds are also given in support of mental health research projects, educational programs, and professional training. Consisting primarily of psychologists and sociologists, the professional staff of the Foundation also teach some advanced classes and seminars within the University.

Special emphasis is given to innovative community mental health programs that have systematic evaluation as an essential part of the project design. Doctoral candidates in the social and behavioral sciences augment the permanent Foundation staff by serving as evaluation research fellows and research associates on community projects under the direction of senior program officers.

The Foundation's grants and technical assistance are often used as catalysts to precipitate major new developments that would otherwise be delayed or not take place at all. For example, following the major report of President Carter's national Commission for Mental Health, the Foundation organized a statewide conference and developed a series of projects to implement the major recommendations of the Commission. Political leaders, health service providers, social activists, university professors, and thousands of other citizens joined forces under sponsorship of the Foundation in a new organization called Citizens for Human Development. Many recent reforms in Texas are an outgrowth of this grass roots movement.

Last year the Foundation appointed three statewide commissions to study issues related to community care of the mentally ill, the mental health of children and their families, and the mental health of adolescents and young adults. Over 50 statewide leaders serve on these commissions which will complete their work in 1990. About $1 million of Foundation resources will be devoted to the work of the commissions and related projects during this three year period. The Commission on Community Care of the Mentally Ill is focusing specifically upon the development of a new system of community care for the chronically mentally ill within our society. Chairman of the Commission is Ira Iscoe, a well-known community mental health leader and professor of psychology at The University of Texas at Austin.

The work of the Commission is carried out largely by professional staff under the Commission's guidance. During the three-year life of the Commission, meetings are being held throughout the state. They range from special hearings and task force activities to major statewide conferences focusing on community care of the mentally ill. The Commission will design and take steps to implement a comprehensive statewide plan for the improvement of community services to the chronically mentally ill in Texas. Severe mental illness is viewed as an incapacitating condition that may yield to some improvement but may always need some kind of constant care. The target population is defined as those individuals who are diagnosed with either a psychotic or severe affective illness, who are experiencing either an acute or chronic state of their illness, and who may have a concomitant substance abuse problem. Special attention is being given to the distinctive aspects of rural communities, regional differences throughout the state, and different ethnic groups.

One example of activities under the auspices of the Commission is the forthcoming Sutherland Seminar on Community Care of the Chronically Mentally Ill. Over 100 mental health specialists, political leaders, and university professors representing all the major stakeholders in community mental health will meet for two days the end of September. Ten background papers by nationally-recognized specialists dealing with legal issues, cost and finance issues, and asylum and community care are being distributed in advance to all participants. Key speakers at the conference itself will present community models of care for the chronically mentally ill, review state agency collaboration on mental health issues from a political perspective, debate whose rights should prevail in intrafamily conflict and the delivery of mental health services, and outline a program of action for the future community care of persons with chronic mental illness.

During the past five years, the Foundation has granted over a half-million dollars to twelve new community-based programs for mentally ill persons. Recipients of these grants include both the state and local chapters of the Mental Health Association, the state Department of Mental Health, the League of Women Voters in Texas, a religious organization, two new organizations that are establishing transitional living programs in Houston, a rural State Hospital, and a major community mental health centre for a metropolitan area. A $250,000 grant to the Austin-Travis County Mental Health Mental Retardation Center to establish community-based lodge training illustrates the cooperative way in which the Hogg Foundation operates.

Two years ago the Robert Wood Johnson Foundation announced a new program for the chronically mentally ill as a national demonstration project in consortium with the U.S. Department of Housing and Urban Development. The Robert Wood Johnson Foundation is providing about $28 million in grants and low-interest loans to support major demonstration projects in nine cities that consolidate and expand services for people with serious mental illness. The

Department of Housing and Urban Development is providing substantial rent subsidies in each city to assist grantees in developing safe, affordable housing for mental patients in their community. Austin, Texas was chosen as one of these nine demonstration sites, largely because the Hogg Foundation was willing to join forces as a sponsor of a project to be undertaken by the local community mental health centre. A smaller grant from the Foundation several years earlier to the Disciples of Christ, a Protestant church group in Central Texas, laid the groundwork for a residential recovery centre for the mentally ill. Still earlier, the Foundation helped implement and evaluate a series of Fairweather Lodge programs associated with the State Hospital system, most of which were operating effectively in the Central Texas area. These lodge programs are based on the earlier successful work of Fairweather, a psychologist who developed a model program that has proven highly successful for ex-patients who can be socialized into synthetic families that are capable of achieving independent living. For these reasons, the Hogg Foundation's five year grant with accompanying technical assistance is designed to demonstrate the effectiveness of a combined community-based housing and vocational training program for the chronically mentally ill as an important component of the Robert Wood Johnson Foundation's national demonstration project.

The Austin project emphasizes community support services, housing, and interagency coordination. These include specifically a client drop-in centre, a partial hospitalization program, expansion of vocational programs to include supported employment, a homeless outreach program, and the training program for community living skills under the Fairweather Lodge model. Over 300 apartment units will be made available in the next two years. The housing plan relies on a $5.5 million line of credit from a local bank, public housing certificates, and owner financing.

The Robert Wood Johnson Foundation's program for the chronically mentally ill has identified five key elements to be tested in the nine cities across the nation. First, there must be a central authority, a single point of clinical, administrative, and fiscal responsibility. In Austin, this authority is represented by the Austin-Travis County Mental Health Mental Retardation Center. Second, there must be continuity of care. Each client must have a designated care-giver who is responsible for coordinating the various components of the service system to meet the client's needs. Third, there must be a flexible financing system so that money can be provided from a variety of sources with a minimum of red tape to meet the client's needs. Fourth, a range of housing options must be developed for the chronically mentally ill; and fifth, there must be a range of psychosocial and vocational rehabilitation programs that support clients in the community. The city and county governments, local church groups and countless volunteers, public programs at the state and national level, private foundations, and university professors are all working together toward a common goal in this highly significant national demonstration of what can be done to reform community-based programs for mentally ill persons.

The Austin mental health project can look forward to four more years of major financial support from the Robert Wood Johnson Foundation and the Hogg Foundation for Mental Health. Although both the state of Texas and the metropolitan area surrounding Austin are still shaking loose from two years of economic troubles due largely to set-backs in the energy business, there is a general statewide determination to do something of lasting significance about the serious problems surrounding treatment and care of the mentally ill. A new state Commissioner, coupled with Federal Court orders to mandate certain system improvements, will provide further impetus for progress in the next several years.

Private initiatives of the kind outlined above are crucial to the success of this endeavour. Although most of the funds for sustained operation of care and treatment programs will come from public appropriations at the national, state, and local levels, major private funds from individual donations, foundation grants, and corporate contributions are essential to assure a successful outcome. The flexible and timely nature of private funding encourages innovation and the testing of new ideas, many of which cannot be supported by public funds accountable to the taxpayers. Even more critical are the many thousands of volunteers from all walks of life who give of their personal time and effort to extend and enrich the quality of care for the mentally ill, thereby creating a more humane environment in which treatment can take place.

CORRESPONDENCE
Hogg Foundation for Mental Health, The University of Texas, Austin, Texas 78712, U.S.A.

Social Applications and Issues in Psychology
R.C. King and J.K. Collins *(editors)*
©*Elsevier Science Publishers B.V. (North-Holland), 1989*

EVALUATION OF COMMUNITY PARTICIPATION IN A HEALTH SERVICE REVIEW

Sharon L. Driscoll

Waikato Hospital Board, New Zealand

Formative and process evaluation techniques were used to analyse the Service Development Group (SDG) approach used to review maternity services for the Waikato Hospital Board. Three major research techniques were used. Analysis of archival data gave an historical perspective of the board and its maternity services, while questionnaires were used to gather information from the three groups involved in the study: an 11 member Service Development Group, the 6 member Board's Steering Committee and several committee members of each of the 7 SDG nominating organisations. Interviews with the SDG and the Board's Steering Committee members provided in-depth qualitative information. One questionnaire was administered to SDG members after pretesting. It was then adapted for use with the Board's Steering Committee and committee members of the SDG nominating organisations. The research was sequential with preliminary data analysis being completed before interviews were conducted with SDG and the Steering Committee. Data analysis consisted of descriptive statistics and qualitative interpretation. Nine themes emerged from the questionnaire and interview data, two of which had importance for client orientation. These were that the SDG approach was positively supported as was the combination of professional and community representation in health services reviews.

BACKGROUND INFORMATION: THE WAIKATO HOSPITAL BOARD

The Waikato Hospital Board area covers one-eleventh of the area of New Zealand and contains one-tenth of the population, 336,143 in 1986 (Waikato Hospital Board, *1985-1986 Annual Report*). The Board is one of the largest in terms of both area and population and covers a diverse range of physical and cultural features. The Board's area incorporates twenty local authorities (six countries, three districts, ten boroughs and Hamilton city). The road network is extensive in the Waikato area but is poor for most of the west coast and other areas, other than the main highways going south and east.

Twenty-eight per cent of the Board's population are found in Hamilton and fifteen per cent in Rotorua with a further twenty six per cent dwelling in the remaining townships. About thirty per cent of the Board's population live in the rural areas of the counties and districts. For New Zealand as a whole, nine per cent of the population are Maori but for the Waikato Hospital Board the figure is eighteen per cent (Sceats & Pool, 1986). The Waikato Hospital Board administered fourteen maternity hospitals in 1985. There were one hundred and five operating public maternity units in New Zealand, many in rural areas (Rosenblatt, 1984).

WAIKATO HOSPITAL BOARD REVIEW OF MATERNITY SERVICES: PUBLIC PARTICIPATION IN PLANNING

In 1982 the Waikato Hospital Board began a review of the maternity services in its area following a request from the Minister of Health. The Board has 14 hospitals providing maternity services and decided to appoint a steering committee and a service development group to initiate the review.

Service development groups have provided a new approach to health service planning in recent years in New Zealand. Experience in pilot projects in Northland and Wellington showed that the service development group approach was valued by participants for community involvement, professional communication, self-learning and improved co-ordination. They also helped to bridge the gap between information and decision-making.

The objectives of the service development group in considering future maternity services in the Waikato were to define an 'ideal' maternity service and to assemble and evaluate data required for planning a co-ordinated maternity service over the Board's area.

The review was also required (i) to prepare a plan to include philosophies, strategies, and future programmes for maternity services which provided an adequate level of service; (ii) to reduce expenditure by five per cent and indicate the effects of 10 and 15 per cent reductions in expenditure; and (iii) to identify hospitals where closures appeared to be justified and/or where alternative functions could be undertaken without significant physical alterations.

Various public and private sector organisations were invited to select representatives to serve on the service development group. The Board decided the objectives and terms of reference for the group. A second committee called the Board's Steering Committee was appointed to advise the service development group.

Reasons for the Research

The idea of inviting community groups to nominate representatives to assist a statutory body to plan for future services and developments was an interesting development in hospital board administration. The service development group set up by the Waikato Hospital Board had no previous models to follow, nor were any direct monitoring provisions established to allow the Board to direct the exercise. The present study was an evaluation of the Service Development Group process carried out independently of the review of maternity services.

ORGANISATIONAL EFFECTIVENESS

Evaluating the effectiveness of organisations requires the selection of appropriate criteria (Cameron 1980). In order to find the most useful approach, the evaluator should first answer critical questions about the assessment of organisational effectiveness (Cameron, 1980). The present researcher decided to make a comparison between Cameron's model of organisational effectiveness and the ways in which the Service Development Group (SDG) functioned in order to understand the SDG's level of effectiveness. The critical questions asked were: How well did the SDG accomplish its goals? Did the SDG acquire needed resources? Was there evidence of participant client satisfaction? and, What were the internal processes and operations of the SDG? Organisational or unit effectiveness .becomes a "summing up", an understanding of the past and "interpretation" (Cummings, 1983, p.189). No single approach to the evaluation of effectiveness can be appropriate in all circumstances. Cameron's (1980) model provided the main framework for critical thinking and for assessing what had occurred during the Waikato Hospital Board's Review of Maternity Services and the involvement of the SDG.

Four major approaches were used to define and assess organisational effectiveness: 1) The Goal Model allows evaluators to focus on the outputs of an organisation and assumes that the closer an organisation's outputs come to meeting its goals, the more effective it is. 2) The Human Resource Model or System Resource approach judges an organisation's effectiveness on the extent to which it acquires needed resources; that is, the more needed resources an organisation can obtain from its external environment, the more effective it is. 3) The Participant Satisfaction Model defines effectiveness as the extent to which all of the organisation's strategic constituencies are at least minimally satisfied. 4) The Process Model focuses on the internal process and operations of the organisation. Effective organisations are those with an absence of internal strain, where members are highly integrated into the system, internal functioning is smooth and typified by trust and benevolence toward individuals and there is a free flow of information. In the process approach, organisations are more effective if they possess a higher degree of these internal characteristics and less effective if they possess a lesser degree of these characteristics (Cameron, 1980).

The present study attempted to create meaning from confusion and complexity (Pfeffer, 1981) by establishing goals that would act as a guide throughout the formation of the research, overall process and end analysis. The objectives provided a conceptual framework for questionnaire and interview research and provide the format for a discussion of the results.

Statistical methods of data analysis were not appropriate for the small sample sizes involved in this research. However, qualitative analyses have facilitated and enhanced the ability to draw conclusions from the information collated.

Assessment of the extent to which aims were achieved, a critique of the methodology and the methods used for analysis will be discussed. Implications of the results, some serendipitous findings and recommendations for future service development groups are outlined. Suggestions are made about methods for further research and emphasis is placed on the importance of monitoring and evaluation for health services reviews.

AIM 1: TO ESTABLISH THE REASONS BEHIND THE BOARD'S DECISION TO REVIEW EXISTING MATERNITY SERVICES

Archival research methods assisted with achievement of this aim. Searches of Board minutes, newspaper clippings, Department of Health's (1977) bed guideline figures and discussion with the Board's Executive Officers provided reasons. These were: demographic changes such as the trend towards smaller families, the guidelines of the *Obstetric Regulations* (1975), oversupply of maternity beds in all of the Board's maternity hospitals, financial constraints and the temporary closure of Te Aroha Maternity due to shortage of nursing staff.

For a period of three to four years before the initiation of the maternity services review the Superintendent-in-Chief stated that he had been recommending closure of at least two underutilised district maternity hospitals. Pressure caused by the need for provision of other health services and a shortage of financial resources made it necessary to review the way existing services, facilities and finances were being used. However, it was the management problems of Te Aroha Maternity Hospital that provided the reason for the Board to write to the Minister of Health and request permanent closure of that hospital. In declining the request the Minister used the issue as a catalyst to ask the Board to conduct a review of all its maternity services. Overall there was a number of contributing reasons for the review but the Minister's letter appears to have been the catalyst that caused the Board decided to review its Maternity Services.

Achievement of Aim One involved acquiring resources such as information about the supply and use of maternity services in order to accomplish this goal. Cameron (1980) described the goal model as the first and most widely used approach of defining effectiveness of "...how well an organisation accomplishes its goals" (Cameron, 1980, p.67). The approach proved useful in systematically assessing what was the major reason for the maternity services review; the power of the Minister's request.

AIM 2: TO DESCRIBE WHAT HAPPENED DURING THE REVIEW PERIOD

The public exercise undertaken by the SDG and Waikato Hospital board support staff involved collecting information from many sources. The system resource approach (Cameron, 1980; Cummings, 1983), judges the extent to which an organisation (the SDG) acquired needed resources.

Commencement of the Review

The Board agreed to proceed with the programme as set out in a Draft Obstetric Service Plan. The plan proposed that there should be two committees: (1) the Board's Steering Committee, made up of Board members and executives who were to assist in the evaluation of objectives within financial constraints, maintenance and quality of services and existing policies; and (2) a service development group, to comprise representatives of providers and users of the maternity services.

Having accepted the general principles of service planning, the Board set up its SDG in October 1982 with membership from professional, public, private and voluntary organisations. Representatives were: Chairman of Obstetrics and Gynaecology, Waikato Hospital Board; Director of New Born Unit, Waikato Hospital; a practising midwife from a district hospital; the Board's adviser on Obstetric Nursing Services; Research and Development Officer (Waikato Hospital Board employee); Representative from: General Practitioners, Parents Centre, Plunket, National Council of Women, Public Health Nurse, a Board Member and Maori Women's Welfare League. General objectives were formulated by the Board from which the SDG was to form its own terms of reference.

Definition of an "Ideal Maternity Service"

Many in the group stated at the time they were interviewed that the definition of an "ideal maternity Service" was the SDG's major achievement. SDG members were united in their approach to the review. Sufficient time was taken to ensure that the "ideal" definition embraced ideas that were potentially worthwhile and feasible for families and health professionals. They pursued that "ideal" philosophy throughout all of their activities. Recommendations were made after careful consideration and discussion. The widespread opposition from local authorities and the general public to the SDG's report was disappointing to the SDG but perhaps inevitable because the recommendations to close five district maternity hospitals overshadowed the worthwhile concepts that the "ideal maternity service" espoused. More publicity about the potential benefits of the SDG's ideal concept may have altered the public's negative perception of the SDG's work. Communication networking, consultation, participatory democracy and the importance of articulating them through skilled public relations programmes and the use of a professional facilitator are all aspects that could have been better handled.

Integration of the service development group's and steering committee's recommendations resulted in a request to the Minister of Health to allow the Board to implement the plan and recommendations. In turn the Minister of Health appointed a two person investigating committee of the Hospitals Advisory council to advise him about the Waikato Board's request. In July 1986 the Minister released and supported the investigating committee's report. By 1988 the overall result of this planning exercise were annual savings to the Board of approximately $NZ7 million in running costs. Service development groups have now been legislated as requirements for health planning for Area Health Boards in New Zealand (*Area Health Board Act,* 1983).

AIM 3: TO DESCRIBE THE REASONS FOR THE BOARD'S DECISION TO USE A SERVICE DEVELOPMENT GROUP TO REVIEW MATERNITY SERVICES

The process model was Cameron's (1980) and the present researcher's third approach to assessing and understanding organisational effectiveness. It focuses on the internal processes and operations of an organisation. Healthy organisations are those that function smoothly, are typified by trust and kindness toward individuals and in which information is allowed to flow smoothly in all directions. In the process approach effectiveness is judged according to how many of the healthy characteristics an organisation possesses (Cameron, 1980). Description of the reasons for the Board's decision to use a service development group to review maternity services, was aided by the process model.

One of the major influences on health services reorganisation has been the then Labor Government's White Paper *A Health Service for New Zealand* (1974). Prior to the "White Paper", planning was determined in terms of numbers of hospital beds. The "White Paper" was modelled on the national Health Service approach in Great Britain. It proposed fourteen regional health authorities for New Zealand by 1 April 1978. Although that did not eventuate, another proposal was developed by a Legal and Administration Consultative Group (1976) that recommended that service development groups should be established for each clinical and front line service and thus become the foundation unit of organisation and planning under the proposed new regional health authorities. Malcolm (1981) commented that the service development group approach was an innovation of international significance as it demonstrated that a democratic participative model could work and that a desire for change could evolve from such a process.

One reason for the use of a service development group approach was the recent history of health planning in New Zealand. A second reason was that the service development group approach had already been used in Northland and

Wellington with reasonable success. A third reason may have been the appointment of a new Chief Executive from North Canterbury Hospital Board who had knowledge and experience of service development groups. The Waikato Hospital Board decided to use a service development group approach because of a succession of events that seemed to provide sufficient evidence to implement the approach.

There was agreement by the Board that there should be community involvement in the review. A suggested plan *(Draft Obstetric Service Plan,* 1982) was endorsed by the Chief Executive, then formally approved by the Board. No alternative courses of action were offered or suggested at the decisive Board meeting *(Waikato Hospital Board Minutes,* 13 September 1982).

AIM 4: TO ASSESS THE EFFECTIVENESS OF EVALUATION RESEARCH TECHNIQUES FOR THIS STUDY

The researcher was assisted in assessing the effectiveness of evaluation research techniques for the present study by the system resource approach or human resource model (Cameron, 1980). The system resource model is most useful when there is a clear connection between resources received by an organisation and what it produces or delivers. Organisations that have resources and do not use them in a productive manner are not effective (Cameron, 1980). The system resource or human resource approach allowed the researcher to understand the importance of the participant observer role in appreciating the significance of the various aspects of the exercise.

Examples of the Ways in Which Various Aspects of Evaluation Research Have Assisted This Study

Technical Aspects. A study of the National Medical Care Expenditure Survey (NMCES; Berk, Wilensky & Cohen, 1984) provided some useful guidelines for the present study because it showed evaluation research techniques were useful and adaptable fro a complex research design and worthwhile for a large study. It had used surveys with different groups of potential clients that allow comparison of different aspects of medical care expenditure. It was decided that questionnaires administered to the three groups involved in the present programme would provide the information needed for analysis of the service development group process and so allow a comprehensive profile about the functioning of a service development group.

Models of Evaluation Research. Four models of evaluation research were used by the researcher to understand how the SDG functioned: 1) the Goal Model; 2) the Human Resource Model; 3) the participant Satisfaction Model; and 4) the Process Model (Cameron, 1980). The goal model approach helped the researcher to develop an awareness about the types of questions required to obtain information from participants about how effective the SDG was in attaining its goals. The SDG had targets such as the "ideal maternity service" and delivery of maternity services that were more cost-effective. Use of this approach highlighted difficulties and showed how achievement of the goals was impeded. One instance was the restrictive terms of reference that had limit~d the SDG's objectives. The goal model also helped show that the SDG's work had had some effects that were not intended.

The human resource model assisted with understanding the ways that the SDG had been used by the Board to carry out a difficult task. The SDG brought a broad knowledge base to the review and the potential for worthwhile recommendations as a result of client involvement (House, 1977; Leviton & Hughes, 1981). The human resource model can be used to judge the extent that an organisation is effective in acquiring needed resources from the external environment (Cameron, 1980). It may be harsh to comment that the Board "used" the SDG to carry out a difficult task but the approach of the human resource model helped in trying to understand what occurred. Resource based theories propose that it is agreement on multipurpose means that binds many social systems together (Cameron, 1980; Keeley, 1984). If the Board was not able to change maternity services by resolution from a Board meeting, they had to find another method. Appointment of the SDG was a means to finding a method of effecting change. SDG members were willing to work on maternity service issues, but at the same time they helped facilitate a change in provision of services and allocation of finance.

The approach of the participant satisfaction model produced the guideline for designing questions about which people were likely to be satisfied in the review of maternity services. Effectiveness is defined as the extent to which strategic constituencies of organisations are satisfied by the review or programme (Cameron, 1980; Keeley, 1978; Pfeffer & Salancik, 1978). Perhaps the only strategic constituency that was fully satisfied was the Board, as all other groups involved lost to a certain extent, especially doctors, nurses, domestic workers, gardeners, pharmacists and florists who lost aspects of their employment or business. At the time of this report (March, 1987) it would appear that the group that lost the most and were least satisfied were young parents.

Social intervention programmes will be affected by the people involved in the project. Aspects of evaluation research to be taken into account include assurance of confidentiality of client information and respect for the procedures and protocols of institutions or organisations where research is undertaken (Finney & Moos, 1984; Patton et al. 1975; Snelgrove, 1983). Involving staff in evaluation studies can be useful and cost-effective for the programme because interest in obtaining successful outcomes is increased and unsuccessful aspects are more easily understood.

The process model describes effective organisation as those that operate smoothly (Cameron, 1980). In order to use the process model the SDG was conceptualised as an organisation and examined to see how smoothly it had operated. Questions were formed to allow responses about the way SDG members perceived the functioning of their group and the overall effectiveness of the service development group approach. Members believed that they were a "good" group. However, they may not have been able to continue to exist as a group. The leaders (the Parents Centre representative and a paediatrician) were finding the terms of reference increasingly restrictive. They shared a mutual and serious commitment to the protection and care of infants and their families. The researcher believed that, given time, they would have convinced the SDG and the Board that relaxation of the terms of reference was necessary to allow useful results and implementation of the "ideal concept".

AIM 5: TO DESCRIBE PARTICIPANTS' ATTITUDES ABOUT THE SDG

Understanding participants' attitudes about the SDG came through the strategic constituencies or participant satisfaction model (Cameron, 1980). This approach defines effectiveness as the extent to which all of the organisation's strategic participants (constituencies) are at least minimally satisfied. The theme of participatory democracy was revealed as important in the SDG process. The methodology used to gather information from the SDG, Board's Steering Committee and selected community groups about their attitudes toward the use of a service group development involved three major techniques. These were: analysis of archival data, questionnaires and interviews.

As an illustration of this model the SDG and nominating organisations were satisfied that the SDG's work had acted as a "catalyst for change" to maternity services. Changes occurred because of the involvement of the SDG and the interest created in maternity services and professional practice. Subsequently the SDG's ideas about family-oriented delivery rooms were introduced in all the Board's maternity hospitals.

Protection of parochial interests was another theme introduced by over half the participants. SDG members were perceived to have put their own needs first. Community representatives wanted to retain hospital services in local districts. Professional people emphasised the quality of care provided for women at local maternity hospitals in an effort to retain local services and ensure the continued use of facilities and maintenance of employment. The researcher believes that interviews with the nominating organisations should have been carried out. They would have provided more in-depth information about the effect on districts and the social costs to people should maternity services be changed or closed. The researcher has learnt that as well as the major tasks it is important to have a key person (facilitator) available to assist service development group members with technical and information resource questions.

AIM 6: TO EXAMINE THE INTERACTION AND CO-OPERATION
BETWEEN THE VARIOUS COMMITTEES INVOLVED IN THE REVIEW

It is argued (Cameron, 1980; Daft & Wiginton, 1979) that it is not possible to produce an overarching framework, or categorisation scheme, that labels and distinguishes organisations one from another. The attempt to examine the interaction and co-operation between the various committees involved in the review was only achieved with the assistance of the process model (Cameron, 1980) that focuses on the internal strengths and weaknesses of the processes and operations of an organisation. Political aspects of evaluation research were useful when attempting to understand the degree of co-operation between the three main groups involved in the review. Many staff members were involved in aspects of the review and had the potential to shape the review's directions and outcomes.

Co-operation varied between the different groups. Interviews with SDG members showed that many had feelings of frustration and resentment toward the Board's Steering committee. The Steering Committee's brief was to advise the SDG about financial, service and policy matters. However it seemed that there was little useful interaction between the Steering Committee and the SDG. Community representatives commented on the rigidity of the Steering Committee's approach while professional representatives worried about the use of power. The hierarchical chain of command in hospitals in New Zealand allocates most power to the position of Superintendent-in-Chief. SDG members felt powerless to deal with it. In the interaction that did take place between the Steering Committee and the SDG, the Superintendent-in-Chief used the power attributed to his position to make sure that decisions made were the way that he thought they should be. Although some issues were only minor, this negativism resulted in feelings of resentment and anger from the SDG.

The Steering committee's comments indicated that more interaction and understanding between the groups may have benefited the review. The power relationships existing between the two groups meant effective communication was impossible. One committee was meant to "steer" the other, but any attempts to do so were met with resentment and frustration from the SDG.

AIM 7: TO ATTEMPT TO MEASURE THE AMOUNT OF SATISFACTION
WITH THE SDG EXERCISE AS PERCEIVED BY PARTICIPANTS

The participant satisfaction model (Cameron, 1980; Keeley, 1978; Pfeffer & Salancik, 1978) was used to understand the extent to which all or key organisation's strategic constituencies were satisfied. The response formats were open-ended to allow different ideas from each of the three groups. Analysis of the responses enabled conclusions to be made about the amount of satisfaction with the service development group exercise.

Facilitation of community participation and communication were listed by all SDG members as positive outcomes by the SDG. The SDG felt that their report had made information about maternity services available to the general public and allowed interactive comment. Conceptualising an "ideal" for maternity services was also counted as an achievement.

All groups consulted commented about the positive way in which community and professional people had worked together as members of the SDG. In retrospect, little acknowledgement was given to the SDG for its work by the Board or the general public, yet its foundation work continues to gain credibility as a health service planning initiative in New Zealand.

In contrast to positive outcomes and satisfaction, there were some major dissatisfactions noted by all groups. These were: parochial interests, restrictive terms of reference, closure decisions and subsequent loss of public confidence. There appears to be a public expectation that hospital boards supply but do not withdraw services. Suggestions of possible maternity hospital closures caused people to worry that further hospital and other general services such as rail, bus and courthouses would be lost to townships. This is evidence of participant dissatisfaction. Criticism of the "terms of reference" for the SDG occurred repeatedly throughout this study.

AIM 8: TO MAKE CONCLUSION ABOUT THE VALUE OF THE SERVICE DEVELOPMENT GROUP PROCESS

Two models, goal and participant satisfaction (Cameron, 1980) allowed analysis and conclusions to be made about the value of the service development group process. Responses from participants indicated that the service development group approach was valuable for reviewing health services. The combination of professional and lay perspectives had resulted in fresh ideas and innovate approaches for maternity services. The importance of the "lay input" should not be underestimated.

A process of change occurred within the SDG. Seating at meetings was strategically changed by the facilitator to encourage wide communication within the SDG and to break down the traditional medical and nursing hierarchical patterns that were operating within the group.

AIM 9: TO MAKE RECOMMENDATIONS FOR FUTURE SERVICE DEVELOPMENT GROUP EXERCISES

A major challenge in the present research was to discover the most useful methods for distinguishing what were the important aspects of the service development group approach in order to make recommendations for the future. It was designed not only to study the process of service development group functioning and people's perceptions of its effectiveness, but also to make recommendations for any other agencies planning a similar type of exercise. Six recommendations were derived from the findings of the present study and the researcher's participant involvement. The recommendations are: 1) that the service development group approach or community involvement and participatory democracy is recommended as a worthwhile method to assist with reviews of health services it involved people in the prescription of their own services and ensures understanding and co-operation; 2) that all service development group members are selected before meetings commence so that non-one feels unequal; 3) that skilled public relations and communication exercises should be employed to help facilitate and communicate the information and thus increase the understanding about such reviews; 4) that adequate time should be given to allow discussion and agreement about any terms of reference before commencement of the task so that SDG members do not feel they are being controlled and directed; 5) that service development groups should be small to ensure optimal SDG performance; 6) that a key person such as a community psychologist should be available to act as a facilitator for the group; and 7) that cultural issues should be taken into account. This is a complex matter that requires careful study and consideration.

REFERENCES

A health service for New Zealand. (1974). Presented to the House of Representatives by Leave. A.R. Shearer, Government Printer, Wellington, New Zealand.

Area Health Board (1983) Act. Wellington, New Zealand: Government Printer.

Attkisson, C.C., Brown, T.R., & Hargreaves, W.A. (1978). Roles and functions of evaluation in human service programmes. In C.C. Attkisson, W.A. Hargreaves & M.J. Horowitz (Eds.), *Evaluation of human service programmes.* New York: Academic Press.

Berk, M.L., Wilsensky, G.R. & Cohen, S.B. (1984). Methodological issues in health surveys. An evaluation of procedures used in the national medical care expenditure survey. *Evaluation Review, 8,* 307-326.

Cameron, K. (1980). Critical questions in assessing organisational effectiveness, *Organisational Dynamics,* Autumn, 66-80.

Campbell, D.T. (1974, September). *Qualitative knowing in action research.* Kurt Lewin Award Address, Society for the Psychological Study of Social Issues. Meeting with the American Psychological Association, New Orleans.

Cummings, L.L. (1983) Organisational effectiveness and organisational behaviour: A critical perspective. In K. Cameron & D. Whetton. *Organisational effectiveness: A comparison of multiple models.* New York: Academic Press.

Department of Health (1977). *Planning guidelines for hospital beds and services.* Issued by the Division of Hospitals in Association with The Management Services and Research Unit, Department of Health, Wellington, New Zealand: Government Printer.

Finney, J.W. & Moos, R.H. (1984). Environmental assessment and evaluation research: Examples from mental health and substance abuse programme. *Evaluation and Programme Planning, 7,* 151-167.

House, E.R. (1977). The politics of evaluation in higher education. In F. Caro (Ed.), *Readings in evaluation research.* New York: Sage Publications.

Keeley, M. (1984). Organisational analogy: A comparison of organismic and social contract models. *Administrative Science Quarterly, 25,* 337-362.

Levine, A. & Levine, M. (1977, November). The social context of evaluation research: A case study *Evaluation Review, 5,* 525-548.

Malcolm, L.A. (1981). Planning primary and community care. In J. Richards, (Ed.), *Primary Health Care and the Community,* 3-16. Auckland: Longman Paul.

Obstetric Regulations (1975/137) Wellington, New Zealand: Government Printer.

Patton, M.G. (1979). Evaluation of prgramme implementation. *Evaluation Studies Annual Review, 4,* 318-346.

Patton, M.M., Grimes, P.S., Guthrie, K.M., Brennan, French B.D. & Blyth D.A. (1975). *In search of impact: an analysis of the utilisation of federal health evaluation research.* Minneapolis: University of Minnesota, Minnesota Centre for Sociological Research.

Pfeffer, J. (1981) Management as symbolic action: The creation and maintenance of organisational paradigms. In L.L. cummings & B.M. Staw (Eds.), *Research in organisational behaviour (Vol 3)* Greenwich, Conn.: JAI Press.

Pfeffer, J. & Salancik, G.R. (1978). *The external control of organisations.* New York: Harper and Row.

Rosenblatt, R.A. (1984). *Regionalisation of obstetric and perinatal services in New Zealand.* A health services analysis. Wellington: New Zealand.

Rjossi, P.H., Freeman, H.e. & Wright, S.R. (1979). *Evaluation a systematic approach.* Beverly Hills: Sage Publications.

Sceats, J. & Pool, I. (1986). Demographic communities of South Auckland-Bay of Plenty. In *Area health boards. What's in them for the community?* Papers presented at a seminar held in Hamilton, June 1986. New Zealand: Waikato Mental Health Association in conjunction with Centre for Continuing Education, University of Waikato.

Snelgrove, T. (1983). Providing evaluation services for social services concerned with children and families. A survey conducted for the Hamilton children's Trust. In D.R. Thomas (Ed.). *Development of evaluation research for social services* (Psychology Research Series No 16. community Psychology Research Record IV. 11-24. Department of Psychology, University of Waikato, New Zealand.

Trend, M.G. (1979). On the reconcilliation of qualitative and quantitative analyses: A Case Study. In T.D. Cook and C.S. Reichardt (Eds.). *Qualitative and quantitative methods in evaluation research.* Beverly Hills: Sage.

Waikato Hospital Board (1986). *Annual report 1985-1986.*

Waikato Hospital Board (1982). *Draft obstetric plan.* Waikato Hospital Board, Hamilton, New Zealand.

Waikato Hospital Board minute book, (September and October, 1982).

Social Applications and Issues in Psychology
R.C. King and J.K. Collins (editors)
©Elsevier Science Publishers B.V. (North-Holland), 1989

MEDICAL PRACTITIONERS AND QUIT-SMOKING ADVICE

Rosemary A. Knight

Australian Institute of Health, Australia, and

David A. Hay

La Trobe University, Australia

Medical practitioners are assumed to be effective agents of change in altering patients' beliefs and behaviour. Nevertheless, they are reportedly often loath to engage in health education and evidence exists that such intervention meets with varied success. The aim of this research was twofold: a) to assess the efficacy of quit-smoking advice from medical practitioners and b) to assess their attitudes to quit-smoking interventions and their beliefs about control over their patients' smoking habits. Adult smokers visiting their general practitioner completed questionnaires about smoking habits and beliefs at time of consultation and at a later time. Half of the patients, randomly allocated to the experimental group, were given quit-smoking advice and literature from their medical consultant. The remainder made up the control group. More of the experimental group tried to quit smoking, had more negative attitudes towards smoking and were more likely to cite 'Doctor's advice' as the reason for attempted quitting.

There were, however, no significant differences between the two groups in the percentage of patients who ceased smoking. This may reflect on the program itself or on the confuting of results by practitioners breaching control groups treatment arrangements. Analysis showed that successful quitting was most strongly related to a set of attitudinal variables, especially prior intention to give up smoking. Although the sample of doctors was mostly committed to the intervention program, and believed their advice to be influential, some were cynical about their own efficacy and the recidivism rates. To be effective agents of change, practitioners must be committed to quit-smoking programs and must first focus on patients' attitudes and intentions prior to implementing any behavioural interventions.

Medical practitioners, especially general practitioners (GPs), are assumed to be in a unique position to influence the smoking habits and beliefs of their patients. Some researchers (e.g., Chapman, 1985) even maintain that stop-smoking clinics and other labour-intensive cessation programs are not cost-effective compared with the quit-smoking advice available from GPs who have daily contact with thousands of smokers and who are able to counsel them in a very cheap and effective way. Despite the claimed advantages of GP intervention, there is, at best, meagre information concerning the beliefs, practices and efficacy of GPs with regard to their health promotion activities (Catford & Nutbeam, 1984).

Perhaps the most dramatic and recent Australian example of the effect of a GP intervention program was given by Richmond and Webster (1985), in which a 33% cessation rate was achieved in the experimental group, compared with only 3% in the control group. Patients assigned to the former group made 6 visits to the GP, were given a demonstration of lung function and blood tests, filled in a detailed questionnaire concerning smoking habits, dependence and motivation to quit and were asked to keep a diary of smoking patterns. In addition, patients were given a handbook containing a sequenced quit program and counselled intensively about progress over a 6 month period.

Although Richmond and Webster (1985) have shown convincingly the value of intense GP intervention, it is unlikely that the majority of GPs in normal busy practices would invest such time and commitment to one health education program. Clearly, as Catford and Nutbeam (1984) and Stewart & Rosser (1982) suggest, more information is needed about the best type of advice to give GPs concerning the promotion of health lifestyles and effective intervention techniques.

Another important factor contributing to patients' cessation of smoking, appears to be the individual features of the GP, especially his or her smoking status. Pederson (1982) cites the findings of Pincherle and Wright (1970) where patient abstinence rates varied between 17% and 30%, the difference partially being accounted for by the variation in practitioners' own smoking habits.

Hallett (1983) found that GPs who smoked cigarettes were less likely to give either helpful quit-smoking advice, or any advice at all, than GPs who smoked a pipe or cigars, or who did not smoke at all. Fortmann et al. (1985) discovered that practitioners who doubted the effectiveness of their anti-smoking advice, or who did not know what to say to smoking patients, were also less likely to provide quit-smoking advice.

Individual patient variables are of great importance when assessing the efficacy of GPs quit-smoking advice. Hill and Gray (1984) and Pederson, Strickland and Deslauriers (1984) found that patient's intention to quit was the best predictor of cessation behaviour. Pederson et al. (1984) concluded that patients' faith in the advice of medical practitioners may be important in explaining varying cessation rates. In an Australian study, Rigby and Mezzer (1984) found that patients did indeed view medical practitioners as "authority figures", emphasising their potential powerful role. However, Rigby and Mezzer also noted strong age and sex effects, such that older people were more inclined to believe in the authority of medical practitioners, as were males. The implication of these studies is that Australian GPs may be differentially successful according to the individual features of their patients, as has been found in several overseas studies (see Pederson, 1982).

The aim of this study was to assess the efficacy of the Australian Capital Territory Give-Up Smoking (GUS) program which combined a survey of patients' attitudes, habits and beliefs about smoking and an assessment of GPs attitudes to quit-smoking programs, their attitudes towards the GUS campaign, an investigation of their own smoking habits and beliefs about control over patients' smoking behaviour.

METHOD

Recruitment of Medical Practitioners

GPs were selected from the Australian Capital Territory medical practitioners registration roll. Recruitment was achieved by a personal approach from a colleague practitioner, who explained the program to both practitioners and receptionists, indicated the success of other similar campaigns and emphasised that the study had the support of the Royal Australian College of General Practitioners' Family Medicine Program and the Australian Medical Association. All 50 GPs who were approached took part in the study.

Selection of Patients

All tobacco smokers aged 16 years and over who attended surgery for the first time were included in the sample. Of the 784 eligible smokers who attended the surgeries during the 4 weeks trial, only 25 patients refused to participate.

Procedure and Materials

Three questionnaires were administered to each patient: an initial survey and two follow-up surveys consisting of a short series of questions about the patient's current smoking habits, attitudes and attempts/intentions to stop smoking. The initial questionnaire was completed in the waiting-room before seeing the GP, while the follow-up surveys were mailed to the patients one month and one year later.

A GPs' questionnaire was administered to each practitioner by the colleague who introduced the program. Information was gathered about the GP's age, gender, own smoking habits, current technique (if any) of giving anti-smoking advice, attitude towards quit campaigns and approval or disapproval of the GUS program. After the 4-week trial period, a further short questionnaire was posted to GPs and receptionists who had participated in the study to assess how they had implemented the program and its perceived effectiveness.

RESULTS

Although we briefly report here the results of the GPs' intervention, they have been documented fully elsewhere (Knight and Hay, 1989). The main purpose of this paper is to document the reaction of the GPs to the program and their attitudes and behaviour.

In Knight and Hay (1989), it was found that GPs' advice to quit smoking was effective. At the follow-up survey, 16.6% of the experimental group had ceased smoking, compared with 11.8% in the control group, although these results are not significant. Significantly more ex-smokers in the experimental group cited "Practitioner's advice" as their reason for quitting and they were more likely to have used the techniques recommended in the GUS booklet. More of the experimental group patients attempted to quit, again citing GP intervention and indicating strengthened desire to stop smoking. In addition, heavy smokers in the experimental group decreased their consumption rate more markedly than did heavy smokers in the control group. Older males who smoked heavily were more willing to try giving up, primarily citing health as their reason for quitting. They were largely successful. The ex-smokers also found quitting somewhat easier than they had expected, an effect more significant among the experimental than control group patients. The results further revealed that ex-smokers were more likely to have tried giving up in the past and were more likely to have non-smoking friends.

In this study, about 55% of patients reported that they had previously been advised by a GP to quit smoking. This compared favourably with Hill & Gray's (1984) Australian data, in which only 8% of smokers listed their medical practitioner as someone who would be in favour of their quitting. When patients were asked how much influence they thought GPs could have in persuading smokers to quit, 51% thought that they could be influential, 22% were unsure and 21% of smokers believed that they could have very little influence.

Although GPs' advice was found to be successful, there is some suggestion that it was differentially effective: some patients were more influenced than others. In addition, the initial beliefs and attitudes held by smoking patients were of paramount importance, such that the best predictor of quitting was prior intention to give up.

A Profile of the GPs

Of the 50 GPs who participated in the program, 40% were females and 60% were males. The GPs were mostly aged between 31-40 years (40%), with an equal proportion of the remainder in the following age ranges: under 30, 41-50

..d 51-60 years. Only 7% were over 61 years of age. Older GPs were more likely to be current or ex-smokers (bi-serial r=.33; df=48; p=.016).

Concerning their smoking habits, only 2 GPs (4%) were current smokers (both being cigar smokers). The majority (71%) had never smoked and 24% were ex-smokers.

All GPs in the sample claimed to give routinely some form of quit-smoking advice to their patients. Most GPs (60%) used a combination of methods (e.g., hypnosis, self-help groups, verbal advice), but the single most common technique was verbal advice only (27%). When asked if they would be willing to arrange a follow-up consultation with patients after giving quit-smoking advice, 80% of GPs said yes, 13% were unsure and 7% said no.

The GPs in this sample typically believed that medical practitioners could have some influence in persuading patients to quit smoking (80%), 13% thought that they could have a lot of influence and 7% believed that they had very little influence. Older practitioners believed they had less influence (r=-.27; df=48; p=.04), that fewer of their patients would quit (r=-.3; df=48; p=.06) and that fewer would cut down their smoking (r=-.38; df=48; p=.03).

GPs' Experiences with the GUS Program

Approximately half the GPs who participated in the program returned a follow-up questionnaire concerning the actual procedure followed and perceived success of the venture. When asked if they would use the GUS method again, 77% said yes, 14% said no, and 9% were unsure. However, only 18% of GPs stated that they had used the kit exactly as intended. During the experimental period, the majority of GPs (64%) gave out quit-smoking advice to all smoking patients, but 27% claimed to have given the advice on an ad hoc basis. Furthermore, 86% gave quit-smoking advice to some patients during the control period, for ethical reasons. Results from the GUS program must be qualified accordingly.

The majority of GPs (59%) found the GUS kit moderately useful in counselling smokers, 14% said it was very useful, 23% said it was mildly useful and 4% claimed it was of little use. In this context, 68% acknowledged that they had promoted the GUS kit quite positively, 23% promoted it enthusiastically and 9% confessed to being lukewarm in their advice. The GPs estimated that 46% of patients responded to it somewhat positively, 41% were neutral, 9% were very positive and 4% were somewhat negative. Overall, 68% did not want to see the GUS program changed in any way and 18% suggested improvements.

As a result of the intervention program, many GPs (41%) estimated that the number of queries about quit-smoking advice had increased, but half the practitioners claimed that there had been no change.

DISCUSSION

It must be said that the primary difficulty of such intervention programs is to get GPs involved, to increase their motivation to participate, to alter their beliefs concerning the efficacy of such health-promotion strategies and to get them to realise that often it is crucial to alter patients' attitudes and intentions to quit smoking before implementing a program. GPs are typically very busy people, dealing with patients' immediate complaints on a tight schedule. Accordingly, it is hard to convince these practitioners that quit-smoking advice needs to be given to all smoking patients, firmly, repeatedly and with the offer of follow-up consultations. In this context, many practitioners complained that the intervention program was time-consuming and demanding. For example, one GP commented, "Without continual follow-up, I find that most people begin smoking again. I cannot justify this continual follow-up in a general practice situation". Clearly, GPs' basic attitudes to such campaigns are crucial. Intervention programs should be as much concerned with recidivism rates as with attempts to induce cessation of smoking.

Encouraging GPs to participate in evaluation research not only requires skilful and persuasive negotiation, but also the full support of all staff, such as receptionists. For example, when receptionists were asked about why the program wasn't always followed exactly, 61% said there was no time. Hence, one receptionist claimed, "Due to the work load, both x (secretary) and myself were unable to participate in your campaign". The fact that this receptionist's comment came from a practice where the GPs were enthusiastic about the program, suggests the absolute necessity of having support staff fully committed to any health promotion campaign one may wish to implement.

Even when the researcher succeeds in involving general practitioners in such programs, ethical considerations and lack of attention to control group requirements may create problems of interpretation. In conclusion, we stress the need to implement health promotion programs which have a low response cost on the part of medical practitioners and staff if we wish them to be involved and committed in any way at all.

ACKNOWLEDGEMENTS

1   Address all correspondence to the first author. These data were collected while the first author was a Research Psychologist within the Research, Planning and Evaluation Unit, ACT Health Authority, Canberra, Australia.

2   Sincere thanks are extended to the following people:
The GPs and patients who took part in the study; The Health Promotion Branch (ACTHA) for financial assistance; Dr A Shroot (AMA & ASH) and Dr H Van Doorn (RACGPs' Family Medicine Program) for initial advice and help with the preparation of the intervention program; Dr A Pritchard (RACGPs' Family Medicine Program) for recruitment of GPs; Ms R Dupont and Ms C Fitzwarryne for their initial contribution to the program; Ms T Theobald for computing assistance; Mr R Barge and Mr E Brinkley (ABS) for initial statistical advice.

CORRESPONDENCE

Dr Rosemary A Knight, Australian Institute of Health, GPO Box 570, Canberra, Australia, and Dr David A Hay, Department of Psychology, La Trobe University, Melbourne, Australia.

REFERENCES

Catford, J.C. & Nutbeam, D. (1984).   Prevention in practice: what Wessex general practitioners are doing. *British Medical Journal, 288,* (6420), 832-834.

Chapman, S. (1985).   Stop-smoking clinics: a case for their abandonment. *The Lancet, 1,* (8434), 918-920.

Fortmann, S.P., Sallis, J.F., Magnus, P.M. & Farquhar, J.W. (1985).   Attitudes and practices of physicians regarding hypertension and smoking: the Stanford Five City Project. *Preventive Medicine, 14,* (1), 70-80.

Hallett, R. (1983).   Intervention against smoking and its relationship to general practitioners' smoking habits. *Journal of the Royal College of General Practitioners, 33,* (254),   565-567.

Hill, D. & Gray, N. (1984).   Australian patterns of tobacco smoking and related health beliefs in 1983. *Community Health Studies, 8,* (3), 307-316.

Knight, R.A. & Hay, D.A. (1989) Practitioners' influence: its relationship to the modification and prediction of patients' smoking behavior.

Pederson, L.L. (1982).   Compliance with physician advice to quit smoking: a review of the literature. *Preventive Medicine, 11,* (1), 71-84.

Pederson, L.L., Strickland, M.D. & Des Lauriers, A. (1984) Factors related to successful smoking cessation in general practice patients. Paper presented to CPA Annual Meeting, Ottawa, Canada.

Richmond, R.L. & Webster, I.W. (1985).   A smoking cessation programme for use in general practice. *Medical Journal of Australia, 142,* (3), 190-194.

Rigby, K. & Mezzer, J. (1984).   Attitudes towards medical practitioners. Paper presented to the Thirteenth Annual Meeting of Australian Social Psychologists, Adelaide, May.

Stewart, P.J. & Rosser, W.W. (1982).   The impact of routine advice on smoking cessation from family physicians. *Canadian Medical Journal, 126,* (9), 1051-1054.

Social Applications and Issues in Psychology
R.C. King and J.K. Collins (editors)
©Elsevier Science Publishers B.V. (North-Holland), 1989

113

MEDICAL SCIENCE, PSYCHOTHERAPY AND THE DOCTOR-PATIENT RELATIONSHIP

G. Duncan

University of Auckland, New Zealand

The changing needs and abilities of societies lead to constant changes in the relationship between consumers and providers of health care. This paper will review some of the important changes in the doctor-patient relationship through the history of the West, leading to a portrayal of some of the problems encountered today in interactions between physicians and sick people. Data collected in New Zealand from patient, physician and complementary-healer populations concerning preferred qualities of doctor-patient relationship will be reviewed. Concepts taken from the psychotherapies, particularly transference, will be brought to bear on these issues, highlighting the difficulties inherent in the institutionalized separation of the organically and psychologically oriented healing professions.

The ancient Greek doctors were fully aware of the importance for healing of the emotional and rhetorical qualities of their relationships with patients (Lain Entralgo, 1969; Mutton, 1985). The Greek word philia was used to describe the doctor's love or affection for both patients and the art of medicine (Lain Entralgo, 1969). I hope to show that the importance of such an awareness has not diminished over the intervening millennia, although our professional awareness of it in modern times may have.

The optimism behind the growth of science and technology and the corresponding metaphor of the body as a machine, which over the last two centuries increasingly dominated medical thought, have diverted the profession's attention away from the emotional issues inherent in health and healing. More often than not, the focus of modern medical consciousness is on physical, organic events exclusively. A few voices in the medical literature of this century have attempted to remind practitioners of the unity of emotional and organic functioning (Bacon et al., 1952; Balint, 1964; Hamman, 1939; Henderson, 1935; Houston, 1938; Lewin, 1946; Osler, 1904). In general, however, the approach to this aspect of healing has been at best superficial and at worst dangerously neglectful. Thus, despite its obvious strengths, medical science has left us a legacy of an institutional division between organic and psychological healing practices. The dualistic tradition that we inherit leaves one group of professionals treating soulless bodies, and a quite separate group treating bodiless souls.

It has been left largely to the psychoanalytical camp to keep alive an awareness of the importance of emotional dynamics in the doctor-patient relationship (Freud, 1912/1950, 1915/1950; Glauber, 1953; McLaughlin, 1961; Menninger, 1959; Nunberg, 1938; Simmel, 1926; Zabarenko et al., 1970). Freud revived the ancient Greek notion of medical philia when, in 1906, he wrote in a letter to Jung that "Essentially . . . the cure is effected by love" (McGuire, 1979, p. 50). Psychoanalysts were also aware of the impact on the body of emotional dysfunction, or unconscious conflicts (Jones, 1938; Glover, 1929). Unfortunately, because psychoanalysis did not always match up to scientific expectations, many of Freud's more fruitful ideas were forgotten along with the less useful ones.

In order to account for these observations psychoanalysts have appealed to their theories of psychosexual development and to their observations of transference in the clinical setting. Freud observed that, in any healing relationship, the patient's deep-seated emotional conflicts, originating in childhood, will be `acted out' with the doctor as a parent-substitute. He believed that this phenomenon was a necessary requirement of successful therapy and that it typically occurs at that stage in therapy where the analyst experiences the greatest resistance from the patient (Freud, 1912/1950). The concept of transference is of great explanatory value in understanding the medical encounter. It is highlighted particularly by patient non-compliance, and by those patients whose symptoms are often clinically unidentifiable but who persist in seeking medical attention and refuse to acknowledge any possible psychosocial aetiology (Balint, 1964; Chancellor et al., 1977; Ford, 1983; O'Hagan, 1984; Whitehouse, 1987). The importance of transference for health professionals is also suggested by the fact that their quality of personal approach and communication in relating to patients is usually at or near the top of the list in studies rating the factors which affect patient satisfaction (Doyle and Ware, 1977; Lebow, 1974; Ley, 1982).

The disadvantage of Freud's formulation of the transference is that, although the patterns of adult interpersonal relationships undoubtedly have precursors in early parent-child interaction, Freud did not seem to think that the analytical relationship should grow beyond a situation analogous to parent and child, into a more equal partnership. In Freud's formulation, the doctor remains a figure of power and authority and, it is hoped, the patient leaves analysis feeling grateful. Such a relationship may encourage inappropriate expectations in both parties, resulting in what some physicians refer to as `malignant dependency' (Ryle, 1987). Freud also forbade the analyst any open acknowledgement of counter-transference, the reciprocal emotional vulnerabilities that the doctor brings into the situation. He was fully aware of the obvious dangers inherent in these situations, particularly when there exists mutual sexual attraction between doctor and patient (Freud, 1915/1950).

Similarly, the medical professional has tended on the whole to maintain an image of power and authority (an image that is legally institutionalized) and has generally avoided any recognition of the reciprocal; emotional vulnerabilities of its members. This is despite the fact that doctors as a group suffer at unusually high rates from illnesses of the type of aetiology which they generally avoid in their discourse with patients: that is, marital break-ups, suicide, mental illness, and addictive substance abuse (Evans, 1985; Ford, 1983; Pearson, 1982; Vaillant et al., 1972.

It is towards an appraisal of these issues of power and authority and the management of strong emotion in the medical encounter that the present study addresses itself. My main assumptions are that healing relationships should involve change in both parties, that such change should develop towards an increasingly equal relationship and that such a relationship would often require an acknowledgement of personal, emotional issues. This would, of course, focus primarily on the patient, but would also require appropriate listening skills and empathic ability in the doctor. The development of such a doctor-patient relationship should be predicated on the awareness that, although acquired institutional power may reside with the doctor, the real healing power itself is an inherent capacity of the patient. I thus ally myself with the community psychologists' concepts of empowerment and competence building (Clarke and Viney, 1979, 1984; Gesten and Jason, 1987; Owen, 1978; Raeburn, 1978; Rappaport, 1977, 1985).

In the past, the self-healing potential of the patient has often been trivialised by the term `placebo effect'. The patient's recovery is thus attributed to an irrational faith in the power and authority of the doctor. This has helped justify professional claims for an unquestioned authority. It has also diverted our attention from the need for patients to develop a `faith' in their own inherent healing process, which ultimately is what counts (Weick, 1983).

Conversely, the vulnerable, or wounded, side of the doctor has also been neglected in favour of a medical persona of benign heroism and ethical and personal invulnerability. Some authors have argued that the physician's desire to be perceived as invulnerable stems from his or her own phobias about disease and death, and the consequent desire to exert control over these phenomena in others (Golloway, 1981; Groesbeck, 1975). I thus also ally myself with the Jungian conception of the wounded healer (Jung, 1983; Groesbeck, 1975). A recognition of the patient's healing potential will require a reciprocal recognition of the physician's vulnerability.

The present study attempts to measure both lay and professional approval or disapproval of these ideals. To achieve this, I constructed a typology of 'styles' of doctor-patient relationship. This owes most to Szasz and Hollender's seminal paper on this topic (Szasz and Hollender, 1956), an early improvement on Parsons' rather rigid 'sick-role' model (Parsons, 1958, 1975; Parsons and Fox, 1952), but also draws on the work of more recent commentators (Barofsky, 1978; Haug and Lavin, 1981; O'Hagan, 1984; Schacht and Pemberton, 1985; Siegler, 1980; Vertinsky et al., 1974).

The first 'model' incorporated is Szasz and Hollender's 'Guidance - Co-operation', wherein the doctor assumes a position of authority and expects the patient to follow his or her orders. To work, this relationship requires complete trust on the part of the patient and selfless altruism on the part of the doctor who makes the decisions. This probably works well in emergency situations or with notifiable infectious diseases such as hepatitis (Szasz and Hollender, 1956).

The second model is 'Informed Consent'. Here the doctor does not assume that the patient should cooperate unquestioningly, but has the right to know about the disease and all treatment options. Decisions are made after negotiation between both parties, and of course with the patient's consent. Such a relationship is not usually possible in emergency situations or with mentally impaired and immature patients, but has become widely recognised as a vital ethical requirement in longer-term treatment (Alexander, 1982; Hull, 1985; Ost, 1984). Informed consent has recently become a public issue in New Zealand due to a judicial inquiry into the treatment of cervical cancer at Auckland's National Women's Hospital (Cartwright, 1988).

The third model is 'Patient Autonomy' or 'Consumerism'. In this case , the patient takes charge and expects the doctor to provide the services requested. The success of this relationship depends on a well-informed patient and a compliant doctor. It is often argued that this model is unworkable because patients lack the skill, knowledge and judgement to be totally responsible for determining their own treatment (Schacht and Pemberton, 1985), and that such an approach undermines the covenantal nature of the doctor-patient relationship, thus making it a purely contractual arrangement (Siegler, 1980).

The fourth model is designated 'Mutual Collaboration', and differs from Szasz and Hollender's formulation (Szasz and Hollender, 1956) insofar as I have given it a greater emphasis on empowerment. This relationship implies an active and responsible role in both parties. The physician provides the best available services, resources and knowledge, but acknowledges that healing itself is achievement by the patient. The physician does not present an ideal image to which the patient can aspire, but attempts to adapt to each patient's individual and culturally acquired qualities and capabilities and build upon these. Rather than maintain the commonly held negative view of patient non-compliance (Klein et al.,

1982) such a physician will treat resistance - and possibly even the illness itself - as an adaptive response on the part of the patient (Fine, 1984; Taylor, 1982). Deliberate non-compliance can be seen as a transference phenomenon, reflecting a breakdown in the doctor-patient relationship itself, rather than the patient's supposed ignorance, stubbornness, malingering or ingratitude. The doctor's best response is therefore to examine and change his or her own personal approach before attempting to change the patient's behaviour.

I have also sought to measure the degree of preference for a counselling role for doctors. In terms of transference then, this study concerns different relationships of relative power and depth of reciprocal emotional bonding. This in turn raises issues of dependency, hostility and sexuality, and the recognition and management of strong emotional in medical practice.

TABLE 1
Sample Characteristics: Laypeople

	Parnell	**Eden**	**Roskill**	**T**
N	28	28	19	75
Age Range	16–65	18–68	19–72	16–72
Mean Age	43	33	48	40
Gender (N)				
Males	7	11	7	25
Female	21	17	12	50
Occupation:				
1. Parent/ Home–maker	10	3	3	16
2. Student	1	4	0	5
3. Managerial/ Financial	8	0	1	9
4. Self–Employed	1	0	0	1
5. Retired	1	2	7	10
6. Clerical	1	2	4	7
7. Unskilled Labour	0	0	1	1
8. Tradesperson	1	4	1	6
9. Semi– Professional	3	10	2	15
10. Professional	0	3	0	3
11. Unspecified	2	0	0	2

METHOD

Subjects. The survey was taken from lay people in three very circumscribed neighbourhoods in urban Auckland (see Table 1). The three areas were chosen in order to reflect a wide spectrum of public opinion, but no claims to the sample's being representative of the wider Auckland population are made. Registered medical and complementary practitioners (see Table 2) from the surrounding areas were also surveyed with a parallel form .

TABLE 2
Sample Characteristics: Professionals

Practitioners	Orthodox	Complementary
N	25	28
Age Range	31–80	30–63
Mean Age	47	41
Gender (N)		
Males	19	11
Females	6	17
Occupations:		
G.P.	15	
Specialist	10	1.
1. Homeopath		2
2. Naturopath		14
3. Body Therapist		4
4. Osteopath		5
5. Acupuncturist		2
6. Massage Therapist		3
7. Chiropractor		1
8. Nutritionist		3
9. Nurse		1*

*   Some complementary practitioners gave two occupations.

Procedure. Respondents were asked to rate their approval or disapproval of items of behaviour relating to each of the different models described above. It needs to be stressed in advance, however, that these data indicate the participants' preferences and not necessarily their actual behaviour in a clinical relationship.

RESULTS

On the whole, the three groups expressed very similar preferences (except for two significantly divergent results), and the two professional groups tended to be on average less emphatic than lay people in rating these preferences. I will only review the most outstanding results.

On items of 'Guidance - Cooperation', no clear overall trend was discernible, apart from the item asking lay people about doctors' use of technical jargon. Ninety-two percent of the lay sample prefer doctors not to use such language. Informed consent was consistently favoured with the relevant items gaining 93-97 percent approval from patients and similarly from practitioners (85-100% approval).

Lay people tended to oppose items concerning 'Patient Autonomy' (7-16% approval), suggesting that there was little desire among patients to ignore the 'competence gap', or that they tended not to trust their own competence. Practitioner opinion in both groups was more evenly divided on this issue (7-39% approval), suggesting that many individual practitioners may more willingly accept a consumerist relationship with patients. Mutual Collaboration was a widely favoured option with lay people (73-85% in favour), and practitioners (60-91% in favour). This included an item regarding the doctor's role as "assisting the patient's inherent healing potential".

The closest to unanimous approval from lay people was in their desire for a counselling relationship with doctors (92-5% in favour), showing that patients clearly prefer doctors who can respond openly, warmly and unhurriedly to emotional issues. On one of these items, however, the responses of both groups of practitioners differed significantly from those of lay people (p<.001). On Carl Rogers' requirement that a counsellor should show a genuine personal liking for the client (Rogers, 1961), only 40 percent of practitioners would commit themselves compared with 92 percent of lay people who believed this important. Obviously health workers are expected to treat all those in need no matter what their personal feelings about the patient may be. But if counselling were seen as an important role for health practitioners, these personal feelings would nevertheless be an important factor in their work.

Another statistically significant difference (p<.001) was between registered medical and complementary practitioners in their estimation of the percentage of working time they spend dealing with illnesses that are wholly or partially psychosocial or emotional in origin. Physicians' estimates averaged around the accepted one third (i.e., 32.8%) (Chancellor et al., 1977; Eastman and McPherson, 1982) whereas complementary practitioners averaged 63.9 percent (see Figure 1). This may be due either to different qualities in their respective client populations, or to different professional attitudes. However, a community health study by senior medical students in Auckland found that complementary practitioners spent on average over one hour with their clients, as opposed to G.P.s' consultations which are rarely longer than fifteen minutes. Complementary practitioners are therefore more likely to take the time required to hear relevant emotional issues.

FIGURE 1

Practitioners' estimates of the percentage of their own time spent dealing with complaints of a fundamentally emotional or psychosocial nature

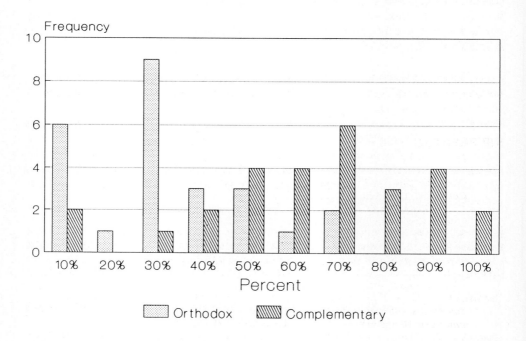

SUMMARY AND DISCUSSION

In the urban Auckland population surveyed, results show a clear preference for an informed partnership relationship in health care. They also underline a need for doctors to be trained in the skills of listening, negotiating, empathising and responding to people's emotional needs. It is widely recognised that these needs are not adequately catered for in medical schools (Evatt, 1977; Metcalfe, 1983; Helfer, 1970; Poole and Sanson-Fisher, 1979), although attempts are being made to change this (Brodaty et al., 1981; Carrick, 1979; Jones et al., 1981; Pendleton et al., 1984; Poole and Sanson-Fisher, 1980; Wakeford, 1983; Winefield, 1982).

The problem will only be fully resolved when medical science breaks through the dualistic ideological dilemma imposed by its Cartesian heritage and institutionalised by the spilt between organic and psychological healing professions. Unlike homeopathy or acupuncture, allopathic medicine does not have the ability to treat both psychic and somatic symptoms with the same remedy. As Zabarenko et al. (1970) observed in their study of physicians, when confronted by the anxious patient presenting a "puzzling, persistent complaint ... the doctors knew something about what was wrong, but lacked a conceptual vehicle which could lead to synthesis, understanding and effective intervention" (p. 113). The understanding and competence that they lacked can only come through self-examination and personal growth, such as any psychotherapist or counsellor would be required to undergo.

ACKNOWLEDGMENTS

I would like to acknowledge the assistance of Dr Barry Kirkwood, who supervised this work, and Ms Susan Harding and Rebecca Hindin who helped distribute the questionnaire.

REFERENCES

Alexander, L. (1982). Illness maintenance and the new American sick role. In N.J. Chrisman and T.W. Maretzki (Eds.) *Clinically applied anthropology* (351-367). Dordrecht: D. Reidel.

Bacon, C. L., Renneker, R. & Cutler, M. (1952). A psychosomatic survey of cancer of the breast. *Psychosomatic Medicine, 14,* 453-460.

Balint, M. (1964). *The doctor, his patient and the illness.* London: Pitman.

Barofsky, I. (1978). Compliance, adherence and the therapeutic alliance: Steps in the development of self-care. *Social Science and Medicine, 12,* 369-376.

Brodaty, H., Andrews, G. & Austin, A. (1981). Training in interviewing and counselling. *Medical Journal of Australia, 1,* 596.

Cartwright, S. R. (1988). *The Report of the Committee of Inquiry into allegations concerning the treatment of cervical cancer at National Women's Hospital and into other related matters.* Auckland: Government Printing Office.

Chancellor, A., Mant, A. & Andrews, G. (1977). The general practitioner's identification and management of emotional disorders. *Australian Family Physician, 6,* 1137-1143.

Clarke, A. M. & Viney, L. L. (1979). The primary prevention of illness: A psychological perspective. *Australian Psychologist, 14,* 7-20.

Clarke, A. M. & Viney, L. L. (1984). The primary prevention of illness: Social systems and personal power. *Australian Psychologist, 19,* 39-63.

Doyle, B. J. & Ware, J. E. (1977). Physician conduct and other factors that affect consumer satisfaction with medical care. *Journal of Medical Education, 52,* 793-801.

Eastman, C. & McPherson, I. (1982). As others see us: General practitioners' perceptions of psychological problems and the relevance of clinical psychology. *British Journal of Clinical Psychology, 21,* 85-92.

Evans, J. L. (1965). Psychiatric illness in the physician's wife. *American Journal of Psychiatry, 122,* 159-165.

Evatt, E. A. (1977). *Final Report of the Royal Commission on Human Relationships* (Vol.2). Canberra: AGPS.

Fine, M. (1984). Coping with rape: Critical perspectives on consciousness. *Imagination, Cognition and Personality, 3,* 249-267.

Ford, C. V. (1983). *The somatizing disorders: Illness as a way of life.* NY: Elsevier Biomedical.

Freud, S. (1912/1950). The dynamics of the transference. In J. Riviere (Ed. and trans.), *Collected papers* (Vol. 2, 312-322). London: Hogarth Press. (Paper first published in 1912.)

Freud S. (1915/1950). Further recommendations in the technique of psychoanalysis: Observations on transference-love. In J. Riviere (Ed. and trans.), *Collected papers* (Vol.2, 377-391). London: Hogarth Press. (Paper first published in 1915.)

Garrick, C. (1979). Teaching for counselling skills. *Medical Journal of Australia, 2,* 358-359.

Gesten, E. L. and Jason, L. A. (1987). Social and community interventions. *Annual Review of Psychology, 38,* 427-460.

Glauber, I. P. (1953). A deterrent in the study and practice of medicine. *Psychoanalytical Quarterly, 22,* 381-412.

Glover, E. (1929). The psychology of the psychotherapist. *British Journal of Medical Psychology, 9,* 1-16.

Golloway, G. (1981). Are doctors different? Reflections on the psychodynamics of physicians. *Journal of the Florida Medical Association, 68,* 281-284.

Groesbeck, C. J. (1975). The archetypal image of the wounded healer. *Journal of Analytical Psychology, 20,* 122-145.

Hamman, L. (1939). The relationship of psychiatry to internal medicine. *Mental Hygiene, 23,* 177-189.

Haug, M. R. & Lavin, B. (1981). Practitioner or patient - Who's in charge? *Journal of Health and Social Behaviour, 22,* 212-229.

Helfer, R. E. (1970). An objective comparison of the pediatric interviewing skills of freshmen and senior medical students. *Pediatrics, 45,* 623-627.

Henderson, L. J. (1935). Physician and patient as a social system. *New England Journal of Medicine, 212,* 819-823.

Houston, W. R. (1938). The doctor himself as a therapeutic agent. *Annals of Internal Medicine, 11,* 1416-1425.

Hull, R. T. (1985). Informed consent: Patient's right or patient's duty? *Journal of Medicine and Philosophy, 10,* 183-197.

Jones, E. (1938). The unconscious mind and medical practice. *British Medical Journal, June 25,* 1354-1359.

Jones, K. V., Hornblow, A. R. & Tiller, J. W. G. (1981). Evaluation of teaching on interpersonal interactions. *Medical Education, 15,* 43-45.

Jung, C. G. (1983). *The psychology of the transference.* London: Routledge & Kegan Paul. (First published 1954.)

Kent, G. G., Clarke, P. & Dalrymple-Smith, D. (1981). The patient is the expert: A technique for teaching interviewing skills. *Medical Education, 15,* 38-42.

Klein, D., Najman, J., Kohrman, A. F. & Monroe, C. (1982). Patient characteristics that elicit negative responses from family physicians. *Journal of Family Practice, 14,* 881-888.

Lain Entralgo, P. (1969). *Doctor and patient.* London: Weidenfeld and Nicolson.

Lebow, J. L. (1974). Consumer assessments of the quality of medical care. *Medical Care, 7,* 328-337.

Lewin, B. D. (1946). Counter-transference in the technique of medical practice. *Psychosomatic Medicine, 8,* 195-199.

Ley, P. (1982). Satisfaction, compliance and communication. *British Journal of Clinical Psychology, 21,* 241-254.

McGuire, W. (Ed.) (1979). *The Freud/Jung letters.* London: Pan.

McLaughlin, J. T. (1961). The analyst and the Hippocratic Oath. *Journal of the American Psychoanalytic Association, 9,* 106-123.

Menninger, K. A. (1959). *A psychiatrist's world: Selected papers.* NY: Viking Press.

Metcalfe, D. (1983). The mismatch between undergraduate education and the medical task. In D. Pendleton and J. Hasler (Eds.) *Doctor-patient communication,* (227-232). London: Academic Press.

Nunberg, H. (1938). Psychological interrelations between physician and patient. *Psychoanalytic Review, 25,* 297-308.

Nutton, V. (1985). Murders and miracles: Lay attitudes towards medicine in classical antiquity. In R. Porter (Ed.) *Patients and practitioners: Lay perceptions of medicine in pre-industrial society,* (23-54). Cambridge: Cambridge University Press.

O'Hagan, J. J. (1984). What influences our prescribing? Some non-pharmacological issues. *New Zealand Medical Journal, 97,* 331-332.

Osler, Sir W. (1904). The master-word in medicine. In *Aequinimitas with other addresses to medical students, nurses and practitioners of medicine,* (369-371). PA: Blakiston.

Ost, D. E. (1984). The `right' not to know. *Journal of Medicine and Philosophy, 9,* 301-312.

Owen, A. (1978). Self-help approaches in health care. *Social Alternatives, 1,* (2), 5-7.

Parsons, T. (1958). Definitions of health and illness in the light of American values and social structure. In E.G. Jaco (Ed.) *Patients, physicians and illness,* (165-187). NY: Free Press.

Parsons, T. (1975). The sick role and the role of the physician reconsidered. *Milbank Memorial Fund Quarterly: Health and Society, 53,* 257-278.

Parsons, T. & Fox, R. (1952). Illness, therapy and modern urban American family. *Journal of Social Issues, 8,* 2-3, 31-34.

Pearson, M. M. (1982). Psychiatric treatment of 250 physicians. *Psychiatric Annals, 12,* 194-206.

Pendleton, D., Schofield, T., Tate, P. & Havelock, P. (1984). *The consultation: An approach to learning and teaching.* Oxford: Oxford University Press.

Poole, A. D. & Sanson-Fisher, R. W. (1979). Understanding the patient: A neglected aspect of medical education. *Social Science and Medicine, 13A,* 37-43.

Poole, A. D. and Sanson-Fisher, R. W. (1980). Long-term effects of empathy training on the interview skills of medical students. *Patient Counselling and Health Education, 2,* 125-127.

Raeburn, J. (1978). Clinical psychology vs. the people: A community psychology perspective. *New Zealand Psychologist, 7,* 41-45.

Rappaport, J. (1977). *Community psychology: Values, research and action.* NY: Holt, Rinehart and Winston.

Rappaport, J. (1985). The power of empowerment language. *Social policy, 16,* 15-21.

Rogers, C. R. (1961). *On becoming a person: A therapist's view of psychotherapy.* MA: Houghton Mifflin.

Ryle, A. (1987). Problems of patients' dependency on doctors: Discussion paper. *Journal of the Royal Society of Medicine, 80,* 25-26.

Schacht, P. J. & Pemberton, A. (1985). What is unnecessary surgery? Who shall decide? Issues of consumer sovereignty, conflict and self-regulation. *Social Science and Medicine, 20,* 199-206.

Siegler, M. (1980). A physician's perspective on a right to health care. *Journal of the American Medical Association, 244,* 1591-1596.

Simmel, E. (1926). The 'doctor-game', illness and the profession of medicine. *International Journal of Psychoanalysis, 7,* 470-483.

Szasz, T. S. & Hollender, M. H. (1956). A contribution to the philosophy of medicine: The basic models of the doctor-patient relationship. *Archives of Internal Medicine, 97,* 585-592.

Taylor, S. E. (1982).   Hospital patient behavior: Reactance, helplessness, or control?   In H.S. Friedman and M. R. DiMatteo (Eds.) *Interpersonal issues in health care*, (209-232).   NY: Academic Press.

Vaillant, G. E., Sobowale, N. C. & McArthur, C. (1972).   Some psychologic vulnerabilities of physicians. *New England Journal of Medicine, 287*, 372-375.

Vertinsky, I. B., Thompson, W. A. & Uyeno, D. (1974).   Measuring consumer desire for participation in clinical decision-making. *Health Services Research, 9*, 121-134.

Wakeford, R. (1983).   Communication skills training in United Kingdom medical schools. In D. Pendleton and J. Hasler (Eds.) *Doctor-patient communication*, (233-247). London: Academic Press.

Weick, A. (1983).   Issues in overturning a medical model of social work practice. *Social Work, 28*, 467-471.

Whitehouse, C. R. (1987).   A survey of the management of the psychosocial illness in general practice in Manchester. *Journal of the Royal College of General Practitioners, 37*, 112-115.

Winefield, H. R. (1982).   Subjective and objective outcomes of communication skills training in first year. *Medical Education, 16*, 192-196.

Zabarenko, R. N., Zabarenko, L. and Pittenger, R. A. (1970).   The psychodynamics of physicianhood. *Psychiatry, 33*, 102-118.

Social Applications and Issues in Psychology
R.C. King and J.K. Collins (editors)
©Elsevier Science Publishers B.V. (North-Holland), 1989

UNDERGRADUATE CURRICULA AND ADMISSION TO GRADUATE PROGRAMS IN PSYCHOLOGY IN THE UNITED STATES

Jon D. Swartz, Robert C. Reinehr, and Jesse E. Purdy

Southwestern University

Data were gathered regarding the requirements for a degree in psychology at 50 leading baccalaureate institutions and the criteria for admission to 106 leading graduate programs in psychology in the United States. Although undergraduate programs differ widely, most were found to have a common core of required courses. Graduate programs are also similar in the criteria which they utilize in making decisions, although there are some differences among Clinical, Counselling, and Experimental programs with respect to the weight given to previous clinical or research experience.

Graduate programs in psychology are currently able to accept only a relatively small fraction of the applicants for graduate training . This selection ratio makes it very desirable for directors of undergraduate programs to be aware of those aspects of undergraduate training which are most crucial with respect to admission to graduate training.

Although some of the more objective requirements for admission are published in the American Psychological Association's annual publication, Graduate Study In Psychology and Associated Fields, the relative weight assigned to each of these varies with each institution, as does the weight assigned to various aspects of undergraduate training. There is an informal interaction between undergraduate training and graduate admission requirements, of course. Graduate programs are to some extent related to the undergraduate experiences of the graduate faculty, and undergraduate programs attempt to develop curricula which will prepare students for graduate study.

Unfortunately, the nature of university training in the United States does not provide for the routine dissemination of such information between institutions. Accordingly, the authors, all of whom are involved in the undergraduate training of prospective psychologists, undertook to gather information regarding the characteristics of undergraduate training in psychology in the United States and the relative importance of various aspects of training and experience in the selection of students for admission to graduate training.

STUDY 1
UNDERGRADUATE CURRICULA OF BACCALAUREATE INSTITUTIONS

Method and Procedure

Current catalogues of the 50 undergraduate institutions listed by Hall (1985) in his survey of the baccalaureate origins of U.S. doctorate recipients in psychology were examined and the course requirements for an undergraduate degree in psychology were summarized for each. Questions regarding the substantial equivalence of courses with similar but not identical titles were resolved by requesting further information if consensus could not be reached among the authors. If the nature of the course could not be clarified by examination of supporting documents or if the nature of a given program was not clear, curriculum information was obtained from telephone interviews conducted with members of the departments involved.

Results and Discussion

Although 7 of the 50 schools surveyed operate on the quarter system, their requirements have been converted to semester hour equivalents for purposes of this summary. The average number of semester hours required for an undergraduate degree in psychology was 30.5, the median number was 30. Only 5 schools required fewer than 26 hours, only 7 required more than 36.

All but one of the institutions studied required an introductory psychology course which was prerequisite to enrolment in the other courses in the department. The number of hours committed to this course varied, but 32 of the 50 institutions surveyed required a 3 hour course, 8 others required a 4 hour course, and 8 others a 5 or 6 hour course. Typically, all of the introductory courses above 3 hours included some laboratory component.

Introductory statistics was nearly as universal a requirement; only 5 of the 50 schools surveyed did not require such a course and 3 of these included instruction in statistics in a required experimental methods course. More than half of the institutions (28) required some specific course or courses in experimental methods; most others arranged the core areas such that a student was forced to include a laboratory course in his or her course selection. Although one institution required the completion of 9 specific psychology courses, the average number of required specific courses was only 4.6. Most programs provided the student with a menu of acceptable courses, usually divided into several content areas, with the requirement that the student choose a given number of courses from each area. In institutions with programs of this sort, a median number of 6 hours was required to be chosen from what might be referred to as traditional experimental courses (Physiological, Sensation and Perception, Learning) and a similar number of hours was required to be chosen from what might broadly be referred to as professional courses (Abnormal, Developmental, Personality). In 9 schools the menu of acceptable courses was not subdivided into core areas. In schools of this sort, students were required to choose a median number of 12 hours from the menu.

Although there is considerable program diversity among undergraduate institutions, there are also some marked similarities. Nearly all programs required similar core courses, although methods of specifying required courses vary. A comparison of the ten most productive of these institutions and the ten least (keeping in mind that all of these institutions are productive) revealed no differences in requirements for total hours, hours of introductory psychology, statistics, or experimental design.

It is thus possible to characterize an undergraduate program that represents the majority of those schools that produce the largest number of successful doctoral candidates. Although there is considerable variation, most programs of this sort require a 3 hour introductory course, a 3 hour statistics course or its equivalent, an experimental methods course, and 12 hours chosen from selected courses. Courses are often grouped into core areas, with the student required to select some courses from each area. The student may select any other courses offered by the department to complete the average 30 hours of required psychology.

STUDY 2
ADMISSION CRITERIA FOR GRADUATE PROGRAMS IN PSYCHOLOGY

Method and Procedure

A one page questionnaire concerning the relative importance of the various information contained in applications for admission to graduate study was mailed to the leading graduate programs in the U.S. as reported by Gourman (1980) and Jones, Lindzey, and Coggeshall (1982). The program directors were asked to indicate whether a given item was very important, moderately important, or not important in the decision regarding admission of the student to graduate training.

Included in the survey were 50 programs in Experimental Psychology, 38 APA accredited programs in Clinical Psychology, and 18 APA Accredited programs in Counselling Psychology. Responses were received from 78% of the experimental programs, 89% of the clinical programs and 83% of the counselling programs. The overall rate was 83%.

TABLE 1
Responses to Graduate Admissions Criteria Questionnaire
Percent Responding

	Important			Not Important		
Item	Coun	Clin	Exp	Coun	Clin	Exp
GRE Quantitative	100	100	100	0	0	0
GRE Verbal	100	100	100	0	0	0
GRE Analytical	55	76	69	45	23	30
GRE Subject	41	68	71	58	32	29
Letters of Recom	100	100	95	0	0	5
Research Exper	100	100	100	0	0	0
Clinical Exper	3	1	30	7	9	70
Prev Grad Study	66	24	19	33	76	81
Overall GPA	93	97	97	7	3	3
Last 2 yrs GPA	100	100	97	0	0	3
Psych GPA	100	97	97	0	3	3
Statistics	100	97	100	0	3	0
Experimental	92	94	100	8	6	0

Results and Discussion

Survey results are summarized in Table 1. Virtually all program directors reported that a course in statistics is at least moderately important, and 65% of the directors of experimental and clinical programs considered that it is very important, as do 47% of the directors of counselling programs. The situation is similar with respect to experimental courses: 95% of all program directors feel that these courses are at least moderately important in the selection process. Laboratory courses are also highly valued, but specific course work is only one important aspect of undergraduate training. Essentially all program directors agree that overall grade point average and psychology grades are at least moderately important and 65% agree that they are very important. Counselling programs are especially concerned with grades achieved in courses completed during the final two years of undergraduate training; 93% of Counselling programs rated this dimension very important.

Graduate Record Examination (GRE) scores and letters of recommendation also play an important role in the decision to admit. Scores on the analytical subtest and on the various GRE subject examinations are seen as less important than the Verbal and Quantitative scores. This is particularly so for Counselling programs . Virtually all programs of all types consider letters of recommendation to be at least moderately important; approximately 75% of Clinical and Counselling programs and over 90% of Experimental programs consider them to be very important.

Marked differences do exist between types of programs with respect to the weight given previous experience. Both Clinical and Counselling programs value previous clinical experience very highly; over 90% of these programs rate this dimension at least moderately important, and over half of the Counselling programs rate it very important. Rather surprisingly, 30% of Experimental programs also view clinical experience as at least moderately important.

Counselling programs value previous graduate training somewhat more highly than do either Clinical or Experimental programs. Approximately two-thirds of these programs rate previous graduate training to be at least moderately important; only 24% of Clinical programs and 19% of Experimental programs show a similar interest in such training.

All types of programs value previous research experience; no program reported that such experience was unimportant, but Clinical and Experimental programs plainly value it more. Only 20% of Counselling programs reported that previous research experience was very important, while 85% of Clinical programs and 82% of Experimental programs did so.

In general, all graduate programs give considerable and approximately equal weight to the completion of certain specific undergraduate courses, overall grade point average, psychology grades, GRE Verbal and Quantitative scores, and letters of recommendation. Programs show considerable differences in the weight assigned previous experience, with counselling programs particularly valuing previous graduate training, Clinical and Counselling programs giving considerable weight to previous clinical experiences, and Clinical and Experimental programs placing particular value on previous research experience.

CONCLUSIONS

Although few formal channels exist for communication between baccalaureate institutions or between these schools and graduate training centres, undergraduate programs often differ more in appearance than in substance, and most programs provide the types of training and experience valued by graduate admissions committees. Graduate programs show considerable agreement regarding the importance of grades, GRE scores, letters of recommendation, and undergraduate courses. Most differences in admission criteria relate to the different value placed on previous experience by Clinical, Counselling, and Experimental programs.

Portions of this paper appeared in two comments to the *American Psychologist* :
>   Purdy, J.E., Reinehr, R.C. & Swartz, J.D. (1987). Undergraduate curricula
>   of leading psychology departments. *American Psychologist, 42* (7),
>   757-758.
>   Purdy, J.E., Reinehr, R.C. & Swartz, J.D. (in press). Graduate admission
>   criteria of leading psychology departments. *American Psychologist.*

Copyright 1987, 1989 by the American Psychological Association. Adapted by
permission of the publisher.

REFERENCES

Gourman, J. (1980). *The Gourman Report.* Los Angeles: National Educational Standards.
Hall, A.E. (1985).   Baccalaureate origins of doctorate recipients in psychology: 1920-
    1980. *American Psychologist, 40,* 120-122.
Jones, L.V., Lindzey, G., & Coggeshall, P.E. (1982).   *An assessment of research-doctorate
    programs in the United States: Social Sciences.*   Washington, D.C.:   National
    Academy Press.

Social Applications and Issues in Psychology
R.C. King and J.K. Collins (editors)
©Elsevier Science Publishers B.V. (North-Holland), 1989

A NATIONWIDE TESTING PROGRAM FOR ADMISSION TO MEDICAL SCHOOLS IN WEST GERMANY

Günter Trost

Institute for Test Development and Talent Research, F.R. Germany

All West German schools of medicine, dentistry and veterinary science are state institutions. The admission procedure is centralised. In 1986, a new "quota system" for admission was introduced, part of which is an aptitude test. Forty-five per cent of the places are awarded according to a combined score of the "Abitur" average mark and the test result; another 10 per cent are reserved to those who do best in the test, no matter what school marks they have earned. The remaining places are awarded according to the length of time the applicants have had to wait for admission, and on the basis of an interview. The "Test for Medical Studies" (TMS) is designed to measure cognitive aptitudes that are needed to meet the requirements of courses in medical studies.

PRESENT ADMISSION PROCEDURE

In West Germany, all schools of medicine, dentistry and veterinary science except one are state institutions. The admission procedure is centralized. In 1986, a new "quota system" for admission was introduced (Kultusministerkonferenz, 1985), part of which is an aptitude test: the "Test for Medical Studies" (TMS). Forty-five per cent of the places are awarded according to a score combining the average mark in the secondary school leaving certificate (Abitur) and the test result; another 10 per cent of the places are awarded to those who do best in the test - no matter what school marks they have earned. Twenty per cent of the places are awarded on the basis of the length of time the applicants have had to wait for admission. Fifteen per cent of the places are awarded on the basis of an interview conducted by members of the faculty staff. The remaining 10 per cent of the places are reserved for special cases (e.g. foreigners, "hardship cases"). If an application is rejected, this rejection is valid for all German state universities at a given admission date. However, all rejected candidates can apply repeatedly without restriction (see table 1). At present, there are about 3 to 4 times as many applicants as there are places available; several years ago, the selection ratio was more unfavourable, that is 1:6 or even 1:8.

STRUCTURE AND FUNCTION OF THE "TEST FOR MEDICAL STUDIES"(TMS)

The "Test for Medical Studies" (TMS) is designed to measure the particular cognitive aptitudes that are needed to meet the requirements of courses in medical studies. Factual knowledge does not play an important part in the test; however, in the science comprehension section, familiarity with typical problems and terminology in biology, chemistry and physics does improve the test results. Personality, motivation or interest scales are not included in the examination (Institut für Test- und Begabungsforschung, 1988).

TABLE 1
System of admission to West German schools of medicine, dentistry and veterinary science (since 1986)

Proportion of Study places	Criterion for Selection	Explanations
Up to 10 %	Special quota for foreigners, "hardship cases" etc.	
45 %	Combination of "Abitur" average mark and test score (proportion 55:45)	— Participation in the test only once
10 %	Top test scores	Test score remains valid for all future applications
20 %	Waiting time	Admission on the basis of time passed since the first application Improvement of chances for admission by — completion of vocational training — service in armed forces, alternative service — occupation after completed vocational training
15 %	Result of an interview	— admission to interview by lottery — conducted by faculty staff — participation in the interview only once

The test consists of 204 multiple-choice items and lasts about five hours. Its 9 subtests focus on basic comprehension of medical and natural sciences, reading comprehension, interpretation of graphs and tables, basic mathematical comprehension, memory for facts and figures (2 subtests), differentiated visual perception, spatial perception, and concentrated and accurate work under speed conditions (see table 2).

TABLE 2
Structure of the "Test for Medical Studies" (TMS)

Name of Subtest	Aptitudes aimed at	Number of items	Time (min.)
Pattern Recognition perception	Differentiated visual	24	22
Basic Comprehension of Medical and Natural Sciences	See subtest title	24	60
Perspectives of Tables	Spatial perception, recognition of spatial relations	24	15
Quantitative and Formal Problems	Competence in dealing with numbers, quantities, units and formulas	24	60
Concentrated and Accurate Work	Concentration, accuracy	1,200 ≙ 20 raw points	8
	N o o n b r e a k		60
Learning Phase: Memorizing Figures	. . . .	20 units	4
Memorizing Facts	. . . .	15 units	6
Reading Comprehension	Comprehension and interpretation of text passages	24	60
Reproduction Phase: Memorizing Figures	. . . Memory of figures, ... visual memory	20	5
Memorizing Facts	. . . Memory of facts, ... verbal memory	20	7
Graphs and Tables	Combination, interpretation and evaluation of . . . information presented in . . . graphs and tables	24	60
Total Test		204	5 hours

The TMS is administered once a year, on the same day, in about 450 test centres throughout the Federal Republic of Germany. Each time a new test form is used; a second form is kept in reserve in case test security is impaired. Taking the test is obligatory for all applicants for studies in medicine, dentistry and veterinary science. Every candidate can take the test only once; his or her test results are valid for all future applications. Participation in the test is free of charge. At present, about 23,000 candidates take the test each year.

In item construction and revision, the psychologists of the Institute for Test Development and Talent Research cooperate closely with representatives of the faculties of medicine and natural sciences. Each item undergoes several revisions by the board of experts and one empirical tryout before it is used in the test.

RESULTS OF TEST EVALUATION

Prior to its introduction as part of the admission procedure, it was possible to try out the test, in its previous form containing 13 subtests, and to evaluate it over a period of six years. For that transition period, participation in the TMS was not yet compulsory; but taking the test did improve chances of admission. About 65,000 applicants took the test during that probationary period. The main results of the test evaluation are presented below.

RESULTS OF TEST AND ITEM ANALYSES

The test and item characteristics as determined according to classical test theory are satisfactory. The index for the average difficulty of the test items is $p = .56$ (no correction for guessing is applied). The reliability of the total test in terms of split-half coefficients is above $r = .90$. The coefficients for the retest reliability of the total test are around $r = .80$. The correlation between different test forms is $r = .87$.

CORRELATION BETWEEN TEST PERFORMANCE AND PERFORMANCE IN SECONDARY SCHOOL

The median Pearson Product-Moment correlation between performance in the test and performance in school is around .45. As a result of this only moderate correlation, those applicants who have not earned top marks in the Abitur examination are also granted a chance of immediate admission by the new admission system as a result of the introduction of the test.

Effects of Experience and Training on Test Performance

Applicants who choose different major subject areas in school also differ in their TMS results. On average, candidates whose majors in school are in the fields of natural sciences and mathematics earn the highest test scores.

Practical experience in the medical field (e.g., as a result of training and practice as a nurse or of volunteer work in a hospital) does not enhance performance in the test.

Several studies have investigated the effects of training or coaching, as it is offered by commercial institutions, on performance in the TMS. The results indicate that "test-wiseness" does have some influence. However, taking a coaching course or using commercial coaching books in addition to studying the authorized information material – two published original versions of the TMS and a free test brochure containing sample items and recommendations concerning the best test-taking strategies – does not seem to improve performance in the test substantially beyond the level that can be reached merely by using the authorized material for preparation.

PREDICTIVE VALIDITY OF THE TEST

Follow-up studies on six samples of medical students, with sample sizes ranging from 1,141 to 1,327 persons, were carried out to determine the predictive validity of the TMS (Bartussek, Raatz, Stapf & Schneider, 1985, 1986; Trost, 1988). In these studies, the samples of students were only slightly preselected in terms of performance in the test and performance in secondary school. The criterion of academic success was performance in the First Medical Examination after two to three years of study. The results are shown in table 3.

TABLE 3
Predictive validity of (a) the total score in the Test for Medical Studies (TMS), (b) the Abitur average mark and (c) the combination of both predictors with the weights of 45 : 55. Criterion: Total score in the First Medical Examination.

Predictor	Pearson coefficients of correlation	
	range (6 studies) (N = 1,141 – 1,327)	median
Total TMS score	.40 – .47	.44
Abitur average mark	.31 – .50	.38
Combination of test score and school mark	.45 – .60	.51

The Pearson correlation coefficients (corrected for restriction of range) vary from .40 to .47 for the total test score; the median value is .44. For the average mark in the secondary school leaving certificate as a rule somewhat lower coefficients were found. The corrected correlation coefficients ranged from .31 to .50; the median value was .38. The median coefficient for the zero-order correlation of a combination of the Abitur average mark and the test result, with weights of 55 per cent for the school average mark and of 45 per cent for the test score, is .51 when corrected for restriction of range.

The results indicate that the TMS has a satisfactory predictive validity with respect to performance in the First Medical Examination. Therefore the prediction of success is substantially improved if both the school average mark and the test score are taken into account.

In another approach, information on the mean overall scores in the First Medical Examination and the percentage of those who passed this examination at the first attempt was collected for all applicants who had taken the test during the first two years of the probationary period (1980-1981) and who had subsequently been admitted to medical schools on the basis of various selection criteria. These criteria were superior test score (the top two per cent of all testees); combination of the school average mark and the test score (20 per cent of all testees); "waiting time" (about 4 per cent of all testees); and "achievement-oriented lottery", in which the better the school average mark, the more lots could be drawn (about 6 per cent of all testees).

As can be seen in Table 4, those who had done best in the TMS (first group) and those who had been admitted on the basis of both school average mark and test score were much more successful in the First Medical Examination than those who had achieved lower test scores and had been admitted according to other criteria. Consequently it may be concluded that, by introducing the test into the selection procedure, a contribution has been made towards raising the average performance of the students in medical schools.

APPLICANTS' ATTITUDES TOWARDS TEST AND INTERVIEW

On the occasion of the test date in the fall of 1986, all applicants were asked to give their opinions of each of the elements of the new admission procedure. Fifty-four per cent considered the introduction of the TMS an improvement of the selection system. The introduction of the interview met with much more approval; 77 per cent of the applicants considered it an improvement of the selection system.

TABLE 4
Mean overall scores and ratio of success of groups of students who
were admitted on the basis of different selection criteria, in the
First Medical Examination

Admitted on the basis of	First Medical Examination:		
	Number of students	Mean overall score	Ratio of success (%)
Superior performance in the test	352	108.9	97.0
Combination of school average mark and test score	3,287	105.6	95.2
Waiting time	683	98.8	76.1
"Achievement-oriented lottery"	973	97.4	71.0
All students who took the test and were subsequently admitted	7,324	102.4	86.2

REFERENCES

Bartussek, D., Raatz, U., Stapf, K.H. & Schneider, B. (1985). Die Evaluation des Tests für medizinische Studiengänge. 2. Zwischenbericht. Bonn: Kultusministerkonferenz.

Bartussek, D., Raatz, U., Stapf, K.H. & Schneider, B. (1986). Die Evaluation des Tests für medizinische Studiengänge. 3. Zwischenbericht. Bonn: Kultusministerkonferenz.

Institut für Test- und Begabungsforschung. (Ed.). (1988). Der neue TMS. Originalversion des Tests für medizinische Studiengänge im besonderen Auswahlverfahren. Göttingen: Hogrefe.

Kultusministerkonferenz. (Ed.). (1985). Die Hochschulzulassung ab Wintersemester 1986/87, insbesondere zu den medizinischen Studiengängen. Informationsbroschüre. Bonn: Sekretariat der Kultusministerkonferenz.

Trost, G. (1988). Ein psychologischer Beitrag zur Regelung des Hochschulzugangs. In F. Lösel & H. Skowronek (Eds.), Beiträge der Psychologie zu politischen Planungs- und Entscheidungsprozessen (pp. 213-224). Weinheim: Deutscher Studien Verlag.

Section 3

PEOPLE AND THE
TECHNOLOGICAL ENVIRONMENT

Social Applications and Issues in Psychology
R.C. King and J.K. Collins (editors)
©Elsevier Science Publishers B.V. (North-Holland), 1989

THE EFFECTIVENESS OF COMPUTER BASED LEARNING IN DEVELOPING CHILDREN'S CLASSIFICATORY ABILITIES

Jean D. M. Underwood

Derbyshire College of Higher Education, England

How effective is the computer as an aid to classroom learning? Three empirical studies were conducted, involving pre- and posttesting of matched subjects, to evaluate the effectiveness of the classroom computer as a stimulus to the development of categorisation skills in children.

The purpose of the group of experiments was two-fold: to establish whether children's (9 to 11 years old) classificatory abilities could be stimulated by a set programme of work, and whether or not the computer as part of the learning/teaching strategy would lead to differential gains in performance over non-computer users. Each experimental programme was based on a specific teaching strategy. In each experiment half the the children used a computer-based package while the control group completed similar work without computer presentation.

In each experiment there was an initial assessment of the children's classificatory abilities using a 'twenty questions' task, followed by one of the specified programmes of work, after which classificatory ability was again assessed. A comparison of the results from the three experiments showed that there was an overall improvement in performance between pretesting and posttesting with the categorisation task, and that these improvements were a result of the teaching strategy. In each experiment the computer-users made differential performance gains over non-computer users. The three investigations taken together show a gradation in performance gains by the computer-users, with children using the Ausebelian information handling packages being the most successful (Expt. 3), followed by children involved in the Piagetian exploration of concepts through a design program (Expt. 2), and with the smallest gains being made by the group receiving a tutorial programme of work (Expt. 1).

Suggestions are presented to account for the results in the three experiments. Firstly, children respond differently to the computer compared with an adult. They appear to be aware that the computer is inflexible and that they must be the ones to adapt if communication is to take place. This inflexibility forces children to greater precision in their own thinking. Secondly, children are more likely to accept novel ideas when presented by the computer.

The experiments reported here investigate the potential influence of classroom computers on the development of children's cognitive abilities. There is a wide range of potential uses of computers in our classrooms. They can be used to develop basic skills, or to develop conceptual understanding and the ability to question (Underwood and Underwood, 1987). Can the use of classroom computers, with appropriate software, be an effective stimulus to children's acquisition of classificatory skills?

Classificatory skills allow the reduction of environmental data into a hierarchy of classes by discrimination, abstraction, generalisation and organisation of common elements or crucial aspects of stimuli. Categorisation is an essential cognitive ability in helping with perceptual organisation, in eliminating the need for constant learning, and thereby, in aiding decisions about necessary actions. It is an ability that provides economy of mental effort, and efficiency in learning.

There is a considerable research literature on the importance of categorisation skills in the development of human thought. The work of Bruner and others suggests that categorisation skills are the key to efficient information storage and retrieval in human memory. The evidence for the use of classificatory criteria in organising and retrieving information is well established (Bousfield, 1953; Bower, Clark, Lesgold and Winzenz, 1969). Each has shown that effective learning is demonstrably dependent upon effective organisation. In classifying our world we are in fact developing concepts which, Bransford (1979) argues, we should view as tools to organise and clarify new experiences. The development of classificatory abilities underpins logical thought but it is also relevant in the development of basic skills of reading. Turner, Scullion and Whyte (1984) have shown that good readers have well developed classificatory skills which allow them to construct a flexible and conceptually organised internal lexicon.

Good classificatory skills should be encouraged because they are vital foundation skills from which our thinking can develop. The initial premise on which this study is based is that the use of readily available data storage and retrieval systems for educational microcomputers should actively encourage information-handling skills. This study asks what will be the effect on children's thought processes, of exposure to information-handling software? Although all information stores, including books, directories and computer data bases, are displays of organised data, the structure of that organisation is more overt in computer data bases. The importance of this transparency of the organisational structure to the efficient retrieval of information is apparent in the work of Durding, Becker, and Gould, (1977) and Underwood and Underwood (1988). It is also recognised by publishers who now highlight the structure of both school and undergraduate texts through the use of colour, script style and skeletal summaries. The very method of constructing and interrogating computer data bases, however, requires a clear understanding of that structure. This is not always so for a directory and certainly not so for retrieval of information from a book. It might be hypothesised, therefore, that the transparency of structure in a computer data base would facilitate the development of classificatory skills.

There is a wide variety of educational computer software incorporating a classificatory component. Following the initial stimulus of working with databases in the classroom the study was widened to include an evaluation of other approaches to teaching. The purpose of the group of experiments was two-fold: to establish whether children's (9 to 11 years old) classificatory abilities could be stimulated by a set programme of work, and whether or not the computer as part of the learning/teaching strategy would lead to differential gains in performance over non-computer users. Three different types of teaching programme were devised. Each experimental programme was based on a specific teaching strategy. In each experiment the children used a computer-based package while the control group completed similar work without computer presentation. In Experiment 1 the children completed a guided tutorial programme of work which was essentially didactic. In Experiments 2 and 3 the approach was one of personal discovery. In Experiment 2 this was a self-discovery or Piagetian approach, while in Experiment 3 the programme emphasized the organisational structure of the information that the children were exploring and could be described as Ausebelian. These three programmes are similar to those used by Lawton, Hooper, Saunders and Roth (1984) who compared the effects of three types of instruction defined as Ausebelian, Piagetian and traditional, on pre-school children's acquisition of logical concepts and classificatory skills.

EXPERIMENT 1: TUTORING PROGRAMMES

This experiment investigated whether children's development of classificatory skills, as measured by a simple pre-post categorisation task, would be stimulated by a learning programme which involved both direct instruction and classificatory skills practice. If so would the teaching strategy employed, in this case teaching with or without the aid of a microcomputer and relevant software, influence the acquisition of classificatory skills?

Method

Subjects. Twenty-nine children, aged 10 to 11 years, were assessed using McLeod's GAP reading test and Raven's Progressive Matrices test (non-verbal ability). The children were further assessed on their ability to complete a simple 'twenty questions' type categorisation task. The three test scores were used to establish two experimental groups, each of which contained twelve children. The mean test scores for the children are presented in Table 1.

Materials. The pre-post categorisation test materials consisted of two matched sets of twenty-four cards with a simple line drawing in black ink on white card. Each set of drawings differed on two dimensions, shape and number of objects. The shapes were equally divided into concrete objects, fruit or toys, and abstract objects, two or three-dimensional geometric shapes. Six examples of each category were represented: cards depicting fruit included oranges, apples, pears, bananas, grapes and strawberries. Within each set of cards the objects occurred singly or as a group. In Set 1, composed of fruit and three-dimensional shapes, the group size was two. In Set 2, which included the toys and two-dimensional shapes, each object occurred by itself and in a group of three identical objects. Two sets of test material were developed to reduce the effects of memory and material familiarity in the post-test situation.

TABLE 1
Ability profiles of the Children in the Two Experimental Conditions

		Mean age	Mean reading score	Mean non-verbal score	Mean Pre-categorisation score
Computer group	LC (N=12)	10.9	24.7	16.6	7.9
Control group Non-computer	LN (N=12)	10.9	24.4	16.0	7.7

The suite of computer programmes LOGIBLOCKS 2 is designed to encourage the development of classificatory abilities through tutorial guidance and practice in the the categorisation of two and three dimensional shapes, the latter being represented by two dimensional drawings. The programmes are carefully graded and offer practice in a games format; the more difficult games have a time element which can be pre-set by the child or the teacher. The games can be played individually or by two or three children together. The programmes draw on familiar primary school activities designed to encourage classificatory skills through the manipulation of concrete materials. The software documentation includes a booklet of support exercises, based on the computer games. In the present study they formed the basis of the work completed by the children in the control group, but were not available to the computer group.

Design. In this mixed factorial design experiment there was one between-subjects factor and one within-subjects factor. The two experimental groups each received the pre- and post- categorisation tests along with all members of the contributing class. All subjects completed a programme of work based on a suite of graded categorisation games. The children worked with the same adult who was not the experimenter on all occasions. The games were presented on the computer to the experimental group LC. The 'knowledge of results' aspects of the computer programs was provided by the adult working with the children in the control condition LN.

Procedure. Subjects were tested individually in both the pre- and post-categorisation task. The twenty-four cards depicting fruit and three dimensional shapes (Set 1) were used in the pretest categorisation task and Set 2 (toys and two-dimensional shapes) was used as the posttest stimulus. In this task, a version of the 'twenty questions' game, the child was asked to discover which of the twenty-four cards the experimenter was thinking about. The experimenter randomly placed one set of twenty-four cards face upwards on a table and the subject identified verbally the object depicted on each card. Once the subjects had identified each card satisfactorily, a necessary pre-condition to limit any disparity in the two sets of stimuli, the child was asked to identify which one of the twenty-four cards the experimenter had chosen. An unlimited number of questions could be asked to aid in the identification but a response would be given only to those questions which could elicit a yes/no answer. Children were asked to generate both legitimate and illegitimate questions on this criterion. If they failed, exemplar questions were given. Once the child understood the type of question needed to elicit information the test proceeded. Ten trials were conducted for each subject. The number and type of questions used to identify the target card were noted.

Developing classificatory abilities. All twenty-nine children in the sample class were involved in a three week work programme which involved the children in graded series of classificatory games. Care was taken not to distinguish the twenty-four members of the experimental groups from the remaining members of the class in order to reduce experimenter bias. The children worked in groups of three which were not fixed; rather they were formed by the availability of any three subjects within a condition. All work took place in the children's normal classroom as part of an integrated programme of work. All groups were led by the same adult who was not the experimenter.

Initially, each triad was introduced to one of the simple games either on or off the computer, depending on the experimental condition it was assigned to. Over the following three weeks the children worked with each of the games and each child played every categorisation game at least twice. All the children proved proficient players of the simplest games but showed greater enthusiasm for the more demanding games. The children were, therefore, allowed to concentrate on those games and each child was involved in the demanding games on six to eight occasions. The term 'more demanding' here refers to both the number of dimensions and level of abstraction upon which the classificatory decision was to be based and to the nature of the game, including the pre-set time penalty. In order to remove, or at least reduce, any perceptions of being treated differently, the children in the control group LN were involved in a programme of work using the computer for text processing.

Results

Scoring. Subjects were assessed on the mean number of questions required to identify the target card on each trial. Note was taken of the overall ratio of constraining questions to specific questions. A constraining question was defined as a question which eliminated several possible cards at a time. For example, the questions 'Is it a fruit?' and 'Do children play with it?' are both constraining questions as they effectively eliminate the geometric shapes. Specific questions and pseudo- constraining questions referred to individually identifiable cards. Such questions might take the form of 'Is it the teddy?' or, more convolutedly, 'Has it got four corners and lines all the same length and right angles?'.'

Analysis. A split-plot analysis of variance was performed on the mean number of questions per trial provided by each subject in each condition. The two factors were teaching strategy (between-subjects factor) and pre-post classification scores (within-subjects factor).There was a significant improvement in performance for subjects as a whole on the pre- versus post-categorisation task (F=6.29; df=1,22; p<0.02). The mean number of questions required to identify the target word was lower on the post test (M=7.24) as compared to the pre-test (M=7.80), but there was no reliable difference in performance between teaching strategies (LC, M=7.45; LN, M=7.59). The interaction between teaching strategy and performance on the pre- post categorisation task failed to reach significance (F=1.62; df=1,22; n.s.).

Further analysis showed that the pretest scores for the computer and non-computer groups were virtually indistinguishable (F<1), nor was there a reliable difference between the pre- and posttest scores for the non-computer group LN (F<1). The computer users LC (Table 2) did show improved performance on the post-categorisation test (F=7.15; df=1,22; p<0.02). Although there was no reliable difference in post-test performance between the two teaching groups LC and LN (F=1.76; df=1,22; n.s.).

TABLE 2

Mean Numbers of Questions and Standard Deviation per Trial and Ratio of Constraining to Specific Questions per Subject for the Pre-Post Test, across Teaching Strategy.

	Computer group LC		Non-computer group LN	
	Pretest	Posttest	Pretest	Posttest
Questions	7.88	7.03	7.73	7.45
	(2.41)	(2.52)	(1.87)	(2.52)
Constraining/ Specific Questions	0.59	0.80	0.61	0.66

An analysis of the ratio of constraining to specific questions (Table 2) showed no difference between groups in the pretest situation (F<1) nor in the posttest situation (F=1.43,; df=1,22; n.s.), and there was no improvement in the performance of the non-computer group LN during the investigation (F<1). This also held for the computer group LC (F=3.64; df=1,22; n.s.) although a trend of improvement suggested that this group was more likely to use a classificatory strategy in the posttest situation.

Discussion

The pre-post categorisation task and the tutorial programme required the children to employ comparable strategies to resolve the problems set in both situations and, because of this, it was anticipated that there would be an overall improvement in performance on the categorisation task by subjects in both experimental groups. Such an improvement in performance did occur, but the gains were small and they were related to the use of the computer. The computer users performed significantly better on the pre- versus posttest, unlike the non-computer users, but they did not significantly out-perform the non-computer users in the posttest situation. The large predicted performance gains due to the similarity of the learning task and the test task were not apparent.

Possible explanations of these results fall into two types: disparity of treatment of the two conditions and the nature of the interaction between the user and the computer. In conducting the experiment great care was taken to match the operations off the computer to those presented on the machine. This was easy to achieve as the programme documentation provided ready made board games which simulated the computer games. Of course, in the control condition the adult had the important role of arbitrator and provider of 'knowledge of results' to the children which was fulfilled by the computer for the experimental condition. It can be argued that the differences between the two conditions were minimised, if not removed, by this careful matching of procedure.

If we reject the disparity argument then the differences in recorded performances need to be explained in terms of child-computer interaction. The motivational aspects of the computer were always evident. The children needed no encouragement to join in the games. Indeed, the class teacher commented that some children were more motivated to complete non-related work in order to be ready when their turn to 'play' came about. His comments did not apply to the control group but the children did exhibit considerable enthusiasm when playing the board games.

There are other factors to be considered. Although care was taken to mimic the computer in all relevant operations, however careful the adult worker was to be machine-like, she still operated as a significant figure in the working group and it could be argued that as arbiter of success in the non-computer group she would be inhibiting to the children. As a consequence the children might have viewed the exercise as a traditional classroom experience, becoming more circumspect in the solutions they put forward, and watching carefully for signs of adult approval or disapproval. The inability of the computer to offer real punishment might be another one of its advantages in the classroom.

A second sequence showed a little boy becoming increasingly irate with the computer which corrected what he felt was a perfectly good answer to the set question. The child eventually abandoned the computer because it was 'unfair' and he went to a different machine. The important point here is that a child with a history of academic failure was willing to question the authority of the computer and to put forward a cogent, if misguided, argument why his answer was correct and the machine's wrong. It is difficult to envisage the same child challenging his teacher in this way. Indeed, Hughes (1986) cites several instances when even highly able children accepted incorrect information from a teacher without raising a single objection.

The children might have benefited from interacting with the computer because of the swift response to the child's actions. This could have led to a greater bonding between the child's input and the correct answer. For the less able subjects, in particular, the immediacy of feedback when playing the computer games, may have proved important as answers could be provided before attention strayed and the memories of the question under review faded, the adult would have provided rapid responses in the simpler games but delays might have occurred in the more complex games.

In summary, the computer group made a small differential gain in performance over the control group. The explanation for this gain lies partly in the power of the computer to motivate children and in the nature of the interactions which occur between the computer and the child.

EXPERIMENT 2: DESIGN PROGRAMMES

This experiment investigated whether children's development of classificatory skills, as measured by a simple pre-post categorisation task, would be stimulated by encouraging children to think in new ways about everyday objects through the use of a design programme based on de Bono's (1978) concept of lateral thinking. If so, would the teaching strategy employed, in this case teaching with or without the aid of a microcomputer and relevant software, significantly influence the acquisition of classificatory skills?

Method

Subjects. Twenty-nine children, aged 10 to 11 years, were assessed for reading ability, non-verbal ability and categorisation ability as for Experiment 1. The three test scores were used to establish two experimental groups, each of which contained eleven children. The mean test scores for the children are presented in Table 3.

Materials. The pre-post categorisation test materials were as described in Experiment 1. The computer programme used was THINKLINKS. In

THINKLINKS, children's ability to design is developed through a series of increasingly complex activities. Initially children are asked to classify, on a range of criteria, five randomly selected objects, for example, to grade the following objects on the criterion of softness: matches, a shoe, water, a spade and a table. The second phase of the game is to use five randomly presented objects to solve a computer selected problem such as crossing a stream, catching a fish, or, getting into a locked house. Finally the children are asked to invent or design a device to solve a problem such as sorting potatoes or catching a mouse (see Underwood, 1985).

TABLE 3
Ability profiles of the Children in the Two Experimental Conditions

		Mean age	Mean reading score	Mean non-verbal score	Mean Pre-categorisation score
Computer group	TC (N=11)	10.8	29.5	19.4	6.89
Control group Non-computer	TN (N=11)	10.9	29.6	16.0	6.89

At first sight this type of lateral thinking exercise is an activity that appears likely to gain little from being computerised, as all that is necessary is a mechanism for providing the random list of words and design problems. Output to the screen is confined to text and the children's only input to the program occurs when they request another list of words or problems. The computer program proved very easy to replicate as a card game with appropriately marked cards and the adult experimenter randomly dealing out the pack .

Design and Procedure. In this mixed factorial design experiment there was one between-subjects factor and one within-subjects factor. The two experimental groups each received the pre- and post-categorisation tests along with all members of the contributing class, and the procedure matched that of Experiment 1. All subjects completed a programme of work based on the design game.The children worked on all occasions with the same adult who was not the experimenter. The games were presented on the computer to the experimental group TC. The problem generation aspect of the computer program was provided by the adult working with the children in the control condition TN.

All twenty-nine children in the sample class were involved in a three week graded programme of work that encouraged them to think in new ways about ordinary, everyday objects, as well as to apply those new insights to the solution of specified problems. The children were randomly assigned to groups of three within a condition. All work took place in the children's normal classroom as part of an integrated programme of work. In order to remove, or at least reduce, any perceptions of being treated differently, the children in the control group TN were involved in a programme of work using the computer for text processing.

Results

Scoring of the pre-post categorisation test was as in Experiment 1. A split-plot analysis of variance was performed on the mean number of questions per trial provided by each subject in each condition. The two factors were teaching strategy (between-subjects factor) and pre-post classification scores (within-subjects factor). There was a significant improvement in performance for subjects as a whole on the pre- versus post-categorisation test ($F=19.45$; $df=1,20$; $p<0.001$). The mean number of questions required to identify the target card was lower for the post ($M=6.18$) as opposed to the pre-categorisation ($X=6.89$) test. There was no reliable difference between teaching strategies (computer, $M=6.39$; non-computer, $M=6.67$), nor was there an interaction between teaching strategy employed and performance on the pre- versus post-categorisation task ($F=3.13$; $df=1, 20$; n.s).

Further analysis showed that the pre-categorisation scores for the computer and non-computer groups were indistinguishable ($F<1$), and there was no difference between pre- and posttest scores for the non-computer users TN ($F=3.48$; $df=1,20$; n.s.). The computer users TC (Table 4) did show a reliable difference in pre- and posttest scores for the computer users ($F=19.10$; $df=1,20$; $p<0.001$) and between posttest scores of the computer TC versus non-computer TN users ($F=6.26$; $df=1,20$; $p<0.05$).

This pattern of improved performance for the computer users was not apparent in the analysis of constraining questions. There was no difference between groups in the pretest situation ($F<1$) nor in the posttest situation ($F=3.13$; $df=1,20$; n.s.). There was no improvement in the performance of the non-computer user group LN over the period of the investigation ($F<1$). This also held for the computer user group LC ($F=3.94$; $df=1,20$; n.s.) although a trend of improvement was discernable suggesting that this group was more likely to use a classificatory strategy in the posttest.

TABLE 4

Mean Numbers of Questions and Standard Deviation per Trial and Ratio of Constraining to Specific Questions per Subject for the Pre-Post Test, across Teaching Strategy

	Computer group TC		Non-computer group TN	
	Pre-test	Post-test	Pre-test	Post-test
Questions	6.89	5.89	6.89	6.43
	(0.91)	(0.78)	(1.02)	(1.38)
Constraining/ Specific Questions	0.91	1.15	0.87	0.98

Discussion

There were overall gains in performance between pre- and post-categorisation tasks governed by the teaching strategy employed. The computer users performed significantly better on the pre- versus posttest, unlike the non-computer users, and they significantly out-performed the non-computer users in the posttest situation.

The question again arises why this disparity in skills acquisition should occur. The arguments for and against explanations involving disparity of treatment between groups and the nature of the interaction between child and machine have been presented in Experiment 1. In this experiment equal care was taken to match operations on and off the machine and, as the operations on the machine were very simple, involving the presentation of randomised lists, this matching process was extremely easy to achieve.

It is difficult, at first sight, to offer any explanation of the advantage of computer use in this experiment. Comments from the children in the non-computer group were illuminating, however. When presented with the task of organising five randomly selected objects along a novel dimension several of the children appeared resistant to the task. Comments on the silliness of discussing the softness of a table were articulated and the adult working with the children was asked to re-deal the cards (randomly select a new group of objects) to produce a more sensible problem. Although the adult resisted these overtures and continued to operate in a similar manner to the computer, there was no doubt that the interactions between the children and the adult were different from those taking place between the children and the computer. In the latter case, although the children were often puzzled by the unusual task, they accepted it. One boy said that the computer was made to act that way by people and it could not change. Other children simply stated that the computer was funny but they carried on the task nevertheless.

The motivational argument appears less acceptable for this class of children. The software cannot be described as exciting as it uses few of the facilities of the computer in this electronic-book-mode. Equally, the argument pertaining to the rapidity of knowledge of results is irrelevant here as there was no interaction between the child and the computer other than when the user asked for another problem to be set. Although a variety of hypotheses can be put forward to explain the results in this experiment, the insights into acceptable interactions between child and adult and child and computer, particularly the awareness that adults can be manipulated but 'machines are machines' and you have to accept that, do present a convincing argument about the differential effectiveness of the two experimental conditions.

EXPERIMENT 3: INFORMATION-HANDLING PROGRAMMES

This experiment investigated whether children's development of classificatory skills, as measured by a simple pre-post categorisation task, would be stimulated by a learning programme that involved the active sorting and classifying of objects and the creation and interrogation of appropriate data files both on and off the computer. If so, would the teaching strategy employed, in this case teaching with or without the aid of a microcomputer and relevant software, significantly influence the acquisition of measures classificatory skills?

Method

Subjects. Fifty-nine children, between 9 and 11 years of age, were assessed for reading ability, for non-verbal ability and categorisation ability as in Experiments 1 and 2. The three test scores were used to establish four experimental groups, each of which contained ten children. In this initial investigation two other factors, the type of organisational structure into which the data was to be placed and factual knowledge, were also measured. These have been omitted here as they have no relevance to the comparative study. A more detailed description of this experiment including a comparison of skills versus factual knowledge acquisition can be found in Underwood (1986). There was no effect of organisational structure and the data have therefore been collapsed and two experimental groups designated. The mean test scores for the children are presented in Table 5.

Materials The pre-post categorisation test materials were as described in Experiments 1 and 2. Two computer programmes were employed in the study. The first programme SEEK allows children to set up and interrogate a binary tree, in which information is sorted or classified linearly through a series of yes/no answers. The second programme FACTFILE operates a matrix classification structure. Again children can set up and interrogate the data base, but in this case the classificatory model is two-dimensional rather than linear. The two programmes are treated the same for the purposes of this analysis.

TABLE 5
Ability Profiles of Children in the Two Experimental Conditions.

		Mean age	Mean reading score	Mean non-verbal score	Mean Pre-categorisation score
Computer group	SC (N=20)	10.5	19.5	17.3	8.4
Control group Non-computer	SN (N=20)	10.6	19.6	17.1	8.4

Design and Procedure. There was one between-subject factor and one within-subjects factor in the experiment. The two experimental groups each received the pre- and post- categorisation tests along with all members of the contributing school classes. All subjects completed a work topic which involved classifying a range of cheeses. The children worked with the same adult who was not the experimenter. One group operated with either the binary tree classification or matrix programme on the computer SC; the control group matched the structure of the computer programme using file cards SN. The interrogative aspects of the programme were provided by the adult worker. The procedure for administering the pre- and post- categorisation task followed that of Experiments 1 and 2.

All fifty-nine children in the two sample classes were involved in a three week project in which the main task was to classify a range of cheeses. The children worked in groups of seven or eight and each group contained five experimental subjects. All groups were led by the same adult who was not the experimenter. Each group was initially shown nine cheeses and, with guidance and following careful observation and description, identified a number of characteristics of each cheese. From this work the children constructed their classificatory criteria and each child was given one cheese to describe in detail using the agreed criteria. The remaining cheese, or cheeses, were described collectively by the group and one child recorded the group's deliberations.

Once the classificatory criteria had been agreed the experimental group (SC), who were to use either the SEEK or FACTFILE programmes, proceeded to enter its data into the computer over the next week and then interrogated the newly-made files. The non-computer users (SN) created hand-made grids with file cards and, with the aid of the adult, simulated the computer interrogation. This simulation consisted of the children asking retrieval queries in the manner of the computer user group and the adult responding to those queries. It was stressed to the children that their questions must be carefully formed, and the adult was instructed to give a nil, or 'do not understand' response to ill-formed questions. For example, a question asking for the 'best' cheese would be unanswerable if the children failed to specify the criteria on which 'best' should be judged. To remove, or at least reduce, any perceptions of being treated differently, the control groups (SN) completed a series of mathematical investigations with the computer. All activities took place in the school library, an area the children frequently used for small group work.

Results

Scoring of the pre-post categorisation test was as in Experiment 1. A split-plot analysis of variance was performed on the mean number of questions per trial provided by each subject in each condition. The two factors were teaching strategy (between-subjects factor) and pre-post classification scores (within-subjects factor). There was a significant improvement in performance for subjects as a whole on the pre- versus post-categorisation task (F=9.07; df=1,36; p<0.005). The mean number of questions required to identify the target card was lower for the post (M=7.13) as compared to pre-categorisation (M=8.44) task. There was a strong interaction between the teaching strategy employed and performance on the pre- versus post-categorisation task (F=6.39; df=1,36; p<0.016).

TABLE 6

Mean Numbers of Questions and Standard Deviation per Trial and Ratio of Constraining to Specific Questions per Subject for the Pre-Posttest, across Teaching Strategy

| | Computer group SC | | Non-computer group SN | |
	Pretest	Posttest	Pretest	Posttest
Questions	8.48	6.07	8.42	8.21
	(3.28)	(0.95)	(3.40)	(3.54)
Constraining/	0.52	1.06	0.49	0.67
Specific Questions				

Further analysis showed that although the pre-categorisation scores for the computer and non-computer groups were virtually indistinguishable (F<1), and there was equally no difference between the pre- and posttest scores of the non-computer users (F<1), the computer users did not follow this pattern of results. This is clearly evident from the overall means of questions per trial shown in Table 6. There was a reliable difference between the pre- and posttest scores of the computer users (F=15.34; df=1,36; p<0.0004) and between the posttest scores of the computer versus non-computer users (F=12.10; df=1,36; p<0.001). The computer users not only showed improved performance in the pre- versus posttest situation, they outshone the non-computer users in the posttest situation although their performance had been indistinguishable from the latter group on the pretest. Analysis of the strength of the improved performance registered between the pre- and posttest situation confirmed the superiority of the computer user group over the non-computer users (F=6.39; df=1,36; p<0.016).

A similar pattern of improved performance was apparent for the computer user group (SC) in the analysis of the type of questions asked by subjects (F=23.67; df=1,36; p<0.0001). Although there was no difference between groups in the pretest situation (F<1), the computer group asked a higher ratio of constraining to specific questions on the posttest than did the control group (F=12.00; df=1,36; p<0.002). There was no improvement in the performance for the non-computer user group over the period of the investigation (F=2.83; df=1,36; n.s.). This suggests that the computer group may have been operating a classificatory strategy in the posttest situation. Indeed, Table 6 shows that in the posttest situation the computer users were asking more constraining questions than specific questions. The non-computer users as a whole remained relatively reluctant to use this strategy, which suggests that the strategy may not have been available to them and that the children might not have come to realise the benefits that it offered in solving the task at hand. It might be argued therefore that the computer users had been primed to a classificatory approach to the data by use of the computer software, but no such priming had taken place for the non-computer users. This argument would be consistent with the view of the superior transparency of organisational structure of computer versus non-computer data bases.

Discussion

There were overall gains in performance between the pre- and post-categorisation task but the strength of those gains was governed by the teaching strategy employed; computer users outperforming the non-computer users. There are several possible explanations of this result. The first two arguments are suggestive of a disparity in the treatment received by the experimental and control groups. It might be argued that the data handling packages on the computer exhibited a superior organisation to the hand-operated system generated in the study. Secondly, it might be argued that the interrogative mode, in both SEEK and FACTFILE, was superior to that operated by the adult worker with non-computer groups. Other explanations stem from the intrinsic nature of the computer. Were the children simply more motivated because they were using this new technology or, was there something more specific than an overall stimulus to work, in the nature of the interaction between the computer and the child?

In conducting the experiment great care was taken to match the operations off the computer to those presented by the machine and the appropriate software. Are we left then with the motivational aspects of the computer as the sole cause of the improved performance in this study? Certainly the comments of the children using the computer were encouraging. The children appreciated the colour, layout and animated aspects of the programmes. Those children in the control groups, using the computer for other activities, were also willing to complete the most mundane of tasks over and over again if the computer was involved.

Although care was taken to mimic the computer in all relevant operations, in human operations it is difficult to operate the same rigidity of control. The demands placed on the learner for precision in data presentation may be significant here. Each user must have thought very deeply about the material to hand not only to enter it into the machine but also to allow worthwhile questions to be asked of that data. This is no easy task, and both adults and children may initially have great difficulty in preparing material for entry into programmes such as FACTFILE (Underwood, 1985).

The precision of field specification and the selection of relevant data are key classificatory skills that had been encouraged during the experimental study. It is this latter process, the process of stripping data down to the essentials, that could be responsible for the differential improvement in performance of the computer and non-computer users in this study. This is a persuasive argument, for it could be asserted that the careful observation and naming of objects should lead to improved classificatory skills. Equally, although in both the construction and interrogation of either a SEEK or FACTFILE data base the programme exercises considerable control over possible operations, the children may have felt a sense of control which was not achievable when the adult took the role of the computer. Such a sense of control might lead to greater self-esteem (Papert, 1981) and be motivating in itself.

Alongside Papert's 'power hypothesis' it could be argued that the swift response of the computer to the children's queries, particularly more complex questions, might have led to a greater bonding between question and answer. Although the adult, under the control condition, would have provided rapid answers to simple searches there may have been delays on the more complex material. For the less able the immediacy of feedback may have proved particularly important as answers could be provided before attention strayed and memories of the question under review faded.

GENERAL DISCUSSION

The purpose of this group of experiments was to establish whether children's classificatory abilities could be stimulated by a set programme of work, and, whether the use of the computer would lead to differential gains in performance over non-computer users. Direct comparisons between types of instruction were not built into this programme of research. Inevitably, questions of the comparative effectiveness of these methods of presenting classificatory problems to the children arise from the results presented here.

A comparison of the results showed that there was an overall improvement in performance on the post-, as compared to the pre-, categorisation task and that these improvements were a result of teaching strategy. In all three experiments the computer users made differential performance gains over the non-computer users. Although the results suggested that improvements occurred for each instructional programme, the results appear most robust in Experiment 3, in which the children were asked to complete a data organisation and retrieval task. The computer users in this experiment not only improved their own categorisation performance and performed significantly better than the non-computer users on the posttest, they also were likely to use the more efficient hypothesis-constraining rather than an hypothesis-scanning strategy to resolve the 'twenty questions' problem.

In Experiment 2 similar differential gains were made by the computer users when compared with the non-computer users but, although the computer users show a trend to use the more efficient constraint strategy in the posttest situation this improvement is below statistical significance. In Experiment 1, the computer users do show significant gains in the posttest situation, but they do not reliably out-perform the non-computer users, although they do show a trend to greater use of the constraint strategy when completing the post-categorisation task.

In each experiment the computer users out-performed the non-computer users. The non-computer programmes of work had disappointingly little effect on children's performances. The three investigations together show a gradation in performance gains, by the computer users, with the children using the information handling packages being most successful, followed by those children involved in the exploration of concepts through a design programme with least gains being made by the group who received a tutorial programme of work.

The low effectiveness of the guided tutorial programme was surprising for it offered activities closely related to the categorisation task. In their work with very young children, Lawton et al. found that what they described as traditional instructional programmes had little effect on children's classificatory skills, but that their young children in the Ausebelian programme. That is, children who were encouraged to emphasise knowledge structures were far more successful on a range of post- versus pre-categorisation tasks, than were children being taught in a Piagetian or in a traditional classroom. The results for the computer-users in these experiments are consistent with those findings. The children using information handling programmes not only made posttest gains, they were also more likely to use the highly effective hypothesis constraining strategy to resolve the classification problems. This did not hold for the THINKLINKS and LOGIBLOCKS 2 programs. Although the pattern appears to be similar this is only so when comparing the computer-user groups. Progress by the non-computer-users was small, if it occurred at all. Yet Lawton et al. did not use computers!

Lawton and Wanska (1979) have shown that knowing the structure of concepts merely in terms of their properties is not sufficient for children (8-10 years old) to produce a hierarchical structure for those concepts successfully, or to compare super and subordinate concepts within the hierarchy. They found that children need more than the knowledge that 'a mammal is a hairy animal which suckles its young,' in order to place that concept in the animal hierarchy. The children must be able to generate the rules governing that hierarchy; for example, that the superordinate concept (animal) is defined by a property shared by all the subordinate concepts. Lawton et al, in their Ausebelian programme, placed a heavy emphasis on this rule generation, and the children made commensurate classificatory progress. In Experiment 3 it was in questioning the data base that a clear understanding of the structure of the information, along with the rules governing it, were most needed. It was in this area that the disparity between computer and non-computer treatment may have occurred. It has already been stressed that to get an answer from the computer required great precision in questioning.

When the adult in Experiment 3 was asked a question, in the simulated computer role, every effort was taken to be computer-like. It has already been suggested that there might have been some loss in immediacy of feedback on more complex questions. Equally, due to the shared knowledge of child and adult, the adult was able to interpret and respond to less precise questions from the non-computer users. This unintentional lack of rigidity in the adult's behaviour could have allowed children to gain information without the precision of thought needed by the computer users.

That child-computer interaction can be different from child-adult interaction was clearly shown in Experiment 2. Here, the children were willing to accept a task defined by the computer, but the same task presented by an adult was rejected as nonsensical. The children in the non-computer group tried to manipulate the adult and change the learning situation. This is a frequent and normal occurrence in the classroom. Holt (1969, 1970) demonstrated that children reduced their role in finding the solution to the problem to hand by encouraging the adult to take on part of the task, or to alter the task and make it simpler. In doing so the children may have reduced those conceptual conflicts that are generally believed to be vital to their own cognitive development.

In summary, the main findings of these three experiments were that the computer can be a powerful tool for encouraging children's classificatory abilities. The arguments presented here, to account for the results in these experiments, are two-fold. Firstly, children respond differently to the computer than to an adult. They appear to be aware that the computer is inflexible and that they must be the ones to adapt if communication is to take place. Some children go as far as treating the computer as a less able peer who must be helped. This inflexibility forces the children to greater precision in their own thinking. Secondly, children are more likely to accept novel ideas when presented by the computer, for the computer is different from a human being.

CORRESPONDENCE

Department of Mathematics and Computing, Derbyshire College of Higher Education, Mickleover, Derby DE3 5GX, England

REFERENCES

Bousfield, W.A. (1953). The occurrence of clustering in the recall of randomly arranged words of different frequencies of usage. *Journal of Genetic Psychology, 52,* 83-95.
Bower, G.H., Clark, M.C., Lesgold, A.M. & Winzenz, D. (1969). Hierarchical retrieval schemes in the recall of categorised word lists. *Journal of Verbal Learning and Verbal Behaviour, 8,* 323-343.
Bransford, J.D. (1979). *Human Cognition: Learning, Understanding and Remembering.* Belmont, Ca., Wadsworth.

de Bono, E. (1978). *Lateral Thinking*. London: Penguin.

Durding, B.M., Becker, C.A. & Gould, J.D. (1977). *Data organisation. Human Factors, 19*, 1-14.

Holt, J. (1969). *How Children Learn*. Harmondsworth, Middlesex, Penguin.

Holt, J. (1970). *How Children Fail*. Harmondsworth, Middlesex, Penguin.

Hughes, M. (1986). *Children and Number*. Oxford: Blackwell.

Lawton, J.T., Hooper, F.H., Saunders, R.A. & Roth, P. (1984). A comparison of logical concept development in three pre-school programmes. *Human Learning, 3* (3), 143-164.

Lawton, J.T. & Wanska, S.K. (1979). The effects of two different types of advance organisers on classification learning. *American Educational Research Journal, 16*, 223-239.

Papert, S. (1981). *Mindstorms: Children, Computers and Powerful Ideas*. Brighton: Harvester Press.

Turner, I.F., Scullion, L.T. & Whyte, J. (1984). Relationship between reading proficiency and two types of classificatory ability. *Journal of Research in Reading, 7*, 123-134.

Underwood, G. & Underwood, J.D.M. (1987). The computer in education: A force for change. In F. Blackler & D. Oborne (eds). *Information Technology and People*. Leicester, The British Psychological Society.

Underwood, J.D.M. (1985). Cognitive demand and CAL. In I. Reid & J. Rushton (eds.) *Teachers, Computers and the Classroom*. Manchester: Manchester University Press.

Underwood, J.D.M. (1986). The role of the computer in developing children's classificatory abilities. *Computers in Education, 10*, 175-180.

Underwood, J.D.M. and Underwood, G. (1988). Data organisation and retrieval by children. *British Journal of Educational Psychology, 57*, 313-329.

FACTFILE (1982). Cambridge Microsoftware.

LOGIBLOCKS 2 (1983). Shiva Mathematics.

SEEK (1984). Longman Microsoftware.

THINKLINKS (1983). Straker, A.

Social Applications and Issues in Psychology
R.C. King and J.K. Collins (editors)
©Elsevier Science Publishers B.V. (North-Holland), 1989

AN INVESTIGATION OF GROUPS VERSUS INDIVIDUALS SOLVING MICROCOMPUTER BASED PROBLEMS

Anita C. Jackson, Ben C. Fletcher & D.J. Messer

The Hatfield Polytechnic, United Kingdom

Microcomputers are now widely used in primary schools and predominantly by groups of children working together rather than one child working alone. This paper reports a series of experiments that examined whether and, if so, in what situations, small groups of children (10/11 year olds) showed superior performance to individual children on a series of microcomputer-based mathematical problems. Groups showed superior on-task performance to individuals, with no loss of efficiency in time to solution. Furthermore, there was an indication that group interaction could be more beneficial for performance over and above the provision of a software-based 'help facility', particularly when problems were more difficult. Surprisingly, task relevant concurrent verbalisation had no significant effects on performance, suggesting that intragroup discussion is not essential in group superiority. Factors found to be important included the presence of peers and the opportunity to watch peers solving the problems. These results are discussed in relation to psychological theory and educational practice.

Microcomputers are now widely found in primary schools in the United Kingdom. Several surveys of microcomputer use in primary schools (i.e. for 5 to 11 year olds) have recently been undertaken (Jackson, Fletcher & Messer, 1986; Jackson, Fletcher & Messer, 1988). In nearly all cases, children were found to use the microcomputer in small groups rather than individually. In the near future, it is unlikely that British primary schools will possess microcomputers sufficient in numbers to permit any degree of individual contact; therefore group use will be the norm for some time to come. However, many of the arguments in favour of the use of Information Technology (IT) in schools have rested on the power of microcomputers to give children individualised instruction, where the microcomputer acts as some sort of personal tutor (e.g., Suppes, 1966). Jackson et al. (1986, 1988) found that much of the most frequently used software in schools was of the 'drill and practice' variety specifically designed for individual use. Moreover, although teachers commonly considered that group interaction at the microcomputer was socially beneficial, few referred to any cognitive benefits. Similar attitudes have been reported by Perret-Clermont and Schubauer-Leoni (1981) who found that teachers typically justified group activities in social rather than cognitive terms. Although the development of good interpersonal relationships and interaction skills is undoubtedly important, it is equally important to investigate whether group interaction at the microcomputer results in improved performance and learning.

There is considerable evidence to suggest that groups should perform better than individuals as superior group performance has been reported for a wide variety of tasks and under a wide variety of testing conditions (for reviews see e.g., Hill, 1982; Johnson & Johnson, 1975; Johnson et al., 1981). For example, in one of the few examinations of group and individual performance on a microcomputer-based task, Fletcher (1985) reported that groups solve problems in fewer moves than subjects working alone. A number of theories attribute better group performance to social factors (e.g., Kelley & Thibaut, 1969; Lorge & Solomon, 1955; Steiner, 1972). That is, a group of people between them can possess a greater number of resources than any single person working alone. It is this that puts them at an advantage. Therefore, in the problem solving environment, group members can combine their abilities and are more likely to solve a problem in fewer moves than an individual working alone.

There is also evidence that superior group performance could be due, at least in part, to cognitive factors. Groups generally engage in conversation, whereas individuals (i.e., subjects working alone) do not. It could be the act of talking, or task relevant concurrent verbalisation, that leads to improved performance. A number of experiments suggest that talking does facilitate group performance (e.g., Doise, 1978; Skon et al., 1981). Talking has also been found to facilitate individual performance when individuals are required to verbalise concurrently during problem solution (Bower & King, 1967; Fletcher, 1985; Schunk & Cox, 1986). In this sense, concurrent verbalisation is said to result in cognitive facilitation.

This paper reports a series of experiments that examined whether and, if so, in what situations, small groups of children showed superior performance to individual children on a series of microcomputer-based mathematical problems. All the experiments were conducted in primary schools with 10/11 year old children.

THE EXPERIMENTS

Experiment 1 examined the relative contribution of social and cognitive facilitation to group superiority. It examined whether groups performed better than individuals on a microcomputer-based problem solving task and whether the requirement to verbalise concurrently had any effects on performance. The basic design is 2 X 2 factorial (group/individual X concurrent verbalisation/silent) and is shown in Table 1.

TABLE 1
Design of Experiment 1

PRETEST ----->	MICROCOMPUTER TASK ----->	POSTEST -------->	TRANSFER TASK
(individually	4 conditions =	(individually	(individually
administered)	Silent Indivs.	administered)	administered)
	(n = 12)		
	Verbal Indivs.		
	(n = 12)		
	Silent Groups		
	(n = 12 grps.)		
	Verbal Groups		
		(n = 12	grps.)

The pretest was a pencil and paper test designed to give an indication of problem solving ability (Jackson, 1987). It involved the solution of mathematical problems of a similar nature to those employed in the experimental tasks. Children were assigned to groups on the basis of similar pretest performance to give similar ability groups of three. Overall, children were assigned to the 4 conditions so that there was a similar ability profile in each condition. The number of correctly answered problems was used as a covariate in the statistical analyses of experimental task performance.

Following the pretest, children were split up into 4 conditions to perform the microcomputer task. Half the individuals and half the groups were required to verbalise concurrently, which meant they had to give reasons out loud for their decisions during problem solution; if in groups, they had to reach group decisions as to how to proceed. Children in both the verbal conditions were asked to talk throughout problem solution. Children in both groups conditions took turns at the keyboard to keep the group members as fully involved as possible. The Silent Group condition required children to work in silence and not to try to help or interfere with each other.

The microcomputer task involved the solution of 6 problems of the same difficulty level. An example of one of the problems is shown in Table 2. This task requires a target unit number (a quantity of 'water') to be obtained by the multiple addition and subtraction of two given number units (filling, emptying, and transferring 'water' from one 'jug' to another). The problems could be solved in a minimum of 4 moves. Five keys of the BBC microcomputer were pre-programmed and labelled to correspond to these moves and, each time one was pressed, it counted as one move. The 'jugs' were always empty to start with, and the aim was to end up with a specified amount of 'liquid' in one of the 'jugs'. No spillage was possible.

After the microcomputer task, the children completed a further pencil and paper posttest that was very similar to the pretest. Any change in problem-solving performance following experience of the microcomputer task and any differential change according to experimental manipulation could thus be examined. Following the posttest, children were given what was called the 'Transfer Task'. They had to solve these 4 problems individually. These were conceptually similar to the microcomputer problems but were 'real-life' problems requiring the manipulation of weights on a balance scale rather than 'water' in 'jugs'. This task was designed to examine whether there was any transfer of learning from the microcomputer problems.

TABLE 2
Example of Microcomputer Problem

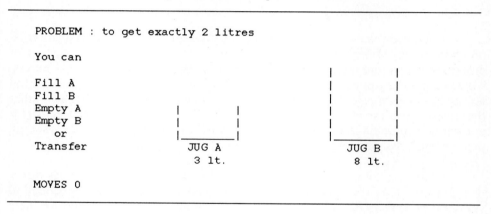

```
PROBLEM : to get exactly 2 litres

You can
                                                        |        |
Fill A                                                  |        |
Fill B                                                  |        |
Empty A              |        |                         |        |
Empty B              |        |                         |        |
   or                |_____|                         |_____|
Transfer               JUG A                              JUG B
                       3 lt.                              8 lt.

MOVES 0
```

Table 3 shows the results of the pre- and posttests. No differences were observed between pretest by condition ($F(3,92) < 1$) nor between posttest by condition ($F(3,92) < 1$). However, there was a general improvement from pre- to posttest. Therefore, there was no observed effect of experimental manipulation. The improvement may have been due to experience of the microcomputer task or a practice effect from having already completed a very similar test.

Table 4 shows the results of the microcomputer task. As expected, there was a main effect of Group versus Individual ($F(1,43)=4.07, p=0.05$) for number of moves to solution; Groups taking an average of 19.5 moves to solve each problem in comparison to 23.5 moves for Individuals. The surprising result was that there was no significant effect of concurrent verbalisation, nor any interaction with the Group/Individual factor. Therefore, verbally interacting groups solved the problems in a similar number of moves to silent groups, and concurrently verbalising individuals showed similar performance to their silent counterparts.

TABLE 3
Results of Pre- and Posttest (Experiment 1)

CONDITION	MEAN NUMBER CORRECT (out of 10)	
	Pretest	Postest
Silent Indivs	6.5	6.8
Verbal Indivs	6.4	7.0
Silent Groups	6.7	7.1
Verbal Groups	6.2	6.6
Mean	6.5	6.9 $p<0.01$

TABLE 4
Results of Microcomputer Task (Experiment 1)

CONDITION (secs)	MEAN PERFORMANCE (of 6 trials)		
	MOVES	TIME (secs)	TIME PER MOVE
Silent Indivs	23	208	10
Verbal Indivs	24	243	9
Silent Groups	19	203	11
Verbal Groups	20	219	11
	Main Effect *p = 0.050*	*Not Signif.*	*Not Signif.*

Table 5 shows the results of the Transfer task. (Only the Control group performed the Transfer task.) The results indicate no differences in performance from that of the control subjects as a result of experience of the microcomputer task, nor of the experimental mainpulation. Therefore, no transfer of learning was observed from the microcomputer to the real-life task. This finding is in accord with many other studies. Even with very similar tasks, previous investigations have failed to demonstrate transfer of children's learning (e.g., Glachan & Light, 1984; Ringel & Springer, 1980).

TABLE 5
Results of Transfer Task (Experiment 1)

CONDITION (secs)	MEAN PERFORMANCE (of 4 trials)		
	MOVES	TIME (secs)	TIME PER MOVE
Silent Indivs	13	277	26
Verbal Indivs	11	212	21
Silent Groups	12	237	26
Verbal Groups	12	267	25
Controls	12	273	29
	Not Signif.	*Not Signif.*	*Not Signif.*

The critical result of this experiment was that groups of children solved the microcomputer problems in fewer moves than children working alone. This finding is in accord with previous studies that have reported group superiority for problem solving tasks. It extends this research into the realm of microcomputer-based activity.

However, it was rather surprising that there was no significant effect of concurrent verbalisation, especially that Verbal Groups performed similarly to Silent Groups. One explanation as to why verbalisation did not help is that the problems involved a large visual component and were not particularly easy to talk about. This problem has also been noted by Light and Glachan (1985). Other research suggests that subjects may need some sort of pre-orientation to the problem for verbalisation to be effective (Berry & Broadbent, 1984; Fletcher & Perman, 1982, 1984).

Because of the potential importance of the Silent Group superiority effect, it was considered important to replicate this aspect of the first experiment and show it to be robust effect. Table 6 shows the design of *Experiment 2* which was very similar to Experiment 1 but with fewer components. The same pretest, microcomputer task and procedure were used as before.

TABLE 6
Design of Experiment 2

PRETEST ----------> MICROCOMPUTER TASK
                   2 Conditions =   Silent Individuals (n = 16)
                                    Silent Groups (n = 16 groups)

Table 7 shows the results of the second experiment. Once again, Silent Groups solved the problems in significantly fewer moves than Silent Individuals ($F(1,29)=5.19$, $p=0.03$) and, in this experiment, they were also faster per move than Individuals ($F(1,29)=4.40$, $p=0.045$). This demonstrates that intragroup discussion is *not* essential for group superiority.

TABLE 7
Results of Microcomputer Task (Experiment 2)

CONDITION	MEAN PERFORMANCE (of 6 trials)		
	MOVES	TIME (secs)	TIME PER MOVE (secs)
Silent Indivs	28	250	9
Silent Groups	21	239	11
	Main Effect *p = 0.0302*	*Not Signif.*	*Main Effect* *p = 0.045*

The question remained as to why Silent Groups should solve the problems in fewer moves than Silent Individuals. One possible explanation as to why this should occur is that Groups may be at an advantage because each group member has the opportunity to watch other group members solve the same type of problem. They may be learning something about effective problem solution by watching each other; a case of observational learning. One group member might use an approach to problem solution that another group member might not have thought of alone, or at least not have arrived at so quickly. In this sense, Silent Group performance could also be a result of pooled resources although in a possibly more restricted manner than that in a verbally interacting group. Thus children can draw on the abilities of other group members by remembering how their colleagues solved the previous problems. This might be particularly useful when the children were unsure of how to proceed. In turn, children working alone might be at a disadvantage because they have no outside resources on which to draw, especially when they are 'stuck'. The opportunity to receive help when needed might improve an individual's performance.

Experiment 3 examined the usefulness of help on request provided by a specially produced computer program. In particular, it examined how such software driven help affects individual and group performance. Table 8 shows the design of Experiment 3. A 'help facility' was written into the same computer task as used in the previous experiments. The same pretest and procedure were used as before, however slightly harder problems were used that required a minimum of 6 moves to solution instead of 4 moves. This was to diminish the likelihood of a 'ceiling effect' in the data in case the 'help' facility had made the problems easier. Children could press a key labelled 'SHOW' which would result in the presentation of the next best move (or moves, if pressed more than once). Therefore, children could draw on this resource when they needed it. It was made available to both Individuals and Groups to use when they wanted. As verbalisation had been shown to have no extra beneficial effect on performance, groups were allowed to discuss the problems during solution as they would under normal classroom conditions.

TABLE 8
Design of Experiment 3

PRETEST ----------------> MICROCOMPUTER TASK
                          2 Conditions = Individuals (n = 16)
                                            Groups (n = 16 groups)

In addition to investigating the effects of the provision of a help facility on group versus individual performance, the frequency of use of 'SHOW' was also noted. It was a possibility that groups and individuals would not utilise this facility with the same frequency. If, as has been suggested, groups have a type of 'built-in' help that partly accounts for their superior problem solution, they should not need to use 'SHOW' as often as individuals. Therefore, overall performance might be similar, but Groups might not use 'help' as frequently.

Table 9 shows that despite the provision of the help facility, Groups solved the problems in an average of 6 fewer moves than Individuals ($F(1,29) = 6.00$, $p=0.021$). This is the total number of moves made which includes the use of 'SHOW'. (Each use of 'SHOW' was counted as one move just like other key presses.) Analysis of the frequency of the use of 'SHOW' revealed that Individuals were also using it about twice as often as Groups ($t(30)=2.57$, $p<0.02$). Therefore, even with the benefit and greater use of the help facility, Individuals could not match the superior performance of Groups.

DISCUSSION

Taken together, the results of the 3 experiments show that group-based microcomputer use leads to superior problem solution compared to individual use. They also demonstrate that providing individuals with software-based help is not as effective as group interaction in producing superior performance. This is not to conclude that software-based help facilities are not helpful in some situations but rather that group interaction can be more effective.

TABLE 9
Results of Microcomputer Task (Experiment 3)

CONDITION	MEAN PERFORMANCE (of 6 trials)		
	TOTAL MOVES	TIME (secs)	TIME PER MOVE (secs)
Individuals	22	134	6
Groups	16	128	7
	Main Effect *p = 0.021*	*Not Signif.*	*Not Signif.*

FREQUENCY OF 'SHOW' USE

Individuals	:	'Show'	=	29% of Total Moves
Groups	:	'Show'	=	15% of Total Moves

One explanation as to why the software-based help was of limited usefulness compared to group interaction can be found in some classroom-based research. Webb (1977) had reported a significant positive relationship between student achievement and receiving help from other children. However, when this was examined in further detail (Webb, 1982a), she found that the type of help was important. When children were told the problem solution only, no improvement was observed; however, when it was accompanied by a brief explanation, higher achievement was recorded. Using the help facility in this experiment is similar to being told what to do but not why you are doing it. Therefore, individuals might be at a disadvantage because they do not receive explanations. Children in groups, on the other hand, are likely to give brief explanations for their actions. A further aspect of group interaction which may partly account for these results is the effect of the presence of others. Whilst the provision of a help facility may reduce an individual's test anxiety by offering him/her some support when 'stuck', it may not be as reassuring as the presence of classmates.

Although no beneficial effects of verbalisation were revealed in this research, it is not suggested that children should not talk in groups. The Silent Group is clearly unnatural and may be less motivating for its members. From a personal observation, it appeared that the Verbal Groups enjoyed the task more and that motivation was an important educational component. However, this research does bring into question the assumption that talking is cognitively beneficial in group interaction. It is clearly an important issue to discover when and how verbalisation does facilitate cognition.

CORRESPONDENCE

The Hatfield Polytechnic, School of Humanities & Education, Wall Hall Campus, Aldenham, Watford, Herts., WD2 8AT, U.K.

REFERENCES

Berry, D.C. & Broadbent, D.E. (1984). On the relationship between task performance and associated verbalisable knowledge. *Quarterly Journal of Experimental Psychology, 36A,* 209-233.

Bower, A.C. & King, W.L. (1967). The effect of number of irrelevant stimulus dimensions, verbalisation, and sex on learning biconditional classification rules. *Psychonomic Science, 8,* 10, 453-454.

Doise, W. (1978). *Groups and Individuals : Explanations in Social Psychology.* Cambridge University Press.

Fletcher, B.(C) (1985). Group and individual learning of Junior school children on a microcomputer-based task : Social or cognitive facilitation? *Education Review, 37,* 251-261.

Fletcher, B.C & Perman, L.M.V. (1982). Knowing and doing: The relationship between verbal knowledge and systems control ability. Paper presented to British Psychological Society Annual Conf., York.

Fletcher, B.C. & Perman, L.M.V. (1984). Why are N + 1 heads better than one: Social psychological or cognitive information processing facilitation? *Bulletin of the British Psychological Society, 37,* A59.

Glachan, M. & Light, P. (1982). Peer interaction and learning : Can two wrongs make a right? In G. Butterworth and P. Light (Eds). *Social Cognition.* Harvester Press.

Hill, G.W. (1982). Group versus individual performance : Are N + 1 heads better than one? *Psychological Bulletin, 91,* 517-539.

Jackson, A. (1987). Group and Individual Performance on Microcomputer Based Problems. Unpublished Ph.D. Thesis. The Hatfield Polytechnic.

Jackson, A., Fletcher, B.C. & Messer, D.J. (1986). A survey of microcomputer use and provision in primary schools. *Journal of Computer Assisted Learning, 2,* 45-55.

Jackson, A., Fletcher, B.C. & Messer, D.J. (1988). Effects of experience on microcomputer use inprimary schools : Results of a second survey. *Journal of Computer Assisted Learning, 4,* 214 - 226.

Johnson, D.W. & Johnson, R.T. (1975). *Learning Together and Alone: Cooperation, Competition & Individualisation.* Prentice-Hall Inc.

Johnson, D.W., Maruyama, G., Johnson, R.T., Nelson, D. & Skon, L. (1981). Effects of cooperative, competitive and individualistic goal structures on achievement : A meta-analysis. *Psychological Bulletin, 69,* 186-192.

Kelley, H.H. & Thibaut, J.W. (1969). Group problem solving. In G.Lindzey & E.Aronson (Eds) *The Handbook of Social Psychology* Vol.4, 2nd Edn., Addison Wesley.

Light, P. & Glachan, M. (1985). Facilitation of individual problem solving through peer interaction. *Educational Psychology, 5,* 217-225.

Lorge, I. & Solomon, H. (1955). Two models of group behaviour in the solution of eureka type problems. *Psychometrika, 20,* 139-148.

Perret-Clermont, A.-N., & Schubauer-Leoni, M.-L. (1981). Conflict and cooperation as opportunities for learning. In W.P. Robinson (Ed.). *Communication in Development* Academic Press.

Ringel, B.A. & Springer, C.J. (1980). On knowing how well one is remembering : The persistence of strategy use during transfer. *Journal of Exptional Child Psychology, 29,* 322-333.

Schunk, D.H. & Cox, P.D. (1986). Strategy training and attributional feedback with learning disabled students. *Journal of Exptional Child Psychology,* *86,* 201-209.

Skon, L., Johnson, D.W. & Johnson, R.T. (1981). Cooperative peer interaction versus individual competition and individualistic efforts : Effects on the acquisition of cognitive reasoning strategies. *Journal of Educational Psychology, 73,* 83-92.

Steiner, I.D. (1972). *Group Processes and Productivity.* Academic Press.

Suppes, P.(1966). The uses of computers in education. *Scientific American, 215,* 206-220.

Webb, N.M. (1977). Learning in individual and small group settings. (Tech. Rep. No. 7), Aptitude Research Project, School of Education, Stanford University, California.

Webb, N.M. (1982). Student interaction and learning in small groups. *Review of Educational Research, 52,* 121-145.

Social Applications and Issues in Psychology
R.C. King and J.K. Collins (editors)
©Elsevier Science Publishers B.V. (North-Holland), 1989

THE ROLE OF RESEARCH IN THE REGULATION OF U.S. CHILDREN'S TELEVISION ADVERTISING

Dale Kunkel

University of California, U.S.A.

There is great variability in the extent of regulation applied to advertising content presented on different countries' commercial broadcasting systems. In terms of restrictions on advertising directed to children, the United States maintains one of the more permissive postures of any country in the world (Murray & Kippax, 1979). This situation has generated substantial controversy among Americans and has led to repeated attempts to forge more stringent regulatory policies to protect the interests of children. The goal of this essay is to review the development of regulations governing television advertising to children in the U.S. and to examine critically the influence of psychological research in the construction of these policies.

THE GROWTH OF RESEARCH ON CHILDREN AND TELEVISION ADVERTISING

Scholarly research on children and television first emerged in the mid-to-late 1950s. Its focus centred almost exclusively on the influence of programs. It was not until more than 10 years later that researchers began to show interest in children's understanding of advertising content. This interest coincided with increasing public concern about the commercial exploitation of children.

In one of the first policy proceedings on the topic, a public interest group called Action for Children's Television (ACT) petitioned the Federal Communications Commission (FCC) in 1969 requesting that all commercials be eliminated during children's programs. This somewhat radical proposal received widespread attention and a surprising degree of public support.

The FCC had been sensitized to policy issues regarding children and television, primarily because of concern within the U.S. Congress about the adverse effects of televised violence (Rowland, 1983). In 1969, the Congress commissioned a series of psychological studies on the effects of violent portrayals that were conducted under the auspices of the U.S. Surgeon General. Because of the growing concern about advertising to children, several studies exploring children's comprehension of television commercials were included in that project.

These studies provided the first published research examining children and television advertising (see Ward, 1972 for a review). The findings suggested that many youngsters experienced difficulty in recognizing the nature and intent of commercials and thus were thought to be particularly susceptible to their influence.

Soon after the Surgeon General's research was published in 1972, literally dozens of children and advertising studies began to appear. Most of the findings pertained to at least one of three basic issues:

1. How well can children tell the difference between programs and commercials?
2. How well can children recognize the persuasive intent in commercials?
3. To what extent are children influenced by commercials?

CHILDREN AND TELEVISION ADVERTISING RESEARCH: THE KEY FINDINGS

By 1977, only five years after the first published studies on the topic, an elaborate research review (Adler et al., 1977) conducted by the National Science Foundation provided relatively thorough answers to the three questions noted above. Additional findings have accumulated since, but the conclusions drawn by the NSF report in 1977 remain essentially unaltered. A brief summary of findings in each of the key areas is offered below.

Program/commercial discrimination. Given the similarities in perceptual characteristics between children's programs and commercials, it is hardly surprising that many youngsters have difficulty distinguishing between the two. Numerous studies of program/commercial discrimination document confusion on the part of a majority of children below the age of about 5 years.

Research using direct verbal questioning to measure discrimination ability indicates that children first recognize the difference based on either affective (e.g., "commercials are funnier than programs") or perceptual (e.g., "commercials are short and programs are long") cues (Blatt, Spencer, & Ward, 1972; Ward, Reale, & Levinson, 1972). This approach typically finds that children below age 5 exhibit "low awareness of the concept of commercials, frequently explaining them as part of the show" (Ward, Reale, & Levinson, 1972, p. 486).

Some have suggested that limited verbal abilities may be masking young children's true competence in distinguishing programs from advertisements when only direct questioning is used to measure such knowledge. However, techniques that avoid dependence on language skills have also generated findings similar to those cited above. For example, Palmer and McDowell (1979) showed 5 to 7 year-olds videotapes of two children's shows with advertisements included. At predetermined points, the tape was stopped and children were asked whether what they had just watched was part of the show or a commercial. Children correctly identified a commercial 64% of the time in one program and 55% in the other. Both results are only slightly above chance for a dichotomous measure.

The evidence overall indicates that a substantial proportion of young children cannot consistently discriminate between television programs and commercials. The ability to apply the marker "a commercial" appears to develop before the actual recognition that a commercial is not part of a program (Kunkel, 1988a). This suggests that the ability to distinguish between these two types of content is not well-developed until at least 5 years of age.

Recognition of persuasive intent. The primary purpose of all television advertising is to influence the attitudes and subsequent behaviour of viewers. For adults, the recognition that a message is a commercial triggers a cognitive filter or defence mechanism that takes into account factors such as the following: (1) the source of the message has other interests than those of the receiver; (2) the source intends to persuade; (3) persuasive messages are biased; and (4) biased messages demand different interpretive strategies than do unbiased messages (Roberts, 1983).

Because of their limited cognitive development, young children generally lack the ability to apply such considerations to television advertising. Below 7-8 years, children are highly egocentric and have difficulty taking the perspective of another (Flavell, 1977; Shantz, 1975). Thus, there is a strong basis for expecting that youngsters will be unable to attribute persuasive intent to television advertising. A substantial body of empirical evidence corroborates this position.

Typical of studies on this topic, Ward and Wackman (1973) interviewed children aged 5-12 to determine their understanding of the purpose of commercials. Rather than conducting analyses by age, however, these researchers used independent measures to categorize children into three levels of cognitive ability, with the lowest one equivalent to Piaget's preoperational stage of development. Fifty-three percent of the 5-6 year-olds and 41% of the 7-8 year-olds were categorized as "low" in cognitive level. Low cognitive level was a significant predictor of a low level of understanding of the persuasive intent of commercials. This study concluded that "low cognitive level children cannot abandon their own perspective and take the perspective of the advertiser when viewing commercials" (Ward & Wackman, 1973, p. 127). Other studies have produced comparable findings that age is positively related with an understanding of commercials' persuasive intent, with such ability typically developing at about 7-8 years.

Commercial influence on children. Children begin to be influenced by television advertising at an early age. Lyle and Hoffman (1972) found that almost 75% of preschoolers' mothers reported their children were singing commercial jingles by age 3. Exposure to television advertising generates different types of effects, such as social learning of modelled behaviour (Bandura, 1977) and consumer socialization (Atkin, 1982), as well as impacts on children's product preferences and purchase requests. Because regulatory policies designed to protect children from advertising have been primarily related to evidence in the latter realm, only that aspect of effects will be addressed here.

Many studies document youngsters' positive reactions to commercials designed for child audiences (see Adler et al., 1977 for a review). Almost all children's commercials are at least moderately successful in achieving their goal of positively influencing desires for the advertised product.

Several different approaches have documented the persuasive effects of commercials on children. One method is to inquire directly about the source of information for desired products. This approach reveals that television is by far the most pervasive influence on children's product preferences. An alternative approach compares the desires of children experimentally exposed to advertising with the desires of control group children. This approach also yields clear evidence of children's susceptibility to commercial persuasion, even for products they are likely to favour on their merits alone. For example, Atkin and Gibson (1978) found that 90% of children who viewed a sugared cereal commercial wanted the product, compared to 66% of a control group who saw no advertising but had the product described to them.

Age-related individual differences play an important role in mediating the effects of advertising exposure. Both desires and requests for products decrease as children grow older (Wartella, 1980). Similarly, children's acceptance of advertising claims is negatively related with age (Rossiter, 1977; Ward, Wackman, & Wartella, 1977). These outcomes are consistent with the age-related changes reported in children's ability to discriminate programs from commercials and to recognize persuasive intent, suggesting such factors help to account for the more powerful effects of advertising on young children.

RESEARCH AND THE REGULATION OF CHILDREN'S TELEVISION ADVERTISING

The evidence of young children's inherent limitations in the skills required for mature comprehension of advertising, coupled with the findings of their unique susceptibility to commercial persuasion, have led to the enactment of specific policies to limit television advertising to child audiences.

The first such restrictions were established by the FCC in 1974. At that time, the agency acknowledged the contributions of relevant research, stating:

> There is ... evidence that very young children cannot distinguish conceptually between programming and advertising; they do not

understand that the purpose of a commercial is to sell a product. Since children watch television long before they can read, television provides advertisers access to a younger and more impressionable age group than can be reached through any other medium. For these reasons, special safeguards may be required to insure that the advertising privilege is not abused.(FCC, 1974, p. 39399)

The FCC then enacted two different types of policies. First, limits were placed on the overall amount of commercial content permissable during children's programs, and second, a requirement was established that broadcasters maintain a "clear separation" between children's programs and commercial content.

In the first area, limits on commercial levels, research was applicable only as it established children's unique vulnerability to advertising. The limits implemented, ranging from 9.5 to 12 minutes per hour, were crafted according to the economic needs of broadcasters rather than the psychological needs or limitations of children. The goal was to "limit advertising to children to the lowest level consistent with programming responsibilities" (FCC, 1974, p. 39400). In other words, because stations must offer some children's programs, they could present advertising to generate the revenue needed to maintain the programming.

In the second area, maintaining a clear separation between programs and commercials, the influence of research was much more palpable. Empirical findings that young children have difficulty discriminating programs from advertising led policy-makers to try to make this task an easier one. The "separation principle," as this ruling is now known, was applied in three different ways:

host-selling - Program characters or hosts were prohibited from promoting products during commercials embedded in or directly adjacent to their show.

program-length commercials - The promotion of products within the body of a program's story was prohibited.

separators - Short program/commercial separation devices were required at the beginning and end of all commercial breaks during children's programs.

All three of these policies were clearly tied to research evidence regarding children's limited ability to discriminate programs from commercials. Indeed, on the face of it, each seems a reasonable policy given the findings, with one key reservation. While empirical evidence weighed heavily in demonstrating the need for regulation and the appropriate area for redress, no research supported or even suggested that the newly established policies would effectively benefit children. That is, there were no specific findings to indicate that host-selling or program-length commercials made it more difficult for children to identify advertising content, or that bumpers would make it easier.

As it turned out, only two of these three FCC policies hit the mark. Research now makes clear that host-selling exacerbates children's difficulty at recognizing commercials and exerts a more powerful persuasive effect than standard advertising (Kunkel, 1988a). Program-length commercials seem to present similar problems, though the direct empirical evidence has been scant (Kunkel, 1989), perhaps because the outcome is so easily anticipated. But the third policy has clearly failed to accomplish its intended goal. Numerous experimental studies demonstrate that the separation devices typically employed do not help children distinguish programs from commercials (Butter, Popovich, Stackhouse, & Garner, 1981; Palmer & McDowell, 1979; Stutts, Vance & Hudleson, 1981). In fact, in some cases children perform better at this task without the separators than with them.

RESEARCH AND THE DEREGULATION OF CHILDREN'S TELEVISION ADVERTISING

The policies noted above were maintained into the 1980s. At that time, however, the government's regulatory philosophy shifted markedly towards a reliance on marketplace factors to serve the public interest better (Fowler & Brenner, 1982). This new philosophy holds that the public will benefit from the increased competition facilitated by the removal of governmental rules and regulations.

Consistent with this perspective, the FCC repealed most of its limited number of television content regulations. When it addressed the realm of advertising, the Commission held that "marketplace forces can better determine appropriate commercial levels than our own rules" (FCC, 1984, p. 33598). The FCC's logic went as follows: if stations exceeded viewers' tolerance for advertising, then the size of the audience would drop, advertising rates would decline (because they are proportional to audience size), and the broadcaster would ultimately be forced by economic considerations to reduce the number of commercials. Accordingly, the FCC (1984) dropped all limits on the amount of commercial time for audiences of children as well as adults.

Surprisingly, none of the FCC's deliberations on this matter addressed the potential impact of its deregulatory decision on the child audience (Huston, Watkins, & Kunkel, 1989). Based on this oversight, the U.S. Court of Appeals ordered the FCC to reconsider the decision to lift its limits on children's advertising, noting:

> Without explanation, the Commission has suddenly embraced what had theretofore been an unthinkable bureaucratic conclusion that the marketplace did in fact operate to restrain the commercial content of

children's television *(Action for Children's Television v. FCC,* 1987).

A fundamental issue obviously related to the FCC's contention that marketplace forces can effectively limit advertising practices is whether or not children will react adversely to excessive commercial content. If not, the FCC's logic would not warrant rescinding the limits on commercials for children. Research offers substantial evidence pertaining to this issue.

First, given the findings that young children have difficulty distinguishing programs from advertisements, it seems unlikely that such viewers would react negatively to a substantial increase in commercials. Indeed, an increase might not be perceived at all by very young children. Even if an increase was perceived, there is little reason to expect that children would dislike it because of their favourable attitudes toward commercials. Positive attitudes toward television advertising are negatively related with age. However, the age at which children actually develop a negative attitude toward commercials, if in fact such a perspective evolves during childhood, has not been precisely defined. Early grade-school children generally like to watch Saturday morning commercials, while older children express ambivalent feelings at worst (Rossiter, 1977; Ward, 1972).

These considerations seem to contradict the assertion that a heavy load of commercials would encourage child-viewers to seek other program alternatives. Younger children lack the basic skills to differentiate programs from commercials, and older children are most likely to find the advertisements sufficiently appealing that they would not choose to turn off a program because of excessive commercials.

The merits of this issue are presently being weighed by the FCC. In response to the U.S. Court of Appeals order to reconsider its decision, the Commission invited comment from researchers about the need for the policies it had rescinded. The arguments described herein were presented to the FCC in a brief prepared on behalf of the American Psychological Association (Kunkel, 1988b). A final ruling in the case is expected sometime in 1989.

CONCLUSION

The relationship between researchers and policy-makers is rarely a simple one. In the case of children's advertising regulation, research has played a meaningful role until the FCC's recent deregulatory action. At that point, the agency apparently chose to rely on its marketplace philosophy to determine appropriate public policy independent of the relevant psychological evidence. That course has now been corrected by the courts and this research must now be weighed in tandem with other factors. That does not necessarily mean the policy outcome will be altered in this case. But the precedent of forcing policy-makers to consider clearly relevant psychological findings in crafting their decisions is an important one. The interests of children will be best served when policy decisions are informed by empirical findings.

REFERENCES

Action for Children's Television v. FCC, 821 F.2d 741 (D.C. Cir. 1987).

Adler, R., Friedlander, B., Lesser, G., Meringoff, L., Robertson, T., Rossiter, J., & Ward, S. (1977). *Research on the effects of television advertising on children.* Washington, DC: U.S. Government Printing Office.

Atkin, C. (1982). Television advertising and socialization to consumer roles. In D. Pearl, E. Bouthilet, & J. Lazar (Eds.), *Television and behavior,* Volume 2, 191-200. Washington, DC: U.S. Government Printing Office.

Atkin, C., & Gibson, W. (1978). *Children's nutrition learning from television advertising.* Unpublished manuscript, Michigan State University.

Bandura, A. (1977). *Social learning theory.* Englewood Cliffs,   NJ: Prentice-Hall.

Blatt, J., Spencer, L., & Ward, S. (1972). A cognitive developmental study of children's reactions to television advertising. In E. Rubinstein, G. Comstock, & J. Murray (Eds.), *Television and social behavior,* Volume 4, 452-467. Washington, DC: U.S. Government Printing Office.

Butter, E., Popovich, P., Stackhouse, R., & Garner, R. (1981). Discrimination of television programs and commercials by preschool children. *Journal of Advertising Research, 21,* 53-56.

Federal Communication Commission. (1974). Children's television programs: Report and policy statement. *Federal Register, 39,* 39396-39409.

Federal Communications Commission. (1984). Revision of programming and commercialization policies, ascertainment requirements, and program log requirements for commercial television stations. *Federal Register, 49,* 33588-33620.

Flavell, J. (1977). *Cognitive development.* Englewood Cliffs,   NJ: Prentice-Hall.

Fowler, M., & Brenner, D. (1982). A marketplace approach to broadcast regulation. *Texas Law Review, 60,* 207-257.

Huston, A., Watkins, B., & Kunkel, D. (1989). Public policy and children's television. *American Psychologist, 44,* 424-433.

Kunkel, D. (1988a). Children and host-selling television commercials. *Communication Research, 15,* 71-92.

Kunkel, D, (1988b). *Children's television commercialization:Policies and practices.* Testimony to the FCC on behalf of the American Psychological Association. Washington, DC: APA.

Kunkel, D. (1989). From a raised eyebrow to a turned back: The FCC and children's product-related programming. *Journal of Communication, 38* (4), 90-108.

Lyle, J., & Hoffman, H. (1972). Explorations in patterns of television viewing by preschool-age children. In E. Rubinstein, G. Comstock, & J. Murray (Eds.), *Television and social behavior,* Volume 4 (pp. 257-273). Washington, DC: U.S. Government Printing Office.

Murray, J., & Kippax, S. (1979). From the early window to the late show: International trends in the study of television's impact on children and adults. In L. Berkowitz (Ed.), *Advances in experimental social psychology,* Volume 12, 253-320. New York: Academic Press.

Palmer, E., & McDowell, C. (1979). Program/commercial separators in children's television programming. *Journal of Communication, 29 ,* 197-201.

Roberts, D. (1983). Children and commercials: Issues, evidence, interventions. *Prevention in Human Services, 2,* 19-35.

Rossiter, J. (1977). Reliability of a short test measuring children's attitudes toward T V commercials. *Journal of Consumer Research, 3,* 179-184.

Rowland, W. (1983). *The politics of TV violence: Policy uses of communication research.* Beverly Hills: Sage.

Shantz, C. (1975). The development of social cognition. In E. Hetherington (Ed.), *Review of child development research,* Volume 5, 257-323. Chicago: University of Chicago Press.

Stutts, M., Vance, D., & Hudleson, S. (1981). Program- commercial separators in children's television: Do they help a child tell the difference between "Bugs Bunny" and the "Quik Rabbit?" *Journal of Advertising, 10,* 16-25.

Ward, S. (1972). Effects of television advertising on children and adolescents. In E. Rubinstein, G. Comstock, & J. Murray (Eds.), *Television and social behavior,* Volume 4, 432-451. Washington, DC: U.S. Government Printing Office.

Ward, S., Reale, G., & Levinson, D. (1972). Children's perceptions, explanations, and judgments of television advertising: A further exploration. In E. Rubinstein, G. Comstock, & J. Murray (Eds.), *Television and social behavior,* Volume 4, 468-490. Washington, DC: U.S. Government Printing Office.

Ward, S. & Wackman, D. (1973). Children's information processing of television advertising. In P. Clarke (Ed.), *New models for mass communication research.* Beverly Hills: Sage.

Ward, S., Wackman, D., & Wartella, E. (1977). *How children learn to buy: The development of consumer information- processing skills.* Beverly Hills: Sage.

Wartella, E. (1980). Individual differences in children's responses to television advertising. In E. Palmer & A. Dorr (Eds.), *Children and the faces of television: Teaching, violence, selling.* 307-322. New York: Academic Press.

Social Applications and Issues in Psychology
R.C. King and J.K. Collins (editors)
©Elsevier Science Publishers B.V. (North-Holland), 1989

OPERANT BEHAVIOURAL MEASUREMENT OF TELEVISION WATCHING

Masashi Ida

Tokiwa University, Japan

In order to examine TV watching behaviour, it is necessary to measure spontaneous responses the viewer emits to watch programs. In the first experiment a modified conjugate reinforcement method was applied, using microcomputers set up in homes of subjects. Results showed that even though a certain channel is tuned in, operant TV watching behaviour is quite different. Another experiment was conducted to estimate how many programs on different channels a subject could follow on the same television set. Results showed that the limit was three channels in recognizing details of programs, but subjects could recount stories of programs on three channels as well as stories on two channels.

It has become important to study and discuss a new concept of people's television watching behaviour, which has become different from that in the past. For instance, some communication researchers report that viewers change from one channel to another quite often now that many channels are offered on television (Heeter and Greenberg,1985; Kaplan,1985). Other researchers say this channel changing or flicking tendency is due to the fact that people do not watch programs as intensely or seriously as in the past (Ishikawa,1986).

However, it may be explained that people have become so familiarized with television watching that they have gained an ability to watch more than one program shown simultaneously by changing channels continuously on the same television set. Furthermore, people may have changed channels frequently before, but their behaviour may not have been observed because there were no methods of recording such behaviour. For instance, program ratings in Japan, similar to those using the A.C. Nielsen Company's Storage Instantaneous Audimeters, monitor changing of channels in units of 60 seconds and cannot record switching at a more frequent pace.

Program ratings today are usually taken by installing the audimeters in homes to record which channels were tuned in, or by having viewers keep diaries on what they watched on television (Smith, 1985; Summers, et al., 1978). Such conventional methods used in studying TV viewing behaviour posed problems in that we cannot know if the audience was actually watching the program even when a certain channel is recorded on the audimeter. Concerning the diary method, the subjects might remember differently when they actually answer the questionnaires from what they actually felt when watching the program, or their answers may be biased, influenced by social factors.

To overcome these problems involving the conventional survey methods, a number of psychological methods have been devised to examine how people actually watch TV programs. For instance, psychophysiological reactions, like galvanic skin response, heart beat, pupil sizes and brain waves have been measured. Such psychophysiological reactions are involuntary actions or respondent behaviours. Therefore, methods of measuring these reactions only focus on the passive aspect of TV watching behaviour.

However, our behaviour incorporates voluntary or active elements and TV watching behaviour is no exception. A method of recording the active and voluntary side of TV watching behaviour was devised by O.R. Lindsley in 1962. Lindsley used a conjugate reinforcement method which was similar to the audio-meter principle used by Bekesy (1960). Lindsley's method focused on measurement of voluntary aspects of TV watching.

An experiment was conducted to develop a method of measuring voluntary aspects of TV watching behaviour in every day setting, by applying Lindsley's method. Another experiment was conducted to study the channel changing behaviour and viewer's capability to follow a number of programs on different channels.

Experiment 1

Method A modified conjugate reinforcement method was applied, using microcomputers set up in homes of subjects.

Subjects The subjects were five undergraduate students living alone.

Procedure Microcomputers, Sharp X-1, programmed with experimental procedures and recording means, were used for the experiment. The computers were capable of showing ordinary TV programs on their screen. A remote controller with two switches was connected to the microcomputer. One switch was for turning on the picture on the screen and the other for choosing a channel. Seven channels were available, each showing an actual TV program. No observation was made concerning a subject's watching a video tape on one of the channels.

The subject was able to watch the program for 10 seconds after pressing the picture switch. If the subject did not react within this 10 seconds, a bluish-grey color was superimposed on the screen and the picture could not be seen. If the subject pressed the picture button again, the picture would reappear on the screen. The 10 minute period became reset from the point of each reaction. Therefore, the subject had to press the switch at least once every 10 seconds in order to watch a continued picture.

By pressing the channel switch, the subject was able to change channels according to a set order. Volume of the sound of the programs was kept at a level appropriate for each subject. The records of subjects' watching behaviour were taken at the apartments of the subjects.

Results

Typical results are shown in terms of channel selection and cumulative records of responses to the picture switch (Fig. 1 & 2). The upper portion shows when and which channel was selected for viewing. This is an equivalent to data taken by audiénce ratings recorded with meters attached to television sets.

The middle figure shows the state of the picture. For instance, when the record takes a concave figure, it shows that the picture did not appear on the screen even though the television set was switched on. The bottom record shows the cumulative record of responses to the picture switch. The cumulative record shows the total numbers of responses as a function of time. Therefore, the slope of the cumulative record indicates the rate of responding to picture switch.

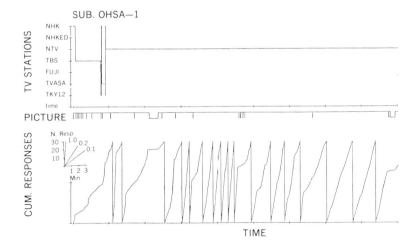

The upper section of Figure 1 shows the subject's channel selection. The middle section shows the state of the TV screen. Downward record shows that the picutre is off. The bottom part of the figure shows cumulative record of responses emitted in order to watch programs.

Figure 2 shows channel selection and operant TV watching behaviour on another occasion.

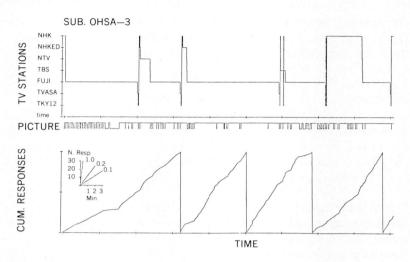

Discussion

As the results of cumulative record and the state of the picture screen show, even though a certain channel is selected, the way the subject is actually watching the programs varied. By using this method, it was possible to measure the exact length of time subjects were watching programs, which was not possible using conventional rating methods.

This method presents an operational definition of voluntary aspects of TV watching; that is, the method directly measures the behaviour emitted by subjects in order to watch television. Having subjects respond to switches does disturb natural TV watching behaviour, but it is indispensable in measuring voluntary aspects of the behaviour. The extra task of pressing the switch is not a great trouble as one might imagine. An experiment has shown that subjects could maintain high rate of response, such as a response per second, for a period of three hours without much fatigue (Ida, 1983). This method focuses on measuring individual behaviour, but solutions must be found to adopt the conjugate reinforcement method to situations where more than one person is watching television together.

Although this method may seem similar to Lazarsfeld's Program Analyzer, the functions of subjects' reactions are quite different. The Program Analyzer does not directly measure behaviour emitted to watch television (Lindsley, 1962). Nielsen's Person Meter and AGB Research's People Meter (Lu & Kiewit, 1987; Smith, 1985), which record who had the television switched on, are equipped with no operational definition of voluntary TV watching behaviour.

Because microcomputers are becoming popular even in ordinary homes, it may be possible to conduct TV watching surveys using this method rather than the conventional rating methods.

Experiment 2

Experiment 2 was conducted to estimate how many programs on different channels a subject could follow by changing channels.

Method

Subjects. A total of 42 university students.

Procedure. The subjects were instructed to select a channel by manipulating a switch for channels, and another switch for a signal detecting task. The subjects were able to change one program to another by pressing on the channel switch.

The subjects were divided into four groups, according to the number of channels they must follow. Group A could only watch one channel, and were instructed to watch carefully because they would be tested later.

Group B could also watch only one channel and at the same time were assigned a signal detecting task. The task required a subject to press the task button, by which the screen switches to a task screen showing a three digit random number signal. If the signal was the right one, 777, the subject was given 20 points, but if it used other numbers, the subject lost 2 points. In five seconds the screen returned to the picture showing the program the subject had been watching before pressing the task switch. The subject was instructed to gain as many points as possible.

The signal was scheduled according to a variable interval of 15 seconds with limited hold of 5 seconds (VI15", LH5"). This means that the right signal, 777, comes at random intervals averaging once every 15 seconds. The subject does not know when it is time for the 777 to appear, so he or she will have to press the task switch occasionally to hit on the right signal. It was assumed that the subject would do so when it did not interfere with following of the TV program. The signal detecting task was assigned to the subject in order to estimate when and how much extra attention the subject can spare for watching other things beside the actual program.

Group C had to watch two programs by switching between two channels and was in addition assigned to the above signal detecting task. Group D had three programs on three channels and the signal detecting task.

After the subjects watched the programs, they were asked to reply to 20 yes-or-no questions about the contents of the programs (content test). The subjects were also asked to rate on a scale of five their subjective comprehension and their subjective feeling of satisfaction of having watched television (subjective rating). Moreover, the subjects were asked to give verbal accounts of the plot of each program, which were tape recorded. Transcriptions of these reports were shown to five subjects, who were asked to evaluate correctness of the reports on a scale of five (evaluation of reproduction).

Twenty-five-minute video-recorded programs, including action dramas for youths, were used for the experiment. Each group watched two different sets of programs. Programs No.1, 2 and 3 - three stories which conclude in 25 minutes of a rerun program (same set) - were shown to Group D during a session, followed by Programs No. 4, 5 and 6 – three completely different programs (different set) – in another session on another day. The order of sessions was counterbalanced within each group.

Results

Results are shown in Table 1. The results of the content test show that there were no differences in test scores between Groups A and B, indicating that having the task did not influence comprehension of the program. This is because subjects could divide attention between the task and the program without it interfering with understanding of the story. However, with groups having more than one channel to watch, the score concerning contents of the story declined linearly. Group D, which had three channels and the task, scored close to 50 points out of 100, the same as the chance level (Fig. 3). Analysis of variance tests showed that the factor of numbers of channels was highly significant.

TABLE 1
Results of Experiment 2. Relation between the number of channels and comprehension.

Group	A	B	C	D
Content Test Score	89.8((6.13)	89.5(9.16)	71.4(14.3)	53.3(16.5)
Number of Choosing Task	---	87.1(55.3)	51.1(44.9)	32.2(30.4)
Subjective Comprehension Rating [a]	1.38(.52)	1.41(.59)	.275(1.33)	-.175(1.31)
Evaluation of Story Reproduction [b]	3.13(.62)	3.26(.90)	2.01(.66)	1.96(.75)

Note. Standard Deviation in ( )
    a,b were rated on a five point scale. a ranged from -2 to 2 and b ranged from 1 to 5.
    The higher the value, the greater the evaluation.

Figure 3. Relation between the content test score and number of channels

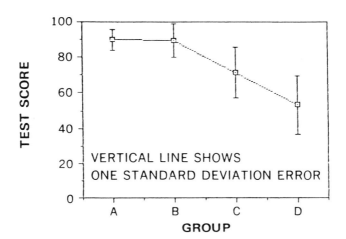

The rate of the subjects choosing the signal detecting task decreased significantly as the number of channels increased, though there were large variances. In conventional experiments involving similar distracting tasks, a distracting object was presented beside the television screen and the subjects reactions to the distracter were observed (Lesser, 1974). By using the distracting task in this experiment, it is possible to standardize the distracter and is easier to make measurements.

Concerning evaluation of reproduction of the stories, the results show that reports of Group A and B were rated higher than those of groups C and D. The above tendencies were observed in the results of the subjective rating in understanding of programs and satisfaction ratings. Channels were chosen almost equally in terms of time.

Discussion

In order to understand channel changing behaviour, it is necessary to consider not only methods of survey, but also to examine a person's ability to follow stories on two or more channels. Some researchers have noted that a viewer acquires this ability through his or her experience in watching television (Greenfield, 1984).

From the results of the content test scores, we can estimate that a person can follow details of only three or fewer programs on different channels at the same time. However, the subjective ratings show that subjects think they keep track of three channels just as well as two channels. This is backed up by the evaluation of reproduction of stories. They also report satisfaction of having watched each program even though they had to switch from one channel to another. People's constant channel changing behaviour may be due to the fact that they do not take television seriously, but it may also be due to their striving to gather information by changing channels.

Although further surveys in ordinary settings are called for, it is important to take into consideration the voluntary aspects of TV watching behaviour and ability to watch a number of programs. This is so whether conducting basic communication studies of television viewing or when surveying rating methods on a more practical level.

AUTHOR NOTES

Experiment 1 was conducted in part with grants from Hideo Yoshida Memorial Fund in 1986. Experiment 2 was run with the help of K. Wakabayashi.

Address requests for reprints to Masashi Ida, Department of Psychology, Tokiwa University, 1-430, Miwa, Mito, Ibaraki Pref., 310 Japan.

REFERENCES

Békésy, G. von. (1960). *Experiments in Hearing* (E.G. Wever, Trans. & Ed.). New York: McGraw-Hill.

Greenfield, P. M. (1984). *Mind and Media: The effects of television computers and video games*. Great Britain: Fontana.

Heeter, C., & Greenberg, B. S. (1985). Profiling the Zappers. *Journal of Advertising Research, 25,* 15-19.

Ida, M. (1983). *Measurement of Operant TV watching behaviour* (Report No. 16, 19-31). (in Japanese). Tokyo, Yoshida Hideo Memorial Foundation.

Ishikawa,H. (1986, No.12). ta-channel CATV to shichou koudou no henyou [Cable Television and changing Television Watching Behaviour in USA]. *Housou Kenkyuu to Chousa [The NHK monthly report on Broadcast Research]*, 22-32,(in Japanese).

Kaplan, B. M. (1985). Zapping - The Real Issue is Communication. *Journal of Advertising Research, 25,* 2, 9-12.

Lesser, G. S. (1974). *Children and Television.* Random House.

Lindsley, O. R. (1962). A Behavioural Measure of television viewing. *Journal of Advertising Research, 2,* 2-12.

Lu, D., & Kiewit, D. A. (1987). Passive People Meters: A First Step. *Journal of Advertising Research,27,* 9-14.

Smith, F. L. (1985). *Perspectives on Radio and Television: Telecommunication in the United States* (2nd ed.). New York, Harper & Row.

Summers, H. B., Summers, R. E., & Pennybacker, J. H. (1978). *Broadcasting and the Public.* (2nd ed.). Belmont, CA, Wadsworth.

Social Applications and Issues in Psychology
R.C. King and J.K. Collins (editors)
©Elsevier Science Publishers B.V. (North-Holland), 1989

ASSOCIATION, IMITATION, AND SYNTHESIS AS COMMUNICATION STRATEGIES IN ADVERTISING ART

Fairfid M. Caudle

The College of Staten Island, USA

Advertising art has long been a selling tool. However, while there is an extensive body of research literature concerned with the effectiveness of verbal components in magazine advertising, relatively little work has been done to determine the role of visual factors (Bettman, 1986). Rossiter and Percy (1983) have reviewed the relatively few studies pertaining to static and dynamic pictorial stimuli and have provided a model of information processing as it pertains to visual stimuli, among other topics, but have not addressed the role of aesthetic values. Caudle (1989) has provided a taxonomic exploration of art forms that are frequently incorporated into magazine advertisements, suggesting a number of issues requiring further research and relating aesthetic factors in advertising art to hypothetical cognitive mechanisms that may affect memorability and persuasiveness. The present paper provides a further development of this discussion together with additional examples.

THE ROLE OF ASSOCIATION IN ADVERTISING ART

One major goal of magazine advertising is to establish desirable and distinctive associations for products so that consumers will distinguish them from others, remember them, and buy them. It has only recently been the case that memory strategies in advertising, as distinct from, for example, copywriting techniques, have received systematic attention. Alesandrini (1983) has reviewed strategies promoting visual and organizational memory, and Caudle (1988a) has provided a taxonomy of the associative strategies frequently employed in magazine advertising. When magazine advertisements employ associative strategies that are primarily visual in nature, the product is usually presented together with an object or setting selected for the associations it is likely to evoke in the reader. The intended association may be based on an existing similarity with the product, or on some contrasting characteristic. Where there are few existing conceptual links between the product and other advertising content, it is nevertheless the case that the contiguous pairing of the product with unrelated objects is an approach often utilized to establish the desired associations for the product.

The range of objects that can be paired with products is indeed extensive. However, the selection of artistic objects to create desirable associations for products is particularly attractive to advertisers because works of art are already recognized by many magazine readers. In addition, many art works have connotations of prestige and status. Included among the art forms incorporated into advertisements for their associative value are recognized works and original works commissioned for the advertisement. Associative value is not limited, however, to the art itself; objects themselves associated with art, such as artists' tools, provide additional routes to association with art.

ILLUSTRATING ADVERTISING COPY WITH RECOGNIZED WORKS OF ART.

One trend that has become increasingly apparent in magazine advertising is the selection of well-known works of art to illustrate advertising copy, although the degree of relatedness between the chosen work and the advertising copy varies considerably. One advertisement in which a well-known painting was selected because it depicted objects similar to the product is an advertisement for crystal that reproduces Manet's A Bar at the Folies-Bergere. In the painting, a blond woman behind the mirrored bar gazes at a customer, reflected in the mirror. On the bar are crystal glasses ready for use in serving champagne and other drinks. The advertisement's caption, "Cabaret by Manet. Crystal by Saint-Louis," leads the reader to compare the crystal shown in the painting with representations of the product, which employs a pattern resembling that in the painted crystal. In this way, the product is given the valuable association of possibly being the same type of crystal painted by Manet.

In other examples, the connection between a product and a work of art reproduced in the advertisement may be less direct but may nonetheless provide an appropriate associative context. An advertisement for a prepared rice product illustrated its copy with Manet's Picnic on the Grass, in which a naked woman shares a luncheon with two men and a woman. The painting provided an attention-getting illustration to support the headline, "Before Savory Classics people went to extremes to make meals interesting." In another example, an insurance company selected a detail from Edward Hick's Noah's Ark, in which many animals are lined up to enter the ark to escape the flood, to illustrate the headline, "We have a better way to deal with inclement weather." Thus, the advertisement utilized a recognized work of art to establish an association based on contrast between a problem, the consequences of flooding and its solution, insurance.

A similar approach has been followed by an advertisement for Casablanca Fans. To reinforce the caption, "What do you mean, no one looks at the ceiling?" Casablanca Fans reproduced a detail from the ceiling of the Sistine Chapel, painted by Michaelangelo. The American Cancer Society recreated a smaller, though as widely recognized, detail from the same work, the hand of God bestowing life on Adam, to accompany the suggestion to "Leave your mark on life."

In these and other examples, recognized paintings are selected that in some way illustrate the text or provide a visual focus for points made concerning the product. Although such paintings appear frequently in magazine advertisements, little is known concerning their effects on attention or memory.

In addition to paintings, well-known statues are also employed to illustrate advertising points. For example, the armless Venus de Milo appears frequently. In one instance it was reproduced in an advertisement for computer software to illustrate that "You don't have to pay an arm and a leg for demonstration software!" Similarly, it has also been depicted as if gazing longingly at a rug to illustrate the caption, "Introducing the oriental rug you'd give your right arm for." Rodin's The Thinker, another frequent choice, was utilized in an advertisement for an investment company that exhorted the reader to "Think first. Then invest." Rodin's The Kiss has also appeared in advertising. Each of these works is so well known that it is instantly recognizable. However, it is not known whether the potential effectiveness of advertisements incorporating such works is dependent on their recognizability or upon their inherent aesthetic characteristics. Advertisements could serve a valuable educational function by incorporating less widely known works of art.

COMPARISONS BETWEEN PRODUCTS AND WORKS OF ART

A second associative strategy utilizing art is to make some comparison between the work of art and the product. One form of comparison often employed is an analogy, which designates conceptual relationships between comparable objects in different categories. Since recognized works of art may already be viewed as superlatives, an advertiser wishing to establish the association that a product is superlative when compared with other products in the same category finds a potent tool in the use of analogies.

Such comparisons need not be between similar objects. For example, Michaelangelo's David is recognized as one of the greatest works of art ever created. The fact that Michaelangelo was an Italian artist has been utilized in advertisements that have made comparisons between the qualities of his artistry and that shown in contemporary Italian products. (Caudle, 1988b, has provided a taxonomy with numerous additional examples of the use of national and cultural symbols to provide desirable associations). The vast range of products that can be presented as superlatives through comparisons with the same work of art is illustrated with two advertisements making analogies based on the David. In one, the David is presented as comparable to an Italian brand of chocolates and, in another, to an Italian brand of condoms. The latter advertisement displayed the statue in all its glory, accompanied by the caption, "Who's better equipped than the Italians to design the world's best condoms?"

Occasionally, products related to the creation or reproduction of visual materials emphasize similarities between their use and existing works of art. For example, Kodak, a photographic company, has often employed analogies between works of art and the results to be obtained from its products. In a recent example, the appropriateness of photography as a contemporary portrait medium is established by presenting two portraits, one by Goya and one by Kodak. The advertisement combines the simultaneous use of association by contrast and similarity.Two portraits are presented side by side, Goya's Blue Boy and a photographic portrait of a young man in a blue baseball uniform. The Goya portrait illustrates the caption, "In 1770 the best way to get a great portrait was to hire a professional," and the caption under the young man's portrait notes, "Today it's still the best way."

A second example of this approach may be seen in an advertisement for a photocopier that presents a colour copy of a Raphael portrait to illustrate the caption, "Original by Raphael, copy by Sharp." An advertisement for computer graphics has depicted Leonardo da Vinci creating the Mona Lisa by using a computer; da Vinci is shown intently staring at the screen of his monitor as the model sits patiently in the background. Each of these examples has reproduced a recognized work of art to suggest that the product provides results of comparable quality.

PORTRAYING THE PRODUCT AS A WORK OF ART

Comparisons between products and recognized works may further focus the consumer's attention by presenting a product as itself being a work of art. Where the associative link is a direct one, an advertisement may display the product together with an assertion that the product constitutes art. One example presented carpets as "paintings for your floor." Similarly, a travel advertisement utilized hand-made quilts to illustrate the point that "In North Carolina, some of our greatest works of art never hang in a museum." The quilts are shown on a clothesline behind a barn.

When the relationship between a product and art is less obvious, the verbal copy may support a claim that the product is a form of art by including reproductions of familiar works. A brochure for French spirits and champagne suggested that "French spirits and champagne are French art" and invited the reader to "picture yourself with a glass of French art." The brochure was illustrated by well-known Impressionist paintings. A more distant association was made in a travel advertisement that reproduced a Van Gogh landscape to illustrate the point that "most people only get to visit great works of art. The Dutch get to live in one." In this instance, the advertisement built on the association that a visit to Holland will enable the tourist to experience first hand the same scenes that have long inspired artists.

PRESENTATION OF ORIGINAL ART

One way in which a company's corporate image may be enhanced is to commission original works of art that are then reproduced in the company's advertisements. In a recent example, Air France presented a painting entitled The Fine Art of Flying, in which a geometric pattern crossing back and forth across the canvas suggested flight paths of planes across the sea. Numerous additional examples could be provided of original art, commissioned by companies to enhance their images, which are thematically related to the products or services of the company. Original art commissioned for advertisements has ranged widely; a textiles company commissioned paintings of rooms in which the furnishings utilized its fabrics while a newspaper, the Phoenix Gazette, reinforced its name and image by commissioning a painting entitled Phoenix in Flight.

ASSOCIATION WITH ARTISTS' TOOLS

So well established is the association between art and enhanced status that it is sufficient merely to include objects that are themselves associated with works of art; this might be viewed as a form of second order association. For example, artists' tools such as palette, brushes or frames are often employed to establish positive connotations for products. An artist's palette has been used to illustrate the range of colours occurring in products ranging from tissues to autumn foliage. A travel advertisement for Texas invited the reader to "Stay in a country where the art is tasteful and the masters still work with brushes." However, the illustration is not of art in the usual sense but of barbecued ribs being brushed with sauce. Finally, the simple expedient of surrounding a product or scene with an ornate frame presents it as having the same status and value as a recognized work of art. Such an approach has been widely employed to sell products as diverse as clothing, hotel interiors, and pickles.

Each of the preceding examples has illustrated the use of art to establish desirable associations. Often, the advertisement has done little more than to pair the product with a work of art, or with something itself associated with art. In many examples, existing works of art have been reproduced essentially unchanged. However, advertisements have also provided a medium for visual representations that carry these associative processes still further, either by imitating recognized works or by employing classic forms and styles.

IMITATION OF CLASSIC STYLES AND FORMS IN ADVERTISING ART

Imitations of recognized styles of art. Just as imitation and parody appear often in works of literature and music, so also do they appear in the visual arts. In advertising, artistic styles are imitated when they provide beneficial associations. Such benefits may result from the use of art that suggests a particular era as well as art that elicits appropriate emotional or cognitive responses. Among the most frequent styles to be imitated in advertising art are Italian Renaissance, Impressionist and Surrealist, although examples could be given of virtually every major period and form in art.

One example of the use of a generic Italian Renaissance style can be found in a painting, appearing in a French magazine, designed to promote financial contributions to an organization dedicated to raising money to preserve the city of Venice. The headline, "Sauvons Venise," (`Save Venice') was illustrated by a portrait that, at first glance, appeared to be a Renaissance painting. However, a closer look indicated that the person portrayed was wearing a scuba diving tube. The advertisement thus graphically portrayed the potential consequences if attention is not paid to the danger that the city of Venice may slowly sink into the sea.

Frequently imitated is the Impressionist style, because of its appropriateness in providing romantic associations. For example, the style that Degas employed in painting ballerinas has been imitated in Nina Ricci advertisements, also portraying a ballerina in hazy, evocative tones.

Surrealist artists and their predecessors have had many imitations and allusions in advertising art. Among the artists whose work has influenced the creation of modern versions is Guiseppe Arcimboldo (1537-1593), who is known for his portraits constructed from objects having a particular theme. For example, his portrait of Spring creates a portrait from flowers, while the face of Summer is fashioned from vegetables. Although the pervasive influence of Arcimboldo on modern art has been documented (Gruppo Editoriale Fabbri, 1987), his influence on advertising art has not been described. Modern versions of his portraits have appeared in contexts as diverse as an advertisement inviting summer travel to France, in which a face made of fruits and wearing a beret illustrated the caption "Summer's Bounty Personified," to an advertisement for salad dressing, in which a face made of salad greens illustrated how "Kikkoman adds personality to your meals." In a minimalist version of an Arcimboldo construction, Bertolli Salad Dressing employed vegetables to create smiling or frowning faces, but suggested the face through providing lettuce hair, tomato eyes and a mouth that was either happy or sad according to the direction in which a stalk of green onion was curved.

Another artist who anticipated the Surrealist movement was the painter Hieronymus Bosch (ca. 1450-1516), known for his bizarre imagery and dream-like themes (see Snyder 1973 for further discussion of his works). Heironymus Bosch's triptych Garden of Earthly Delights is filled with grotesque figures, bizarre animals, distortions of size and other constructions, including giant birds, among other creatures. The eerie and dream-like quality of this painting is suggested, in part, by an advertisement for Karastan carpets. Portrayed are bird-people in formal dress, walking through an archway into a large room. The caption notes, "Some of us have more finely developed nesting instincts than others." The advertisement depicts a startling and vivid image of bird-people to convey the idea that birds and people share nesting instincts.

The surrealist style of the twentieth century artist Magritte is widely imitated in advertising. For example, his Portrait of Madame Recamier (1951), itself a spoof of an well-known portrait of a woman in empire-style dress reclining on a chaise, presents a coffin (bent into a reclining position) on a similar chaise. In a modern version, a wine company has replaced the coffin with a bunch of grapes to illustrate the headline, "The confessions of a one-grape wine."

Magritte's man in a bowler hat, who appeared in many paintings, was adopted by Gore-Tex Fabric for a series of Magritte-like paintings that illustrate how the waterproof fabric "keeps you warm and dry regardless of what falls out of the sky," the caption for a painting of the man being pelted with cats and dogs. Another advertisement in this series presented the bowler-hatted man and companion in modern rain hats and coats, surrounded by falling buckets, to illustrate how the fabric "keeps you warm and dry even when it's raining buckets."

Finally, one notable example of the imitation of a sculptural style should be mentioned. Black Label Scotch presented a Calder-like mobile that incorporated a representation of the product to illustrate the caption, "The upwardly mobile."

CLASSIC FORMS IN ADVERTISING ART.

Among the forms utilized by advertising art are, not surprisingly, the still life, landscape, portrait and abstract composition. Advertising artists continue to employ the same subjects that have attracted painters for centuries. For example, products as diverse as gin, coffee, wine and ceramic ware have been presented in the form of a still life. Cosmetic advertisements frequently utilize paintings of women engaged in such familiar activities as brushing hair or looking into a mirror that have often appeared in museum counterparts. A continuing favourite with advertisers is the creation of reclining portraits; many have suggested classic paintings by Renoir, Goya and others. One interesting addition to the twentieth-century gallery, however, has been the creation of the product portrait, such as the series of portraits commissioned from Andy Warhol and other artists for Absolut Vodka.

SYNTHESIS IN ADVERTISING ART

One technique frequently employed in advertising art is what the author has termed "synthetic" art that alters or reproduces a recognized work of art in order to incorporate the product (Caudle, 1989). Both the Mona Lisa and Grant Wood's American Gothic have had a number of reincarnations in advertising, as have paintings by Renoir, Degas, Seurat and others. Recently recreated paintings include Monet's 1899 Water Lilies - Harmony in Green. The original painting portrays a bridge over the water lily pond that appears often in Monet's paintings. In the modern version, a diamond advertisement, a romantically involved couple has been placed on the bridge; however, the details and style are similar to the original. Another recent recreation was of the 1955 painting by Balthus entitled Figure in Front of a Mantel. Its modern version appeared in a lingerie advertisement. The nude model in the original was replaced by one wearing the undergarment being advertised; however, details such as posture and position were virtually identical.

By incorporating a product into a well-known painting, synthetic art simultaneously provides a visual incongruity that may attract further attention as well as providing a pictorial association. The mnemonic value of such characteristics of visual stimuli has yet to be investigated.

A FINAL WORD

Each example noted in this paper has utilized art as a communicative medium. However, little is known concerning the effectiveness of such advertisements or, in fact, what is communicated. It is hoped that this paper will both call attention to, and stimulate empirical research concerning, the role of association, imitation, and synthesis as communication strategies in advertising art.

1 This paper is an adaptation and elaboration of material originally presented in "Advertising art: Cognitive mechanisms and research issues," published in Cognitive and Affective Responses to Advertising, edited by Patricia Cafferata and Alice Tybout (Lexington, MA: Lexington Books, D.C. Heath and Company. Copyright 1989, Lexington Books). It has been adapted with the permission of the publisher.

CORRESPONDENCE

The College of Staten Island, The City University of New York, Staten Island, New York, USA   10301

REFERENCES

Alesandrini, K. L. (1983).   Strategies that influence memory for advertising communications.   In R. J. Harris (Ed.), *Information processing research in advertising* (pp. 65-82).   Hillsdale, NJ: Erlbaum.

Bettman, J. R. (1986). Consumer psychology.   *Annual Review of Psychology, 37*, 257-289.

Caudle, F. M. (1989). Advertising art: Cognitive mechanisms and research issues.   In P. Cafferata and A. Tybout (Eds), *Cognitive and affective responses to advertising* (pp. 161-217).   Lexington, MA: D.C. Heath, Lexington Books.

Caudle, F. M. (1988a). Associative strategies in magazine advertising: An illustrated taxonomy. In L. F. Alwitt (Ed.), *1987 Proceedings of the Division of Consumer Psychology* (pp. 84-91). Washington, DC: Division of Consumer Psychology, American Psychological Association.

Caudle, F. M. (1988b, August). National and cultural symbols in magazine advertisements. Paper presented at the Ninth International Congress of the International Association for Cross-Cultural Psychology. Newcastle, New South Wales, Australia.

Gruppo Editoriale Fabbri (1987). *The Arcimboldo effect.* London: Thames and Hudson.

Rossiter, J. R. & Percy, L. (1983). Visual communication in advertising. In R. J. Harris (Ed.), *Information processing research in advertising.* Hillsdale, NJ: Erlbaum.

Snyder, S., (Ed.) (1973). *Bosch in perspective.* Englewood Cliffs, NJ: Prentice-Hall.

Section 4

COMMUNITY ISSUES

Social Applications and Issues in Psychology
R.C. King and J.K. Collins (editors)
Elsevier Science Publishers B.V. (North-Holland), 1989

COMMUNITY ATTITUDES TOWARDS WATER PRICING POLICIES AND DOMESTIC WATER QUALITY STANDARDS

Geoffrey J. Syme and **Katrina D. Williams**

CSIRO, Western Australia

While much research has been undertaken on the physical and biological aspects of water policy, little consideration has been given to the social and psychological aspects of planning. Two important policy areas where social psychological information would provide a useful input to policy are those of water quality and pricing. With increased urban development has come increased demands for expensive development of additional water distribution systems. This has led to water authorities considering methods of optimising the provision of water services within existing economic constraints. Pricing is an important component of ensuring economically efficient planning, involving complex equity and social considerations. In setting water quality standards, Australian water authorities have generally adopted those provided by the World Health Organisation. There is a need to understand how planners' views coincide with those of the community, to ensure that the costs of providing "pure" water are worth the benefits as perceived by the community. This paper reports results from continuing psychological research into formulation of quality and pricing policies. Suggestions for future psychological research priorities in this field are also made.

Despite the importance of water and water supplies for the development of various countries, its management is an issue not often studied by psychologists. This is regardless of the fact that in many regions it is a limited commodity and competition between various sectors of the community for its use is increasing. Community values will become paramount determinants in deciding how water will be allocated and managed.

The relatively small psychological literature in water management reveals that it has largely followed the pattern evident in the earlier energy crisis-generated literature. This literature concentrated largely on assessing householders' attitudes and their relationship to conservation behaviour and devising successful interventions to encourage conservation (e.g., Geller, Winett &Everett, 1982).

A similar priority has been given to understanding household water conservation (see Syme & Seligman, 1987 for review). Research has focused on identifying those attitudes which correlate with individual conservation behaviour (e.g., Hamilton, 1983), evaluating the potential effectiveness of publicity campaigns on encouraging water conservation (e.g. Hamilton, 1985) and the effects of feedback and rebates on water use (e.g., Winkler, 1982). While such research has capitalised on the research tradition of energy research it has tended to lose the differences in significance of the two resources for householders. Firstly, the bulk of water resource issues centre around the fact that it is primarily a limited renewable resource. Water can only be "manufactured" by expensive desalination. On the other hand energy is more often derived from the combustion of nonrenewable resources. Renewable energy resources play a far less prominent role in overall planning, although there are exceptions. The fact that water is renewable is likely to play a very important role in governing householders' attitudes to conservation and other policy issues.

Apart from the general perceptions of water as a renewable resource it also has other characteristics that make the personal psychology of water different from the personal psychology of energy. For example, the effects of water conservation are often not immediate as is the case for energy use. Not using water now may result in the death of a plant or garden at some unknown point in the future if unpredicted heat stress is caused by climatic factors. If one turns down the air conditioning the effects of this action are immediately apparent.

Secondly, energy has a uniform quality while water can vary in terms of salinity, organic content, colour and so on. Finally, water can be regarded as a low cost investment in maintaining an often highly valued asset, the home garden. In fact, estimates of the garden's potential contribution to the resale value of one's home was the perception most highly correlated with consumption in a recent study, (Syme & Salerian, 1987). While a similar comment could be offered for electricity, within limits, a television or an oven do not deteriorate if not used for short periods.

At a practical research level, water also provides problems different from those of energy, even liquid fuel. For example, the pricing studies that have been pursued for electricity have largely followed the behavioural experimental paradigm relying on the concepts of feedback and rebates. In the case of water, such studies are much more difficult to relate to current pricing policies (which are seldom pay-for-use) and often provide some sort of basic allowance on the basis of welfare. Water is costed sometimes even on the basis of property values rather than usage. For some users in some cities consumption is not even metered. If you add to this the problem in providing easy access feedback for indoor and outdoor use, the operational difficulties in conducting and interpreting such studies are magnified.

In summary, there is a case for a separate research program for water as opposed to electricity or liquid fuels. The extrapolation of findings or research priorities from one resource to the other may not be justified.

Nevertheless, there is also a case for following some recent trends in energy research. Recent attention in energy research has tended to concentrate more on policy formulation and decision making (e.g., Marks & von Winterfeldt, 1984) than household attitudes towards conservation. While it is interesting in resource management to know what social perceptions are formed it is more important in both the energy and water spheres to know how people will respond to the values dilemmas facing planners. It is this new direction that psychological studies of water management must take if they are to gain maximal benefit from energy resource studies. Water policy orientated research could consider basic issues such as pricing philosophy, quality standards, allocation issues and so on.

In this paper we will review existing literature and examine the potential for psychologists to contribute to policy development in two areas; those of development of pricing policies and quality standards for provision of water supply as a public utility and for human "consumptive"purposes.

Pricing Policies and Water Quality Standards

In our region of Perth, and in many other cities in the world, water authorities are generally charged with providing the cheapest possible water for their consumers. This means that per capita demand for water is consistently rising as it is a cheap input to a consumerist life style. As a result, the demands of cities on their surrounding environments, both in ecological and social terms, are constantly mounting. Increasing provision of dams alienates catchment ecologies. City demand for water may threaten supply for nearby communities which may themselves rely on irrigated agriculture.

In the case of drinking or public water supply quality standards, most major cities adopt a standard which is usually as consistent as possible with those formulated by the World Health Organisation or a nationally based medical agency. The major benefit of such policies is that there is a low health risk for the consumer population. But these standards impose costs on the community. These costs are evident either in economic terms in treating water or in environmental terms in that human land use (including recreation) can be severely curtailed on catchments. Further, it has been suggested that the community is increasingly becoming risk averse (Rayner & Cantor, 1987) so that the standards and the cost of maintaining them, may become increasingly high as less risk is tolerated.

Another issue is the assumption in many cities that all water needs to be provided at this high standard regardless of whether it is being used for human use or garden irrigation. Many may argue that such standards are a luxury that may soon move out of reach of the average city. Others would argue that expenditure and inconvenience associated with maintaining such uniformly high standards is a basic component of quality of life for urban dwellers. Development and maintenance of water quality standards is, therefore, as much about human expectations and perceptions as objective medical or economic decision making.

Since psychologists study communities, environmental perceptions, values and decision making, they should be capable of making useful contributions to setting pricing policies and water quality standards. We could provide an extremely valuable contribution to planners by helping to clarify and resolve the values trade-offs inherent in deciding where and how our water is to be used in the future.

To facilitate discussion we have divided both the pricing and water quality research spheres into five categories: (a) Perceptual and Attitudinal Research; (b) Behavioural Research; (c) Applications of Psychological Economics; (d) Organisa-tional/Social Psychology; and (e) Community Psychology. Most of the research conducted to date can be placed in the first two categories and are of a reflective "how people respond now" variety.

PRICING POLICY RESEARCH

Pricing policy has two major components, that of its effect on demand for water and that associated with the philosophy of pricing both within and between market segments.

The first issue is one which is frequently dealt with by economists using longitudinal data or a combination of longitudinal and cross-sectional data in a regression analysis format. The price elasticity (or predicted change in demand per unit change in price) calculated, not only estimates for the planner the savings in water used by raising prices, but also the effect of this change on income received by the water authority. Rather than a conservation tool it is regarded as an input into a demand management policy.

The second issue strays into the area of ethics. Questions such as "Are restrictions a fairer mechanism than prices for governing water demand?" "Should water pricing be pay-for-use or should there be an initial welfare component which ensures basic household needs?" and "Should the cheapest sources of water always be developed first for urban needs?" can be addressed for domestic users. Cross-sectoral equity questions such as whether tariffs should be the same for all sectors of the community and whether there should be a pricing or administrative basis for the allocation of water to public or private use are also of importance in this area.

(a) Attitudinal and Perceptual Research

This research can be divided into simple attitudinal assessment of pricing as a mechanism for controlling demand, both in comparison with other mechanisms such as adoption of technological standards or restrictions or in terms of differing tariff structures (e.g., increasing price as more water is used, rebate systems and so on).

In general, in a number of Perth studies (e.g., Syme & Salerian, 1987), it has been found that pricing is regarded as the least favourable alternative for managing demand, compared with alternatives such as restrictions on lawn and garden watering. The use of rebate systems in conjunction with pricing options is, however, more popular. In the above study, 75% of the sample responses showed approval for the introduction of a rebate system. While such studies are useful for reflecting current perceptions and have probably been repeated by a number of studies in other locations, they are not sufficient in themselves to assess the community's considered opinion on policy in the demand management area. Such studies are also of a routine nature and do not contribute to our general understanding of water use. Nevertheless they do provide a useful starting point for considering social perceptions.

(b) Behavioural Research

One point that might be generalised from these studies and that may have significance for policy, is the public acceptance of rebates. In an experimental study of the effects of rebates in Perth, Winkler (1982) offered consumers one dollar per kilolitre saved as compared to their weighted weekly average consumption for summer. The rebate was calculated on the marginal cost savings to the water authority of a kilolitre of water at that time of the year. Despite substantial rebates being possible to individuals, the rebates resulted in no observed effect. Further, both in this and a series of studies in the USA (Butram and Geller, 1981, Erickson and Geller, 1981) no effects on consumption were observed for usage feedback.

The finding that rebates were not successful motivators of change in use of water is,perhaps, not surprising given the findings of attitudinal work in Perth about the same time. This research indicated that social and citizenship reasons were greater motivators of conservation than potential monetary savings (Kantola, Syme & Nesdale, 1983).

The reasons advanced by Winkler for the lack of effect of rebates included the low value of the rebate as compared with investment in gardening and the fact that the study was conducted during a cool summer. Participants in this study suggested that they may have responded to rebates if there had been evidence of water shortage. Money as a motivator may therefore interact with environmental ethics in determining its effectiveness in modifying consumption. Winkler's findings are, however, compatible with the econometric studies conducted throughout the world showing that the price elasticity of water is generally low.

A more recent study evaluating the effects of rebates on encouraging water-conserving garden design in Mesa, Arizona has been more positive. It showed that offering a small rebate on a fee paid for a building permit, if a desert style garden was adopted, was cost-effective in encouraging both desert gardens and water conservation (Agthe, Garcia & Goodnough, 1986-87).

More comprehensive rebate studies are therefore required. Perhaps rebate systems can be successfully applied to a number of water-consuming activities (e.g., adoption of dual flush toilets, restricted shower flows and so on). As new sources of water become more expensive, rebates may be a useful way by which efficiency, supposedly produced by pay-for-use water systems, can be introduced in a palatable form. The evidence provided by the current rebate studies does not allow us to make this judgement.

Further research on billing feedback may also be useful. Currently most water authorities (at least in Australia) bill their customers on a six monthly or a yearly basis. Perhaps more frequent billing with more readily accessible feedback on consumption may at least create the climate for such feedback to be an effective demand management tool.

(c) Psychological Economics

To date, the little research in this area has concentrated exclusively on the development of contingent valuation techniques to establish household responsive- ness to price. Contingent valuation techniques have been increasingly used by economists and others to assess the value of commodities that are usually not part of the market economy (e.g., valuation of nature reserves). The valuation obtained is used to provide a quantitative assessment that is readily able to be integrated with market figures.

Much literature is now available about avoiding bias in such techniques, about the role of anchoring and so on (e.g., Cummings, Brookshire & Schultze, 1986). With some exceptions in regard to anchoring effects and methodological issues, psychologists have had relatively little input to the development of these techniques, despite the obvious relevance of their skills.

The technique can frequently become relevant to estimation of price elasticity in water when adequate longitudinal data such as price change and consumption level is not available. It can also be used when the regression technique is not capable of coping with a wide variety of variables occurring at the same time as a price change. In the Perth domestic water use study (Metropolitan Water Authority, 1985) we were faced with the task of estimating price elasticity in a situation in which over the previous few years there had almost simultaneously been water restrictions, a conservation campaign, a substantial growth in the number of private bores and a change in price and tariff structure. We felt that the coincidence of all these factors precluded reasonable statistical estimation of the price variable alone.

It was decided to adopt a contingent valuation method that asked how households would respond if the price was to change (Thomas & Syme, in press). For example, householders were asked to consider a hypothetical situation in which water costs increased by x% and whether they would reduce their water usage in some way. The problem with just asking a question, however, was that respondents' knowledge of how water using behaviour relates to overall household consumption had been shown to be poor. A person may suggest that if they had to pay $x more for their water they would cut down by 30% without realising what they would have to do to achieve this level. In this case, it may be that the behavioural costs (Verhallen & Pieters, 1984) are not worth the monetary savings in reality and that the savings intention response is unreliable.

A contingent valuation technique has, therefore, been developed that assesses what householders would do in the face of pricing changes. This technique provides them with feedback as to how much money they would save on their subsequent bill. Since the interview is conducted on a family basis, discussions would result as to the realistic family response; for example, endangering plants to save $5 is likely to be unacceptable.

The price elasticity estimation from contingent valuation was comparable with those obtained by econometric methods. Validation of the technique was undertaken when households who said they would install their own private bores or wells were followed up eighteen months after the questionnaire. The intention was found to be an excellent predictor of behaviour.

The development of such a technique offers invaluable assistance to planners. Often for public acceptability reasons, pricing changes are often associated with water shortages, 'save water' information campaigns and restrictions (but not elections). As a result, estimation of elasticity by statistical means can often be difficult. In addition, as tastes change, the determinants of water use can also change. For example, new appliances may appear or new tastes in gardening may become fashionable. Thus consumption and pricing data from 10 or 15 years ago, which are necessary for adequate regression analysis, may no longer be relevant.

However, perhaps the main advantage is that effects of pricing change on differing sectors of the community can be established. In addition to demographic segmentation, elasticities can be calculated on a lifestyle basis: for example, we have been able to demonstrate differences in price elasticities for groups with different lifestyle preferences.

(d) Organisational/Social Psychology

There has been little or no research in this area. Issues which do need clarification are what organisational arrangements and/or decision making systems are seen to be appropriate for allocating water. Are freemarket mechanisms or institutional means the most appropriate way of allocating water between differing groups? The application of distributive justice theory, for example, may be one way in which psychologists can provide planners with an understanding of the public's perception of fairness in this area (e.g., Heuer & Penrod, 1986)

Organisational questions could confront the problem as to whether water authorities, which are generally public monopolies, should have the role of setting pricing policies for all segments of the community. On many occasions, water authorities are relatively large and economically powerful competitors with other sectors (e.g., small irrigation farmers). If water authorities should not set the pricing policy, what alternative organisational arrangements would be preferable?

(e) Community Psychology

There are increasing pressures for the public to be involved in pricing and other water management policy formulation. Problems are encountered, however, in designing programs that enable the costs and benefits of underlying values implicit in planning, to be effectively discussed by the community at large. To date, though, most interest in the conduct and evaluation of public involvement in this area has been undertaken by planners rather than psychologists.

Attention could be given by community psychologists to establishing how to motivate individual participation in regional issues, how trade-offs can sensibly and efficiently be presented and how to design public involvement programs within the limitations of budget and manpower of both participant and planner. Issues related to negotiation between planner and participant during public participation should also be investigated to establish processes that seem both adequate and fair to the community. The decision making and negotiation literature are replete with insights and decision aids that could enhance this process (e.g., Sandole & Sandole-Staroste, 1987).

WATER QUALITY RESEARCH

Water quality research can be categorised in the same way as pricing (e.g. see Syme, 1983 for review).

(a) Perceptual and Attitudinal Research

Most research conducted has been perceptual or attitudinal and has concentrated largely on taste (e.g., Dillehay, Bruvold & Siegel, 1967). Thresholds for ability to taste various aspects of water quality such as salinity have been established although they vary substantially from study to study (e.g., Bruvold, 1971). Further, Bruvold's extensive attitudinal work on deriving perceived acceptability of the level of total dissolved solids (TDS) has shown that it can be reliably measured and can be related to the actual level of TDS in the water supplied.

By providing extremely reliable attitudinal measures in relation to acceptability it was hoped to provide consumer based standards for future water supplies in California. Although such research is extremely useful, there is an obvious problem of maintaining constant expectations between differing communities. People living in the country, for example, are often likely to accept poorer water quality standards because of their differing expectations and experiences.

A demonstration of the importance of understanding the dynamics leading to water quality perceptions is shown vividly in Ingolds' (1964) study of the perceived water quality of two Georgian towns both taking water from mostly the same source. Ingolds found that one town rated the water quality as satisfactory while the other complained of poor quality water. The reason for the difference in perception between the two towns turned out to be that for very limited periods the dissatisfied town drew water from a very high quality spring. Consequently, they had a different baseline from which to make judgments on their usual water quality.

Although such vivid differences between adjacent locations should not often occur, this example reminds us of the relativity of standards. Choosing a standard is a judgment consisting of a compromise between the values of managers and the expectations of the community. When this compromise is not obtained, especially in the area of perceived health risk, political controversy occurs.

Despite the expectation problem there is still plenty of research that can be conducted. This could answer pertinent questions such as how many attitudinal dimensions of water quality there are and how the burgeoning risk perception literature should be applied to the area of drinking water standards (e.g., Covello, Lave, Moghissi & Uppuluri, 1987). Preliminary data collected in Perth seems to indicate that judgments of water quality are unidimensional and that overall attitudes towards water quality do not seem to vary according to physical indices within the water quality variability of Perth. Complaints made to the water authority also do not correlate with objective water quality indices. This work needs expansion both within the general community and with planners.

(b) Behavioural Research

There has been very limited research in this area. Drinking water quality standards have been discussed mostly in the context of health or aesthetics contexts. Nevertheless, an interesting study (Rotton, Tikofsky & Feldman, 1982) has shown effects on motor behaviour of quite low concentrations of fluoride and nitrates. No replications of this study have been reported and no new research on the effects of these substances on cognitive behaviour has been published. Clearly this work has left room for expansion, as has our discussion of how such findings, if replicated, should be incorporated into water quality standards.

There is also need for simple research to define how households would cope behaviourally (e.g., by fitting water filters etc.) if water standards were lowered. This research would have value in assessing the overall economic costs and benefits to public utilities and private households, of changes in their water quality.

(c) Psychological Economics

There have been some applications of contingent valuation techniques on willingness to pay for improvement in water quality in streams and catchments (e.g., Smith & Desvousges, 1986). Nevertheless, in relation to the issue of public water supply quality, our literature search has revealed no comprehensive studies. Clearly though, it would be of great benefit for us to develop techniques where community trade-offs between the expense in providing high water quality and the health, aesthetic and economic benefits of purer water can be measured in a pragmatic manner. Taken into account also would be the community's perception of risks associated with any lessening of current water quality standards and variables moderating this perception. This topic is the subject of a current project by our own research group, but there are still many methodological possibilities and many research opportunities yet to be taken up by psychologists.

(d) Organisational/Social Psychological Research

The same issues as discussed for pricing policies would be relevant for water quality standards. In addition though, in many countries of the world, including Australia, groundwater is now being used for drinking water (after treatment). This leads to problems in coordination of water supply, land use and health and pollution planning. These problems should lead to the useful application of research in creating decision making aids for planners in this area (e.g., Kaplan & Schwartz, 1977).

(e) Community Psychology

There is little community psychological work done in the area of drinking water quality standards by community psychologists. The preliminary conceptualisations of Edelstein and Wandersman (1987), in terms of creating consensus rather "dissensus" communities in establishing a proactive stance to potential hazards, could be a useful starting point. Although their view was developed largely in the context of the response to the Love Canal disaster there is good reason to consider similar issues in creating acceptable and affordable water quality standards for communities.

CONCLUSION

In this paper we have presented two of many possible water management problems in which psychologists can and should make theoretical and applied contributions. Issues such as water restrictions policy, dam safety standards, and climatic change and its effect on water management, are all issues in which even less research has been conducted.

It can be seen from our two examples that there is no need for us to restrict our interest to the traditional reflective research paradigms of measuring perceptions and attitudes. There is plenty of scope for wider policy orientated research and practice which can be addressed to water's unique psychological and management problems. Currently, water planners are facing mounting pressures to cope with social and psychological problems in decision making. Our water resources are increasingly becoming the focus of major community conflict. The time should be right for us to offer our skills in this hitherto neglected area.

CORRESPONDENCE

CSIRO, Division of Water Resources,, Floreat Park, Western Australia

REFERENCES

Agthe, D.E., Garcia, M.W. & Goodnough, L. (1986-87). Economic evaluation of a rebate program for saving water: The case of the Mesa. *Journal of Environmental Systems, 16,* 81-86.

Bruvold, W.H. (1971). Scales for rating the taste of water. *Journal of Applied Psychology, 52,* 245-253.

Buttram, B.A. & Geller, E.S. (1981). Analyses of behavioral, educational and engineering strategies for motivating residential water conservation. Unpublished manuscript, Department of Psychology, Virginia Polytechnic Institute and State University.

Covello, V.T., Lave, L.B., Moghissi, A. & Uppuluri, V.R.R. (Eds). *Uncertainty in Risk Assessment, Risk Management and Decision Making.* New York: Plenum.

Cummings, R.S., Brookshire, D.S. & Schulze, W.D. (1986). *Valuing Environmental Goods: An assessment of the Contingent Valuation Method.* New Jersey: Rowman and Allanheld.

Dillehay, R.C., Bruvold, W.H. & Siegel, J.P. (1967). On the assessment of potability. *Journal of Applied Psychology, 51,* 89-95.

Edelstein, M.R. & Wandersman, A. (1987). Community dynamics in coping with toxic contaminants. In I. Altman and A. Wandersman (Eds.), *Neighbourhoods and Community Environments* . New York: Plenum.

Erickson, J. & Geller, E.S. (1981). *Applications of educational versus engineering strategies to promote residential water conservation.* Final Report for Grant #NSF SPI-8003981 from the National Science Foundation.

Geller, E.S, Winett, R.A. & Everett, P.B. (1982). *Preserving the Environment: New Strategies for Behavior Change.* New York: Pergamon.

Heuer, L.B. & Penrod, S. (1986). Procedural preference as a function of conflict intensity. *Journal of Personality and Social Psychology, 51,* 700-710.

Ingolds, R.S. (1964). Task Test Tax Theories. Engineering Experiment Station, Georgia Institute of Technology, Reprint 176, Atlanta,Georgia.

Kantola,S.J., Syme,G.J. & Nesdale,A.R. (1983). The effects of appraised severity and efficacy in promoting water conservation: An informational analysis. *Journal of Applied Social Psychology, 13,* 164-182.

Kaplan, M.F. & Schwartz, S. (Eds.). (1977). *Human Judgement and Decision Processes in Applied Settings*. New York: Academic Press.

Kunreuther, H.C. & Ley, E.V. (1982). *The Risk Analysis Controversy*. Berlin: Springer Verlag.

Marks, G. & von Winterfeldt, D. (1984). "Not in my back yard": Influence of motivational concerns about a risky technology. *Journal of Applied Psychology, 69*, 408-415.

Metropolitan Water Authority (1985). *Domestic Water Use in Perth, Western Australia*. Perth, Western Australia.

Rayner, S. & Cantor, R. (1987). How fair is safe enough? The cultural approach to societal technology choice. *Risk Analysis, 7*, 3-9.

Rotton, J., Tikofsky, R.S. & Feldman, H.T. (1982). Behavioral effects of chemicals in drinking water. *Journal of Applied Psychology, 67*, 230-238.

Sandole, D.J.D. & Sandole-Staroste I. (1987). *Conflict Management and Problem Solving*. London: Frances Pinter.

Smith, V.K. & Desvousges, W.H. (1986). *Measuring Water Quality Benefits*. Boston, Kluwer Nijhoff.

Syme, G.J. (1983). Community perceptions and water quality standards. In *Water Quality: Its significance in Western Australia*. Water Research Foundation of Australia: Seminar Proceedings. Perth Western Australia.

Syme, G.J. & Salerian, C. (1987). Socio-economic, attitudinal and behavioral influences on scheme water use in Perth 1981-82. In *Domestic Water Use in Perth Western Australia*. Working Papers, 3, 125-174. Perth, Water Authority of Western Australia.

Syme, G.J. & Seligman, C. (1987). The planning and evaluation of public information campaigns to encourage water conservation. In *Proceedings of the National Workshop on Demand Management*. Australian Water Resources Council Conference Series No. 14, 601-656. Canberra:AGPS.

Thomas, J.F. & Syme, G.J. (in press). Estimating residential price elasticity of demand for water: a contingent valuation approach. *Water Resources Research*.

Verhallen, T.M.M. & Pieters, R.G.M. (1984). Attitude theory and behavioral costs. *Journal of Economic Psychology, 5*, 223-249.

Winkler, R.C. (1982). Water Conservation. In E.S. Geller, R.A. Winett & P.B. Everett (Eds). *Preserving the Environment: New Strategies for Behavioral Change*. New York: Pergamon.

Social Applications and Issues in Psychology
R.C. King and J.K. Collins (editors)
©Elsevier Science Publishers B.V. (North-Holland), 1989

A NOTE ON COST CONCEPTIONS IN ECONOMIC PSYCHOLOGY

Rik G.M. Pieters

Erasmus University, Netherlands

Cost and value play a central role in economic explanations of behaviour. Three general dimensions in cost can be distinguished: outlay versus opportunity, private versus social, and objective versus subjective. On the basis of these dimensions, several conceptions of costs are described. Non-monetary from monetary costs are distinguished. It is argued that social psychology, in particular, attitude theory, has largely neglected cost and that much can be gained from including cost notions into social psychological theories of behaviour. Implications of distinguishing different cost conceptions and cost types for research on social behaviour are formulated.

Psychological economics (Katona, 1980) or economic psychology studies "... the behaviour of consumers/citizens that involves economic decisions, and the determinants and consequences of economic decisions "(Van Raaij, 1981, p.2). Economic decisions are defined broadly to include money, time, and effort to obtain products, services, work, leisure, the choice between product alternatives, spending versus saving decisions. Economic psychology is not merely another form of applied psychology. Since "... in fact, all decisions that involve a choice or trade-off of some alternative or an investment that will bring future profits or benefits may be called an economic decision" (Van Raaij, 1981, p.2.). In economic psychology, economic behaviour is analyzed using conceptional tools developed in both economics and psychology. More decisions than lay people would imagine are governed by economic considerations (Lea, Tarpy & Webley, 1987).

In this contribution an issue that is relevant to economic psychology is briefly introduced; cost and the nature of cost. Cost is a central topic in economic reasoning. Accounting theory was developed to 'account' for it. In mainstream psychology only occasional attention has been given to the costs associated with behaviour. Recently, Meyer (1982) argued that social psychological theories of attitudes have generally placed a strong emphasis on the benefits of behaviour, without paying much attention to the costs people have to accept in order (to be able) to behave. This statement may apply to social psychological theory in general.

Insight into the nature of costs, the categories of costs and the location of costs may help in building better models of human behaviour. Insight into the way economics has been dealing with the nature of cost may help to show that economics and psychology are dealing with a common set of questions. It is for these reasons that costs will be focused upon here. Cost is so intertwined with the domain of both psychology and economics, i.e., decision making and behaviour, that it may serve as a starting point for much closer collaboration between the two disciplines.

First, the relationship between cost and value will be explored. Next, the way cost is treated in social exchange theory is briefly introduced. Then the role of cost in attitude-behaviour relationships is discussed. Consequences of the analysis for modelling the relationship between attitudes and behaviour are specified. Suggestions for future collaboration between social psychology and economics are given.

COST AND VALUE

The theory of costs is not one of those parts of economic analysis that has been neglected. It has always occupied a more or less central position and it has been the subject of a formidable body of work.

Different conceptions of what constitutes a cost have appeared and disappeared in economics. Many of the differences in conception depend essentially, as Robbins (1973) states, on differences of object and assumptions. To present a definition of cost that does not violate any of the assumptions underlying the different conceptions of the nature of cost is difficult. Buchanan (1969) offers a general definition explaining that cost refers to a loss of value. He argues (Buchanan, 1969, p.7) that the elemental meaning of cost is that of pain or sacrifice. So, asking a person how much a certain behaviour did actually cost is analogous to asking the person how much s/he had to sacrifice, how much pain s/he had to bear.

Three general dimensions in cost conceptions can be distinguished. The dimensions refer to: (a) what kind of general value is lost; (b) whose value is lost; and (c) how the value loss is determined.

Outlay cost and opportunity cost

There are two ideas of the 'real' or 'true' nature of cost and value, i.e., of what kind of general value is lost.

The central element in outlay cost is the so called labour-cost doctrine of value. This doctrine focuses on the sacrifice of giving up scarce resources in order to acquire a commodity. The cost of a commodity is defined as the labour needed to acquire the commodity (Smith, 1776). The required labour may involve pain, "... something that can within limits be measured by sweat, muscle fatigue and tears" (Buchanan, 1969, p.7). So, cost is associated with the outlays for a commodity and cost is called pain cost, real cost, out-of-pocket cost or outlay cost (see, e.g., Buchanan, 1969; Thaler, 1980). We will use the neutral term *outlay cost* hereafter.

The central element in opportunity cost is the choice-cost doctrine of value. This doctrine focuses on the pain one has to bear when choosing between mutually exclusive alternatives. Smith (1776, chpt. 6) employed the choice-cost doctrine when he stated "... if among a nation of hunters, for example, it costs twice the labour to kill a beaver which it does to kill a deer, one beaver should naturally exchange for, or be worth, two deer". In this example, the 'real' cost is no longer defined in terms of the amount of labour. Cost is defined in units of another commodity in the market place. So, "If the choice lies between the production or purchase of two commodities, the value of one is measured by the sacrifice of going without the other" (Davenport, 1894, p.567—568). This can simply be reformulated as "... the cost of beaver is deer and the cost of deer is beaver" (Knight, 1928, p.359).

Cost in this conception is called opportunity cost, alternative product cost or alternativity cost (e.g., Stigler, 1966). Opportunity cost is not an attribute of a commodity but an attribute of the choice between alternatives. It is defined as "... the value of the best alternative necessarily forsaken" (Alchian, 1969).

Private cost and social cost

A second relevant distinction in cost conceptions concerns the bearer of the costs. Private cost (sometimes called commercial cost) is the cost borne by the decision maker, i.e., by the unit that chooses between alternatives. Social cost is the cost borne by society at large (see, e.g., Klein, 1977). An analogous distinction in benefits can be made.

The differences between private and social cost are so called 'spillover' or external effects. Private cost equals social cost if all positive and negative consequences of a choice between alternatives are borne by the decision-making unit. This would be the case if (a) the choice had consequences for the decision-making unit only, or (b) the decision making unit received a full compensation for the positive or favourable spillover effects and if the decision-making unit would fully compensate society for the negative or unfavourable spillover effects. In option (a) all effects are internal, while in option (b) the external effects of a choice are internalized; they are 'priced' for the decision-making unit.

Unfavourable spillover effects arise when the net social cost (social cost minus social benefit) exceeds the net private cost. Mishan (1970) argues that such a situation arises in the case of the automobile. He conjectures that by far the greater part of its cost is borne by the public at large and not by the owner (driver). The public at large is confronted with motor noise, exhaust gases, accident risks, less space and so on. The owner (driver) does not fully compensate the public at large for these costs, so his/her private cost is lower than the social cost. Favourable spillover effects arise when the net private cost exceeds the net social cost. This is the case when a certain decision has benefits for the public at large exceeding the costs for the public at large, next to the benefits to the decision-making unit. For instance, timber growing for the furniture industry may have a positive effect on air quality. If this positive, non-marketed, effect exceeds the social costs (resource depletion, noise and so on), the net private cost of timber growing exceeds the social cost.

Objective cost and subjective cost

Cost can be treated as an objective attribute of a commodity or of a choice between alternatives. In such a view, cost can be objectively measured by an outside observer, or through consensus among a group of outside observers. Then, cost is extra- or inter-individual. This is the objective cost conception (Buchanan, 1969, p.47).

Cost can also be treated as an intra-individual quality. Then, cost is associated with the experience of value loss and is viewed as the result of a more or less complex process in which a decision-maker transforms expected or experienced attributes of a commodity or choice situation into subjective evaluations. Evaluations of a certain commodity or choice situation may differ between individuals due to differences in the valuation process and thus can not be determined extra- or inter-individually. In this view costs are always subjective cost.

The difference between objective and subjective cost is a difference in the conception of the nature of cost, not in the unit or scale to measure cost. Objective cost is measured in some common agreed unit, e.g., money, time or, if appropriate, beaver. Subjective cost can also be converted into the same units. A person can be asked to attach a money price to the annoyance that is caused by the heavy trucks that pass his house all day long (a form of 'shadow pricing'). In this example, money is used as a convenient measuring rod to assess the value of a subjective experience. However, the extent of value loss is still treated as subjective, i.e., intra-individual.

GENERAL CONCEPTIONS OF COST

Combining the three dimensions, eight specific cost conceptions could be construed thus: objective private outlay cost, and subjective social opportunity cost. In practice, the social cost conception is only applied in formal cost-benefit analyses, usually as objective opportunity cost. Formal cost-benefit analysis is concerned with the welfare of society at large (Mishan, 1982). When decisions of individuals or organizations are concerned a private cost conception is most relevant. The four general private cost conceptions are introduced.

Objective outlay cost is a central element in the classical and neoclassical schools of financial accounting (hence the term 'accountant cost', via Thirlby, 1946), where objective past outlays are used as the appropriate basis to value commodities (Belkaoui, 1981, p.138). Commodities are valued at their market price at the date of acquisition and are shown in the financial statements at that value or an amortized portion of it. Objective outlay cost is sometimes called historical cost, or sunk cost, to stress that they refer to past outlays. Valuation on the basis of historical cost may produce incorrect figures of the present value of commodities if value changes over time are ignored. For example, the present value of Manhattan Island is probably somewhat higher than the $24 that the Dutch paid for it to the members of a native tribe some centuries ago (see, e.g., Stigler, 1966, p.104 for this example). At the Erasmus University library, the value of a book is determined on the basis of past financial outlays. The fine when not returning a book equals the price for which the book was originally bought.

Subjective outlay cost refers to the experienced and/or expected loss of value when giving up scarce resources to acquire a commodity. In this conception, cost is sometimes called choice-influenced cost or 'ex post' cost, to distinguish it from opportunity cost that is viewed as choice-influencing or 'ex ante' cost (Buchanan, 1969). Decisions have a number of consequences. After a commitment to an action, the individual (and sometimes others as well) bears the consequences. Although the person may not regret the decision, the 'pain' or 'sacrifice' of giving up scarce resources may still be experienced. Subjective outlay cost may be experienced both after, while, or before the actual outlays are made in much the same way as the coward may experience the pain caused by the needle even before the nurse gives the shot.

Objective opportunity cost deals with the objective value of the best alternative forgone. This conception is the basis of modern price theory in economics. Stigler (1966) illustrates it by arguing that the cost of an acre of land to agricultural uses is the amount the land could yield in nonagricultural uses, and that the cost of the acre of land to wheat growing farmer X is the amount the land would yield to other wheat farmers, as well as all other non-wheat uses. If the value of the best alternative changes, so does the opportunity cost of the acre of land.

Subjective opportunity cost refers to the opportunity cost as experienced by the decision-maker. Forgone value, it is argued in this conception, can not be determined by anyone else than by the decision-maker. In this conception, cost can be called choice-influencing cost or ex ante cost.

Is cost only financial in nature?

Traditionally economic models of decision-making do not include other than monetary cost (implying either that the 'total value loss' is incorporated in the monetary cost, or that the former is not the case but that the non-monetary cost does not exist, cannot be measured, or is too small to make a difference).

In modern economic theories, time is incorporated as a scarce resource next to money (Becker, 1976). Marks (1977) includes effort as a scarce resource that can be allocated to attain a goal. Verhallen and Pieters (1984) argue that in order to perform an act, an individual has to make use of the totality of his monetary and behavioural resources at hand. The behavioural resources comprise time and physical and mental energy. Physical energy refers to labour and strength. Mental energy refers to the general and situation specific cognitive capacity of individuals.

When behavioural resources are sacrificed, behavioural costs are made.

When attempting to build a cost accounting framework in social psychology, all cost conceptions treated in the preceding section are relevant. First, objective cost has its place in a theory of decision-making and behaviour, since it indicates the price of alternatives. Monetary price can be distinguished from the behavioural price (time demand, demand on thinking capacity and strength and so on). Second, the social cost conception is relevant. It is relevant to analyze the extent to which people have internalized externalities. Although these preceding cost conceptions are relevant, the main cost conceptions for a descriptive theory of decision making are the subjective private outlay and opportunity cost concepts. In applying these cost concepts, both monetary and behavioural costs are relevant.

In the next sections, the cost conceptions infused in social psychological theories of human behaviour are analyzed. Social exchange theory and attitude theory will be focused upon.

SOCIAL EXCHANGE THEORY AND COST

The concept of cost is present in several theories and models of social behaviour. Yet, only in social exchange theory does cost receive more than superficial attention.

Social exchange theory is concerned with the general processes and principles that govern the provision, trade or transfer of more or less valued psychological, social, and material commodities or resources. Social exchange theory is not a homogeneous theory; in fact it is more a collection of theories that share a number of characteristics (McClintock, Kramer and Keil, 1984).

In social exchange theory, both outlay cost and opportunity cost are treated. Homans (1961, p.58—60) explicitly defines cost as opportunity cost. A central element in the social exchange theory of Thibaut and Kelley (1959) is the exchange of valued resources between members of dyadic and more complex relationships. Interactions between persons in dyads are treated as exchange relationships. Interactions lead to outcomes that are valued by the participants in the interaction. Two general criteria are used in this valuation process: (a) the Comparison Level (CL), and (b) the Comparison Level for Alternatives (CLalt).

The Comparison Level (CL) is a standard to judge the value of the outcomes in terms of what the person feels s/he deserves. If the outcomes fall below the CL, the interaction is valued negatively, if they fall above the CL, the interaction is valued positively. The CL is influenced by one's personal history and by expectations of attaining certain outcomes. The CL refers to the rewards and benefits of a relationship relative to the outlays.

The Comparison Level for Alternatives (CLalt) is "... the standard the member uses in deciding whether to remain in or leave the relationship" (Thibaut and Kelley, 1959, p.21). CLalt is defined informally as the lowest level of outcomes a member will accept in the light of available alternatives. In Thibaut and Kelley's words (1959, p.22) "... The height of the CLalt will depend mainly on the quality of the best of the member's available alternatives". The Comparison Level for Alternatives is the opportunity cost.

Recently, Rusbult (1980) has extended the work of Thibaut and Kelley by specifying an investment model of romantic associations. The primary goal of the investment model is to predict the degree of commitment to, and satisfaction with a variety of forms of ongoing associations (e.g., romantic, friendship, business) with wide-ranging duration. The relevant aspects of the investment model can be expressed simply as:

$$Com_X = O_X + I_X - O_Y$$

$$I_X = \sum_{i=1}^{n} w_i * r_i$$

$$O_X = \sum_{j=1}^{n} w_j * a_j$$

where Com_X is the commitment to action X, O_X is the outcome value of action X, I_X is the investment value of action X, O_Y is the outcome value of action Y, assuming Y is the best available alternative to X, r_i is the size of the investment of resource j in relationship X, a_i is the individuals's subjective estimate of the value of attribute i available in relationship X and w is the subjective importance of the resources and attributes.

The investment model of ongoing relationships specifies that the commitment to remain in a certain relationship X is a simple function of the subjective benefits of X, the subjective historical outlay cost of X and the subjective opportunity cost of X. In two studies Rusbult (1980) tested and found support for the investment model.

Rusbult's study is one of the few recent studies that treat the costs and benefits of interpersonal relationships as a central topic. Hays (1985), studying friendship development, argues that although notions of costs and benefits are at the core of a number of models of friendship development, "... little data exist on individuals' perceptions of the various costs and benefits accruing from their relationships or possible changes in the types of costs and benefits that emerge at different stages of relationship development" (Hays, 1985, p.909).

Social exchange theory is one of the few attempts to infuse economic concepts and models in social psychological theory. These attempts do not seem to have had a considerable impact on social psychological theorizing.

COST IN ATTITUDE—BEHAVIOUR MODELS

Attitude is by far the most frequently studied concept in social psychology. Studies on attitude formation and change and on attitude-behaviour relationships are so numerous that any review of the literature either is deemed to be incomplete or takes more pages than an average dictionary. In particular, the literature on attitude-behaviour relationships is relevant for the present purpose, for as economic cost and choice are fully intertwined, so are attitude and behaviour, for social psychology.

The utility of the attitude concept largely derives from its assumed property to direct behaviour. Models that specify the relationship between the attitude of individuals and their behaviour have been developed. The model that has dominated research on attitude-behaviour relationships in recent years is the well known Fishbein and Ajzen (1975) model of Reasoned Action.

The question of how cost is treated in attitude theory, in particular in the Fishbein and Ajzen type of attitude model, is relevant. The general form of the Fishbein and Ajzen model can be summarized as:

$$B \approx BI = w1 \, A_{act} + w2 \, SN$$

B stands for 'behaviour', BI is the behavioural intention, A_{act} is the attitude towards the act, and SN is the subjective norm. The model specifies that behaviour that is under volitional control is determined by two general factors, a personal factor, the attitude, and a social factor, the subjective norm.

Attitude is a positive or negative affect with respect to the act. The attitude is determined by the summed expected consequences of the behaviour, called beliefs (b), weighted by the evaluation (e) of these consequences. The subjective norm is the generalized pressure from relevant others. It is determined by the social norms of salient referents (nb), weighted by the motivation to comply (mc), with these social norms. The relevant equations are well known and are presented by, e.g., Fishbein and Ajzen (1975).

Recent research with the model has focused on whether (a) the specified direct and indirect relationships in the model are empirically retrieved, whether (b) other variables than the ones included in the model influence behaviour, and whether (c) factors may moderate relationships between constructs in the model (see Pieters, 1988).

In the literature on attitude-behaviour relationships hardly any mention is made of the cost of behaviour. The conclusion of Meyer (1982) that attitude does not seem to capture the non-zero opportunity cost of behaviour is repeated and extended.

Subjective outlays and revenues and attitudes

Verhallen and Pieters (1984) argue that the subjective outlays and revenues of a behaviour are to be found in the beliefs—times—evaluation expression. A typical belief statement in research on, e.g., residential energy saving might be: " In order to save electricity in the home ... I have to ... spend time."

This belief-statement represents the time-demand of "saving electricity in the home", referring to the outlays in time one has to make. Other belief—statements represent revenues, e.g., the psychic revenue of "being a good citizen when saving energy", or the monetary revenue, when paying a lower electricity bill.

In the Reasoned Action Model, the belief is multiplied by an evaluation of the expected outcome. An evaluation of a belief indicates whether an expected consequence of behaviour is liked or disliked by the person, i.e., whether a consequence is perceived as an outlay or whether it is perceived as a revenue. Negatively evaluated consequences constitute costs, positively evaluated consequences constitute benefits. In other words, a combination of a belief and an evaluation forms a subjective cost or benefit element.

Cost and benefit elements are not distinguished in the Reasoned Action Model. As a consequence, most research with the model does not provide much insight into the structure of the subjective costs and benefits of people. Analogous to the investment model of Rusbult (1980), the costs and benefits of behaviour (subjective outlays and revenues) can be treated as separate constructs (see Pieters and Verhallen, 1986; Pieters, 1987).

Subjective opportunity cost and attitudes

The opportunity cost of performing a certain action is not represented in the Reasoned Action model and similar attitude models. Usually the attitude toward one specific act (or object) is determined. To represent the opportunity cost of performing this act, the attitude towards performing the best alternative should be taken into account. If behaviour involves a choice between alternatives, one should (a) determine which alternatives are contained in the subjective choice set of individuals and (b) which alternative is valued highest next to the target action.

Frey and Foppa (1986) argue that behaviour is crucially determined by the set of possibilities open to an individual. Therefore, the constraints determining the individual's choice set should be analyzed more in depth. Individuals act on the basis of their personal knowledge about the choice set, which may often differ systematically from the actual choice set. Frey (1983) argues that in, e.g., political decision-making, the opportunity cost of behaviour often receives a low weight. Thaler (1980) found in his research that compared to outlay cost, opportunity cost is often underweighted (referred to as the endowment effect).

More research is needed concerning the factors influencing the size and content of the individual's choice set and the role opportunity cost plays in determining behaviour. The opportunity cost of behaviour can be incorporated in attitude models analogously to the way it has been done in the investment model.

The treatment of cost in attitude theory has been introduced briefly. In the next section conclusions are drawn about the collabouration between psychology and economics, in particular with respect to the field of cost and choice.

CONCLUSION

Cost and value are concepts that may connect economic and psychological theories of human functioning. These concepts may provide the starting point for an intensive joint research programme in the disciplines of psychology and economics.

Many economic issues need joint study. Entrepreneurial decision-making is just one of such issues. The list of aspects to study, provided by Hayes (1950) almost 40 years ago, includes decisions to establish an enterprise, to buy into an ongoing enterprise, to increase investment in an enterprise, to sell a portion of the enterprise, to invest in certain projects and not in others, to take a loan, to hire certain professionals and so on. Consumer decision-making has been studied extensively in the last few decades. Yet more intense cooperation between social psychology and economics may be fruitful in this domain.

There are also several traditionally non-economic issues where collabouration between economics and psychology might be fruitful. Research on altruism and moral behaviour might be such an issue. Both psychologists and economists have been working in this domain, with a more common focus than they might think at first sight. Becker (1976) on interdependent utility functions and Dovidio (1984), on personal norms of aiding and fairness and on cost and reward considerations in helping, demonstrate the point. Among the other issues, intimate relationships, marriage and romantic associations might also be fruitfully studied in cooperation (Frey and Foppa, 1986).

At the level of model and theory building, more cooperation is possible as well. In economics, value and cost have been central constructs. The utility of commodities and alternatives and the way (subjective expected) utility relates to choice have been studied in depth. In social psychology, attitude and attitude-behaviour models have dominated research. Analysis of the relationships between values, cost and choice should attract more joint research. Combining the theories and methods developed in economics and social psychology is needed here (see also Antonides, 1984)

In *Behaviour Cost Accounting* the expected and experienced consequences of a behaviour are analyzed from a cost perspective. Analyzing behaviour from such a perspective does not imply that individuals are highly involved and rationally adding and subtracting costs and benefits when deciding about alternative courses of action. The contrary may be the rule. The present approach is descriptive in nature. Costs are distinguished from benefits, outlay costs from opportunity costs. Consequences that directly affect the individual (private) can be distinguished from all other consequences. We can determine to what extent individuals have internalized consequences of their behaviour for others (other people, the environment and so on), i.e., to what extent they have internalized externalities. We can assess when individuals are relying on opportunity cost in choosing between alternatives, when they are relying on outlay cost and when they are doing both.

In the past, interest from economics in psychology has mainly focused on the descriptive models and theories of motivation and choice that psychology could offer. Psychology has been most interested in the domain, the topics, of economics. The study of economic behaviour has long been treated as merely a new domain to which to apply the general psychological theories. Although this has been a profitable operation, even more might be gained for Economic Psychology when attention is paid to the concepts, models and theories developed in economics. Cost may be of value when trying to understand and predict human behaviour.

CORRESPONDENCE

Rik G.M. Pieters, Department of Economics, Erasmus University, Box 1738, 3000 DR Rotterdam, NL.

REFERENCES

Alchian, A. A. (1969). Cost. In: D. L. Sills (Ed.), *International encyclopedia of the Social Sciences*, *3*, 404-414. New York: The Macmillan Company & The Free Press.

Antonides, G. (1984). An attempt to integration of economic and psychological theories in consumption problems. *Papers on Economic Psychology no. 31*. Rotterdam: Department of Economics, Erasmus University.

Becker, G. S. (1976). *The economic approach to human behaviour.* Chicago, Il.: The University of Chicago Press.

Belkaoui, A. (1981). *Accounting theory.* New York: Harcourt Brace Jovanovich.

Buchanan, J. M. (1969). *Cost and choice.* Chicago: Chicago University Press.

Davenport, H. J. (1894). The formula of sacrifice. *Journal of Political Economy, 2,* 561-573.

Dovidio, J. F. (1984). Helping behaviour and altruism: an empirical and conceptual overview. In: L. Berkowitz (Ed.), *Advances in experimental social psychology 17,* 361-419. New York: Academic Press.

Fishbein, M. & Ajzen, I. (1975). *Belief, attitude, intention and behaviour: an introduction to theory and research.* Reading, MA: Addison-Wesley.

Frey, B. S. (1983). *The economic model of behaviour: shortcomings and fruitful developments.* Discussion paper. Zürich: Institute for Empirical Research in Economics, University of Zürich.

Frey, B. S. and Foppa, K. (1986).Human behaviour: possibilities explain action. *Journal of Economic Psychology, 7,* 137-160.

Hayes, S. P. jr. (1950). Some psychological problems of economics. *Psychological Bulletin, 47,* 289-330.

Hays, R. B. (1985). A longitudinal study of friendship development. *Journal of Personality and Social Psychology, 48,* 909-924.

Homans, G. C. (1961). *Social behaviour: its elementary forms.* New York: Harcourt, Brace.

Katona, G. (1980). *Psychological Economics.* Amsterdam: North Holland.

Klein, T. A. (1977). *Social costs and benefits of business.* Englewood Cliffs: Prentice Hall.

Knight, F. H. (1928). A suggestion for simplifying the statement of the general theory of price. *Journal of Political Economy, 36,* 353-370.

Lea, S. E. G., Tarpy, R. M. & Webley, P. (1987). *The individual in the economy: a survey of Economic Psychology.* Cambridge: Cambridge University Press.

Marks, S. R. (1977). Multiple roles and role strain: some notes on human energy, time and commitment. *American Sociological Review, 42,* 921-936.

McClintock, C. G., Kramer, R. M. & Keil, L. J. (1984). Equity and social exchange in human relationships. In: L. Berkowitz (Ed.), *Advances in experimental social psychology, 17,* 183-228). New York: Academic Press.

Meyer, W. (1982). The research programme of economics and the relevance of economics. *British Journal of Social Psychology, 21,* 81—91.

Mishan, E. J. (1970). *21 Popular Economic Fallacies.* New York: Praeger Publishers.

Mishan, E. J. (1982). *Cost-Benefit Analysis.* London: Allen & Unwin, 3rd. edition.

Pieters, R. G. M. (1987). Perceived costs and benefits of buying and using a subsidized compost container. *Resources and Conservation, 14,* 139-154.

Pieters, R. G. M. (1988). Attitude-behaviour relations. In: W. F. van Raaij, G. M. van Veldhoven and K-E. Wärneryd (Eds.), *Handbook of Economic Psychology,* 144-204. Dordrecht: Kluwer Scientific.

Pieters, R. G. M. & Verhallen, Th. M. M. (1986). Participation in source separation projects: design characteristics and perceived costs and benefits. *Resources and Conservation, 12,* 95—111.

Van Raaij, W. F. (1981). Economic Psychology. *Journal of Economic Psychology, 1,* 1—24.

Robbins, L. (1973). Remarks upon certain aspects of the theory of costs. In: J.M. Buchanan and G.F. Thirlby (Eds.). *L.S.E. Essays on cost.* 21-41. London: Weidenfels and Nicholson.

Rusbult, C. E. (1980). Commitment and satisfaction in romantic associations: a test of the investment model. *Journal of Experimental Social Psychology, 16,* 172-186.

Smith, A. (1776/1983). *The Wealth of Nations.* Harmondsworth, Middlesex: Pinguin Books.

Stigler, G. (1966). *The theory of price.* New York: Macmillan Publishing, 3rd. edition.

Thaler, R. (1980). Toward a positive theory of consumer choice. *Journal of Economic Behaviour and Organization, 1,* 39-60.

Thibaut, J. W. & Kelley, H. H. (1959). *The Social Psychology of groups.* New York: John Wiley.

Thirlby, G. F. (1946). The subjective theory of value and accounting "cost". *Economica, 13,* 32-49.

Verhallen, Th. M. M. & Pieters, R. G. M. (1984). Attitude theory and behavioural costs. *Journal of Economic Psychology, 5,* 223-249.

Social Applications and Issues in Psychology
R.C. King and J.K. Collins (editors)
©*Elsevier Science Publishers B.V. (North-Holland), 1989*

THE COGNITIVE STRUCTURE OF RESIDENTIAL DECISIONS: A LONGITUDINAL FIELD STUDY

B. Rohrmann (University of Mannheim, Germany) and

K. Borcherding (Technical University of Darmstadt, Germany)

In this social-scientific field study the following questions have been studied: What information is relevant for the evaluation of residences? How can the multi-criteria evaluations in successive decision situations be modelled? Which residential characteristics (house-related, environment-related, person-related) most influence the final decision? Which cognitive changes occur during the search and decision making process?

The study is based on a conceptual framework that connects perspectives from behavioural decision theory, mobility research and environmental psychology. Empirical data have been gathered in a longitudinal approach: A group of 92 movers was surveyed during the search for a new residence; data were collected at 6 subsequent times by personal or mail or telephone interviews. Additionally, a control group of 72 non-movers was included.

Main topics of the statistical analyses are: identification of crucial determinants of residence evaluation and selection, comparison of various multi-attribute utility models and their relation to holistic judgments and changes in evaluations over time. Finally, consequences for further research and use are discussed.

PROBLEM

The decision-making problem of movers

In the highly industrialized countries of Europe, North America or Australia, every year between 10% and 20% of the population change their residence. Two kinds of decision processes are related to such migration behaviour:

- Deciding *whether* to move: People unsatisfied with their current residential quality can either stay (with or without activities against the causes of deficiencies) or they can leave and try to obtain a better residence.
- Deciding *where* to move: Excluding cases of forced choice, the mover has to choose between the available housing alternatives. This is

usually a sequential process, based on the search and inspection of potential new residences.

The aim of the present investigation is to analyze the cognitive structure of the underlying evaluations, and to determine the crucial influences on housing decisions. A particular interest is related to the relevance of environmental quality versus the other residential factors (i.e., features of the house and its location).

Housing decisions have been studied in the context of mobility research (see e.g., McHugh, 1984; Michelson, 1980, Rossi, 1980; Weichhart, 1988) and within decision research (e.g., Aschenbrenner, 1977; Borcherding, 1981; Lindbergh et al., 1987, Winterfeld & Edwards, 1973). The environmental aspects of housing have received only moderate attention (Rohrmann, 1986, Shumaker & Stokols, 1982). Altogether, the available knowledge is restricted for two reasons: often the individual decision making process has not been analyzed in detail and, in some studies, the issue of residence selection was a vehicle for decision-theoretic questions rather than of substantive interest.

Theoretical framework: Determinants of housing decisions

The investigation is based on a conceptual framework that connects perspectives from migration research (see e.g. De Jong & Gardner, 1981; Clark, 1986), behavioural decision theory (e.g., Borcherding, 1983; v. Winterfeldt & Edwards, 1986) and environmental psychology (e.g., Fisher et al., 1984; Tognoli, 1986). Figure 1 illustrates the assumed structure of the main concepts that are relevant for decisions about residences.

FIGURE 1

Conceptual Framework for Analyzing Decisions on Residences

DETERMINANTS OF HOUSING DECISIONS

ER	Evaluated Residential Quality	
OR	Objective Residential Conditions	
EE	Evaluated Environmental Quality	
OE	Objective Environmental Conditions	
DR	Demands on Residential Quality	
HD	Housing Decision	
DE	Demands on Environmental Quality	
PC	General Personal Characteristics	
SI	Situational & Social Influences	
CE	External Conditions/Constraints	

Previous Living Situations

Actual Situation

Personal Decision Context

The model states that the subjective evaluation of a residence is dependent on its objective characteristics (e.g., costs, size, noise level and shopping facilities) and on the demands (standards, preferences) that people hold in respect of their housing. Two classes of residential features are separated: Aspects of the apartment/ house and its location on the one hand and aspects of the environment (particularly stressors like noise, or lack of nature) on the other hand. The decision about residences is a consequence of those evaluations, but it is also influenced by various internal factors and external constraints that are not related to the residence, i.e., the personal decision context. Furthermore, previous experiences in housing are to be considered.

The evaluation of housing options has been modelled in regard to multi-attribute utility theory (MAUT) (Keeney & Raiffa, 1976). Such model-derived evaluations can be compared with holistic judgments of the decision alternatives (see Fischer, 1979, for a review).

Objectives of the study

With regard to 'real' housing decisions, the following questions have been studied: What information is relevant for the evaluation of residences? How can the multi-criteria evaluations in successive decision situations be modelled, and are multi-attribute utility models sufficiently valid? Which residential characteristics (house-related, environment-related, person-related) influence the actual final decision the most? Do cognitive changes occur during the search and decision making process?

METHOD

Longitudinal research design

To investigate the issue discussed, empirical data have been gathered in a longitudinal approach (see Fig. 2): A group of movers (M) was surveyed during the search for a new residence. At six subsequent points (t1: before moving; t2/t3/t4: during search; t5: after the decision; t6: four months later) responses were collected by personal interviews, mailed questionnaires and telephone interviews. A matched control group of non-movers (N) was included at two points (t1, t6).

Variables and psychometric instruments

Altogether six questionnaires have been constructed, according to the various conditions and interview types (cf. Fig. 2).

FIGURE 2

```
  L O N G I T U D I N A L   R E S E A R C H   D E S I G N


  Point in time:  .  t1  .  t2  .  t3  .  t4  .  t5  .   .  t6  .
  ------------------------------------------------------------------

  Situation:      before      search for a    after the    4 month
                  moving      new residence   decision      later


  SURVEY M:
  M O V E R               M1-----M2---M3---M4-----M5---//---M6


     Sample n =    92        74     56    28       34          45

  SURVEY N:
  N O N - MOVER           N1-----------------------------------------N6


     Sample n =    71                                            63

  ------------------------------------------------------------------

  Considered  M:  old r.    potential residences  new r.    new r.
  residence:  N:     old r.                                    old r.

  ------------------------------------------------------------------

  Survey          personal    mailed questi-   telephone   personal
    type:         interview   onnaire (3x)     interview   interview
```

The set of included variables refers to the conceptual framework shown in Figure 1. The main concepts of demands, objective conditions and evaluations are operationalized with regard to 12 key attributes (cf. Tables 1 to 4); five of these are related to features of the dwelling/house, three to location criteria, four to environmental aspects. In order to measure residential preferences, for each of these attributes four relevant levels were defined in either quantitative or qualitative terms. Some examples are:

- Size of the residence = Number of rooms : (A) 5 or more; (B) 4; (C) 3; (D) 1 or 2.
- Shopping facilities in the area (walking distance): (A) several different shops, banks, services; (B) supermarket or a few shops; (C) one grocery shop; (D) no shops (only kiosks or snack bars).
- Availability of parks/nature: (A) house directly adjacent to gardens, public parks, greens; (B) within 5 minutes walking distances; (C) 15 minutes distances; (D) car or public transport necessary to reach parks/nature.

Responses were scaled by either standardized rating schemes or ratio judgments.

Data collection

The surveys were conducted in Darmstadt and its suburban areas during 1986/87. When establishing the samples, four variables were controlled so as to distribute 50:50%: sex, age (below versus above 30 years), township (urban versus suburban); and family versus "single". All respondents were tenants. The sample sizes are shown in Fig. 2.

FINDINGS

The longitudinal approach yielded a rather large data deck with several hundred variables. It consists of 8 data sets which are designated by M1 to M6 and N1, N2 (cf. the design in Fig. 2). In the following, selected results of the statistical analyses are presented; for a full report see Rohrmann and Borcherding (1988).

Judgments on residential attributes

In order to explore the demands and preferences of movers, they were asked to evaluate the importance of various residential attributes, the acceptability and the favourableness of relevant housing conditions, as well as the most aspired levels within each attribute. Altogether, the respondents expressed moderate and rather realistic demands; however, most people do not accept, for example, a rent above 1.000 DM, apartments lacking any technical comfort, distances to working place or shopping centres above 30 minutes, exposure to frequent smell or noise nuisance and urban quarters without parks. As can be seen from the weights in Table 1, costs and size of the residence and noise/quietness are the most important aspects within the considered set of attributes.

TABLE 1
Residential Preferences

Data Set: M1 (n = 92)	ATTRIBUTE LEVEL				ATTRIBUTE WEIGHT
	A	B	C	D	
HOUSING ATTRIBUTE	RATED FAVORABLENESS				
Costs of residence	5.8	4.2	1.9	0.4	.120
Number of rooms, size	3.5	4.2	4.0	1.8	.111
Comfort, state/repair	4.6	5.3	2.4	0.3	.090
Balcony/terrace/garden	4.5	5.4	3.2	0.9	.076
Type/size of building	4.2	4.6	3.1	0.8	.068
Distance to city center	4.8	4.6	2.8	1.1	.080
Distance to place of work	5.3	4.9	2.9	0.7	.083
Shopping facilities	5.2	5.0	3.7	0.5	.059
Smell nuisance	5.8	2.6	1.2	0.3	.080
Noise/quietness	5.4	3.3	0.8	0.1	.092
Avail. of parks/nature	5.7	5.0	3.5	0.8	.077
Aesthet. qual./decayment	5.4	5.1	3.2	1.2	.055

Favorableness scale: 0 = unacceptable to 6 = very desirable.
Weights: measured by ratio scaling; standardized to E = 1.

In the following Table 2 the mean evaluations of the respondents' actual residences are given. These data show that:

- The overall evaluation of the new residence which may be interpreted as satisfaction is significantly better than for the old residence (see M1 vs. M5) and for the average inspected residence (M2 to M4), but decreases after some months (M6).
- Non-movers express higher satisfaction than the movers at time t1, but not at t6.
- Dissatisfaction occurs most frequently in regard to the availability of balcony or garden and to noise versus quietness.
- Nearly all evaluations are in the positive range of the underlying evaluation scales.

TABLE 2
Residential Satisfaction

Data Set: n:	M1 92	M234 173	M5 34	M6 45	N1 71	N6 63
Overall evaluation of the residence						
(M, scale 0..10)	6.1	5.9	7.6	7.4	6.9	6.8
Attribut-specific evaluations						
(M, Scale 1..5)						
Costs of residence	3.4	3.2	3.5	3.3	3.4	3.4
Number of rooms, size	3.2	3.7	4.0	4.0	3.8	3.7
Comfort, state/repair	3.3	3.5	3.9	3.7	3.4	3.5
Balcony/terrace/garden	2.9	2.9	3.4	3.4	3.2	3.3
Type/size of building	3.5	3.6	3.9	3.8	3.5	3.5
Distance to city center	3.8	3.6	4.0	4.1	4.2	4.1
Distance to place of work	3.6	3.5	3.9	4.0	3.9	3.9
Shopping facilities	3.3	3.5	4.0	4.0	3.6	3.3
Smell nuisance	3.6	3.7	4.2	4.0	3.5	3.5
Noise/quietness	3.0	3.3	3.8	3.3	3.2	3.1
Avail. of parks/nature	4.0	3.9	4.3	4.1	3.9	3.9
Aesthet. qual./decayment	3.4	3.5	3.9	3.8	3.3	3.5

Multiple prediction of residence evaluations

To what extent can the overall satisfaction with a residence be predicted by the attribute-specific evaluations? As can be seen from the multiple regressions in Table 3, R^2 ranges from .37 to .58 and the best single predictors correlate about .50 with the criterion. (Note that subjective judgments of the residences were used as predictors). Neither environmental attitudes nor socio-demographic variables have relevant influence.

The structure is similar for movers in t1 and t6 although predictability is higher for the new residence (see models 3 and 4). Environmental aspects seem to be more predictive for the non-movers' satisfaction (models 5 and 6).

TABLE 3:
Multiple Prediction of Residential Satisfaction

Criterion: overall evaluation of the residence

Data set	M1	M1	M1	M6	M6	M6	N1	N1	N1
n:	91	91	91	45	45	45	71	71	71
Analysis:		(1)	(2)		(3)	(4)		(5)	(6)
mult. R:		61	65		73	76		65	70
mult. R<:		37	43		53	58		42	49

Predictors:	r-PC	Beta	Beta	r-PC	Beta	Beta	r-PC	Beta	Beta
Costs of residence	12	10	10	34	30	32	23	17	11
Number of rooms, size	47			41			35		
Comfort, state/repair	45	36	30	43	36	41	36	26	22
Balcony/terrace/garden	34			34			51		
Type/size of building	38			41			49		
Distance to city center	09	-12	-09	37	22	25	26	26	23
Distance to place of work	19			11			16		
Shopping facilities	30	29	30	14	09	11	-04	-17	-17
Smell nuisance	14			28			50		
Noise/quietness	36	22	28	49	43	36	42	25	24
Avail. of parks/nature	26	17	15	33	-12	-18	40	27	25
Aesthet. qual./decayment	32			44			35		
Age	09		07	20		13	-23		-15
Sex (f=1)	01		05	08		-03	-03		00
Urban vs. suburban res.	05		05	03		-14	02		05
Family/single	-24		-18	09		02	-09		-04
Duration of residence	09			-10			19		
Identification with area	49			-24			37		
Environmental concern	03		14	01		-03	-31		-08
Importance of env. qual.	-02		-18	04		13	-24		-20

r-PC = correlation between predictor and criterion; Beta = standardized beta-weights; all coefficients mulitiplied by 100.

The cognitive structure of residence evaluations has also been analyzed by means of the LISREL approach (Joereskog & Soerbom, 1981). Figure 3 gives a first example (these analyses are not yet finished). In this path model the various evaluations of a residence were dichotomized into dwelling/location aspects and environmental aspects (referring to the concepts ER and EE in the theoretical framework in Figure 1). The results indicate that environmental quality is more relevant in t6 (lower scores) than in t1 (upper scores); MAU-models (to be explained in the next section) are predictive for subjective satisfaction; and attitudes such as environmental concern or local identification have low influence on residential satisfaction.

FIGURE 3

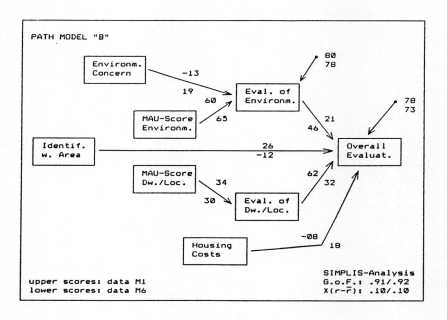

The evaluations of residences discussed so far can be considered as general *intentions,* as a kind of pre-decision about housing alternatives. In order to identity relevant determinants of residential *choice,* discriminant analyses were run (see Table 4).

These analyses are computed about residences that have been inspected during the movers' search phase. Criterion (1) refers to an acceptability statement about all considered residences; analysis (2) compares desired versus unwanted residences (excluding not available ones). The set of included predictors equals that in Table 3.

Evidently the resulting prediction pattern for the choice responses is somewhat different, with costs now being the dominating influence.

TABLE 4
DISCRIMINANT ANALYSIS: DETERMINANTS OF RESIDENTIAL CHOICE

Criterion:	(1) Residence accepted			(2) Residence desired		
Data set:	M2+M3+M4+Mx			M2+M3+M4+Mx		
n (n+/n−):	161 (58/103)			88 (29/59)		
Canon. Corr.:	47			52		
Wilks' Lambda:	78			74		
Predictors:	r−PC	CDF	SWC	r−PC	CDF	SWC
Costs of residence	31	61	77	29	51	81
Number of rooms, size	19			26		
Comfort, state/repair	20	41	39	21	36	46
Balcony/terrace/garden	13			26		
Type/size of building	14	27	11	06	11	−32
Distance to city center	04	08	09	−01	−01	02
Distance to place of work	11			06		
Shopping facilities	16	30	33	12	22	22
Smell nuisance	23			32		
Noise/quietness	23	45	40	27	48	36
Avail. of parks/nature	12	22	14	21	41	37
Aesthet. qual./decayment	20			30		
Age	−03	−07	−16	−05	−10	−20
Sex (f=1)	−03	−09	−22	02	−04	−05
Urban vs. suburban res.	08	10	22	−13	−17	13
Family/single	−07	−15	−09	07	15	30
Identification with area	−06	−11	−09	07	13	35

r−PC = correlation between predictor and criterion; CDF = correlation v. discriminant function; SWC = standardized weight coefficients; all coefficients multiplied by 100.

Multi-attribute utility models

Analyzing the appropriateness of models derived from multi-attribute utility theory was a main goal of the project. The 12 attributes shown above were considered as components and five variants of the basic additive model were defined (see Table 5).

Models MAU1 and 2 use standardized utility measures whereas MAU3 and 4 are based on raw scores. In models MAU2 and 4 attributes are treated with equal weights (i.e., unweighted); however, in MAU5 the weights of those attributes are added up for which the actual state of the residence is within the individual acceptability range, as determined by the respondent (corresponding roughly to Simon's "satisficing" concept).

TABLE 5
Analyzed "MAU"—Models: Overview

| Model | Basic model: U(Ai) = E u(Xij) * wj | | Weights |
	Residence data X	Preference judgments u	w
MAU 1	t1..t6	Partial Utility, t1	t1
MAU 2	t1	Partial Utility, t1	—
MAU 3	t1..t6	Favorableness judgments, t1	t1
MAU 4	t1	Favorableness judgments, t1	—
MAU 5	t2..t5	Acceptability level, t1	t1

Scales:
Attribute outcomes (X): levels A/B/C/D = 1/2/3/4
Favorableness: rating scale 1..6
Partial utility (u): favorableness transformed, 0..100
Acceptability of an attribute level: yes/no = 1/0

These approaches were used to compute model-derived evaluations of all residences that had been judged by either the movers (data sets M1 to M6) or the non-movers (N1, N6). Additionally the elicitation of utilities and weights was repeated in phase t6, enabling stability checks and also the determination of two different MAU-scores for M6 and N6-data.

Evidence on the prescriptive validity of MAU-based evaluations of residences can be gained from correlations with "holistic" overall evaluations of the respective housing alternatives. In Table 6 the correlational analyses are summarized. The *inter*individual coefficients are computed across n respondents; the *intra* individual analyses are based on m residences (m = 3..6).

TABLE 6
CORRELATIONS (r) BETWEEN MAU—VALUES AND HOLISTIC EVALUATIONS

Criterion: Overall evaluation of the quality of the residence

	inter-individual									intra-individual
Data set:	M1	M2	M3	M4	M5	M6	N1	N6	Mdn	Data M1...M6
Model: n:	92	74	56	28	34	45	71	63		Mdn (N:66)
MAU 1	40	48	41	36	49	38	48	35	42	61
MAU 2	37						43			
MAU 3	36	50	29	38	41	40	46	39	40	63
MAU 4	36						47			
MAU 5		26	41	08	23				25	56

Coefficients: Pearson-r. Empty fields: not yet analyzed.

According to these results, MAU models are only moderate predictors of residential satisfaction; models using attribute weights are slightly better than unweighted ones; the use of standardized partial utilities instead of (untransformed) favourableness scores seems not to increase validity; and the acceptability-based approach (MAU5) is less effective. Concerning model MAU5, it has to be taken into account that the acceptability of outcomes was scaled only by yes/no and that, on average, only 1.1 attributes were in the non-acceptance range; thus the variance (and possibly the stability) of MAU5 values is restricted.

Changes in evaluations over time

In this context it is instructive to compare the evaluations of residences across the considered 6 points in time. For both overall and partial judgments it has already been shown in Table 2 (see above) that residential satisfaction is considerably increased for the chosen residence but somewhat reduced after 4 months in the new home. This is particularly true for the evaluation of noise/ quietness, an environmental stressor that is often underestimated (cf. Paechter et al. 1988).

The same structure is obvious for the MAU data (see Table 7): as expected, the lowest means occur for the rejected dwellings, the highest means for the selected residence after the decision has been made.

TABLE 7
MAU-DATA: LONGITUDINAL COMPARISONS (MOVERS, n=45)

Considered residence:	old residence	inspected but rejected residences	inspected and accepted residence	new residence after 4 months
Point in time:	t1	t234	t2345	t6
MAU 1	67.3	66.8	75.6	71.9
MAU 3	67.3	64.9	74.7	71.3
MAU 5	84.8	88.1	93.2	90.2

All MAU models based on 12 attributes; values range from 0.0 to 100.0. Given are means across residences.

The results for the non-movers show no significant differences between phases t1 and t6. (Both holistic evaluations and MAU values yield N1/N6 correlations between .70 and .80, which can be interpreted as stability coefficients).

Difficulties and constraints of housing decisions

Some further findings on the decision making process, including qualitative data, shall be summarized briefly (see Rohrmann & Borcherding, 1988, for details): The attention of those inspecting a prospective home is mainly focused on the immediately salient features (such as characteristics of the building and the rooms) whereas environmental and location aspects which are highly weighted in "principal" considerations get less interest in this situation. The consequences and long-term impacts of adverse environmental conditions seem to be underestimated by most people. When finally deciding about their future residence, people are often considerably influenced by social constraints (e.g., family needs) or external influences (e.g., the availability of an apartment or time pressure). On average, the movers visited a dozen houses, spending not more than about 40 minutes for each inspection. Due to the complex (and mostly incomplete) information, the decision problem is rated as a very difficult task.

Finally, it should be mentioned that many movers have no clear and stable preferences and, in the case of couples/families, their demands can be rather heterogenous.

CONCLUSIONS

Consequences for further research

The study has clarified the main determinants of residential judgments and decisions, but also demonstrated the restricted validity of formal evaluations of decision alternatives. The (in-)appropriateness of the employed MAU models might be due to substantive problems, e.g., too simple additive modelling or crucial external influences that are not considered in the analyzed variable set, or it might be due to methodological reasons, e.g., measurement problems with attribute weights or utilities or acceptance scores.

Thus it seems necessary to develop and test modified MAU models, e.g., conjunctive approaches (that will be tried in further analyses of the present data); to increase the reliability and the practicability of the necessary scaling procedures (particularly under the conditions of a field study); and to include contextual factors/constraints (transformed into quantified variables) in the evaluation model. With respect to the external validity of findings on residential decision making, larger and more differentiated samples are needed. Relevant issues are regional differences (e.g., urban versus rural), the role of attitudes and life values within different populations and the social decision process within moving couples/ families.

Applicability aspects

The results are relevant not only for theoretical issues, but may also have practical significance. Prospective users of research findings are, for example, city planners, urban administration, or residence agents.

How about the movers, the actual "problem owners"? Apparently, these decision makers are stressed by their task (as also noted by Weichhart, 1988) and they suffer from some cognitive overload. Besides various social and economic constraints, the realistic anticipation of future impacts of a housing decision seems to be a crucial difficulty.

If there is a need for "better decisions in moving or choosing a house" (McKenzie, 1980), it could be useful to provide movers with something like a "guideline for assessing and evaluating residences", serving as an aid for people's decision making about their future homes.

NOTE

The project was funded by the German Research Society within the program 'Ecological Psychology'.

CORRESPONDENCE

Institut fuer Psychologie der THD, Steubenplatz 12, D-6100 Darmstadt, Germany (FRG), Phone (6151) 16.5113; BitNet: XBR1DB1M@DDATHD21

REFERENCES

Altman, I., & Werner, C.M. (Eds.) (1985). *Home environments.* New York: Plenum.

Aschenbrenner, K. M. (1977). Influence of attribute formulation on the evaluation of apartments by multiattribute utility procedures. In H. Jungermann & G. de Zeeuw (Eds.), *Decision making and change in human affairs* 81-97. Dordrecht: Reidel.

Borcherding, K. (1981). *Successive evaluation of multi-attribute decision alternatives.* Contribution to the 8th Research Conference on Subjective Probability, Utility and Decision-Making, Budapest.

Borcherding, K. (1983). Entscheidungstheorie und Entscheidungshilfeverfahren fuer komplexe Entscheidungssituationen. In M. Irle (Ed.), *Methoden und Anwendungen in der Marktpsychologie* (Bd. D/III/5 der Enzyklopaedie der Psychologie). 64-173. Goettingen: Hogrefe.

Clark, W.A.W. (1986). *Human migration.* Beverly Hills: Sage.

DeJong, G., & Gardner, R. (Eds.) (1981). *Migration decision making.* New York: Pergamon Press.

Fischer, G.W. (1979). Utility models for multiple objective decisions: Do they accurately represent human preferences? *Decision Sciences, 10,* 451-479.

Fisher, J. D., Bell, P. A., & Baum, A. (1984). *Environmental psychology.* New York: Holt, Rinehart & Winston.

Joereskog, K. G., & Soerbom, D. (1981). *LISREL User's guide, Version 5.* Chicago: National Educational Resources.

Keeney, R. L., & Raiffa, H. (1976). *Decisions with multiple objectives: Preferences and value tradeoffs*. New York: Wiley.

Lindberg, E., Gärling, T., Montgomery, H., & Waara, R. (1987). People's evaluation of housing atributes. *Scandinavian Housing and Planning Research, 4*, 81-103.

McHugh, K. E. (1984). Explaining migration intensions and destination selection. *The Professional Geographer, 36*, 315-325.

McKenzie, W. M. (1980). *Toward better decisions in moving or choosing a house*. Melbourne: CSIRO, Built Environment Group, Division of Building Research.

Michelson, W. (1980). Long and short range criteria for housing choice and environmental behaviour. *Journal of Social Issues, 36*, 135-149.

Paechter, M., Rohrmann, B., Wertenbroch, K., & Wetzel, S. (1988). The relevance of noise for evaluating and selecting residences. In B. Berglund, U. Berglund, J. Karlson, & T. Lindvall (Eds.), *Noise as a public health problem* (vol. III) 71-77. Stockholm: Swedish Council for Research.

Rohrmann, B. (1986). *Environmental stressors and housing decision A review* (Contribution to the 21th International Congress of Applied Psychology Jerusalem 1986). Darmstadt: Bericht Nr. 86-2, Institut fuer Psychologie der THD

Rohrmann, B., & Borcherding, K. (in prep. (1988)). *Der Stellenwert der Umweltqualitaet bei Wohnentscheidungen Forschungsbericht ueber eine Laengsschnitt-Feldstudie*. Darmstadt: Bericht Nr. 88-1, Institut fuer Psychologie der THD.

Rossi, P. H. (1980). *Why families move* (sec. ed.). Beverly Hills: Sage.

Shumaker, S. A., & Stokols, D. (1982). Residential mobility as a social issue and research topic. *Journal of Social Issues, 38*, 1-19.

Tognoli, J. (1986). Residential environments. In D. Stokols & I. Altman (Eds.), *Handbook of environmental psychology* (pp. 65-84). New York: Wiley.

Weichhart, P. (1988). Wohnsitzpraeferenzen und "neue Wohnungsnot" Das Beispiel Salzburg. *DISP, 94*, 44-51.

Winterfeldt, D. v., & Edwards, W. (1973). *Evaluation of complex stimuli using multi-attribute utility procedures*. Ann Arbor: Technical Report, Engineering Psychology Laboratory, University of Michigan.

Winterfeldt, D. v., & Edwards, W. (1986). *Decision analysis and behavioural research*. Cambridge: University Press.

Social Applications and Issues in Psychology
R.C. King and J.K. Collins (editors)
©Elsevier Science Publishers B.V. (North-Holland), 1989

MODERN HEALTH TECHNOLOGIES AND QUALITY OF LIFE MEASURES

David R. Evans, Margaret T. Hearn, Lynn M. L. Levy and Lisa A. Shatford

The University of Western Ontario, Canada

The research was designed to evalutate the impact of three divergent and discrete health technologies on quality of life. The three technologies were liver transplant, *in vitro* fertilisation (IVF) and stress management. In the first study, liver recipients completed selected scales from the Quality of Life Questionnaire-D (QLQ-D) before and after their liver transplant was performed. The second study involved a similar paradigm, however, the participants were couples participating in an IVF program. In the final study, middle managers were exposed to an exercise program, skill-training or no training condition. The QLQ-D was administered pre- and posttraining and six and 12 months following training. In the case of liver recipients, it was demonstrated that after their transplant their quality of life was restored to normal. IVF couples were shown to have better than average quality of life. At follow-up, the stress management training procedure involving exercise had an impact on quality of life in general and interpersonal domains in particular. The results of these studies indicate that QLQ-D has utility as an evaluative measure with respect to a broad range of modern health technologies. The instrument also has potential as both a diagnostic and predictive instrument, but its generalisability to these uses has yet to be demonstrated.

Interest in the assessment of quality of life can be traced to the early 1940s. However, since the mid 1970s there has been increasing interest in the development and impact of health interventions upon an individual's quality of life (Croog et al.,1986; Mayou, 1986; Platt Furst et al., 1987). A proportion of this research has been directed at identifying factors that impact upon quality of life, in order that more effective prevention programs can be designed (Haug & Folmar, 1986; Osberg et al., 1987). Other studies have been concerned with the evaluation of primary,secondary or tertiary prevention programs for a range of health related problems (Lawson, 1985; McDaniel, 1987; Packa, 1987).

Evaluations of the impact of primary prevention programs on quality of life have involved wellness programs (Lawson, 1987),antihypertensive therapy (Croog et al., 1986), and health promotion behaviour activities with older adults (McDaniel, 1987). Impact studies of secondary prevention programs on quality of life have focussed on bypass surgery (Mayou, 1986) and interventions involving transplantation of organs (Evans, Manninen et al., 1985; Packa, 1987). Finally, the impact of tertiary prevention factors on quality of life has been evaluated with such groups as rheumatoid arthritis patients (Baird, 1986; Marnell, 1986; Platt Furst et al., 1987), post mastectomy patients (Meyerowitz, 1983) and patients suffering from childhood leukemia (Fife, Norton & Groom, 1987).

As discussed in an earlier paper (Evans, Burns, et al., 1985), there remains considerable confusion concerning the definition and measurement of quality of life. A small minority continues to define quality of life as the absence of physical and/or emotional dysfunction (Haug & Folmar, 1986). Others employ combinations of affective and/or life satisfaction measures (Croog et al., 1986; Evans, Manninen et al., 1985). Still others use a range of measures in areas such as work, family, social life and leisure, reflecting the multivariate character of the concept (Mayou, 1986). The Quality of Life Questionnaire(QLQ-D) was developed to address some of the definitional and measurement concerns in this area of research (Evans, Burns, et al., 1985). The purpose of the present paper is to investigate the utility of the Quality of Life Questionnaire in evaluating a range of health technologies.

QUALITY OF LIFE AFTER LIVER TRANSPLANTATION

As health care costs have increased the cost/benefit of organ transplant programs has been questioned. Evans, Manninen, et al., 1985) demonstrated that kidney transplantation had a positive impact on both subjective and objective measures of the quality of life of recipients. Recently, Grant, et al. (1987) evaluated the impact of liver transplantation on the quality of life of recipients. Selected scales from the Quality of Life Questionnaire were used in the latter study.

Method

Subjects. The participants in this study were 15 men and 16 women who had undergone liver transplants at University Hospital, London, Ontario. When compared to the 1981 census data for Canada, demographic characteristics for the participants did not differ markedly from those for the population as a whole. The average time since last transplant was 19.3 (3.4 to 48.5) months, and the majority (n=25, 80.7%) had had only one transplant.

Measures. Participants completed a demographic questionnaire, paper-and-pencil versions of the Campbell, Converse and Rodgers (1976) Life appraisal and Life satisfaction questions, along with selected scales from the Quality of Life Questionnaire.

Procedure. Consecutive adult recipients of liver transplants in the program were mailed a set of questionnaires. They were asked to complete them, and return them by mail.

Results and Discussion

The scores of the participants on the Campbell, Converse and Rodgers (1976) indices of quality of life and the selected scales from the Quality of Life Questionnaire were compared to the normative data for each measure. None of the t values for the comparisons reached significance, suggesting that the liver transplant recipients had normal levels of well-being, general affect, and life satisfaction. Further, they appeared to have normal levels of Material well-being, Personal growth, and Marital, Extended family and Extrafamilial relations. In general their life quality appeared normal. In that the majority (n=24, 77.4%) indicated that their quality of life had changed markedly for the better since their transplant, it was concluded that the impact of the transplant was to restore their quality of life to normal.

In order to explore further the relationship between measures, factor analysis was performed on the independent measures of quality of life. A principal components factor analysis was performed, followed by oblique rotation of factors meeting the Kaiser criterion, with delta set at 1.0 (see Table 1). Factor I, which accounts for 44.7% of the variance among measures, indicates the quality of extrafamilial and extended family relationships and is related to a sense of personal well-being and general well-being as measured by the Campbell, Converse, and Rodgers (1976) general index. The second factor represents a sense of personal well-being and functional ability that, like Factor I, is related to. general well-being.

TABLE 1
Factorial Structure of the Quality of Life of Liver Transplant Patients

Measure	Factor	
	I	II
Extrafamilial relations	.84	
Extended family relations	.77	
Well-being	.75	.74
Marital relations	.56	
Material well-being	.54	.47
Personal growth	.62	.80
Functional impairment		-.77
Common variance	44.7%	16.4%

QUALITY OF LIFE AND *IN VITRO* FERTILIZATION

Since the inception of the *in vitro* fertilization procedure in 1979, hundreds of pregnancies have been reported worldwide using this method. As Hearn et al. (1987) have noted there has been little study of the psychological characteristics of couples seeking *in vitro* fertilization. They demonstrated that on selected scales from the Quality of Life Questionnaire a sample of three hundred couples entering the IVF program at University Hospital, London, Ontario were found to have above average quality of life in most domains. The study presented here evaluated the impact of having a successful IVF treatment upon quality of life.

Method

Subjects. Sixteen couples who were successful in the *in vitro* fertilization program at University Hospital, London, Ontario made up the sample.

Measures. Each participant completed all of the Quality of Life Questionnaire - D scales, with the exception of the Physical well-being, the Altruistic and the Political behaviour scales. As indicated in Hearn et al. (1987) participants also completed a number of other personality, behavioural and environmental self-report measures at intake.

Procedure. Couples meeting the medical criteria for inclusion in the program were sent two sets of questionnaires 3 months prior to their entry into the program. They were asked to complete a set of the questionnaires each and to return them for scoring prior to their first visit to the Hospital. The pretest was administered approximately 12-18 months prior to delivery of the child(ren). Couples were mailed a second set of questionnaires approximately 12 months following the delivery of the child(ren).

Results and Discussion

The questionnaires were scored and a Quality of Life Score was computed for each person on each occasion. A Spouse (2) by Time (2) repeated measures analysis of variance was completed for each measure. The significant main effects for Time and the means and standard deviations for each of these measures are shown in Table 2. The main effect of Time on Material well- being, Personal growth, Extended family relations, Occupational relations, Sports activity, Vacation behaviour and Social desirability was not significant. These results compare with the study reported by Harriman (1986) for couples achieving parenthood by natural means. As with most critical events, the arrival of children affected the marital relationship by producing a reduction in its quality. No doubt the time demands of parental responsibilities had an impact on interaction with friends and creative/aesthetic activities. Finally, the change in life interest from job to family might explain the impact of parenthood on the job related scales. In general, the quality of life of successful IVF couples moved closer to the norm.

TABLE 2

The Impact of Successful *in vitro* Fertilization on Selected Scales from the Quality of Life Questionnaire

Scale	Pre-scores		Post-scores		
	M	SD	M	SD	F
Marital relations	10.67	1.42	9.67	2.14	7.96**
Extrafamilial relations	9.32	1.62	8.6	2.08	7.27*
Job characteristics	9.81	1.60	8.58	2.10	6.30*
Job satisfiers	8.96	2.22	7.65	1.99	5.80*
Creative/aesthetic behaviour	6.47	2.21	5.80	2.61	4.79*
Quality of life score	135.42	13.95	126.19	18.99	12.59**

* p<.05   ** p<.01

STRESS MANAGEMENT STRATEGIES AND QUALITY OF LIFE

Stress has long been recognized as a pervasive problem with many detrimental effects, including physical and psychological health problems (Monroe, 1983). In addition, there is a small but growing body of research that has identified a relationship between stress and the disruption of performance at work (Moos & Moos, 1983) and that shows decreases in job satisfaction (Mclean, 1982). In recent years a number of training programs have been developed to facilitate the ability of individuals to cope with stress and, hence, to offset the detrimental effects of stress noted above. The purpose of the present study was to evaluate the impact of two such programs, coping skills training, and aerobic exercise/fitness training on alleviating the effects of stress and producing an enhancement in quality of life.

Method

Subjects. Forty five managers/supervisors from a total of 25 businesses in London, Ontario voluntarily participated in this study. At the beginning of the study the participants had a mean age of 43 years (30-61). They were randomly assigned to one of three groups: coping skills training; aerobic exercise/fitness training; or waiting list control.

Measures. Each participant completed the Quality of Life Questionnaire - D, and the Index of Organizational Reactions.

Procedure. The measures were completed by all participants prior to the training period, then immediately, at six months and at 12 months after the training period. Each of the three groups received a two hour stress-educational package during the first week of the training program. The remaining ten weeks were then devoted to coping skills training, aerobics exercise/fitness training or no training. The training groups met for one 45 minute period each week. The coping skills training was modelled on stress inoculation training (Meichenbaum & Cameron, 1983) and was focused on developing self talk, relaxation and problem solving skills. The aerobic exercise/fitness training involved the development of aerobic exercise skills to develop cardiovascular fitness and an ability to relax to offset the impact of stress.

Results and Discussion

A one-way groups (3) multivariate analysis of variance was performed on the data for the Quality of Life Questionnaire scales taken together for each assessment time. The results of these analyses are shown in Table 3. The groups effect was not significant at pre-intervention, post-intervention or at 12 months post-intervention. The groups effect was significant at six months follow up. At this time both intervention groups had a higher quality of life than the no training group. It appears that the interventions had an impact on day to day stress management and, by six months follow, on quality of life. In turn this effect was diminished by 12 months follow up. It is possible that if the initial training period had been more intense and of longer duration the impact at six months would have continued.

TABLE 3

Group Effect on QLQ-D Scales at Pre-, and Post-intervention, and at Six and Twelve Months Following the Intervention

Time	Wilks Lambda	F	p
Pre-intervention	0.47	0.86	0.67
Post-intervention	0.41	1.04	0.43
Six Months Follow Up	0.25	1.88	0.02
Twelve Months Follow Up	0.34	1.34	0.17

GENERAL DISCUSSION

The results of these three studies indicate that the Quality of Life Questionnaire is a useful tool in the evaluation of a variety of new health technologies in both the primary and secondary prevention areas. Current research suggests that the instrument can be used to assess the needs of specific groups and communities. It has potential also as an alternate means of assessing an individual such that enhancement interventions can be employed rather than reactive treatments. Perhaps at some point, individuals will find it useful to have an annual psychological checkup, in which the QLQ-D will form an integral part .

CORRESPONDENCE

The University of Western Ontario, London, Ontario, Canada

REFERENCES

Campbell, A., Converse, P. E., & Rodgers, W. L. (1976). *The Quality of American Life: Perceptions, Evaluations, and Satisfactions.* New York: Russell Sage.

Croog, S. H., Levine, S., Testa, M. A., Brown, B., Bulpitt, C. J., Jenkins, C. D., Klerman, G. L., & Williams, G. H. (1986). The effects of antihypertensive therapy on the quality of life. *New England Journal of Medicine, 314,* 1657-1664.

Evans, D. R., Burns, J. E., Robinson, W. E., & Garrett, O. J. (1985). The Quality of Life Questionnaire: A multidimensional measure. *American Journal of Community Psychology, 13,* 305-322.

Evans, R. W., Manninen, D. L., Garrison, L. P., Hart, L. G., Blagg, C. R., Gutman, R. A., Hull, A. R., & Lowrie, E. G. (1985). The quality of life of patients with end-stage renal disease. *New England Journal of Medicine, 312,* 553- 559.

Fife, B., Norton, J., & Groom, G. (1987). The family's adaptation to childhood Leukemia. *Social Science and Medicine, 24,* 159-168.

Grant, D. R., Evans, D. R., Hearn, M. T. Sherlock, M., Ghent, C. N., Duff, J. H., & Wall, W. J. (1987). The quality of life after liver transplantation. Paper presented at the Annual Meeting of Canadian Association of Clinical Surgeons, St. John's, Newfoundland.

Haug, M. R., & Folmar, S. J. (1986). Longevity, gender, and life quality. *Journal of Health and Social Behaviour, 27,* 332-345.

Harriman, L. C. (1985). Marital adjustment as related to personal and marital changes accompanying parenthood. *Family Relations, 34,* 233-239.

Hearn, M. T., Yuzpe, A. A., Brown, S. E., & Casper, R. F. (1987). Psychological characteristics of in vitro fertilization participants. *American Journal of Obstetrics and Gynaecology, 156,* 269-274.

Lawson, B. R. (1985). The identification and analysis of selected wellness programs in educational institutions in the state of Texas. *Dissertation Abstracts International, 46,* 3610A.

Mayou, R. (1986). The psychiatric and social consequences of coronary artery surgery. *Journal of Psychosomatic Research, 30,* 255-271.

McDaniel, R. W. (1987). Relationship of participation in health promotion behaviours to quality of life in older adults. *Dissertation Abstracts International, 48,* 1940B.

McLean, A. A. (1982). Improving mental health at work. *Psychiatric Hospital, 13,* 77-83.

Meichenbaum, D., & Cameron, R. (1983). Stress-inoculation training: Toward a general paradigm for training coping skills. In D. Meichenbaum & M. E. Jeremko (Eds.), *Stress Reduction and Prevention.* New York: Plenum.

Monroe, S. M. (1983).   Major and minor life events as predictors of psychological distress: Further issues and findings. *Journal of Behavioural Medicine, 6,* 189-205.

Moos, R. H., & Moos, B. S.   (1983).   Adaptation and the quality of life in work and family settings.   *Journal of Community Psychology, 11,* 158-170.

Osberg, J. S., McGinnis, G. E., Dejong, G., & Seward, M. L.   (1987).   Life satisfaction and quality of life among disabled elderly adults.   *Journal of Gerontology, 42,* 228-230.

Packa, D. R. (1987).   Quality of life of adults after a heart transplant.   *Dissertation Abstracts International, 48,* 91B.

Platt Furst, G., Gerber, L. H., Smith, C. C., Fisher, S., & Shulman, B.   (1987).   A program for improving energy conservation behaviours in adults with rheumatoid arthritis.   *American Journal of Occupational Therapy, 41,* 102-111.

Social Applications and Issues in Psychology
R.C. King and J.K. Collins (editors)
©Elsevier Science Publishers B.V. (North-Holland), 1989

NECESSARY PREREQUISITES FOR DEAF'S SELF ACTUALIZATION IN A HEARING SOCIETY

Gunnel A.M. Backenroth

University of Stockholm, Sweden

Communication and interaction are vital for the individual's development and self actualization regardless of hearing status. Many childhood deaf people have grown up without sign language, resulting in less favourable developmental possibilities according to reported studies. Despite a common language and a common culture, not all of the deaf people participate in the deaf community. About 10 % are psychosocially isolated with limited possibilities for self actualization. The paper stresses the necessity to work with the deaf person's social network at different levels. Self actualization in the deaf culture is discussed on the basis of an investigation of 20 deaf people as well as on the basis of a case study of a deaf woman of 26 years. The application of humanistic psychology in deaf research is described. Two models are presented, a conceptual model and an action model. The discussion focuses mainly on necessary prerequisites at different levels for facilitating the deaf's self actualization.

TO BE DEAF IN A HEARING COMMUNITY

"Do you know what a language is ? Bridges. It is these bridges that make us human. It is only when we have mastered words, have a language, that we have access to the mutuality of the human world and to the understanding that we give to and receive from each other" (Lerner, 1987, p.16). The quotation is taken from a play by the English dramatist Harold Pinter. One of the factors limiting the possibility for self actualization for the deaf is the lack of opportunities for them to participate in the language, information and culture of the hearing community.

The most important problem that has confronted the deaf over the years is not the deafness itself but rather the attitudes and lack of understanding that they meet for the consequences of deafness, whether cognitive, emotional or social. Since the deaf have been, and continue to be, a minority group, few resources have been allocated them (Award, 1978; Denmark & Eldridge, 1969; Pyke & Littman, 1982; Schein, 1983; Thoreson & Tully, 1971; Williams & Sussman, 1971).

There have been several positive developments in Sweden in the deaf area that give rise to satisfaction. Sign language has been recognised as an official language; there is a special high school for the deaf; a deaf person has been awarded an honorary doctorate; the culture of the deaf has been exposed in various ways to the community, exemplified in cultural festivals for the deaf; and there are several different educational courses for the deaf in their own language that have thereby broadened the career opportunities for the deaf (in linguistics, child and psychiatric care, for nursing assistants, dental technicians, and in media/video courses for the deaf).

The most important and decisive factor for a child's development, regardless of the child's hearing status, is the interaction and communication between the child and its environment (e.g. parents, siblings, relatives, friends, teachers). Many childhood deaf have grown to adulthood without sign language, during the period when sign language was not officially recognised in Swedish schools. This has resulted in less favourable developmental potential for the deaf (Backenroth, 1980; Backenroth & Hanson, 1986.)

There is international research that maintains that the absence of sign language in a hearing family with a deaf child can result in depression, introversion and an inability to establish close relations with others as an adult for the deaf person (Backenroth, 1986a, 1986b; Magen, 1987). There is also research that shows the importance and necessity of early, recurrent and adequate support for the parents if deaf children are to have favourable developmental conditions (Backenroth, 1983; Jongkees, 1983; Mindel & Vernon, 1971; Vernon, 1971). If accepted when they are children, deaf people are presumably much less inclined to isolate themselves as adults (Backenroth, 1986b).

SELF ACTUALIZATION AND DEAFNESS

How is self actualization defined? Self actualization is the attempt to develop latent potentials (Bühler, 1971; Maslow, 1971; McMullen, 1982; Steele, 1976). A person's readiness to be committed beyond self is also related to self actualization (Magen, 1987; Maslow, 1971). Maslow and Goldstein saw self actualization as the goal of life (Bühler, 1974a, 1974b).

The culture of the deaf is a culture in itself, but in many respects reflects the culture of the hearing. Perhaps the deaf culture unconsciously also tries to copy the hearing culture. Cultural differences between the deaf and the hearing can sometimes hinder an initial contact. That such differences can sometimes also make cooperation difficult finds support in Goldstein (1986) and Sue & Zane (1987). In their article, Sue and Zane discuss the role of cultural competence and culture-specific techniques in psychotherapy with minority groups.

What does the concept of self actualization involve in the area of deafness? In a recent investigation of relevance (Backenroth, 1988a) it was found that 12 of 20 deaf subjects claimed they knew what self actualization meant, namely developing oneself, developing one's interests, participating in two cultures, succeeding with something one strives for, breaking down barriers; doing what one has dreamed of and accepting challenges.

Despite the fact that the deaf now have a common language and culture, not all deaf people participate in the deaf community. On the contrary, many remain apart. An estimated 10% of the childhood deaf are psychosocially isolated (Backenroth, 1986b). Working with a deaf person's social network is therefore important in helping to liberate energy for new developments (Backenroth & Hanson, 1987). Other humanistically oriented researchers have also stressed the importance of building social networks (Bühler, 1974a, 1974b; Steele, 1976).

Being deaf and psychosocially isolated, regardless of whether the isolation is self-imposed or forced upon one, involves feelings of being an outsider and lacking membership of the deaf community, perhaps the only group that deaf people have. We who are hearing can choose between many different hearing groups. The deaf do not have that opportunity and isolation is therefore unmercifully hard upon them (Backenroth, 1986a).

APPLICATION OF HUMANISTIC PSYCHOLOGY IN DEAF RESEARCH

Research work utilizes two models; a conceptual model that includes some important concepts in the acceptance of one's own deafness such as identification, reality testing, working through (Backenroth, 1983, 1984, 1986b); and an action model for the interventions that are carried out (Morrill et al, 1974; Drapela, 1983).

It is important to point out that in the first model i.e., the conceptual model (see Backenroth, 1983, 1986b) the four key concepts differ in meaning compared with the psychoanalytic usage. Furthermore, they should not be thought of in isolation from each other but rather as parts in a complicated interaction (Backenroth, 1983, 1986b). For counselling work with the deaf, the concepts have the following implications:

Identification. By identification is meant the creation of a network of contacts with other deaf people through activity groups, discussion groups, deaf associations.

Reality Testing. Reality testing refers to accommodation to reality. This includes taking realistic decisions and recognising the consequences of deafness in a hearing society. A grasp of reality can be developed and strengthened in such a way that one becomes more aware of the demands and responsibilities of others and of oneself.

Working Through. The working through of problems can be of various types; for example, relationship problems, conflicts, life experiences, one's own deafness and the problems that relatives experience in accepting the deaf's deafness' and thereby the deaf person himself or herself.

Acceptance. Identification, reality testing and working through could all be included in the concept of acceptance, which, among other things, means to work at the handicap as constructively as possible (Backenroth, 1984). Assuming that deaf individuals have good conceptions of their own identity, good self-esteem, positive attitudes to sign language, worked through attitudes to their own handicaps, ability to see their assets and resources as persons in a wider and realistic perspective, then one can say that they will have reached intellectual and emotional acceptance.

On the basis of the action model (see Morrill et al, 1974; Drapela, 1983) various work models can be carried out and evaluated. Furthermore, various aims, goals and methods can be combined to offer the deaf adequate measures of support. As the model shows, interventions can take place at different levels. Besides humanistic psychology (primarily inspired by Goldstein, 1986; Raubolt, 1985; see also Backenroth & Hanson, 1986), psychodynamic theory has also figured as a theoretical base. Humanistic psychotherapy focuses on the positive, growth-oriented ego-capacities of the individual. Empathy, a here-and-now focus and interpersonal and psychosocial forces are of importance (Raubolt, 1985).

The "rule of experts" has been very prominent in the deaf area throughout the years. This approach has not been competence-enhancing. Humanistic psychology and a firm belief in and respect for an individual's own activity, problem solving ability, potential and personal development, have still failed to achieve a sufficiently potent position in the professional approach that confronts deaf persons and their families. Deaf clients who, when evaluated from a hearing and non humanistic perspective seem to have a conspicuous lack of developmental potential, have, on the contrary, demonstrated their resourcefulness when a humanistic approach has pervaded all contacts with them. (Backenroth, 1987a, 1987b; Backenroth & Hanson, 1987).

In practical work with clients, the professionals' active involvement is important for the therapeutic process (Backenroth & Hanson, 1986; Raubolt, 1985; Steele, 1976). Seen in an international perspective there is a direct relationship between rehabilitation results and active participation of the deaf themselves in the rehabilitation process (Evans, 1984; Vernon, 1970, 1975).

SELF ACTUALIZATION : A CASE STUDY

Charlotte Bühler maintains that scientific studies of the process of self actualization should include examining the person as a whole, including a personal history where the emphasis lies primarily on intentionality, motivation, determination, creativity, integration, social relations and existential aspects. Bühler suggested the use of both biographical and autobiographical material when studying an individual.

The client in the present study is Karin, a 26 year old deaf woman, well-qualified and working with people. She is unmarried and has no children. She is categorised as group 3 as regards psychosocial isolation (see Backenroth & Hanson, 1987) i.e., deaf persons with minor isolation and lacking clear psychosocial problems. Group 3, seen as a group, is rather well-prepared from childhood to handle difficulties. There is a need for support in identification, reality testing, working through and acceptance.

Karin has been in therapy a couple of times, most recently 1 1/2 years in individual therapy. The therapy, just goes on. In therapy Karin works through her family relationships, her friendships, dependence and independence, intimacy and distance, alienation, deaf identity, female identity, professional identity, self-confidence, self esteem, sense of ambition, feelings of guilt and shame. Before summer, Karin felt that the problems remained. She now dares to confront them and work on them. Furthermore, she says: "I am starting to become more aware of how I function in relation to others. I begin to dare to believe in myself."

What does the concept self actualization mean to Karin? "Self actualization, to make oneself (as far as possible) real. Trying to reach the innermost core. To see who you are and strive to be the person you want to be. Get rid of the unnecessary baggage you are carrying from the past. Re-pack so to speak."

Are there situations in life where Karin feels she can actualize herself? "Therapy. My work finding my professional identity. Chatting with friends, when we get close to each other. Books which help me widen my perspective. Every day, every moment is actually an opportunity. It's seldom that I realise it ... a little more often now than before."

Are there areas in life that Karin would like to realize? "Lots, oh yes! I want to try and achieve the absolute most I can (that is the absolute most for me, not according to anyone else's ideas). Want to find my place amongst the deaf. Want to write, to tell about the misery of integration. Want to become good at work, a good person, become harmonious with myself and with others. Want to understand the creative act".

Karin has many thoughts as to what forms a person. The following quotation is an abridged excerpt from her diary, as summer approaches: "Thinking of myself now... feel that I am so very insecure deep down. I have thoughts and ideas but don't know how I am going to carry them out... and so everything comes to nothing. My commitment has come up a couple of times in therapy. Have a feeling that all my commitment and activity, when it comes down to it, is an escape from myself. Much of what I do is in fact purely mechanical. Whenever I am personally responsible for something I always feel a sense of failure. But what has happened? How have I become so unsure? At school I was always the one that knew everything. I could read and write better than most. I studied hard for all my exams. I got good grades. Though there is one memory which is very strong, every time I think of it a sense of shame comes over me. It was a failure at school... But it was the only time I can remember failing at school. Throughout my school days I was rather strong. I was cheerful and had my own opinions, wasn't afraid to say no. What happened on the way to who I am today ?... I got work immediately... Two memories remain with me however from that period. Two memories of failure... Otherwise I was harmonious. Was out with my friends, boyfriend, active in sport, travelled... I was abroad for a year. That year was fun, though at the same time really hard. Looking back I wonder if the difficult feelings didn't take over. I was lonely, became shy, and didn't always dare to make contact... That's how it is, if you live in another country for a longer period your whole way of thinking changes. The most difficult thing was not having anyone from the family, or a close friend, there..."

"I took up my education again. I had planned to ever since high school. Wonder if I chose myself or whether some outside influence was behind the choice?...Took a course at the special high school for deaf...Since I hadn't been to a school for the deaf it was great, strengthened my identity as a deaf person... Up to the last minute I was unsure as to whether I would continue my education or not. Decided however to complete the course. I now feel that I have chosen an important job. I want a job that is meaningful and fun. So long as I get over this insecurity, I think I will manage it. What I find most difficult with the work now is that I must look to myself for the answers. And I often lack guidance".

SUMMARIZING DISCUSSION

Research on the disablement area requires an interdisciplinary profile. To ensure optimal developmental conditions for the deaf, measures at different levels are required aiming to increase the deaf person's ability to establish social networks, i.e., identification, increasing working through capacity, reality testing and acceptance of the deafness in a hearing majority culture. The attitudes, values and possibilities provided by the society are of outermost importance. Buss (1976) claims that we do not have a humanistic society. Whether or not we do, depends on ourselves. Society is what we make it. For self actualization to be possible for the deaf in a hearing society the following is required :

a) that society's *attitudes* towards the deaf continue to develop in a positive direction (Garstecki, 1982; Krauft et al., 1976; Schein, 1983; Sussman, 1983; Vernon, 1970)

b) that the *interpreter service* offered to the deaf is expanded (Backenroth, 1988b, 1988c)

c) that society recognises the need for *a variety of supportive measures for the deaf and the deaf family* (Backenroth, 1987b) and recognises the need for *support at various levels* (Backenroth, 1986b; Backenroth & Hanson 1986, 1987)

d) that the establishment of *psychiatric outpatient facilities* for the deaf continues in various parts of the country (Backenroth, 1986a, 1986b)

e) that measures aimed at the deaf take *psychological* and *psycho-social factors* into consideration (Backenroth, 1983; Backenroth & Hanson, 1986, 1987)

f) *early and recurrent support for the deaf family* (Backenroth, 1975, 1980, 1983; Jongkees, 1983; Mindel & Vernon, 1971; Vernon, 1971)

g) that the *deaf person's own resources* are recognised in e.g. teaching situations, in rehabilitation and research (Backenroth, 1987a, 1987b; Vernon, 1970, 1975) and that *parents* of deaf children are accepted as partners, as a competent group with extensive influence (Backenroth, 1987a, 1987b)

h) that the deaf are encouraged to continue their education in areas where they can use their *"expert knowledge"* Backenroth, 1986a, 1987b)

i) that the *professional "cultural competence"* in this area is developed further (Levine, 1976; Schein, 1983; Sussman, 1983)

j) that *personnel* who work with the deaf have the opportunity of airing and *working out their feelings* (Backenroth, 1988b, 1988c)

k) that *more research* is undertaken in this area (Backenroth, 1987a, 1987b)

"A humanistic psychology helps to implement what people are longing for" (Bühler, 1974, p.203). This should be the starting point for all research, according to Polkinghorne (1982). One of the primary aims of research on deafness as regards its practical significance is to influence and improve life for the deaf family in our society. In this respect the researcher is like a politician.

In conclusion I quote Woolpert (1982): "To be a humanist is to be political... The humanistic perspective provides not only a new vision of the possible human, but also a new look at our political life. It points to the dangers and opportunities politics offers for actualizing our potential as individuals, as groups, and as a species" (p. 65).

Despite many positive developmental trends in the area of deafness in Sweden, the ideas of humanistic psychology need to be increased in the "professional approach" deaf people encounter. The deaf person must always play the key role in situations that concern him since it is his own future and life situation that is at stake (Backenroth, 1989, in press).

ACKNOWLEDGEMENTS

The author acknowledges financial assistance for the research from DSF; Allmänna Arvsfonden (Delegation for Social Research; National Inheritance Foundation). The author also wish to express thanks to Sveriges Dövas Riksförbund; SDR (Swedish National Association for the Deaf) for co-operation in the course of the research program and to Psykologförbundet (Swedish Psychological Association) for partial financial support to participate in the XXIV International Congress of Psychology in Sydney in 1988. Last, but not least, the author is deeply indebted to the deaf people participating in this study, especially to the deaf woman named Karin in the case study and to colleagues in the research program.

All correspondence concerning this article and request for reprints should be addressed to Gunnel A.M. Backenroth, Department of Psychology, University of Stockholm, S-106 91 Stockholm, Sweden.

REFERENCES

Award, G. Mental health services for the deaf. *Hospital and Community Psychiatry*, 1978, *29*, 674-677.
Backenroth, G. Forskning om föräldrar. *SDR-Kontakt*, 1975, *23*, 6-7, 11.
Backenroth, G. Föräldrastöd. *Nordisk tidskrift för dövundervisningen*, 1980, *6*, 319-323.
Backenroth, G. *Group counseling for parents of deaf and hearing impaired children*. Doctoral dissertation. University of Stockholm: Department of Psychology, 1983.
Backenroth, G. *Föräldrars accepterande av hörselhandikappet i ett flerårigt perspektiv*. University of Stockholm: Department of Psychology, 1984, *45*.
Backenroth, G. Psykosociala interventioner bland döva med varierande brister i det sociala nätverket. Stockholm: Meeting of national medical congress (unpublished speech), 1986. (a)
Backenroth, G. Counselling with the psycho-socially isolated deaf. *International Journal for the Advancement of Counselling*, 1986, *9*, 125-131. (b)
Backenroth, G. Behovet av psykologiska stödinsatser i den döva familjen. Conference: Sign language and the deaf's psychiatric health. Stockholm: Swedish National Association for the Deaf (SDR) in co operation with Department of Psychology and Department of linguistics (unpublished speech), 1987. (a)
Backenroth, G. The role of the family and society in providing favourable conditions for the deaf family member. Conference: Counselling disabled people and their families.Vienna: IRTAC's (International Round Table for the Advancement of

Counselling) conference in cooperation with Rehabilitation International (unpublished speech), 1987. (b)

Backenroth, G. Enkät om temakvällar. Många saknar aktiviteter i dövföreningen. *SDR-Kontakt*, 1988, *6*, 12. (a)

Backenroth, G. Tolkyrket ett bristyrke och ett riskyrke. *DHB-Dialog*, 1988, *2*, 32-34. (b)

Backenroth, G. *Personalhandledning för tolkar som arbetar bland döva*. University of Stockholm: Department of Psychology, 1988, *55*. (c)

Backenroth, G., & Hanson, G. *En modell för psykosocialt rehabiliterings arbete bland barndomsdöva*. University of Stockholm: Department of Psychology, 1986, *48*.

Backenroth, G., & Hanson, G. *Sociala nätverk bland döva som sökerpsykologiskt stöd*. University of Stockholm: Department of Psychology, 1987, *50*.

Backenroth, G. Counselling with the deaf and his social network. In R.I. Brown & S.E. Robertson (Eds). *Rehabilitation counselling. A series in rehabilitation education*. London: Routledge, Chapman & Hall, 1989, *5* (in press).

Buss, A.R. Development of dialectics and development of humanistic psychology. *Human Development*, 1976, *19*, 248-260.

Bühler, C. Basic theoretical concepts of humanistic psychology. *American Psychologist*, 1971, *26*, 378-386.

Bühler, C. The scope of humanistic psychology. *Education*, 1974, *95*, 2-8. (a)

Bühler, C. Humanistic psychology as a personal experience. *Interpersonal Development*, 1974, *4*, 197-214. (b)

Denmark, J.C., & Eldridge, R.W. Psychiatric services for the deaf. *The Lancet*, 1969, Aug. 2, 259-262.

Drapela, V.J. *The counselor as consultant and supervisor*. Springfield, Illinois: Charles C Thomas, 1983.

Evans, H.M. Increasing patient involvement with therapy goals. *Journal of Clinical Psychology*, 1984, *40*, 728-733.

Garstecki, D.C. Rehabilitation of hearing-handicapped elderly adults. *Ear and Hearing*, 1982, *3*, 167-172.

Goldstein, H. A cognitive-humanistic approach to the hard-to-reach client. *The Journal of Contemporary Social Work*, 1986, *67*, 27-36.

Jongkees, L.B.W. Psychological problems of the deaf. *Ann. Otol. Rhinol. Laryngol.*, 1983, *92*, 8-13.

Krauft, C.C., Rubil, S.E., Cook, P.W., & Bozarth, J.D. Counselor attitude toward disabled persons and client program completion: a pilot study. *Journal of Applied Rehabiltation Counseling*, 1976, *7*, 50-54.

Lerner, M. *Psykosomatik. Ett psykologiskt perspektiv*. Stockholm: Natur & Kultur, 1987.

Levine, E.S. Psychological contribution. *Volta Review*, 1976, *78*, 23-33.

Magen, Z. Positive experience of the deaf and their readiness for transpersonal commitment. Conference: Counselling disabled people and their families. Vienna: IRTAC's (International Round Table for the Advancement of Counselling/consultation in cooperation with Rehabilitation International, 1987 (unpublished speech).

Maslow, A. Some basic propositions of growth and self-actualization psychology. In Southwell & Merbaum (Eds). *Personality* (2nd ed.). Belmont, Cal.: Brooks) Cole, 1971.

McMullen, T. A critique of humanistic psychology. *Australian Journal of Psychology*, 1982, *34*, 221-229.

Mindel, E.D., & Vernon McCay. *They grow in silence. The deaf and his family*. Silver Spring, Maryland: National Association of the Deaf (NAD), 1971.

Morrill, W.H., Oetting, E.R., & Hurst, J.C. Dimensions of counselor functioning. *Personnel and Guidance Journal*, 1974, *52*, 354-359.

Polkinghorne, D.   What makes research humanistic?   *Journal of Humanistic Psychology,* 1982, *22,* 47-54.

Pyke, J.M., & Littman, S.K.   A psychiatric clinic for the deaf.   *Canadian Journal of Psychiatry,* 1982, *27,* 384-389.

Raubolt, R.R.   Humanistic analysis: Integrating action and insight in psychotherapy. *Journal of Contemporary Psychotherapy,* 1985, *15,* 46-56.

Schein, J.D.   Cognitive and emotive aspects of deaf youth's selfconcepts. Palermo, Italy: Seventh World Congress for the Deaf, 1983 (unpublished speech).

Steele, R.L.   Humanistic psychology and rehabilitation programs in mental hospitals. *American Journal of Occupational Therapy,* 1976, *6,* 358-361.

Sue, A., & Zane, N.   The role of culture and cultural techniques in psychotherapy. *American Psychologist,* 1987, *42,* 37-45.

Sussman, A.E.   Attitudes toward deafness: Psychology's role, past, present and potential. Palermo, Italy: Seventh World Congress for the Deaf, 1983 (unpublished speech).

Thoreson, R.W., & Tully, N.L.   Role and function of the counselor. In A.E. Sussman & L.G. Stewart (Eds). *Counseling with deaf people.* New York University School of Education: Deafness Research & Training Center, 1971.

Vernon, McCay.   Potential, achievement, and rehabilitation in the deaf population. *Rehabilitation Literature,* 1970, *31,* 258-267.

Vernon, McCay.   Current status of counseling with the deaf people. In A.E. Sussman & L.G. Stewart (Eds). *Counseling with deaf people.* New York University School of Education: Deafness Research & Training Center, 1971.

Vernon, McCay.   Major current trends in rehabilitation and education of the deaf and hard of hearing.   *Rehabilitation Literature,* 1975, *36,* 102-107.

Williams, B.R., & Sussman, A.E.   Social and psychological problems of deaf people. In A.E. Sussman & L.G. Stewart (Eds). *Counseling with deaf people.* New York University School of Education: Deafness Research & Training Center, 1971.

Woolpert, S.   A comparison of rational choice and self-actualization theories of politics. *Journal of Humanistic Psychology,* 1982, *22,* 55-67.

Social Applications and Issues in Psychology
R.C. King and J.K. Collins (editors)
©Elsevier Science Publishers B.V. (North-Holland), 1989

ATTITUDE OF TEACHERS, WITH OR WITHOUT SPECIFIC EXPERIENCE, TOWARDS EDUCABLE MENTALLY OR PHYSICALLY HANDICAPPED PUPILS

Renzo Vianello

University of Padova, Italy

The basic hypothesis of this research is that teachers with direct, continual and committed experience of teaching handicapped pupils in ordinary classes demonstrate more favourable attitudes to their presence than those of teachers without such experience. Teachers from elementary schools in Italy, with or without experience of teaching physically handicapped children were interviewed. Topics discussed during the interviews were: voluntary acceptance of the presence of handicapped pupils, usefulness of special schools, socially unacceptable (unstable, aggressive, embarrassing) behaviour and difficulties in conducting classes. Results supported the basic hypothesis. In particular, teachers with direct experience showed a greater sense of openness to new experiences. Moreover, results showed that problems regarding the inclusion of physically handicapped children in ordinary classes, noted by teachers with experience, are fewer than those presumed by teachers without experience. The results of this research are compared with those of similar research carried out by the same author with the same method, involving subjects with a mental handicap.

The insertion of handicapped pupils into normal schools, begun in many countries all over the world in the 1970s (see law 94-142 of 1975 in the United States of America and law 517 of 1977 in Italy), has stimulated numerous investigations into attitudes towards handicapped pupils. In most cases, teachers were interviewed. This is understandable, given the current interest in scholastic integration (or mainstreaming, as it is termed in the U.S.A.).

Mitchell (1976) and Hughes (1978) have shown how, in many cases, successful mainstreaming depends to a significant extent precisely on teachers' attitudes. Good & Brophy (1972), Kiesler, Collins & Miller (1969), Silbermann (1969) and Triandis (1971) have also found that teachers' behaviour often reflects their attitudes. Although these attitudes are sometimes based on negative stereotypes (Moore & Fine, 1978; Parish, Eads, Reece & Piscitella, 1977; Shotel, Iano & McGettigan, 1972) appropriate professional training programs may improve them (Brooks & Bransford, 1971; Glass & Mackler, 1972; Harasymiw & Horne, 1975; Haring, 1957; Larrivee, 1981; Mandell & Strain, 1978; Smith, 1983).

Many variables have been considered in studies aiming for improved understanding of the nature of the possible changes in attitudes, e. g., teachers' personalities and handicap characteristics. Different experiences in contacting handicapped pupils have also been investigated (Combs & Harper, 1967; Feldman & Altman, 1985; Harasymiw & Horne, 1976; Warren & Turner, 1966).

In Italy too, research has been carried out on the attitudes of the general population and of parents and teachers towards handicapped people (Bellotto & Bolla, 1982; Cacciaguerra, 1978; Catullo, 1984; Gius & Landucci, 1974; Tettamanzi & Vianello, 1982; Vianello, 1988). In one of our previous studies (Vianello, Bertasini, Lucamante & Tettamanzi, 1988), we aimed in particular at evaluating the effects of direct contact with educable mentally handicapped (EMH) pupils on teachers' attitudes. The general hypothesis of our research was that the attitudes of experienced teachers would be more favourable towards inclusion and that they would encounter fewer difficulties than those expected by inexperienced teachers. In other words, we hypothesized that lack of experience would lead inexperienced teachers to believe that problems regarding inclusion would be greater than those effectively found by experienced teachers.

In this report we compare data obtained in previous research on teachers of EMH pupils with data that have emerged from a new study on teachers of physically handicapped (PhH) pupils.

METHOD

As already mentioned, we first of all distinguished experienced teachers (ET) from inexperienced teachers (IT). We considered as experienced, those teachers who had had the same pupil continually in their class for at least one school year. None of them had specialized training in teaching handicapped pupils.

In order to find teachers with the above characteristics, different local health authorities operating in Northern Italy were asked if they could indicate schools in their areas with EMH pupils (specifically those with IQs between 30 and 70) or with PhH pupils (specifically with a hard physical handicap, but without mental handicap). On the basis of the information received, we were able to contact 25 primary school teachers of EMH pupils and 18 primary school teachers of PhH pupils. For each experienced teacher we randomly selected one inexperienced teacher in the same school.

We gave our subjects a semi-structured interview on the following subjects:

a.   Acceptance of the proposed inclusion of a handicapped pupil. In particular, teachers were asked whether they would accept handicapped pupils in their classes if they were asked to do so by the headmaster or headmistress, with the real possibility of refusing.

b. Socialization and learning. In order to analyse this problem, the interview included discussion on the learning rhythms and possibilities of handicapped children, their capacity to cooperate with teachers and other children, acceptance of (and by) school friends, contrast or coordination between socialization-oriented activities and other activities aiming more at how to read and write and learn about mathematics, history, geography and science.

c. Usefulness of special schools. Like opinions on the socialization-learning relationship, those regarding special schools seem to be crucial in revealing fundamental aspects of teachers' attitudes towards the problem. This subject was seen as closely linked to socialization. In every case, questions explicitly referred to the majority of pupils with handicaps; in other words, teachers were asked not to consider the problem of the so-called "very seriously handicapped cases".

d. Socially unacceptable behaviour. With the aim of going depeer into the problem, we believed it would be useful to focus part of our interviews on possible behavioural difficulties, with particular emphasis on psychomotor instability, aggression towards people or objects and embarrassing behaviours such as spitting or undressing.

e. Difficulty in conducting classes. After having focused attention mainly on handicapped children's needs, potentialities and behaviour, towards the end of the interviews we asked questions regarding possible disadvantages which the inclusion of handicapped children could involve for normal school activities.

Although giving ample time for the expression of personal opinion (almost all the interviews lasted more than one hour) the interviewer, having already established some basic grids for data processing, asked questions aimed at obtaining comparable responses. For example, if teachers responded in highly differentiated ways to the question regarding special schools, at the end of that part of the interview, the interviewer asked them if they were overall in favour, uncertain, or against them.

In regard to analysis of results, we carried out the following comparison, using X^2 (with the correction for Yates continuity, where necessary) for each table shown: teachers with experience of EMH versus teachers without experience of EMH; teachers with experience of PhH versus teachers without experience of PhH; teachers with experience of EMH versus teachers with experience of PhH; and teachers without experience of EMH versus teachers without experience of PhH. When opportune, as stated, we also carried out other comparisons and established two response categories. However, for the sake of brevity, we only report the significant X^2 results here.

ANALYSIS OF THE RESULTS CONCERNING THE TEACHERS OF EMH PUPILS.

In regard to acceptance of the interview, the ETs who accepted the interview unhesitatingly were more numerous than the ITs: 92% compared with 56%; $X^2(1, n=50)=8.40$, $p<.005$. Nobody, however, refused.

TABLE 1
Acceptance of interview

	n	Immediate acceptance	Acceptance after hesitation	Refusal
		About EMH		
Experienced	25	23	2	0
Inexperienced	25	14	11	0
		About PhH		
Experienced	19	18	0	1
Inexperienced	21	16	2	3

$X^2(1, n=50) = 8.40$, $p<.005$. (about EMH: experienced versus inexperienced; immediate acceptance versus others).

In regard to acceptance of the proposed inclusion of a handicapped pupil, with the real possibility of refusing, very few refusals were found: 3 ITs. However, more ETs than ITs expressed their own acceptance unhesitatingly: 84% compared with 48%; $X^2(1, n=50)=7.20$, $p<.01$.

TABLE 2
Acceptance of "proposed" inclusion

	n	Acceptance	Uncertainty	Refusal
		About EMH		
Experienced	25	21	4	0
Inexperienced	25	12	10	3
		About PhH		
Experienced	18	14	2	2
Inexperienced	18	12	3	3

$X^2(1, n=50) = 7.20$, $p<.01$. (about EMH: experienced versus inexperienced; acceptance versus others).

In the area of priority of socialization and learning aims, most of our subjects (84% compared with 68%) agreed on the priority of socialization, without significant differences.

TABLE 3
Priority of socialization aims

	n	Agreement	Disagreemen
		About EMH	
Experienced	25	21	4
Inexperienced	25	17	8
		About PhH	
Experienced	18	5	13
Inexperienced	18	12	6

$X^2(1, \underline{n}=36) = 5.44, \underline{p}<.025$. (about PhH: experienced versus inexperienced).
$X^2(1, \underline{n}=43) = 13.81, \underline{p}<.001$. (experienced teachers about EMH versus experienced teachers about PhH).

On usefulness of special schools, the majority of our subjects were opposed . However the ETs were more numerous than the ITs: 84% compared with 52%; $X^2(1, \underline{n}=50)=5.80, \underline{p}<.025$.

TABLE 4
Usefulness of special schools

	n	In favour	Uncertain	Against
		About EMH		
Experienced	25	0	4	21
Inexperienced	25	4	8	13
		About PhH		
Experienced	18	1	3	14
Inexperienced	18	4	9	5

$X^2(1, \underline{n}=50) = 5.88, \underline{p}<.025$. (about EMH: experienced versus inexperienced, against versus others).
$X^2(1, \underline{n}=36) = 11.12, \underline{p}<.001$. (about PhH: experienced versus inexperienced; against versus others).

On the subject of manifestation of socially inappropriate behaviours, we found many differences. As can be seen in Tables 5, 6, and 7, the number of ETs, who noted or expected in the future aggressive or embarrassing behaviour, is smaller than that of the ITs. Differences are significant in 5 out of 6 possible comparisons. There were no significant differences on the matter of difficulty in conducting class.

ANALYSIS OF RESULTS REGARDING THE TEACHERS OF PHH PUPILS.

In terms of acceptance of the interview, 4 teachers (1 ET and 3 IT) did not wish to be interviewed. The majority (85%) accepted unhesitatingly, without significant differences between the ET and the IT. On acceptance of the "proposed" inclusion with the real possibility of refusing, no significant differences were found. The majority (77.8% ET and 66.7% IT) accepted unhesitatingly a proposal of inclusion.

In the area of priority of socialization and learning aims, the ET, who maintain the importance of learning aims and not only those of socialization, were more numerous [72.2% versus 33.3%; $X^2(1, n=36) = 5.44, p<.025$]. On usefulness of special schools, the ETs who were opposed to these schools were more numerous than the ITs [77.7% versus 27.8%; $X^2(1, n=36) = 11.12, p<.001$].

TABLE 5
Manifestation of unstable behaviour

	n	Never	Occasionally	Often
		About EMH		
Experienced noted behaviour	25	7	9	9
Experienced expectations	25	17	4	4
Inexperienced expectations	25	5	3	17
		About PhH		
Experienced noted behaviour	18	17	1	0
Experienced expectations	18	18	0	0
Inexperienced expectations	18	12	2	4

$X^2(2, n=50) = 11.68, p<.005$. (about EMH: experienced noted behaviour vs experienced expectations).

$X^2(2, n=50) = 12.34, p<.005$. (about EMH: experienced expectations vs inexperienced expectations).

$X^2(1, n=36) = 4.98, p<.05$ (about PhH: experienced expectations vs inexperienced expectations).

$X^2(1, n=43) = 15.25, p<.001$. (experienced noted behaviour about EMH vs experienced noted behaviour about PhH; never vs others).

$X^2(1, n=43) = 5.10, p<.025$. (experienced expectations about EMH vs experienced expectations about PhH; never vs others).

$X^2(1, n=43) = 9,52, p<.005$. (inexperienced expectations about EMH vs inexperienced expectations about PhH; never vs others).

Regarding manifestation of socially inappropriate behaviour, we found 3 differences out of 6 possible comparisons. The ET expected a smaller amount of unstable behaviour than the IT [0% versus 33.3%; $X^2(1, n=36)=4.98, p<.05$]. They noted and expected a smaller number of aggressive behaviours than those expected by the IT [5.6% versus 50%; $X^2 (1, n=36) = 8.86, p<.005$ -0% versus 50%; $X^2(1, n=36) = 9.46, p<.005$]. Neither the ET nor the IT expected difficulties in conducting class.

TABLE 6
Manifestation of aggressive behaviour

	n	Never	Occasionally	Often
		About EMH		
Experienced noted behaviour	25	11	6	8
Experienced expectations	25	17	4	4
Inexperienced expectations	25	2	6	17
		About PhH		
Experienced noted behaviour	18	17	1	0
Experienced expectations	18	18	0	0
Inexperienced expectations	18	9	2	7

$X^2(2, n=50) = 9.46, p<.01$. (about EMH: experienced noted behaviour versus inexperienced expectations).
$X^2(2, n=50) = 20.28, p<.001$. (about EMH: experienced expectations versus inexperienced expectations).
$X^2(1, n=36) = 8.86, p<.005$. (about PhH: experienced noted behaviours versus inexperienced expectations; never versus others).
$X^2(1, n=36) = 9.46, p<.005$. (experienced expectations versus inexperienced expectations; never versus others).
$X^2(1, n=43) = 13.54, p<.001$. (experienced noted behaviour about EMH versus experienced noted behaviour about PhH; never versus others).
$X^2(1, n=43) = 9.67, p<.005$. (inexperienced expectations about EMH versus inexperienced expectations about PhH; never versus others).

TABLE 7
Manifestation of embarrassing behaviour

	n	Never	Occasionally	Often
		About EMH		
Experienced noted behaviour	25	14	6	5
Experienced expectations	25	19	3	3
Inexperienced Expectations	25	4	7	14
		About PhH		
Experienced noted behaviour	18	18	0	0
Experienced expectations	18	18	0	0
Inexperienced expectations	18	14	2	2

$X^2(2, n=50) = 8.48, p<.025$. (about EMH: experienced noted behaviour vs experienced expectations).
$X^2(2, n=50) = 18.48, p<.001$. (about EMH: experienced expectations vs inexperienced expectations).
$X^2(1, n=43) = 8.81, p<.005$. (experienced noted behaviour about EMH vs experienced noted behaviour about PhH; never vs others).
$X^2(1, n=43) = 16.38, p<.001$. (inexperienced expectations about EMH vs inexperienced expectations about PhH; never vs others).

TABLE 8
Difficulties in conducting class

	n	Yes	No
		About EMH	
Experienced	2 5	4	2 1
Inexperienced	2 5	1 0	1 5
		About PhH	
Experienced	1 8	1	1 7
Inexperienced	1 8	1	1 7

$X^2(1, \underline{n}=43) = 5.67$, $\underline{p}<.025$. (inexperienced about EMH vs inexperienced about PhH).

COMPARISON BETWEEN THE RESULTS OF THE TWO STUDIES

No significant difference existed in terms of acceptance of the interview. Acceptance of "proposed" inclusion of handicapped students was similarly comparable. The number of teachers who agreed on the priority of socialization aims was greater among the ET of PhH pupils than the ET of EMH pupils, although on usefulness of special schools, there was no significant difference.

In 7 out of 9 possible comparisons, the teachers interviewed in the second study, that is the one concerning PhH pupils, affirmed that they noted and expected in the future fewer incidents of socially inappropriate behaviour.

The number of IT who were worried about the difficulties in conducting class was greater among the teachers interviewed about the EMH pupils than the teachers interviewed about PhH pupils [40% versus 5.6%; $X^2(1, \underline{n}=43) = 5.67$, $\underline{p}<.025$].

CONCLUSIONS

Some distinction may now be made regarding our general hypothesis that direct experience favours a more positive attitude towards the inclusion of handicapped pupils into normal classes. The data confirm our hypothesis that the ET are more positively oriented toward the interview and more open towards new teaching experiences with handicapped pupils. These teachers hold stronger views against using special schools for EMH pupils. It is, moreover, confirmed by the data concerning socially inappropriate behaviour: generally, the IT considerably overestimate the difficulties yhat EMH pupils may cause from the behavioural viewpoint.

The data concerning the PhH pupils show that the hypothesis that the IT overestimate the difficulties caused by the insertion of a PhH pupil, is confirmed only in part (in 3 out of 6 possible comparisons). Regarding other matters, only two differences emerge: the ET were more opposed to special schools and believe less that socialization aims are more important than those of learning. The comparison between the results of the two studies emphasized overall that generally teachers are more worried about the EMH than the PhH pupils. This confirms the results from other studies (Bellotto & Bolla, 1982; Combs & Harper, 1967; Moore & Fine, 1978; Shotel, Iano & McCettigan, 1972) from which it is possible to conclude that the order of preference in the acceptance of handicapped pupils is: the physically handicapped, the learning disabled, the Down's Syndrome children, the emotionally disturbed, the mentally handicapped and the psychotic.

REFERENCES

Brooks, B. L., & Bransford, L. A. (1971). Modification of teachers' attitudes toward exceptional children. *Exceptional Children, 38*, 259-260.

Bellotti, M., & Bolla, M. C. (1982). La relazione tra insegnanti e handicappati: credenze, atteggiamenti e aspettative nei confronti del problema. Distretto Scolastico Mestre Sud.

Cacciaguerra, F., Marciani, A., & Marciani, E. (1978). Handicappati mentali e socializzazione nella scuola. *Quaderni Oasi, 1,* 9-48.

Catullo, D. (1984). Come i bambini percepiscono l'handicappato fisico. *Psicologia italiana, 1,* 16-20.

Combs, R. H., & Harper, J. L. (1967). Effects of labels on attitudes of educators toward handicapped children. *Exceptional children, 33,* 399-403.

Feldmann, D., & Altmann, R. (1985). Conceptual systems and teacher attitudes toward regular classroom placement of mildly mentally retarded students. *American Journal of Mental Deficiency, 4,* 345-351.

Gius, E., & Landucci, G. (1974). *L'inserimento sociale dell'handicappato.* Roma: A.N.Fa.Fa.S.

Glass, R. M., & Meckler, R. S. (1972). Preparing elementary teachers to instruct mildly handicapped children in regular classrooms: a summer workshop. *Exceptional Children, 39,* 152-156.

Good, T. L., & Brophy, J. E. (1972). Behavioural expression of teacher attitudes. *Journal of Educational Psychology, 63,* 617-624.

Harasymiw, S.J., & Horne, M. D. (1975). Integration of handicapped children: its effect on teacher attitudes. *Education, 96,* 153-158.

Harasymiw, S. J., & Horne, M. D. (1976). Teachers' attitudes toward handicapped children and regular class integration. *Journal of Special Education, 10,* 393-401.

Haring, N. G. (1957). A study of the attitudes of classroom teachers toward exceptional children. *Dissertation Abstracts, 17,* 103-104.

Hughes, J. (1978). Attitude is the keystone to success. *School Shop, 37,* 76-80.

Kiesler, C. A., Collins, B. E., & Miller, N. (1969). *Attitude change.* New York: Wiley.

Larrivee, B. (1982). Factors underlying regular classroom teachers' attitude toward mainstreaming. *Psychology in the Schools, 19,* 374-37.

Mandell, C., & Strain, P. (1978). An analysis of factors related to the attitudes of regular classroom teachers toward mainstreaming mild handicapped. *Contemporary Educational Psychology, 3,* 154-162.

Mitchell, M. (1976). Teacher attitudes. *High School Journal, 59,* 302-311.

Moore, J., & Fine, M. J. (1978). Regular and special class teachers' perceptions of normal and exceptional children and their attitudes toward mainstreaming. *Psychology in the Schools, 15,* 253-259.

Parish, T., Eads, G., Reece, N., & Piccitello, M. (1977). Assessment and attempted modification of future teachers' attitudes toward handicapped children. *Perceptual and Motor Skills, 44,* 540-542.

Shotel, J. R., Iano, R. P., & McGettigan, J. F. (1972). Teacher attitudes associated with integration of handicapped children. *Exceptional Children, 38,* 677-683.

Silbermann, M. L. (1969). Behavioural expression of teacher attitudes toward elementary school students. *Journal of Educational Psychology, 60,* 402-407.

Smith, D. K. (1978). Teacher styles of classroom management. *Journal of Educational Research, 5,* 277-283.

Tettamanzi, A., & Vianello, R. (1982). Ricerca di sondaggio sull'atteggiamento dell'insegnante, con o senza esperienza diretta di inserimento, nei confronti del bambino handicappato grave dell'intelligenza, inserito in classe normale. *Ricerche di psicologia, 24,* 105-114.

Triandis, H. C. (1971). *Attitude and attitude change.* New York: Wiley.

Vianello, R., Bertasini, M., Lucamante, M., & Tettamanzi, A. (1988). Attitude of teachers, with or without specific experience, towards educable mentally retarded pupils. Padova: Dipartimento di Psicologia dello sviluppo e della socializzazione dell'Università di Padova.

Vianello, R., & Bolzonella, G. F. (1988). *Il bambino portatore di handicap e la sua integrazione scolastica.* Terza edizione. Bergamo: Juvenilia.

Warren, S. A., & Turner, D. R. (1966). Attitudes of professionals and students toward exceptional children. *Training School Bulletin, 62,* 136-144.

Social Applications and Issues in Psychology
R.C. King and J.K. Collins (editors)
©Elsevier Science Publishers B.V. (North-Holland), 1989

ARE WE CLOSE TO A SOLUTION FOR THE PROBLEM OF TRANSFER?

Lyn Gow

Hong Kong Polytechnic, HONG KONG, and

Earl Butterfield

The University of Washington, U.S.A.

An earlier version of this paper was published in the *Bulletin of the Hong Kong Psychological Society.* The editor of the journal, Dr. J. Blowers, has given copyright permission.

Determining how to teach students so they generalise or transfer their learnings is arguably the most important problem of both education and psychology. Unless students transfer their learnings to their non-school lives, the teachers have failed. Unless psychologists' experimental manipulations have external validity, their theories are not basic understandings. Teachers' lessons and psychologists' manipulations must produce behavioural changes that transfer; otherwise their enterprises are invalid. Unfortunately, transfer has been difficult to demonstrate. In this paper, we describe five approaches that have been used to promote transfer, and we discuss the inconsistency of their effects. Limits of prior approaches are analysed and we discuss the potential of combining two of the approaches. We present some new data and answer the question: "How close are we to a solution of the problem of transfer?" We offer reasons to suggest that we may be close.

INTRODUCTION

The main goal of education is to produce adaptable and flexible students who can cope with changing environments. Our teaching should produce intelligent novices, that is, people who have enough general knowledge, strategies and problem solving skills to be broadly effective in life, not just in school. Determining how to induce students to transfer their learning may be the most important unsolved problem of educational psychology. Current methods of teaching seldom produce transfer (Gow & Butterfield, in press; Gow, Butterfield & Balla, in press). Students often fail to use skills they have been taught when it would serve them well to do so outside the teaching environment.

What is transfer?

Speaking behaviourally, transfer is the use in one setting of overt responses taught in another. On the behavioural view, failures to transfer result from dissimilarities among settings, and efforts to promote transfer concentrate either on increasing the physical similarity or reducing learners' discriminations among teaching and transfer settings (Stokes & Baer, 1977).

Speaking cognitively, behaviour depends upon underlying knowledge and strategies, some of which are situationally specific and some of which are transituational. The latter are called metacognitive components. Transfer is the use in one setting of underlying knowledge and strategies taught in another. Whether such use promotes transfer in the behavioural sense depends upon the specific knowledge and strategy requirements of the teaching and transfer tasks (Butterfield, 1988). If the specific requirements are not identical, then metacognitive components must be used to adapt, subtract, or add to – even invent – untaught specific knowledge and strategies required by transfer tasks (Butterfield & Ferretti, 1987). On the cognitive view, failures to transfer result from incomplete teaching, at either the specific or metacognitive levels. Because teaching is under the control of teachers, but similarity of (largely unknown) transfer settings to (known) teaching settings is not, we prefer the cognitive view of transfer.

Why Study Transfer?

Speaking either behaviourally or cognitively, transfer is not distinguishable from learning (Hebb, 1949). We only learn in situations we experience but this learning has value only if we can use it in situations we have not experienced yet, because no two situations are identical.

Transfer is the chief social goal of education. We justify schooling by what it teaches people that is valued in society and by what it prepares people to do outside of school. Empirically, failures to transfer are a key problem for many students, particuarly for those with intellectual disabilities. The empirical gap between what is taught in school and what is used in life, whether you think of it behaviourally or cognitively, signals a technological gap: we lack a technology of transfer (Stokes & Baer, 1977). As is always the case, this technological gap signals a theoretical gap. We have not yet analysed transfer(s) and how to produce it (them).

What sort of approaches are being used to solve the transfer problem?

1.   The longest standing approach is to *teach fully the underlying knowledge and skills* The idea is that if transfer is not achieved, teaching must have been too incomplete or too little practice provided.

On this view, metacognition need not exist. The required approach is to know better what task-specifics to teach and to provide more practice in the teaching setting.

2.   *Provide supports or further instruction in transfer settings.* Examples are supported employment and enlisting the help of parents and/or peers outside the teaching environment. However it is done, this approach amounts to giving up on the possibility of transfer. It amounts to teaching in every setting where the taught knowledge and skills are relevant.

3.   *Teach in various settings,* especially in ones like those to which we hope skills will transfer. When we know what will be asked of students, we can provide relevant transfer practice. When we don't know about transfer settings (as we seldom can), this approach provides occasion for pupils to practise what they have been taught. That is, it reduces to the practice part of the first approach.

4.   *Teach at a higher level of abstraction* by using "general case programming" (Gersten & Maggs, 1982; Horner, Sprague & Wilcox, 1982) and teaching general rules (Gow, 1986). According to Becker & Engelmann: "The general case has been taught when, after instruction on some tasks in a particular class, any task in that class can be performed correctly" (1978: 325). The learner is taught to attend to the relevant, rather than irrelevant features of the task. Taking an example of screwdriver use, relevant features are the hole and the screw; irrelevant stimuli are the time of day and the trainer. Teaching should also be general in nature and applicable across situations. In the case of screwdriver use, instead of teaching only this limited class of problems, applications of the core skills (i.e. align, turn and push) are taught across tasks requiring use of these same core skills. These might include putting a spark plug into a lawn mower or screwing in a light globe.

5.   In addition to teaching task–specific knowledge and skills, ***teach problem solving skills*** such as planning, monitoring and evaluating. The idea is that transferring learned understandings and skills to new settings is a matter of problem solving. Therefore, if we teach our pupils to manage their own problem solving, they will transfer more regularly and broadly the more specific things we teach them.

None of these five approaches has been very successful in securing transfer (Butterfield, 1988; Butterfield & Gow, 1987; Gow, 1984; Gow & Butterfield, in press). There is some evidence in favour of each approach, but none always produces transfer.

What kinds of difficulties seem to limit all research approaches to the question of how to promote transfer?

There are at least four, potentially serious, problems with prior studies of transfer (Butterfield, 1988; Butterfield & Gow, 1987).

1.   *Knowledge and processes underlying success on the problems studied have been too incompletely analysed.* All of the approaches mentioned above assume that the instructed behaviours or underlying knowledge and skills are all that is necessary for success on the transfer problem. If the initial teaching does not convey all of the behaviours – or underlying components – then transfer should not occur. In as much as many studies of transfer do not demonstrate that they have effected large improvements in performance on the teaching task, it is uncertain whether they have taught all of the behaviours – overt or covert – needed for transfer. It remains a possibility that fuller teaching would produce transfer.

2.   *Too few distinctions have been drawn among kinds of transfer.* One implication of viewing transfer cognitively rather than behaviourally is that there are several kinds of transfer (Butterfield, 1988). This is so because there are a number of ways that teaching and transfer tasks can differ with respect to the underlying knowledge and skills required for their successful performance. They may require the same underlying knowledge and skills, but differ in their surface structure, e.g. word problems versus straight arithmetic problems. The teaching problem may require only part of the knowledge and skills of the transfer problem, or it may require more skills. A lesson may teach several approaches, each of which applies to a different variant of a problem, requiring separate instruction in discriminating problem types. If there are different kinds of transfer, then securing them requires full analysis of both teaching and transfer problems so that the kind of transfer being tested is known. The assumption is that different kinds of transfer will require different kinds of teaching (Butterfield, 1988).

3.   *Too few analyses have been conducted to identify the processes underlying transfer.* Stokes and Baer (1977) were the first to suggest that transfer needs to be analysed in its own right. They argued that the usual approach to securing transfer is to assume that full teaching will promote it, but it might be that teaching for acquisition and teaching for transfer depend upon different principles. Their

suggestion was to try reinforcing transfer, as if it were a teachable behaviour. The cognitive approach is to analyse the skills required for transfer and to teach them. The usual cognitive hypothesis is that transfer is a problem to be solved, just like any other problem, and that one can teach self-management of problem-solving routines, which will promote transfer.

4. *Quantitative metrics of transfer distance have not been used.* It is generally believed that transfer tests can differ in their distance from teaching tasks. However, investigators seldom use any metrics of transfer distance. Rather, they intuit their way to classifications of "near" and "far" transfer. Our reading of experiments that refer to transfer distance says that more often than not different types of transfer are involved. Even when this is not true, objective metrics of transfer distance are not used. It is not surprising that under these conditions no simple pattern of results emerges from studies that purport to measure transfer "distance".

Two of these problems seem especially noteworthy. The failure of investigators to base their teaching on a full and explicit understanding of the knowledge and skills required for success in the task being taught means that the simplest hypothesis about how to produce transfer – teach fully – has yet to receive an adequate test. Second, viewing transfer as if it were a single process means that we may have been comparing apples and oranges when trying to evaluate our success at promoting transfer. In this paper, we will report an experiment in which we combined two of the five approaches using three fully analysed tasks in an effort to produce three kinds of transfer.

We compared full teaching and problem solving instruction. The first approach (discussed above) to promoting transfer is to teach fully all of the knowledge and skills required by the transfer tests used to evaluate the teaching. To apply this approach in our experiment meant using teaching and transfer problems that had been fully analysed so that we would know what to teach and that the teaching and transfer tasks depended on the same knowledge and skills. We used three two-dimensional integration problems, analysed partly by Piaget, then more fully by Siegler and finally by us (Butterfield & Gow, 1987; Ferretti & Butterfield, 1986; Ferretti, Butterfield, Kahn & Kerkman, 1985). These analyses concern the actions of balance scales, inclined planes, and shadow projection devices. These problems are similar to those used in schools to teach principles of physics.

PROCEDURES

Apparatus

We used three pieces of apparatus for teaching. Our balance scale had an aluminium arm centred on a fulcrum on either side of which were six equally spaced pegs to receive small metal weights. The arm was locked during the placement of weights on either side of the fulcrum and then unlocked to show its action after a subject predicted what would happen when it was free to move. Our inclined plane apparatus consisted of two identical sets of tracks adjustable in their angle. A model train car, into which weights could be placed, could be pulled up the tracks by a releasable counterweight attached by string fed through a pulley located at the top of the tracks. After a subject predicted which plane's car would move up its tracks, the counterweights were released to test the subject's prediction. The shadow projection apparatus consisted of two lights and a screen onto which shadows could be projected by pegs of varying weights placed – one per light – at various distances from the screen. After the child subject predicted which peg would cast the tallest shadow, the lights could be turned on to provide a test of the prediction.

Instruction of knowledge and strategies

Prior analyses have shown that to predict the actions of each of these devices, one must do five things. **First,** one must identify the two relevant dimensions for each problem. For the balance scale, the two relevant dimensions are the number of weights on each side of the fulcrum and their distances from the fulcrum. In our study, variable numbers of weights were placed on only one peg for each side of the scale's arm. Number of weights could be counted directly, and distance could be assessed indirectly by counting pegs from the fulcrum to the weights' locations. For the inclined plane apparatus, the two relevant dimensions are the angles of the tracks and the number of weights in each car. Angle was set by placing the track on stops, the number of which could be counted to assess angle. The number of weights in each car could also be counted. For the shadow projection task, the relevant dimensions are the distance of the pegs from the light and the height of the pegs. The pegs were placed in holes, the number of which could be counted to assess distance, and the pegs had stripes, which when counted indexed their height.

Second, having identified the relevant dimensions, one must assess each by counting weights and pegs, angle-determining stops and number of weights, or pegs' heights and distances from the lights. **Third,** one must judge whether the two sets of relevant dimensions yield the same predicted action. Thus, for the balance scale, one must judge the predictions from weight and from distance measurements. For example, if one side has more weights and they are placed farther from the fulcrum, both weight and distance predict that that side of the scale will go down when the stops are released. **Fourth,** if both dimensions yield the same prediction, the subjects should give that as their prediciton. Thus, if the side of a balance scale that has both more weight and more distance, one should predict that that side will go down. If both sides have the same weight and distance, one should predict that the scale will balance. The inclined-plane and shadow-projection devices have three analagous predictions. Thus, a light with a taller peg closer to it will cast a taller shadow.

Fifth, if the two relevant dimensions yield different predictions, one must integrate the values on those dimensions and predict from the integrated value. So, if the car on one set of tracks has more weight, but a lower angle of incline than the other side, weight predicts against it, but angle predicts for it. To solve such problems, for which the relevant dimensions yield conflicting predictions, one must integrate the conflicting dimensions and predict for the smaller integrated value. For all three devices, integration required adding the values of the two relevant dimensions, basing one's predictions on the sums.

We trained our subjects how to do each of the five steps for each of the thee tasks. That is, for each of the three tasks, we taught them [1] to identify the relevant dimensions, [2] to assess the magnitudes of each, [3] to compare the predictions from each dimension, [4] to predict from these assessments if they agreed, but [5] to resolve conflicting predictions between dimensions by integrating with addition the values of the conflicting dimensions and predicting from the integrated values. Taken together, instruction in the first four steps is called dimensional comparison instruction, allowing solution of any problem for which the dimensions yield nonconflicting predictions. Adding instruction in the fifth step, called integration instruction, allows solution of any problem whose dimensions yield conflicting predictions, called conflict problems.

We began by administering pretests for each of the three problems, and selecting only subjects who [1] showed no evidence of using dimensional integration for conflict problems and [2] compared only one of the two relevant dimensions for nonconflict problems. We then gave dimensional comparison instruction on all three problems to all subjects in small *groups*, following which we administered posttests to assess all subjects' use of dimensional comparison and integration strategies on all three problems. Subjects were then given *individualised* training in the use of dimensional comparison. Following dimensional comparison training on each of the three tasks, posttests were administered to assess its use. All pretests and posttests contained unique items, none of which was used during instruction.

Transfer testing

Our examination of transfer concerned the effects of the individualised, dimensional integration training. All training was conducted with mechanical versions of the three problems. All posttesting was done with paper-and-pencil tests which required the subjects to predict from schematic versions of the devices what the actual device would do if configured like the schematic version. In other words, all transfer tests used problems with a format different from training and could be said to tap transfer across problem formats. Nevertheless, our focus was on three other types of transfer. Transfer across instances was studied by testing subjects with different instances of a problem type for which dimension integration instruction had been given. Thus, when a subject was tested with paper-and-pencil items of the balance scale type following balance scale integration training, we could examine **transfer across instances**. Tests of transfer across instances required only that the subjects use dimensional integration on novel items of a sort on which they had received dimensional integration training. Transfer across types was studied by testing subjects with problems of a type for which they had not received integration training. Thus, when a subject was tested with paper-and-pencil items of the inclined plane type following training on only the balance scale or the balance scale and shadows projection problems, we could examine **transfer across types**. Transfer across types required the subject to use dimensional integration on a type of problem for which it had not been taught.

Because simple problems could be solved without dimensional integration, but conflict problems required integration, we could also examine discrimination transfer. That is, we assessed whether, following integration instruction, subjects used the earlier taught dimensional comparison strategy for simple problems. Dimensional integration would solve all problems, so our test of discriminative transfer was not as definitive as it would have been if some problems could be solved only by comparison and others only by integration.

Subjects

Our subjects were 32 mildly intellectually disabled students between 13 to 20 years old with mental ages ranging from 6.6 to 15.0 years (mean = 10.37 years) and IQs ranging from 40 to 74 (mean = 58).

Self-management instruction

Apart from training fully the task-specific knowledge and skills required for problem solution, we also examined the fifth approach, described above, which is to teach self-management of problem solving as well as task-specific knowledge and skills.

We tested the hypothesis that self-management instruction would produce more transfer than task-specific instruction. We also tested whether two different self–management skills would be required by our three kinds of transfer test. To transfer to new problem instances, subjects would only need to recognise that they had been taught how to solve problems of the type with which they were being tested and apply what they had been taught. On the other hand, to transfer to new problem types and to transfer discriminatively, the subjects would need to recognise that they had been taught to solve simple problems of the type being tested, but not conflict problems. Thus, they were taught to decide what they had been taught about simple problems of the same and another type meant that what they were taught about conflict problems of the other type would work as well on the new, untaught conflict problems.

To promote transfer to new problem instances, we taught our subjects a self–management scheme for keeping track of whether they had fully applied what they had been taught, called application instruction. To promote transfer to new problem types, we taught the ways to judge whether a new problem was similar to the one they had been taught to solve, called similarity instruction. Thus, we divided our subjects into four groups, each of which received a different combination of self–management instruction: application alone, similarity alone, both, or neither application nor similarly.

RESULTS AND DISCUSSION

If full instruction on task–specific knowledge and processes is enough to produce transfer across instances and transfer across types and discriminative transfer, then there should be no differences among our four self–management groups. On the other hand, if any of the three types of transfer requires self–management instruction, then the four groups should differ.

In fact, there were no differences among the four self-management groups for either transfer across instances or transfer across problem types. All four showed high rates of both kinds of transfer. Our design allowed two opportunities to examine transfer across instances. Following dimensional comparison training, but prior to integration training, only six of the 32 subjects showed evidence of using dimensional integration on the problem that was taught first (order of problem type instruction was counterbalanced across subjects). Following integration training on their first problem, 30 of the 32 subjects used integration on the test of transfer across instances. This is a significant ($p < .001$) increase in use of integration. Another test of transfer across instances for the first problem taught was administered after teaching integration for the second problem. On this delayed test, 28 subjects used the dimensional integration strategy, which is also a significant ($p < .001$) increase over the pre-instruction test. Our design also allowed two tests of transfer across types. Prior to any instruction, only one of 32 subjects showed evidence of integration on the third problem type. Following training on the first problem, 11 subjects used integration on the third, as yet untrained problem, which is a significant ($p < .001$) increase. Following training on the second problem type, 18 subjects used integration, again a significant ($p < .001$) increase compared with pre-instruction use of integration.

Apparently, transfers across instances and across types of problems both depend only, or primarily, on full problem-specific instruction. Why should this be so? After all, the earlier literature reports lower rates, or none at all (Gow & Butterfield, in press).   The answer probably lies in two facts.   First, our instructions were based on extensive prior analyses of the knowledge and skill required for solution of the problems we studied. In other words, our instruction was probably fuller than the instruction of most earlier studies of transfer. Second, we examined relatively simple kinds of transfer. We have shown elsewhere (Butterfield, 1988; Butterfield & Gow, 1987) that there are several more complex types of transfer that we might have examined. Thus, had we used transfer tests that require subjects to add untaught skills and knowledge to what we had taught them, self-management instruction might have been required. Full evaluation of that possibility awaits further experimentation.

Partial evaluation of the need for more than full process instruction comes from our examination of discriminative transfer. For both tests of transfer across instances and both tests of transfer across problem types, we judged whether our mentally retarded subjects showed discriminative transfer by using dimensional comparison for simple problems and integration for conflict problems. To do this, we scored each of the 28 problems in each transfer test according to whether a subject's written work indicated use of dimensional comparison or integration. Subjects were then classed as predominantly comparison (at least 23 of 28 problems solved by dimensional comparison), integration (at least 23 of 28 problems solved by adding to integrate), or as discriminative (comparison on 7 of 8 simple problems and integration on 18 of 20 conflict problems).

Whether subjects transferred discriminatively depended upon the nature of the test (across instances or problem types), whether it came immediately or sometime after integration training, and whether subjects received metacognitive instruction in strategy application. For the first posttest across instances, 11 of 16 subjects who had received application instruction transferred discriminatively, compared with only 2 of 16 ($Z = 8.29$, $p<.01$) who did not receive application instruction. For the immediate posttest across instances, there were no significant differences between subjects who did or did not receive application instruction, nor were there significant differences for either delayed test.

Although our subjects were far more likely to transfer discriminately during tests across instances immediately after receiving metacognitive instruction in strategy application, they shifted thereafter to exclusive reliance on integration. That may have been the most sensible thing to do, because integration would solve all the problems, and it may have taken less work overall to integrate only rather than to compare dimensions on all problems as well as integrating on those with conflicting dimensions. Whether using problems that require choice among strategies would prevent the abandonment of discriminative transfer remains to be seen. Nevertheless, the immediate effect of metacognitive instruction upon discriminative transfer suggests the utility of continuing to study whether different kinds of metacognitive instruction facilitate different kinds of transfer.

The present results suggest that we are now very close to being able to promote transfer of the simpler varieties. What seems to be required is full instruction based on thorough analysis of the knowledge and skills required by the training and the transfer problems. However, transfer across types was less frequent than across instances. Achieving higher rates across types may require other sorts of self-management instruction (Day & Hall, 1987). We may be close as well to promoting more complex varieties of transfer. How close may depend upon how difficult it is to identify appropriate self-management skills for each of the more complex varietes of transfer (Butterfield, 1988).

CORRESPONDENCE

Dr. Lyn Gow, Reader, Applied Social Studies, Hong Kong Polytechnic, Hung Hom, Kowloon, HONG KONG.

REFERENCES

Becker, W.C. & Engelmann, S. (1978). *Teaching 3: evaluation of instruction.* Chicago: S.R.A.

Butterfield, E.C. (1988). On solving the problem of transfer. In M.M. Grunesberg, P.E. Morris & R.N. Sykes (Eds.), *Practical aspects of memory (Vol. 2)* (pp. 377-382). London: Academic Press.

Butterfield, E.C. & Ferretti, R.P. (1987). Toward a theoretical integration of hypotheses about intellectual differences among children. In J.B. Borkowski & J.D. Day (Eds.), *Cognition in special education* (pp. 195-233). Norwood, N.J.: Ablex.

Butterfield, E. & Gow, L. (1987). Does self-management instruction provide a solution to the problem of transfer for people with an intellectual disability? In: E.A. Bartnik, G.M. Lewis & P.A. O'Connor (Eds.), *Technology, resources and consumer outcomes for people with intellectual disabilities* (pp. 199-206). Perth: PE Publications.

Day, J.O. & Hall, L.K. (1987). Cognitive assessment, intelligence and instruction. In J.O. Day & J.G. Borkowski (Eds.), *Intelligence and exceptionality* (pp. 57-80). Norwood, N.J.: Ablex Publishing Co.

Ferretti, R.P. & Butterfield, E.C. (1986). Are children's rule assessment classifications invariant across instances of problem types? *Child Development, 57,* 1419-1428

Ferretti, R.P., Butterfield, E.C., Kahn, A. & Kerkman, D. (1985). The classification of children's knowledge: development on the balance-scale and inclined-plan problems. *Journal of Experimental Child Psychology, 39,* 131-160.

Gersten, R.M. & Maggs, A. (1982). Teaching the general case to moderately retarded children: analysis of a five year project. *Analysis and Intervention in Developmental Disabilities, 2,* 329-343.

Gow, L. (1984). The use of verbal self-instruction to enhance learning in retarded adults: a study of techniques for improving acquisition, generalisation and maintenance. *CORE, 8* (3), Fiche 5 D10.

Gow, L. (1986). Enhancing far generalisation of strategy use. In: J. Berg (Ed.), *Perspectives and progress in mental retardation: proceedings of the seventh congress of the international association for the scientific study of mental deficiency (IASSMD)* pp. 345-352. London: Methuen.

Gow, L. & Butterfield, E. (in press). Education of people with an intellectual disability. In J. Taplin, G. Maple & T. Miller (Eds.), *An Introduction to Developmental Disability.* Sydney: Williams & Wilkins.

Gow, L., Butterfield, E.C. & Balla, J. (in press). The relative efficacy of cognitive and behavioural approaches to instruction in promoting adaptive capacity. *Proceedings of the Eighth World Congress of IASSMD,* Dublin, August, 1988.

Hebb, D.O. (1949). *The organisation of behavior.* New York: Wiley.

Horner, R.H., Sprague, J. & Wilcox, B. (1982). General case programming for community activities. In B. Wilcox and G.T. Bellamy (Eds.), *Design of high school programs for severely handicapped students.* Baltimore: P.H. Brookes.

Stokes, T.F. & Baer, D.M. (1977). An implicit technology of generalization. *Journal of Applied Behavior Analysis, 10,* 349-367.

Social Applications and Issues in Psychology
R.C. King and J.K. Collins (editors)
©Elsevier Science Publishers B.V. (North-Holland), 1989

PSYCHOSOCIAL FACTORS IN ARCHITECTURAL BARRIERS

Jean LaCour

California State University, U.S.A.

Local laws restricting architectural barriers and the promotion of barrier-free environments for the disabled have resulted in informational efforts directed towards those designing and constructing public buildings.

A model of the psychosocial factors was developed and presented to urban planners, architects and builders. Theories utilized included: Maslow's Hierarchy of Needs, Goffman's Presentation of Self in Everyday Life, McClelland's need for achievement, Seligman's concept of learned helplessness and Selye's concepts of stressors and their impact in the environment. From organizational psychology, concepts of "quality of life", participative management and active consumerism were utilized.

It is suggested that awareness of the psychosocial effects of architectural barriers would sensitize key players to the needs of disabled consumers and that the model may be useful in training counsellors and other mental health professionals.

It is proposed that architectural barriers (those buildings that deny access to, or are unusable by the disabled) impose a constellation of psychological effects on those with limited mobility and other types of disabilities.

A model of psychological factors presumed to be involved has been developed for consideration by key participants - those responsible for the conceptualization, design, construction and conformity to codes of structures, as well as the consumers both in the public and private sector.

RELEVANT THEORIES

From the literature of behavioural science in the areas of social psychology, learning , personality theories and organizational psychology, a range of relevant theories has been incorporated into a model of psychosocial factors relevant to the experiencing of architectural barriers.

STATISTICS ON DISABILITIES

According to a survey in 1979, some 31.5 million Americans, or 14.6 per cent of the non-institutionalized population, were limited in some way by a chronic health condition. An estimated 7.9 million (or 3.7%) were considered severely disabled and, as the population ages, some 46% of those who are 65 years or older will have a chronic activity - limiting disability, with 16.9% unable to carry on a major activity (Dejong & Lifchez, 1983).

Recent figures show some 1.23 million disabled persons reside in Los Angeles County, with over 600,000 located within the boundaries of Los Angeles city. In Los Angeles, the Mayor's Office for the Disabled (MOD) was formed in 1974 to respond to needs and concerns of the disabled and to coordinate the services of various agencies. A series of conferences on Barrier - free design has been convened by this agency to which have been invited consumers, designers, architects, contractors, developers and involved public and private agency representatives to discuss laws, implementation, cost-effectiveness and other concerns.

LEGISLATIVE TRENDS

Major legislation, policies and standards directed toward ensuring equitable modification and/or design of public buildings has been increasingly common in the United States over the past 15 years. The aim has been to render these buildings more accessible to the disabled.

From a prior period of bland acceptance by architects, lawmakers *and* the disabled regarding accessibility, there has emerged a series of laws and actions directed toward encouraging and enforcing accessibility - in essence protecting the civil rights of and "enhancing the quality of life for disabled people" (Dejong & Lifchez, 1983; Greer, 1987).

At present all 50 states in the United States require that most buildings utilizing state revenues for construction be accessible, while another 4/5ths of the states also require accessibility in some private buildings used by the public (Greer, 1987). Yet, in spite of increased awareness in recent years, it is not clear that clients (i.e., builders, contractors and architects) are more interested today in making their facilities accessible to the consumers - the disabled (Dejong & Lifchez, 1983).

NEEDS AND MOTIVATION

A humanist in the behavioural sciences, Maslow (1970), formulated a "need hierarchy theory" that applies to motivation and includes five different classes of needs from basic or deficiency needs (e.g., biological safety) through to actualization needs.

He proposed that these needs are common to all humans and are arranged in a hierarchy of prepotency. Maslow refers to need gratification as "the most important single principle underlying all development". He added that: "the single, holistic principle that binds together the multiplicity of human motives is the tendency for a new and higher need to emerge as the lower need fulfils itself by being sufficiently gratified. Maslow proposed that although we have a desire to satisfy our growth needs, the tendency to meet higher needs can emerge only when basic needs are fulfilled.

Self-actualization growth needs can be defined as the need to grow and develop psychologically, to find one's identity and realize one's potential.

If we are stuck at the bottom of this hierarchy, coping with basic physiological needs, (e.g., environmental barriers) we are not going to be able to move up to higher needs. This theory has some value in conceptualizing our need to grow relative to our need to survive.

THE "SICK ROLE" AND THE DISABLED

The concept of the "sick role", attributed to sociologist Parsons (1951) and addressed by others (Mechanic, 1962; Siegler and Osmond, 1973) is an interesting one as applied to the disabled person. The sick role consists of a set of *exemptions* and *obligations. Exemptions:* sick persons are exempted from normal, social activities and responsibility for their illnesses and are not morally accountable for their conditions. In exchange for these exemptions, sick persons have certain *obligations:* to define the state of being sick as aberrant and undesirable and to do everything possible to facilitate their recovery (in other words, to cease being disabled eventually!); and to seek technically competent help and to cooperate with physicians in attempting to get well.

Further, in fulfilling the "sick role", disabled persons are relieved of the obligation to take charge of their own affairs. However, the impaired role carries with it a loss of full human status. The sick role then would imply *acceptance* of physical and psychological barriers - as being sick means being willing to give up control.

STRESS AND DISABILITY

Adjustment to life situations is always taking place as social, psychologic and biologic needs are constantly changing. In addition, changeable environments require additional adaptive behaviour change. The subsequent need to adjust to those changes is an integral and natural part of living - a state also referred to as coping, that can lead to stress (Goodwin, 1980).

Although all of us experience stress in coping with both the highs and the lows in our daily lives and with the resultant physiological upset, individuals with disabilities are more vulnerable to anxiety than persons without them (Lindermann,

1981; Wright, 1960). Those who experience little mastery in their environment show higher stress (Levitan, 1971).

The potential for stress is greatly enhanced for individuals with disabilities because the environment has many barriers or restrictions that also create stressful situations (Goodwin, 1980; Langer and Michael, 1963; Levitan, 1971).

Depending upon the severity of his or her disability, an individual may encounter stress associated with getting an education, participating in social events and obtaining health services, as well as obtaining gainful employment. All of these are dependent upon securing access to buildings (Henderson & Bryan, 1984).

Uncertainty is one of our more threatening life experiences, as in addition to potential social stigmatization, an individual does not know what to expect in many settings. It is difficult and stressful for any of us to prepare for and live with the unknown (Zola, 1981).

POWER & RESOURCES

"Powerlessness is corrupting...absolute powerlessness is absolutely corrupting" (R.M. Kantor). Zola (1981) writes of a personal experience of having his leg brace snap while aboard a plane to New Delhi, India, detailing his resultant sense of total panic. He points out that disabled persons need financial resources to avail themselves of such amenities as helpers, limousines, first class travel and accommodation, custom made clothes and sufficient "clout" to have meetings take place in accessible environments. But, he asks, what happens to all those without sufficient money or power to alter their environments? These persons may ultimately give up and, unable to change or manipulate the world, they may simply cut out that part of their lives which requires such encounters. This contributes to social invisibility and isolation, loss of identity and self-esteem (Langer & Michael, 1963).

BLAMING THE VICTIM

The ultimate and most pervasive of environmental barriers are the attitudinal ones, in particular the view that disabled people are helpless, pathetic victims (Lifchez, 1985) and that if something does not fit, it is the fault of the disabled person. Ryan (1971) termed this "blaming the victim".

Ryan discusses power or "clout" which, he suggests, has at least two aspects: political and psychological. It includes the power to control the social institutions that affect one's life and the psychological well-being that comes from a sense of internal locus of control (Rotter, 1966).

Rappaport (1975) refers to power as a resource perhaps even more basic than money.

LEARNED HELPLESSNESS

The concept of learned helplessness and self-esteem assumes that a helpless feeling has been learned through experiences and through the reactions of others and a sense of loss of control over the important things in one's life. In addition, it has been shown that learned helplessness in both sexes leads to depression (Seligman, 1975).

Theorists have documented the important relationship between locus of control as a psychological variable and power or powerlessness which is also termed "alienation" in the literature of sociology (Rotter, 1966; Seeman, 1972). Rotter (1966) showed that a person who is alienated does not expect to "engage in mastering his environment and become more involved in social action". Rappaport et al (1975) link control over the outcomes of one's own personal life with social and political control over institutions of which one is a part.

COUNSELLORS AND THE DISABLED

Counsellors and helpers working with disabled persons may consider only the negative aspects of a disability; a helper trying to assist an individual with an access problem may see the *person* as the difficulty rather than the *environmental features*. This is another form of "blaming the victim" (Ryan, 1971).

Some helpers also see the access problem as that of the disabled needing to adapt to, rather than attempting to modify the environment (Hamilton, 1950; Hohenshil, 1979).

THE DISABLED PERSON AS CONSUMER/PARTICIPANT

The "hottest" topic in organizational/industrial psychology and writings directed to managers in the 1980s is that of "participative management". The premise is that workers have expertise and ideas to contribute; they need to be brought into decision-making, to be given more responsibility and, as a result, are more likely to experience job satisfaction (Ouchi, 1981; Saal and Knight, 1988).

There is support for the proposition that disabled persons, by becoming part of the decision-making process, stand to gain maximum mastery or control of their environment. This process has been termed participative management, self-empowerment, self-advocacy or active consumerism (Bowe, 1980; Henderson & Bryan, 1984; Lunt, 1982; Vash, 1981).

empowerment, self-advocacy or active consumerism (Bowe, 1980; Henderson & Bryan, 1984; Lunt, 1982; Vash, 1981).

While everyone concerned with human rights and the rights of people with disabilities must become active participants in achieving barrier-free environments, the brunt of the battle will continue to be borne by people with disabilities as the *consumers* of specialized environments (Hull, 1979; Mart'nelli & Dellorto, 1984).

It follows that disabled persons will need to work with public policy planners, those enforcing building codes, as well as with designers and architects, toward this goal of creating aesthetically pleasing barrier-free environments. Gurus will not lead the way. The expertise and the responsibility belongs to those with disabilities (Koop, 1979).

REFERENCES

Bowe, F. (1980). *Rehabilitating America Toward Independence for Disabled People.* Harper & row, New York.

DeJong, G. & Lifchez, R. (1983). *Physical Disability and Public Policy,* June, *248,* 6, 40-49.

Goodwin, L.R. Jr. (1980). Stress Management for Rehabilitation Clients, *Rehabilitation Counseling Bulletin,* March, 193-201.

Greer, N.R. (1987). The State of the Art of Design of Accessibility, *Architecture Magazine,* January. American Institute of Architects.

Hamilton, K.W. 1950. *Counseling the Handicapped in the Rehabilitation Process.* Ronald Publishing, New York.

Henderson, G. & Bryan, W.V. (1984). *Psychosocial Aspects of Disability,* Chase C. Thomas, Chicago.

Hohenshil, T.H. (1979). Renewal in Career guidance and Counseling: Rationale an Programs. *Counselor Education and Supervision, 18,* 1988-208.

Hull, K. (1979). *The Rights of Physically Handicapped People. An American Civil Liberties Unit Handbook.* Avon Books, New York.

Koop, S.B. (1979). *If You Meet the Buddha on the Road, Kill Him.* Bantam, New York.

Langner, T.S. & Mihael, S.T. (1963) *Life Stress and mental Health,* Free Press of Glencoe, New York.

Levitan, U.M. (1971) Status in Human Organizations as a Determinant of mental Health and Performance. Unpublished doctoral dissertation, Michigan State University.

Lindermann, J.E. (1981). *Psychological and Behavioural Aspects of Physical Disability: A Manual for Health Practitioners.* Plenum Press, New York.

Lunt, S. (1982). *A Handbook for the Disabled Ideas and Innovation for Easier Living.* Chas Scribner & sons, New York.

Martinelli, R.P. & Dellorto, A.E. (1984). *The Psychological and Social Impact of Physical Disability,* Springer Publishing, New York.

Maslow, A. (1970). *Motivation and Personality* (2nd Ed.) Harper and Row, New York.

Mechanic, D. (1962). Concept of Illness Behaviour, *Journal of Chronic Disability, 15,* 189-194.

Ouchi, W.G. (1981). *Theory 3: How American Business Can Meet the Japanese Challenge.* Addison-Wesley, Reading, MA.

Parsons, T. (1951). *The Social System,* The Free Press, Glencoe, Illinois, 428-479.

Parsons, T. (1972). Definitions of Health and Illness in Light of American Values and Social Structure, In E.G. Jaco, (Ed.). *Patients, Physicians and Illness:*

Rappaport, J., Davidson, W., Mitchell, A. & Wilson, M.N. (1975).   Alternatives to Blaming the Victim or the Environment: Our Places to Stand Have Not Moved the Earth. *American Psychologist, 30,* 525-528.

Rotter, J.B. (1966).   Generalized Expectancies for Internal Versus External Control of Reinforcement.   *Psychological Monographs, 80,* No. 609.

Ryan, W. (1971).   *Blaming the Victim.* Random House, New York.

Saal, F.E. & Knight, P.A. (1988).   *Industrial/Organizational Psychology, Science and Practice,* Brooks/Cole Publishing Company, Los Angeles.

Seligman, M.E.P. & Maier, S.F. (1967).   Failure to Escape Traumatic Shock, *Journal of Experimental Psychology, 74,* 1-9.

Siegler, M. & Osmond, H. (1973).   The Sick Role Revisited, *Hasting Center Studies, 1,* No. 3.

Vash, C. (1981).   *The Psychology of Disability,* Springer Publishing, New York.

Wright, B. (1960).   *Physical Disability: A Psychological Approach,* Harper & Row, New York.

Zola, I.K. (1981).   Communication Barriers Between the Able-bodied and the Handicapped, *Archives of Physical Medicine and Rehabilitation.   62,* 355-359.

Section 5

SOCIAL PATHOLOGY

AND WELL-BEING

Social Applications and Issues in Psychology
R.C. King and J.K. Collins (editors)
©Elsevier Science Publishers B.V. (North-Holland), 1989

RELAPSE PREVENTION WITH SEXUAL AGGRESSORS

William D. Pithers
Georgia F. Cumming
Linda S. Beal
Kris Pettit

Vermont Center for Prevention and Treatment of Sexual Abuse,
United States

Relapse Prevention (RP) is a cognitive-behavioural program of assessment
and treatment designed to enhance maintenance of change in sexual
aggressors. The model proposes that no "cure", which would eradicate
deviant fantasies, exists. RP dispels the misconception of therapeutic "cure"
and delineates more realistic, attainable treatment goals. RP also assesses
clients' behaviour in order to detect situations which pose a high risk of
relapse. The sequence of "apparently irrelevant decisions" made by each
client, which ultimately led to the final decision to commit a sexual offence,
are detailed. Thus, a thorough analysis of each offender's offence precursors
is attained. Finally, systematic treatment is conducted. Treatment under the
RP model is designed to provide the sexually aggressive client with
cognitive and behavioural skills which will better enable him to control his
decision-making process and behaviour so that he may disrupt the chain of
events leading to sexual offences. Identification of a relapse process unique
to each offender also facilitates supervision of the offender in the
community by probation and parole officers. Analyses of outocme data from
treatment programs employing RP is presented and compared to other
outcome data to demonstrate the efficacy of this approach to maintenance of
change. Information regarding cost-efficacy of treatment for sexual offenders
is also revealed.

Pithers, Kashima, Cumming, Beal, and Buell (1987, 1988) identified
precursors to the sex offences of 136 pedophiles and 64 rapists. Multiple
determinants were found to exist (See Tables 1 and 2), demonstrating that sexual
aggression represents a process occurring over time rather than poor impulse
control.

Precursors toward offences followed a common sequence. The first
change from the client's typical functioning was affective. The second alteration
involved fantasies about the abusive act. Fantasies were converted into cognitive
distortions in the third step of the relapse process. Distortions served to justify or
legitimize abuse, ascribing inaccurate traits to potential victims, characterizing all
women as emotionless or attributing adult decision-making abilities to children.

Offenders then engaged in a process of passive-planning, which often was accomplished during masturbatory fantasies. Since planning appeared intended to create conditions that might enable offenders to claim their acts were impulsive, we refer to this phenomenon as "planned impulsiveness". In the final step of the relapse process, the plan was acted out. Minimal substance use was noted as an immediate precursor, being used to diminish inhibitions against abuse.

In this relapse process, the earliest sign of increasing danger involved affect. The relapse process entailed a distinct sequence of functional alterations: affect-fantasy-cognitive distortion-passive planning-behaviour. Thus, the relapse processes of sex offenders reveal specifiable precursors that may be addressed during treatment to enhance maintenance of change.

Many theorists propose that sexual offences, particularly rapes, are impulsive acts. While many offences appear impulsive upon first review, closer inspection reveals a different conclusion. In our analysis of precursors to assaults, more than half of all offenders appeared emotionally overcontrolled (See Table 2). Frequently, these men left a hostile interaction without expressing anger. As they brooded about the incident over time, their animosity grew. Although they failed to express anger at the appropriate moment, their amplification of emotion led to an explosive release later. Because their outburst, or assault, was so far removed from the instigating event, the behaviour might appear situationally non-contingent, or impulsive. In reality, the act was not impulsive, but motivated by a delayed emotional response.

Psychological treatment modalities effectively induce beneficial modifications of behaviour, including that in the sexual arena. Unfortunately, short-term benefits often fail to become long-term changes. A major therapeutic concern with sexual aggressors involves maintenance of change after formal therapy has ended.

If successful treatment permanently eliminated abusive sexual interests, relapse rates of sex offenders would be low. Such is clearly not the case. Repetition of sex offences is not an infrequent occurrence (Sturgeon & Taylor, 1979). Recidivism data have been used to argue that efficacy of treatment for sexual offenders has not been proved (Brecher, 1978). Rather than attributing sexual re-offending to ineffective treatment, the therapeutic goals for sex offenders may require examination. The anticipated outcome of treatment that is most likely to lead to re-offence may be that therapy *should eliminate* fantasies about sexual abuse.

TABLE 1
Immediate Precursors to Sexual Abuse

	OFFENDER SUBTYPE	
PRECURSOR	RAPISTS*	PEDOPHILES*
ANGER	88	32
ANXIETY	27	46
BOREDOM	45	28
COGNITIVE DISTORTIONS	72	65
DEPRESSION	3	38
DEVIANT SEXUAL FANTASIES	17	51
DISORDERED SEXUAL AROUSAL PATTERN	69	57
DRIVING CAR ALONE WITHOUT DESTINATION	17	1
EMOTIONALLY INHIBITED/OVERCONTROLLED	58	51
INTERPERSONAL DEPENDENCE	30	48
LOW VICTIM EMPATHY	61	71
OPPORTUNITY (E.G., FINDING A HITCHHIKER	58	19
PLANNING OF SEXUAL OFFENCE	28	73
PORNOGRAPHY USE	2	7
PSYCHIATRIC HOSPITALIZATION	0	7
SOCIAL ANXIETY	25	39
SUBSTANCE USE/ABUSE		
ALCOHOL	42	23
OTHER SUBSTANCES	14	7

*Percentage of sample

TABLE 2
Early Precursors to Sexual Aggression

	OFFENDER SUBTYPE	
PRECURSOR	RAPISTS*	PEDOPHILES*
EXPOSURE TO VIOLENT DEATH OF		
HUMAN OR INFRAHUMAN	22	2
FAMILIAL CHAOS	86	49
MATERNAL ABSENCE/NEGLECT	41	29
PARENTAL MARITAL DISCORD	59	45
PATERNAL ABSENCE/NEGLECT	59	54
PHYSICALLY ABUSED AS CHILD	45	7
PORNOGRAPHY USE (HABITUAL)	14	33
PRECOCIOUS SEXUALITY		
(<12 YEARS AT TIME OF FIRST ACT OF		
PENETRATION NOT CONSIDERED ABUSE)	14	30
PRIOR ARREST FOR NONSEXUAL OFFENCE	44	15
SEXUAL VICTIMIZATION		
PRIOR TO AGE 12	5	56
BETWEEN AGES 12 AND 18	11	6
USE OF FEMALE PROSTITUTES	30	8

*Percentage of sample.

Few therapists, experienced with sex offenders, regard the abuser as curable. No existing therapeutic intervention eradicates, across time and situations, the offender's abusive fantasies.

However, the sex offender may enter treatment believing that therapy will cure him. When suffering from physical illnesses in the past, medication usually eliminated the disorder. Treatment was something done to him, rather than an activity requiring his active involvement. Thus, the sex offender may enter therapy expecting a quick cure that makes few personal demands.

Unfortunately, treatment programs promote the offender's misconceptions by failing to prepare him for the likelihood of lapses (i.e., precursive moods, thoughts, and fantasies). In a similar fashion, institutional programs, that do not offer follow-up outpatient therapy, promote the deception that treatment ends upon discharge. Clients leaving therapy with such misconceptions are primed for relapse. Fortunately, options exist that enhance maintenance of therapeutic gain.

Relapse prevention (RP; Marlatt, 1982) is designed to enhance maintenance of change of compulsive behaviour. Pithers (1982) modified RP for application with sexual offenders. RP is designed to help clients maintain control of problem behaviour over time and across situations.

RP proposes that the determinants of relapse are embedded in a distinct process. First, we assume that the individual experiences a sense of personal control while abstinent and that this perception grows until a high-risk situation is encountered. A high-risk situation is one which threatens an individual's personal control, thus increasing risk of relapse. If a pedophile in a high-risk situation (e.g., condominiums housing young families) enacts a coping response (e.g., moves to an adult apartment house), the probability of relapse decreases. But if he fails to cope, a decreased sense of control and feelings of helplessness ensue. If these reactions occur in a situation containing cues associated with past abusive behaviour, relapse becomes more probable. This is particularly the case if the person selectively recalls only the immediate, positive effects of the prohibited behaviour. The pedophile might remember the pleasant refuge from loneliness offered by his last victim, forgetting that the relief was fleeting, followed by a heightened sense of isolation.

In the sequence of precursors to abuse (i.e., affect-fantasy-cognitive distortion-passive planning-behaviour), the first stage differentiating most sex offenders from other individuals is the *predominance* of sexually abusive fantasies. Therefore, for most sex offenders, the first *fantasy* about sexual aggression may be considered the initial *lapse.* Recurrence of sexually aggressive *behaviour* is defined as a *relapse.* Treatment under RP provides clients with skills to interrupt the relapse process at the earliest possible point in order to reduce the likelihood of another sex offence.

Whether or not a lapse becomes a relapse depends on several factors, one of which is the Abstinence Violation Effect (AVE). A major source of the AVE is a conflict between the individual's previous self-image as an abstainer and his recent experience of prohibited behaviour (e.g., abusive sexual fantasy). To the extent that the person views a lapse as a personal failure, his expectancy for continued failure increases and the chances of relapse grow.

Thus far, the relapse process has been depicted from the point at which a person encounters a high-risk situation. RP also examines events which precede high-risk situations. While some sex offenders relapse in situations that would have been difficult to anticipate, most set the stage for relapse by placing themselves in high-risk situations. One can covertly set up a relapse by making a series of Seemingly Unimportant Decisions (SUDs), each of which represents another step toward a high-risk situation. While there may be little a sex offender can do to deter relapse once he is in an extremely high-risk situation, he must accept responsibility for initiating the chain of events that got him there in the first place. He can learn to recognize the conditions that precede relapse and be prepared to intervene before it is too late.

RP begins by dispelling unrealistic misconceptions regarding the outcome of treatment and describing attainable goals. RP continues by assessing the client's high-risk situations, the internal and external conditions under which relapse has occurred, or is likely to occur. The client's coping skills are also assessed, since situations are considered high-risk only to the extent that the client has difficulty coping with them. Treatment activities enable the client to minimize the frequency and intensity of lapses and to keep lapses from becoming relapses.

In introducing RP, we encourage an active, problem-solving approach on the part of the client. We inform clients that no cure exists for their disorder. Clients learn that treatment may decrease their attraction to abusive sexual behaviours, but that abusive fantasies will recur at least momentarily. Clients are informed that return of an abusive fantasy does not signify a total loss of control and that a critical part of treatment involves learning what to do when they feel drawn to abusive acts again. We instruct clients that they will discover a variety of situations in which they make SUDs which actually lead them closer to re-offending, or which take them away from that danger. They are encouraged that recognizing these situations for what they are and enacting alternatives, will reduce the likelihood of acting out abusive fantasies.

RELAPSE PREVENTION ASSESSMENT PROCEDURES

The RP approach to treatment is highly individualized. Therefore, thorough assessment of the client's needs is required. Assessment under the RP model includes three major tasks: (a) analysis of high-risk situations (including the decisions that create those situations), (b) assessment of coping skills, and (c) identification of specific determinants and early antecedents of abuse. Several methods are used to identify the conditions, both internal and external, that increase the threat of relapse for a given offender. These include self-monitoring, direct observation and self-report measures.

Assessment of High-risk Situations

Self-Monitoring.. Self-monitoring is useful if the offender is still experiencing precursive moods and fantasies (e.g., masturbating to sexually aggressive themes). Self-monitoring represents an effective means of enhancing a client's awareness of his relapse process.

Direct Behavioural Observation. Physiological measurement of penile response to auditory or visual depictions of various sexual scenarios may reveal risk factors that the client has not recognized or reported. Such measurements also provide information about the relative strength of non-deviant sexual interests – information that may be useful in treatment.

Self-Report Measures. In a structured interview, clients provide detailed descriptions of circumstances associated with past offences. Both situational and personal (cognitive and affective) antecedents should be identified and SUDs made en route to the offence should be explored. Once the client begins to recall SUDs he has made, the pace with which he remembers them will accelerate. By integrating information from self-monitoring, direct observation and a structured interview, the constellation of factors heightening risk of relapse may be identified.

Assessment of Coping Skills

Since any situation represents risk only to the extent that the offender is unprepared to cope with it, assessment includes measures of his coping skills. A combination of behavioural and self-report measures are used to evaluate the client's strengths and weaknesses in coping. These measures include the Situational Competency Test, self-efficacy ratings and relapse fantasies.

Situational Competency Test. In this test, the client is required to respond to descriptions of common problem situations. The client's response is later scored along a number of dimensions. A problematic situation is considered to exist whenever the client is unable to formulate a coping response, articulates a strategy that is unlikely to be successful, or verbalizes a response only after a prolonged latency.

Self-Efficacy Ratings. In this procedure, the client is presented with a list of specific high-risk situations, which he rates (on a seven-point scale) according to how difficult or easy it would be to cope with the situation without experiencing a lapse.

Relapse Fantasies. In this procedure, the client is asked to fantasize a future relapse. By reviewing these fantasies, the absence of adaptive coping responses and use of maladaptive coping behaviour can be noted.

Assessment of determinants of sexual aggression

Assessment is not complete until the client and therapist have generated hypotheses about why the client's response to a stressful situation involved a sex offence instead of some other (even maladaptive) response.

A variety of tools are available to assess specific determinants of abusive behaviours. Structured interviews can be used to explore the importance of common determinants such as hostility toward women, deficient social and sexual skills and sexual arousal to abusive fantasies. For this final determinant, the direct measurement methods described previously should be used if available. If not, self-report instruments such as the Clarke Sexual History Questionnaire (Langevin, 1983) can be employed, along with self-monitoring records, to assess this determinant.

In addition to identifying determinants of abusive behaviour, assessment should include exploration of early antecedents, or lifestyle variables, that predispose abuse. Examples of such predispositions include unrealistic expectations of others, rigid defensiveness, a sense of worthlessness, and excessive power needs.

RELAPSE PREVENTION TREATMENT PROCEDURES

Since Relapse Prevention is an individualized program, a variety of interventions must be available to address each client's needs. RP interventions are divided into two groups: (a) procedures designed to help the client avoid lapses and (b) procedures designed to minimize the possibility of a lapse precipitating relapse.

Avoiding Lapses

The first step in teaching a client to avoid lapses is an extension of the assessment process: recognizing the chain of precursive events involved in the relapse process. As the client becomes more skilled in analyzing his own behaviour, he will discover more subtle decisions that led to high-risk situations. Continued self-monitoring of thoughts, fantasies, and urges sensitizes the client to recognize his abusive process. Study exercises can be used to help the client discover how he covertly plans offences by making a series of SUDs.

As a result of these exercises, a discrete point in the relapse process, tha will be considered the client's "lapse", may be identified. For most offenders, the lapse will be one of the cognitive steps (fantasy, cognitive distortion, passive-planning) that precedes an offence. For others, the lapse may be an emotional state (e.g., intense anger toward a potential victim), particular behaviour (e.g., "cruising"), or a combination of behavioural and cognitive events (e.g., buying child pornography and fantasizing).

In the RP model, once a lapse is identified, the situations and decisions preceding it are analyzed. Lapses are viewed, not as signs of therapeutic failure, but as opportunities to learn. Examining factors that led to a lapse and developing coping strategies for them, enables the offender to develop enhanced self-management skills.

Stimulus control procedures. To the extent that the client's relapse process includes external stimuli, he can exercise control by removing these from his everyday environment. If a pedophile's abusive fantasies are elicited by pornography, he can remove these cues from his surroundings.

Avoidance strategies. Avoidance strategies can decrease the frequency with which a pedophile encounters problematic situations. A pedophile whose daily commuting to work takes him by an elementary school can easily travel another route.

Escape strategies. When clients discover themselves in risk situations that challenge their coping skills, escape strategies are advisable. A client who quickly escapes a risk situation will be more successful than one who attempts to figure out how to cope with the situation while remaining amid cues associated with his abusive acts. Previous research has demonstrated that adequacy of a coping response appears less positively correlated with relapse than the speed with which the response is emitted (Chaney, O'Leary & Marlatt, 1978).

Specific Coping Skills

Although some lapses can be prevented by training the client to recognize, avoid and escape risk situations, maintenance also requires acquisition of programmed coping responses and problem-solving skills.

Programmed coping responses. Development of coping responses always begins with problem-solving. The client initiates the problem-solving procedure by describing his highest-risk situation in detail. Once the situation has been detailed, brainstorming is used to generate potential coping responses. Potential consequences of each option are listed to evaluate whether that response would have the desired effect of lessening the likelihood of relapse. The most effective, feasible, coping response is selected for performance. Focusing on the client's thought processes while problem-solving is important in providing clues which suggest additional problem areas for further exploration.

Continued practice of the behaviour should be conducted throughout treatment. Practice on such behaviour resembles the repetitive drills used by musical instructors who wish their pupils to play instinctively. Instinctive musical skills result from hard work. By practising over time, the client performs programmed coping responses in many situations and moods, enhancing generalization.

Interpersonal skills. Acquisition of interpersonal skills is an important part of treatment for many sex offenders. For some, basic skills necessary for establishing and maintaining relationships with adults are deficient. Others show deficits in sexuality skills, communicate ineffectively, misinterpret social cues, or are severely inhibited by anxiety. Many sex offenders are unable to express feelings constructively, then react to conflict with unexpressed anger, which is later overexpressed in abusive outbursts.

Anger and stress management. Since negative arousal states are common precursors of relapse, skills for managing affective antecedents are important coping strategies for many offenders. Our general approach to management of negative arousal states is stress inoculation training, a cognitive-behavioural program which has been successfully applied to problems of anxiety (Meichenbaum, 1977) and anger (Novaco, 1977).

Coping with urges. Sexual abuse is typically characterized by some type of immediate gratification (e.g., a restored sense of power and control). Negative consequences (e.g., guilt, decreased self-esteem, arrest, and incarceration) are typically delayed. Selectively recalling positive aspects of offences, while neglecting the negative after-effects (for both the victim and himself), increases the probability of abuse recurring. Positive outcome expectancies for the immediate effects of behaviour become especially potent when the client is faced with a high-risk situation and is beginning to feel unable to cope. Under such conditions, the client may experience a strong urge to commit a deviant act. We teach the client that his overall response to sexual aggression is biphasic in nature. The initial sense of gratification is frequently followed by a delayed negative effect. Clients are also taught to use self-statements to disrupt urges. Inclusion of aversive outcomes in self-statements enhances their potency in counteracting urges.

Modification of Specific Determinants of Lapses

RP would be incomplete if it did not address specific determinants of sexual aggression. The most important response-relevant interventions are behaviour therapy procedures designed to alter deviant arousal patterns that are critical precursors to relapse for many offenders. The importance of including behavioural assessments (i.e., penile plethysmography) and interventions with sexual aggressors has been emphasized by many experts (Abel, Blanchard & Becker, 1978; Laws & Osborne, 1983; Quinsey & Marshall, 1983). As a general rule, we employ treatment procedures that are direct, simple and transferable to the client's home (e.g., masturbatory satiation, orgasmic reconditioning and olfactory aversion).

Interventions for Early Antecedents

The final set of interventions is designed to modify early antecedents, or global predispositions that contribute to lapses. Among these techniques are didactic sessions on human sexuality, cognitive restructuring to correct "thinking errors" supporting the offender's interpersonal aggression (Yochelson & Samenow, 1976), and re-education groups (Groth, 1983).

Minimizing the Extent of Lapses

Specific RP procedures have been developed to prepare the client to cope with lapses so that a lapse does not become a relapse. First, we teach the client behavioural skills to moderate lapses. Second, in order for these moderating skills to be successful, we instruct the client in cognitive restructuring procedures to cope effectively with the various components of the AVE. Third, lapse rehearsals are staged to practise skills he has acquired to handle the occurrence of a lapse. Finally, an individualized maintenance manual is constructed to provide the offender with general reference material, specific refresher exercises, and emergency coping strategies to use if all else fails and he is on the brink of relapse.

CONCLUSIONS

RP is a comprehensive training program designed to help sex offenders avoid re-offences. The basic premise of the RP model is that clients should *be prepared;* that is, they should be able to recognize SUDs, avoid or effectively cope with high-risk situations, restructure interpretation of urges and prevent a lapse from becoming a relapse.

No final therapy session is conducted under the RP model. Offenders who believe that their treatment ends with the termination of formal therapy have failed to learn the crucial lesson that *maintenance is forever.* The client who has adequately learned the RP philosophy continues his own therapy every day of his life. Relapse rates of clients involved in RP treatment after a 6 year follow-up are presented in Table 3. Based on these data, RP appears to be a highly effective method of deterring sexual aggression.

TABLE 3
Two to Six Year Follow-up Data of Maintenance of Change in Sex
Offenders Treated Under Relapse Prevention Model

	Rapists	Pedophiles	Total
Abstaining	16	144	160
Relapses	4	3	7
Total Number of Offenders	20	147	167
Relapse Rate*,**	20%	2%	4%

* Relapse defined as arrest for an alleged sexual offence.
** Two relapses occurred within 2 months after start-up of outpatient treatment groups; a third relapse took place 3 weeks after offender's parole officer permitted him to discontinue treatment against therapists' advice.

TABLE 4
Estimated Costs Associated with Processing of One Instance of Sexual
Abuse in Vermont in 1987.

Source	Cost	Total Cost
Intake Investigation	$US250	$US250
Child in Custody	$US3,000–10,000/year	$US6–20,000
Police Investigator	$US120	$US120
Emergency Room Physician	$US210	$US210
Emergency Room Tests	$US150	$US150
Prosecutor's Investigator	$US575	$US575
Defender's Investigator	$US575	$US575
Evaluation of Victim	$US350–600	$US350–600
Victim Treatment	$US2,500/year	$US5,000
Presentence Investigation	$US250	$US250
Offender Psychosexual	$US500–600	$US500–600
Prosecuting Attorney	$US1200	$US1200
Public Defender	$US1200	$US1200
District Court Judge	$US888	$US888
Incarceration of Offender	$US17,000/year	$US85,000
Welfare to Offender's Family	$US6,600/year	$US33,000
Parole Supervision	$US1,500/year	$US3,000
Total Cost	**$US138,268**	**— $US152,618**

(Parameters: Married offender with two children, adjudicated to 10 year maximum sentence (serves 5 years in prison with 2 years parole), one victim who receives treatment for 2 years.)

Treatment is also cost-effective. Residential treatment of one sex offender costs $US5,500 per year. In comparison, the costs associated with the investigation, arrest, prosecution, incarceration, parole supervision, and victim's care resulting from a single sexual offence range between $US138,268 and $US180,118 (See Table 4). Thus, each offence and re-incarceration prevented by effective treatment saves society between $US110,768 and $US117,118. If one assumes that the long term recidivism of untreated sexual offenders reaches 50%, while the recidivism rate of treated offenders is 15%, savings resulting from effectively treating 80 offenders would fall between $US1,671,504 and $US2,073,304 (savings created by a 35% reduction in recidivism - cost of treating 80 offenders = savings attributable to treatment). No way of estimating the emotional savings to the potential victims of sexual abuse exists.

CORRESPONDENCE

William D. Pithers, PhD., Georgia F. Cumming, B.A., Linda S. Beal, M.A., Kris Pettit Vermont Center for Prevention and Treatment of Sexual Abuse, 12 South Main Street, Waterbury, Vermont 05676, United States.

REFERENCES

Abel, G. G., Blanchard, E. B., & Becker, J. V. (1978). An integrated treatment program for rapists. In R. Rada (Ed.). *Clinical aspects of the rapist.* New York: Grune & Stratton.

Brecher, E. M. (1978). *Treatment programs for sex offenders.* Washington, DC: U.S. Government Printing Office.

Chaney, E. F., O'Leary, M. R. & Marlatt, G. A. (1978). Skill training with alcoholics. *Journal of Consulting and Clinical Psychology, 46,* 1092-1104.

Groth, A. N. (1983). Treatment of the sexual offender in a correctional institution. In J. G. Greer & I. R. Stuart (Eds.), *The sexual aggressor: Current perspectives on treatment* New York: Van Nostrand Reinhold.

Langevin, R. (1983). *Sexual strands: Understanding and treating sexual anomalies in men.* Hillsdale, NJ: Lawrence Erlbaum Associates.

Laws, D. R. & Osborne, C. A. (1983). How to build and operate a laboratory to evaluate and treat sexual deviance. In J. G. Greer & I. R. Stuart (Eds.), *The sexual aggressor: Current perspectives on treatment.* New York: Van Nostrand Reinhold.

Marlatt, G. A. (1982). Relapse prevention: A self-control program for the treatment of addictive behaviours. In R. B. Stuart (Ed.). *Adherence, compliance, and generalization in behavioural medicine.* New York: Brunner/Mazel.

Meichenbaum, D. (1977). *Cognitive-behaviour modification.* New York: Plenum Press.

Novaco, R. W. (1977). Stress inoculation: A cognitive therapy for anger and its application to a case of depression. *Journal of consulting and clinical psychology, 45,* 600-608.

Pithers, W.D. (August, 1982). *The Vermont Treatment Program for Sexual Aggressors: A program description.* Waterbury, VT: Vermont Department of Corrections.

Pithers, W.D., Kashima, K., Cumming, G.F., Beal, L.S. & Buell, M. (1987). *Sexual aggression: An addictive process?* Paper presented at the New York Academy of Sciences. New York, NY.

Pithers, W.D., Kashima, K., Cumming, G.F., Beal, L.S. & Buell, M. (1988). Relapse prevention of sexual aggression. In R. Prentky & V. Quinsey, (Eds). *Human sexual aggression.* New York: New York Academy of Sciences.

Quinsey, V. L. & W. L. Marshall. (1983). Procedures for reducing inappropriate sexual arousal: An evaluation review. In J. G. Greer & I. R. Stuart (Eds.). *The sexual aggressor: Current perspectives on treatment.* New York: Van Nostrand Reinhold.

Sturgeon, H., Taylor, J., Goldman, R., Hunter, & Webster, D. (1979). Atascadero, CA: Atascadero State Hospital.

Yochelson, S. & Samenow, S. (1976). *The Criminal Personality. Vol. 1: A profile for change.* New York: Jason Aronson.

Social Applications and Issues in Psychology
R.C. King and J.K. Collins (editors)
©Elsevier Science Publishers B.V. (North-Holland), 1989

A FORM OF CAPITAL PUNISHMENT -
DOMESTIC VIOLENCE IN CANBERRA, AUSTRALIA

Rosemary A Knight

Australian Institute of Health, Australia, and

Suzanne E Hatty

University of New South Wales, Australia.

Violence against women by a male sexual partner in a private sphere (typically called 'domestic violence') is, unfortunately, as prevalent in Australia's capital city as elsewhere. The research reported here examined the main features of domestic violence as revealed by 120 Canberra women. Information was elicited through telephone interviews, following mass media advertising. As well as documenting common features of the violence incurred by women (such as its frequency, duration and type) and some socio-demographic data about both partners (such as education level, employment conditions and age) information was sought concerning which personnel, if any, were consulted (such as doctors/hospitals, the police, friends and community agencies). In analysing the data, special emphasis was given to the factors implicated in terminating abusive relationships. Three models (the attitudinal, behavioural and socio-demographic accounts of violence) were fitted using logistic regression analysis. The following factors emerged as critical: Type of violence experienced, intervention of medical and police personnel and marital status. The implications of these findings for women who incur domestic violence are discussed, with particular reference to the difficulties victims experience in extricating themselves from abusive relationships.

Violence perpetrated by a male against a female sexual partner is usually labelled 'domestic violence' and has been described by Ellis (1984; p.56) as 'a crime of momentous proportion'. Indeed, the social cost of this physical abuse is exorbitant: serious injury and, sometimes, death to the woman; psychological disturbance in children raised in the culture of violence (Hughes & Barad, 1982); and the allocation of a significant proportion of policy, judicial and medical resources in an attempt to intervene, prosecute or heal (Goldberg and Tomlanovich, 1984; Parnas, 1967).

Research on domestic violence has typically focused on 3 aspects: (i) estimating the incidence of domestic violence, (ii) determining the extent to which the victims make use of police, medical, legal and other community resources, (iii) investigating factors which facilitate the termination of the abuse, such as ways of helping women to get out of the relationship.

The present study addresses all three issues. It may help to explain the context in which the data were gathered. In 1985, the Australian Law Reform Commission undertook an investigation of the adequacy of the laws in the Australian Capital Teritory in relation to domestic violence. As part of this investigation, we were asked to devise a study to provide information on the extent and type of domestic violence in Canberra, the Capital City of Australia, partly since sceptism was widespread concerning whether it was indeed a problem.

METHOD

The methodology employed in this research was victim-initiated, anonymous telephone interviewing following mass media advertising. Trained interviewers were rostered at both day and evening times over the full 7 day period. Respondents were asked to respond to a detailed questionnaire by describing their violent relationships, with particular reference to the last violent incident. Information elicited included the type of violence inflicted (mental or physical abuse), the way in which it was enacted (involvement of weapons or character of physical assault), type of injury sustained and the date of the last violent incident.

The victims gave information regarding their response to the violent incidents (e.g., leaving the scene, fighting back) and their psychological reaction (e.g. guilt, shame, shock). They were also questioned about the extent to which they sought police intervention, medical treatment and support and counselling from other community agencies. In addition, the degree to which these services were helpful or judgmental was assessed.

Victims were further asked to describe the general features of the violence they typically experienced, such as the duration and frequency of the violence and the time of its initiation. Socio-demographic features of the victim and perpetrator (e.g., age, marital status, number and sex of children, occupation and education) were also sought.

Although this victim-initiated approach to the collection of data may initially appear to present potential difficulties with sampling (self-identified, self-selecting respondents) and the quality of responses generated (retrospective reporting by one party), such difficulties are comparable with the problems in other domestic violence data-collection techniques. Critics of official statistical collections for instance, have contended that a gross underestimation of criminal activity and victimisation is inherent in official data sources (Skogan, 1974). In addition, it has been claimed that reported trends contained within official statistics must be interpreted with caution due to the fluctuations in the ratio of reported to unreported crime (Walker, 1971). Other difficulties associated with the use of official data sources include the loss of information on unreported or undetected crime, the use of varying definitions by differing agencies and disparities in the employment of reporting techniques (Skogan, 1981).

RESULTS

The total number of interviews conducted throughout the week was one hundred and twenty, which represents 0.05% of the Australian Capital Territory adult population.

General Features Of The Sample

Most victims were female (98%) and husbands were the main perpetrators of the violence (71%). Regarding marital status, 54% were currently married and 29% were separated or divorced. The remainder were 'never married'. Most commonly, both victims and perpetrators were within the 30-34 years age range. The mean age of the first child ranged from 10 to 14 years. The general level of educational attainment was high (29% of victims and 27% of perpetrators had completed tertiary education).

In over one-third of cases, children were involved as witnesses to the violence and frequently, the children became integral to the violence. For instance, one woman said: "He grabbed me and twisted my hands 'til three of my fingers broke. My two kids tried to help me. He just went for them." Another explained: "He was just punching, punching, punching at me, and then he raped me in front of the four year old."

Contrary to popular myth, the violent males were not characterised by unemployment or membership of low-status occupations. Few were unemployed (13%) and a substantial proportion (38%) were in professional, managerial, or senior administrative positions. In contrast, the majority of the victims (42%) were not employed outside the home. If in paid employment, they typically occupied secretarial or sales positions (28%), but many victims (20%) were in professional or top administrative jobs. Of the women who were were employed, approximately half claimed to have control of their earnings, or to possess their own money. In terms of educational level, 29% of victims and 27% of attackers had some tertiary qualifications. The socio-economic data also compare favourably with national census data, suggesting that the above findings are not attributable to sampling biases.

For the majority of victims, the violence occurred with a marked regularity (once per week for 24% and daily for 16% of victims). In a quarter of the sample, the violence had been going on for 15 to 20 years or longer and, for 37% of women, the violence had continued for 5 to 10 years. In over half the reported incidents, there was evidence of both mental and physical abuse. Mental abuse was defined as constant verbal abuse, harassment, denigration, excessive possessiveness and deprivation of physical and economic resources. Physical abuse was most often inflicted through punching, kicking or hitting (43%), attempted strangulation/smothering (18%) or use of a weapon (15%). Sexual assault was the main form of abuse for 4% of women, verbal abuse only was experienced in 8% of cases, and 11% of victims did not report the type of abuse used.

The level of abuse common to many was described by one woman thus: "I was kept isolated from my parents and my friends. I was literally locked in when he went to work. He still constantly accused me of having affairs, of doing the most terrible things. He'd wake me up at night by punching me; then he'd violently rape me."

The victims responded to the violence in a number of ways. One third of the women reported that they were unable to fight back, leave or do anything to end the violence. Following the cessation of the violent incident, the majority of victims consulted medical personnel and/or community agencies. Medical practitioners were most often consulted (43%), followed by friends (30%), social workers or psychologists (8%) and parents (8%). Friends were typically reported to be most supportive and doctors were typically not supportive. One woman said: "Personally, I've found male doctors to be very sceptical. They're unsympathetic and they don't believe you. They just don't understand."

The data on reported injuries showed, however, that many women required medical treatment but did not seek it. In some cases, the attacker actively prevented the victim from seeking help. For instance, one woman reported: "He said he'd kill the baby if I went to hospital."

Only one-third of victims sought police intervention. The figures for arrest show that the attacker was arrested in 31% of cases, although 75% of victims had wanted arrest. Of extreme significance is that in no case was the perpetrator arrested against the victim's wish. Women's reasons for not seeking police intervention varied. Some victims reported feeling guilt or shame; others were cynical about police effectiveness. One woman commented: "I was told they would not come unless my life was in jeopardy. They told me to leave the house."

Terminating the Abusive Relationship

The decision to quit an abusive relationship may be informed by the success or failure of a victim's previous help-seeking behaviour or the characteristic features of the violence, or perhaps correlated with socio-demographic features. Logistic regression analysis was applied to the data to test whether particular variables could predict or explain the likelihood that the last reported violent incident occurred recently (within the last twelve months :n = 60) or in the past (more than two years ago :n = 52). Three statistical models were fitted on *a priori* theoretical grounds as detailed below.

The Attitudinal Model Of Domiciliary Intersexual Abuse

This model focuses upon the psychological characteristics of the male aggressor and the female victim as interpreted within the pattern of violence displayed; for example, the involvement of mental abuse, physical abuse or both. In studying the dynamics underlying the violent interaction between sexual partners, Dobash and Dobash (1984, p. 282) isolated a predictable pattern of events culminating in violence: "[The incidents] begin with verbal confrontations, usually of short duration and often perceived as challenges to the man's authority. This is followed by attempts on the part of the woman to avoid or avert violence, and then proceeds to the physical attack." (Authors' emphasis)

We decided to look at the effects of type of violence so that we could see whether the probability of recent violence was a function of: (a) the kind of violence experienced (ie. mental, physical abuse, or both); or (b) the average frequency of the violence (ie. once or more a week, once a month/intermittent violence); or (c) the length of the violence (ie. less than 2 years, or 5, 10, 15 years or more).

If p represents the probability that a victim experienced violence recently, then the logistic regression model can be formulated thus: for mental abuse p = 0.8, for physical abuse p = 0.3, and for mental and physical abuse p = 0.6. That is, victims are more likely to have experienced recent violence if they are subject to mental violence only, than if they suffer physical violence only, or both mental and physical violence. The length and frequency of violence are not salient factors. They do not add further to the explanatory power of the model. Clearly, the presence of physical violence is a strong factor in accounting for the occurrence of past violence. One possible interpretation is that the use of mental abuse may hamper the victim's ability to extricate herself from the violent relationship.

The Behavioural Model: Degree of Victim Passivity

The second model investigated was Ferraro's (1983) contention that domestic violence was associated with the employment of certain defence mechanisms by the victim, such as denial of injury or denial of victimisation. Such strategies involve passivity on the part of the victim. It was postulated that any victim action, such as calling the police, seeking medical treatment or consulting community agencies would be positively related to the cessation of the violence.

A logistic regression model was fitted for recent versus past violence, using variables defined as requiring victim action (i.e., seeking police intervention, medical treatment, counselling). If p represents the probability that a victim experienced violence recently, then the logistic regression model can be formulated as follows.

		Police Intervention Sought	
		Yes	**No**
Medical Treatment Sought	Yes	$\hat{p} = 0.29$	$\hat{p} = 0.55$
	No	$\hat{p} = 0.20$	$\hat{p} = 0.78$

Thus, there is a probability of only 0.29 that victims who have experienced recent violence are likely to have sought any intervention.

The victims who have experienced past violence are more likely to have sought medical treatment and to have called the police $(1 - p = 0.71)$. The victims' use of community agencies does not add anything to the regression model. This behavioural model indicates the significance of the victims' active seeking of police intervention and medical treatment. Such strategies may be tantamount to a public disclosure of the violence and an explicit avoidance of denial, supporting Ferraro's (1983) assertions.

The Socio-demographic Model

The third model tested was concerned with socio-demographic features, since, in contradiction to the popular image, the data from the present study show that intersexual violence is not confined to particular socio-demographic groups.

The following socio-demographic variables were used in a logistic regression model to test the critical factors in recent versus past violence: marital status (i.e., living together or separated); education of victim and attacker (tertiary education or high school education only); occupation of victim and attacker (high status occupation or low status occupation); and age of first child (child <10 years, adolescent 11-19 years, adult 20+ years). Many permutations were possible, all of which were tried. The only significant effect was marital status; victims of recent violence were more likely to be married or in a de facto situation than victims of past violence, who were more likely to be separated or divorced.

If p represents the probability that a victim experienced violence recently, then the logistic regression model can be formulated thus: for married victims p = 0.74, for separated victims p = 0.22.

The remaining socio-demographic variables are unimportant in predicting whether or not victims have experienced recent violence. Clearly, victims with tertiary education, employed in high status positions, are no less susceptible to recent violence than their less educated, possibly unemployed counterparts. This finding supports Johnson's (1981) contention that we need to challenge the assumption that "wife bashing is a lower-class pastime apart from the occasional middle-class psychopath."

DISCUSSION

The results of this study have shown that violence against women in the private domain is remarkedly similar across international samples. In particular, violence in Australia's capital city is clearly not confined to any particular socio-demographic grouping, but is distributed throughout the community, is of momentous proportion and made more difficult to endure by the image that Canberra is free of such violence. One woman's agony expresses this well: "Canberra is like a small town; someone always knows someone else who knows you or your family. I'm afraid that if anything is said, or help sought, it could affect my husband's career. Then everyone suffers."

Despite the empirical relationships demonstrated in the present study associated with the termination of abuse, it needs to be stated that, leaving a violent situation is, nevertheless, a complex process. For instance, many women described a process of accommodating to the violence, despite the serious and long-term consequences of maintaining such a relationship. Attempts to endure the violence may incur both physical and psychological injury on the part of the victim. Resolving to terminate the relationship also poses extraordinary difficulties. Statements by one of the women attested to the dilemma: "I wish people would realise that the pain does not end on parting. Even now, I have nightmares. I am afraid of the dark. I know I have low self-esteem."

ACKNOWLEDGEMENTS

1.   Address all correspondence to the first author. These data were collected while the first author was a Research Psychologist within the Research, Planning and Evaluation Unit, ACT Health Authority, Canberra, Australia.

2.   We wish to acknowledge the assistance of the following people: The women who responded to our questionnaire, some of whom have survived the violence and some of whom continue to suffer; Ross Cunningham for advice on regression analyses; Karen Fogaerty, Paul Faithfull and Beth Tyerman for computing; Anne-Marie Slattery for clerical duties; The anonymous interviewers and coders; The Office of the Status of Women for training interviewers and assisting with media coverage; The Australian Law Reform Commission for financial support for coding; and The ACTHA for the use of their computing facilities.

CORRESPONDENCE

Dr Rosemary A Knight, Australian Institute of Health, GPO Box 570, Canberra, Australia, and Dr Suzanne E Hatty, University of New South Wales, Kensington NSW, Australia.

REFERENCES

Dobash, R. E. & Dobash, R. (1984). The nature and antecedents of violent events. *British Journal of Criminology, 24,* 269-288.

Ellis, J. W. (1984). Prosecutorial discretion to charge in cases of spousal assault: A dialogue. *Journal of Criminal Law and Criminology, 75,* 56-102.

Ferraro, K. J. (1983). Rationalising violence: How battered women stay. *Victimology, 8,* 203-212.

Goldberg, W. G. & Tomlanovich, M. C. (1984). Domestic violence victims in the emergency department. *Journal of the American Medical Association, 251,* 3259-3264.

Hughes, H. M. & Barad, S. J. (1982). Changes in the psychological functioning of children in a battered women's shelter: A pilot study. *Victimology, 7,* 60-68.

Johnson, V. (1981). *The Last Resort: A Women's Refuge.* Ringwood: Victoria.

Parnas, R. I. (1967). The Police Response to the Domestic Disturbance. *Wisconsin Law Review, 36,* 914-960.

Skogan, W. G. (1974). The validity of official crime statistics: An empirical investigation. *Social Science Quarterly, 55,* 25-38.

Skogan, W. G. (1981). Issues in the measurement of victimization. Washington, D.C.: USA Bureau of Justice Statistics.

Walker, N. (1971). *Crime, courts and figures: An introduction to criminal statistics.* Harmondsworth, Middlesex: Penguin.

Social Applications and Issues in Psychology
R.C. King and J.K. Collins (editors)
©Elsevier Science Publishers B.V. (North-Holland), 1989

THE PREDICTION OF MARITAL VIOLENCE

Meir Teichman

Tel-Aviv University, Israel

Spouse abuse is viewed within the general framework of interpersonal relationships and is analyzed in terms of resource-exchange. Foa's interpersonal resource theory, and Gelles' exchange/social control theory are synthesised to form a theoretical proposition which classifies and predicts situations in which violence between spouses, as a mode of exchange, is more likely to occur and vice versa.

The phenomenon of family members resorting to violence is not unique to modern society. The Bible describes the first known act of violence within the family: "...Cain turned on his brother and killed him" (Genesis, 4, 8). The book of Genesis, thereafter, describes several cases of family frictions that have lead to jealousy and envy, frustration, anger and even aggression. The fact that the Bible, in its early Books, deals with such an issue suggests that this phenomenon was of great concern to society at such an early time. Indeed, one may quote the ancient philosopher, King Solomon, who declared: "Generations come and generations go, but the world stays just the same" (Ecclesiates, 1, 4).

EXPLAINING MARITAL VIOLENCE

The analysis of Biblical stories suggests these events are often due to dissatisfaction, frustration and conflicts within the family. Therefore, family violence, especially violence between spouses, may be understood within the general context of the interrelationship among the members of the family, a product of interpersonal behaviours, psychological tensions and external stresses affecting families at all social levels (Skolnick & Skolnick, 1977; 1983).

Gelles (1981, 1982, 1983, 1985) proposed an exchange/social control model of family violence. The theoretical proposition rests upon two principles: The first principle states that people will exercise violence in the family if the *cost* of being violent does not exceed the *reward*. The second, which is derived from control theory, states that people will use violence in the absence of social controls that restrain such a pattern of behaviour.

According to Gelles (1985), the relationships between the cost and reward of being violent are determined, in part, by three elements which are all in favour of the man. The elements are (a) the inherent biological as well as social inequality between man and woman; (b) the private nature of the family which prevents or minimizes outside (legal) intervention in cases of family violence; and (c) the societal attributions of "manhood" and "machoism". All these elements are in favour of the man in most known societies and significantly contribute to the reduction of costs to the violent person (i.e., usually, the man).

The cost and reward of being aggressive constitutes only one aspect of marital violence. Social exchange approaches may also provide some explanations about the nature of interpersonal relationships preceding the eruption of violence, as well as explanations about the patterns of exchange that may reinforce and maintain violence. Likewise, social exchange approaches may help identify the specific "rewards" or "costs" that keep the victim in the relationship in spite of the "costs" on her (his) part while reinforcing the aggressor's exercise of "power". Finally, exchange theories may suggest which patterns of responses may prevent, reduce or eliminate violent behaviour. The identification of such patterns of social exchange may instigate and guide preventive and therapeutic interventions within the violent family.

In order to analyze systematically the patterns of social exchange among family members, a classification-system of interpersonal relationships is needed. In the following section, a systematic and dynamic classification system of interpersonal resources involved in interpersonal behaviour is presented. This system may be useful to the study of marital violence.

CLASSIFICATION OF REWARDS AND COSTS

Interpersonal Resources. A dynamic approach to resource exchange and a systematic classification of resources transacted through interpersonal encounters was proposed by Foa and Foa (Foa, 1971; Foa & Foa, 1974, 1980; Hinde, 1979). It empirically divides the interpersonal resources into six classes which are related to each other in a circular fashion (See Figure 1). The resource-classes are labelled Love, Status, Information, Money, Goods, and Services. Love is defined as an expression of affectionate regard, warmth, and comfort; status is an expression of evaluative judgement that conveys high or low prestige, regard, or esteem; information includes advice, opinions, instructions, or enlightenment, but excludes those aspects of behaviour that could be classified as love or status; money is any coin, currency, or token which has some standard unit of exchange value; goods are tangible products, objects, and materials; and services involve activities on the body or belongings of a person, which often constitute labour for another.

FIGURE 1
The classification of interpersonal-resource classes

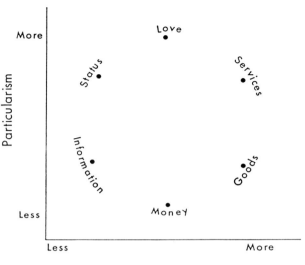

Concreteness

The resource-classes in Figure 1 are plotted along two attributes or coordinates: Concreteness vs. abstract (or symbolism), and particularism vs. universalism. Observation of interpersonal behaviour shows that behaviour may vary from concrete to symbolic: Whereas language, posture of the body, a smile, a gesture, or facial expressions are more symbolic, performing an activity upon the body or the belongings of another individual or delivering an object or cashing a cheque are quite concrete. The other dimension, particularism vs. universalism, pertains to the significance attributed to the person who provides the resources. Whereas the changing of a cashier will not affect the client who intends to pay his/her bill, a change of the personal physician is less likely to be accepted with indifference. Furthermore, a person is even more particular with regard to a friend, a spouse, or parents. Thus, it may be concluded that the more particularistic the resource, the stronger the influence of the person providing it (or taking it away) on the value received (or lost).

Each of the six resource-classes can be classified on the basis of these two coordinates. Services and goods that involve tangible activities and products are considered as concrete resources. Status and information are conveyed in a more symbolic fashion. Love and money, on the other hand, are exchanged in both concrete and symbolic forms and therefore occupy intermediate positions on the concrete-symbolic coordinate. By contrast, love and money occupy opposite positions on the particularistic coordinate. We do care who loves or hates us. Money, on the other hand, is the least particularistic resource. Money, regardless of the person who provides it, retains the same value. Services and status are less particularistic than love, but more so than information and goods.

The circular structure of the resources depicted in Figure 1 determines the ordinal distance among the resources: Love is always closer to services and/or status than to goods or information and is most distal from money. The predicted circular order of resources was validated in several investigations using different instruments, procedures and situations (Foa, 1971; Foa & Foa, 1974, 1980; Foa & Bosman, 1979; Foa, et al., 1987; Garner, 1985; Rahav & Teichman, 1984; Teichman, 1977; Teichman & Foa, 1975; Teichman & Rahav, 1986).

VIOLENT BEHAVIOUR AS RESOURCE-EXCHANGE

In the family, violent behaviour appears to serve structural as well as dynamic/functional purposes. The basic assumption underlying this article is that violent behaviour between husband and wife is a specific form of exchange relationship and therefore is governed by the same principles that explain exchange relations in general. In such an exchange one person, the *actor*, is violently obtaining *power* over and *taking away* or *denying* interpersonal resources from another person, the *object* (Foa, 1971; Rahav & Teichman, 1984; Teichman & Rahav, 1986). Thus, when analyzing the patterns of resource-exchange and power relationships within the family, the norm of reciprocity, credit building along time, the distributive-justice and feelings of equity/inequity, reward and cost (i.e., the pay-off matrix), satisfaction vs. frustration and, finally, mutual expectations should be considered.

Family power and violence. The issue of power within the family seems to play an important role in the development of violent patterns of behaviour among spouses. Family power and marital violence are interrelated in the following modes: First, violence may serve as a social commodity. By behaving violently or by witholding violence the actor may exert power over others. Indeed, in many cultures, violence is often regarded as the man's prerogative. Second, potential violence (the person's readiness and intention to exercise aggression) is also a source of power over other family members. Third, the victim is too often horrified, appalled and dismayed and loses her (his) resolution, and initiative to cope effectively with the aggressor. Finally, because of violent expectations, the victim is willing to relinquish power in exchange for non-violent conduct on the part of the potential aggressor. Thus, in terms of the interpersonal resource theory, when violence is exercised, the violent person exerts control over interpersonal resources that are actually provided by and belonging to the other. At that point, the patterns of resource-exchange within the family are shifting in favour of the aggressor and a new balance of resources is established. This balance will be shaken up and realign with each episode of violent behaviour toward the spouse.

The power-position of each family member and patterns of decision-making are also determined by societal factors. The male, in many traditional [as well as modern] cultures and societies, may be able to exert strong influence because of societal ruling principles and dictates. The woman, on the other hand, is devoid of strength and resources. The male has the right to control resources by virtue of his position as a male, regardless of the actual resources he produces and controls. On the other hand, the woman, in many instances, does not control resources that are actually produced or owned by her.

A resource-exchange model of familial power was first formulated by Wolfe (1959) and Blood and Wolfe (1960). According to this model, the balance of power between husband and wife is closely related to the resources each of them brings to the relationship; the decision-making power is determined by the relative control over needed resources. The family member who controls most of the resources which enable him or her to meet the needs of other family members, is perceived as the powerful member of the family. In a family in which these needed resources can be attained only from a specific member, the member of the family - a spouse (the wife) - is willing to relinquish power in exchange for the desired resources (Cromwell & Olson, 1975; Gray-Little & Burks, 1983).

Thus, the power-position of each family member may be defined by the actual and perceived distribution of specific interpersonal resources and by the actual and perceived need for resources of each member. A great need for resources on one hand and the deprivation of specific resources on the other hand may lead to frustration (Foa & Foa, 1974, 1980). As a result, if society permits the exercise of violence against a family member and if personal intentions for violence do exist, patterns of aggressive behaviour may ensue. In this case, one spouse – the violent one – is attempting to maintain control over the family resources and to achieve dominance by intimidating and abusing the other spouse, usually the wife.

The relationships between interpersonal resource-exchange, power and violence are complex. The more resources a spouse controls the more power he or she may exert upon other family members. However, as suggested by Goode (1971), violence may represent attempts to compensate for deficient resources and to gain control over these resources by those who lack or perceive themselves as lacking interpersonal resources. Following this line of reasoning one may imply that the more resources people have or perceive themselves as having, the more power they command and the less they will use violence. On the other hand, the fewer the resources a person controls, the less power he or she commands, but the more that person is likely to use force. However, it should be mentioned that a different script could be outlined - a script that followed an ancient understanding of human nature: The more you get the more you need. Therefore, obtaining control over resources by force may reinforce and perpetuate the use of violence. In violent families, both scripts are evident.

Status and marital violence: Status, respect, recognition or esteem are goals in and of themselves. Status is, on the one hand, a generalized social reinforcer and on the other hand an acceptable manner of reciprocity. That is, status is a significant social commodity – an interpersonal resource that people will do a lot to obtain, maintain and protect. Indeed, striving for superiority and needing social approval, status and esteem are fundamental motives of men and women (e.g., Hall & Lindzey, 1970).

Status may be related to marital violence in several ways. Often, a person who accepts resources from or is helped by another and who cannot repay appropriately, incurs inferiority (loss of status) as a cost of receiving the help. Inferiority increases frustration and the person will do his or her best to compensate that loss. Compensation may be achieved either by successfully obtaining control over various resources or by degrading the other (Teichman, 1971). Physical aggression is a degrading act. Thus, by battering the spouse, the aggressor degrades and devalues the spouse. He is reciprocating by taking away status from his spouse and, in turn, by increasing his control, power and status.

The effects of status relationships on spouse abuse were investigated by Hornung, McCullough and Sugimoto (1981). They found that status inconsistency of either partner and status incompatibility between partners were associated with an increased risk of abusive conduct within the family. Two surveys, that have been recently conducted in Israel, provide further support to the notion of inconsistency and incompatibility of interpersonal resources, status in particular, between the victim (the battered woman) and the aggressor (the violent spouse) (Lev-Ari, 1986; Teichman, in preparation). Both surveys clearly indicated that (Israeli) battered women were more educated, held more prestigious jobs and earned larger sums of money, as compared with their husbands. Furthermore, the findings clearly pointed out the inequity in certain resources between the violent husband and his wife. The inequity seems to emanate from the following sources. The first source of inequity stems from the differences in education and prestige of jobs between the husbands and the wives; the second is related to the lower income level of these men as compared with the women's earnings; the third source of inequity stems from some cultural differences between men and women, which allocate power to the man regardless of the available interpersonal resources. Thus, cultural norms that permit men to control interpersonal resources regardless of their origin, instigate the use of force by men as a means to achieve balance. The likelihood for violence is increased when the man believes that the provision of interpersonal resources is unfair from his point of view.

Frustration and marital violence. Violent behaviour may also be viewed as an expression of anger and frustration of one person against the other following (inappropriate) resource-exchange. This view is based on the "frustration-aggression" hypothesis, which was first proposed almost fifty years ago by

Dollard, Doob, Miller and Sears. The hypothesis suggests that frustration instigates aggression. The "frustration-aggression" hypothesis can be operationally defined in social-exchange terms. Dissatisfaction and frustration may be caused by specific patterns of decision-making, by inappropriate forms of resource exchange or by deprivation of one's need for resources by his or her partner.

Studies applying Foa's resource theory and assessed frustration from social exchange framework, clearly showed that the level of frustration may vary in accordance with the *mode* of the exchange (e.g., instead of giving a resource, taking it away or denying it) as well as with its *amount* and *appropriateness* (e.g., the proximity between the resources reciprocated) (Foa & Foa, 1974, 1980; Garner, 1985; Rettig & Bubolz, 1983; Teichman & Foa, 1975; Teichman & Rahav, 1986). For example, a spouse's need for love and affection which are met only with gifts and money, represents an exchange between distal resources. Although, receiving goods (gifts) has its own merit, as time elapses and affection and love are not conveyed, deprivation of these resources is deepening and the level of frustration increases.

Such trends are strengthened in family relationships which are characterized by particularistic or affective exchanges. The level of involvement in the relationships significantly enhances the degree of mutual satisfaction or dissatisfaction (Teichman & Foa, 1975). Alienation that characterizes western society has brought the members of the nuclear family closer to each other for emotional as well as for instrumental support. Thus, the contemporary nuclear family's specialized function of affectivity also makes it a particular powerful source of frustrations, conflicts, and violence towards the wife and children (Foa & Donnenwerth, 1971; Weibert & Hastings, 1977). The dissatisfied spouse, more often the man, is more likely to use aggression as a means of retaliation and to restore balance. Indeed, Gray-Little and Burks (1983) suggested that marital dissatisfaction may be related to coercive control techniques.

Previous work based on Gouldner's (1960) norm of reciprocity, Homans' distributive justice, Adams' (1965) notion of equity, and Foa's resource theory (Foa & Foa, 1974; Hinde, 1979) has clearly shown that feelings of inequity, dissatisfaction, and frustration and aggression can be created by varying the amount and kind of resources exchanged among people over time (e.g., see Teichman & Foa, 1975).

The amount of resources exchanged and the appropriateness of the reciprocal relationships are determined during each specific transaction as well as over time. Thus, satisfaction and frustration from family relationships are also cumulative measures of reciprocal relationships and mutual credit-building along time. Being deprived from certain resources increases the expectation for unbalanced exchanges in the future. Dissatisfaction and frustration are increasing regardless of other exchanges that are taking place in the family. Too often, such a prophecy fulfils itself. However, this is not the case when the expression of rejection is rare and the spouse has been able to establish a positive credit.

PREDICTING MARITAL VIOLENCE

The classification system of interpersonal resources enables one to offer several predictions with regard to the probability that violence may occur between spouses. These predictions, which as of now have not been directly tested, are based on the assumption that the violent behaviour is a form of interpersonal behaviour.

Table 1 presents the predictions derived from the theory of interpersonal resources. The table presents the balance of resources between spouses in three positions: (a) The woman is in a superior position with regard to interpersonal resources she actually dominates, (b) the man is in a superior position, and (c) a balance is maintained between the spouses. As can be seen, the predictions presented in Table 1 are skewed. The woman, because of prevailing societal norms and beliefs, is more likely to encounter violence when the resource-exchanges between the spouses are unbalanced in her favour. On the other hand, as previously indicated, when the balance is turning in favour of the man, the likelihood of violence within this relationship is very low.

TABLE 1:
Prediction of marital violence

| Resource | Balance of resource-exhange between spouses | | |
	In favour of woman	Equal	In favour of man
Love	L	N	N
Status	H	M	N
Information	H	M	N
Money	H	M	N
Goods	M	L	N
Services	L	N	N

H - High probability for violence
M - Medium probability
L - Low probability
N - No violence is predicted

A note of caution should be made. The predictive power of social-exchange principles may change under unique societal/cultural norms and may decrease when factors such as personal and social deviance and psychopathology take a dominant role in the person's social behaviour. Societal upheaval such as economic stress due to unemployment, immigration and wars aggravate potential violence and trigger quicker and more frequent incidents.

INTERVENTION

Clinicians and other professionals, who encounter cases of marital violence, often face a mixed and even a paradoxical picture. Each one of the people involved (husband vs. wife) perceives the chain of events in an entirely different way. In many cases, it seems that both spouses perceive themselves as being victimized by the other member. Whereas the wife is abused and battered, the man perceives himself as being neglected, rejected, and stripped of his honour and status.

In this paper, marital violence is viewed as resulting from incongruent perceptions and cognitions regarding "Man and Woman" within a given society, from the actual provision of interpersonal resources in the family and from inappropriate behavioural patterns of resource-exchange. If this assumption is valid, then a comprehensive intervention that will focus on the change of cognitions and on the modification of actual patterns of resource-exchange, should be a promising intervention method. Cognitive-behavioural and interpersonal psychotherapies and interventions are well established therapeutic modalities. Various modes of individual and group, couple and family therapies, that emphasize interpersonal aspects such as social skills training, have been applied in almost every form of psycho-pathology and social deviance. The reasoning for such interventions ranged from economical arguments to theoretical considerations. Steinfeld (1986), in a recent review of clinical implications of theory and research on the control of aggression, summarized several methods to control aggression and violence. Among those methods, cognitive interventions and social skills training were well documented.

The classification system of interpersonal resources may provide us with a systematic framework for analyzing [a] the individual's and the family's perceived and actual needs for interpersonal resources, [b] the patterns of exchange relationships among the members of the family, and [c] an additional intervention modality.

The provision of resources and the perceived as well as the actual distribution of interpersonal resources among the family members are, quite often, the source of stress, frustration and aggression. One may assume that increasing the provision of resources to the frustrated member of the family, should be the goal of the intervention. When the violent person considers the relationships as balanced, no cause for aggression exists. However, this alone, as many battered women have experienced, has only a short-term positive effect. Too often, the balance is repeatedly shattered in the eye of the beholder – the spouse – and a new cycle of violence erupts. Indeed, changes only in the provision of interpersonal resources and in the relative need for resources of each family member produce only short-term effects. However, if core attitudes and beliefs about the relationships between Man and Woman are unchanged, if mutual expectations are unrealistically biased, if the communication difficulties between the spouses persist and if behavioural (i.e., social skills) deficits remain unchanged, the actual or imagined resource-deficit will reappear and violence may erupt again. Thus, without changing spouses' cognitions relevant to manhood and womanhood, and modification of resource-exchange relationships, no long-lasting effects will be produced.

REFERENCES

Adams, J.S. (1965). Inequity in social exchange. In L. Berkowitz (Ed.) *Advances in experimental psychology*. NY: Academic Press.

Blood, R.O., & Wolfe, D.M. (1960). *Husbands and wives*. NY: Free Press.

Cromwell, R.E., & Olson, D.H. (1975). *Power in families*. NY: Wiley.

Foa, E.B., & Foa, U.G. (1980). Resource theory: Interpersonal behavior as exchange. In K.J. Gergen, M.S. Greenberg, & R.H. Willis (Eds.) *Social exchange: Advances in theory and research*. NY: Plenum.

Foa, U.G. (1971). Interpersonal and economic resource. *Science, 171*, 345-351.

Foa, U.G., & Donnenwerth, G.V. (1971). Love poverty in modern culture and sensitivity training. *Social Inquiry, 41*, 149-159.

Foa, U.G., & Foa, E.B. (1974). *Societal structures of the mind*. Springfield, Ill.: Thomas.

Gelles, R.J. (1981). *Family violence*. Beverly Hills: Sage Publications.

Gelles, R.J. (1982). An exchange/social control approach to understanding intrafamily violence. *Behavior Therapist, 5*, 5-8.

Gelles, R.J. (1983). An exchnage/social control theory. In D. Finkelhor, R.J. Gelles, G.T. Hotaling & M.A. Straus (Eds.) *The dark side of families: Current family violence reseach*. Beverly Hills: Sage Publications.

Gelles, R.J. (1985). Family violence. *Annual Review of Sociology, 11*, 347-367.

Gelles, R.J., & Straus, M.A. (1979). Determinants of violence in the family: Toward a theoretical integration. In W. Burr et al. (Eds.) *Contemporary theories about the family*. NY: Free Press.

Gouldner, A.W. (1960). The norm of reciprocity: A preliminary statement. *The American Sociological Review, 25*, 161-179.

Gray-Little, B., & Burks, N. (1983). Power and satisfaction in marriage: A review and critique. *Psychological Bulletin, 93*, 513-538.

Hall, C.S., & Lindzey, G. (1970). *Theories of personality* (2nd edition). NY: Wiley.

Hinde, R.A. (1979). *Towards understanding relationships*. London: Academic Press.

Homans, G.C. (1961). *Social behavior: Its elementary forms*. NY: Harcourt, Brace & World.

Hornung, C.A., McCullough, B.C., & Sugimoto, T. (1981). Status relationships in marriage: Risk factors in spouse abuse. *Journal of Marriage and the Family, 43*, 675-692.

Lev-Ari, R. (1986). *Family violence: A survey of referrals to the Family Violence Center*. Tel-Aviv, Israel: NAMATH (Hebrew).

Lips, H.M. (1981). *Women, men, and the psychology of power*. Englewood, NJ: Prentice-Hall.

Rahav. G., & Teichman, M. (1984). Assessing the seriousness of deviant behaviors: The effect of interpersonal resources. In D.J. Muller, D.E. Blackman & A.J. Chapman (Eds.) 161-169. *Law and psychology*. NY: Wiley.

Rettig, K.D., & Bubolz, M.M., (1983). Interpersonal resource exchange as indicators of quality of marriage. *Journal of Marriage & the Family, 45,* 497-509.

Skolnick, A.S., & Skolnick, J.H. (1977). *Family in transition* (2nd edition). Boston: Little, Brown.

Skolnick, A.S., & Skolnick, J.H. (1983). *Family in transition* (4th edition). Boston: Little, Brown.

Teichman, M. (1971). Antithetical apperception of family members by neurotics. *Journal of Individual Psychology,   27,* 73-75.

Teichman, M. (1977). Affiliative behaviors among soldiers during war time. *British Journal of Social & Clinical Psychology, 16,* 3-7.

Teichman, M. (In preparation). Women in a shelter: A sociodemografic survey.

Teichman, M., & Foa, U. G. (1975). Effects of resource similarity on satisfaction with exchange. *Social Behavior & Personality, 3,* 213-224.

Teichman, M., & Rahav, G. (1986). The severity of deviant behaviors and the preferred reaction. *Criminal Law, Criminology & Police Science, 1,* 69-82 (Hebrew).

Weibert, A.J., & Hastings, R. (1977). Identity loss, family and social change. *American Journal of Sociology, 82,* 1171-1185.

Wolfe, D.M. (1959). Power and authority in the family. In D. Cartwright (Ed.) *Studies in social power.* Ann Arbor, MI: University of Michigan.

Social Applications and Issues in Psychology
R.C. King and J.K. Collins (editors)
©Elsevier Science Publishers B.V. (North-Holland), 1989

DELINQUENCY RISK AS A FUNCTION OF EARLY INTELLIGENCE SCORES

Paul D. Lipsitt, Stephen L. Buka and **Lewis P. Lipsitt**

Harvard Medical School; Brown University Child Study Center, U.S.A.

Most early studies found that delinquents obtained lower IQ scores than non-delinquent controls. A criticism of early findings related to sample selection subsequent to identification as juvenile offenders. Of 3164 births enrolled in the Brown University cohort of the National Collaborative Perinatal Project, 13.6 percent appeared in Family Court charged with juvenile offences prior to age 18. In this study, those delinquency cases were compared with controls at three age levels. At 8 months, based on the Bayley Scales of Mental and Motor Development, there were no significant differences in mental or motor development scores between delinquents and non-offenders. At 4 years, Stanford-Binet scores were significantly lower among the delinquent sample. Similarly, at age 7, the delinquent sample scored lower on the Wechsler Intelligence Scale for Children (WISC) on both verbal and performance measures. Verbal scores were consistently higher than performance scores in both the delinquent and non-offender groups. These findings support the view that intelligence scores at an early age are a factor in the vulnerability of children towards future delinquency, an observation which has relevance for treatment options of children who may later enter the juvenile justice system.

This study documents a relationship between intellectual performance and delinquency, a topic that has received extensive attention in the research literature over the years, amid intense debate. Throughout the last century and into the early 1900's the common characterization of a criminal was as a mental defective. Many early studies found that delinquents typically obtained lower IQ scores than their non-delinquent controls (Glueck & Glueck, 1934, 1950; Kvaraceus, 1945; Merrill, 1947). However, Caplan (1965) concluded that the relationship of intelligence test scores to delinquency is either non-existent or "so small as to be of theoretical interest only." In contrast, Wilson and Herrnstein (1985) assert that "there appears to be a clear and consistent link between criminality and low intelligence."

Since the 1930's, with the introduction of more objective and valid tests such as the Stanford-Binet and the Wechsler-Bellevue, there has been a growing number of investigations of the association of intellectual or cognitive factors and delinquency. Much of the early research encountered methodological difficulties, resulting in ambiguous and inconsistent findings.

A range of approaches, often difficult to compare, frequently without controls and including heterogeneous socio-economic status (SES) samples, confounded opportunities for comparison. Biases affecting results included such factors as a poorly chosen time of evaluation (e.g., after arrest or after incarceration), selective processing of court cases and failure to take into account intervention by other community resources. The present study has avoided some of these methodological pitfalls, with a data base obtained from a cohort selected when they were younger than the age of potential interception by the juvenile justice system.

METHOD

Study Population

The study sample was drawn from the Brown University cohort of the National Collaborative Perinatal Project (NCPP) of the National Institute of Neurological and Communicative Disorders and Stroke (Niswander & Gordon, 1972). This was a major interdisciplinary study of the antecedents of childhood mental, neurological and physical disabilities. Over 56,000 pregnancies (enrolled between 1959 and 1966) were prospectively followed until age seven. Brown University was one of fifteen universities in the United States to document developmental events to seven years of age in this cohort. Major findings from the NCPP have been presented by Broman, Kennedy & Nichols (1975), Nichols & Chen (1981) and Niswander & Gordon (1972).

The cohort upon which this study is based were recruited from a 50% sampling of all registered clinic patients at a major maternity hospital in Rhode Island. The study sample consists of 3164 subjects who were born from March, 1960 to August, 1966. The sample includes information on a broad spectrum of conditions during pregnancy and delivery, as well as follow-up data, some of which is analysed in this study.

Procedure

Through the cooperation of the Chief Judge of the Family Court of Rhode Island, which has statewide jurisdiction over juveniles, all NCPP cases with court contact were identified, with proper safeguards of confidentiality and anonymity. Court involvement was determined after each member of the cohort had reached age 18, at which time juvenile court jurisdiction ends. Court records were matched with the cohort by linking names and birthdates with computerized court listings. Mothers' names, siblings' names, and in some cases home address and fathers' names were used for additional verification. Among the cohort of 3164 subjects, 431 juvenile delinquency cases were found in the court records. The cases were reviewed and coded according to age, as well as to the nature and disposition of each offence petition.

To assess the reliability of the juvenile offence data obtained through this process a random 5% sample of the entire cohort was recoded. There was 100% concordance for classification as having a court record or not. For the subjects with court records there was an 85% agreement on the number of delinquent petitions filed, with 97% of the comparisons accurate within one petition.

Subjects were classified as having only one (single) delinquency offence or more than one (repeat). Those with repeat offences were of particular interest. First, from the vantage point of the juvenile justice system, subjects with repeat offences are of special concern because they place a particular burden upon the legal system. Secondly, assuming that recorded offences are an accurate index of actual offences, recurrent offenders are of greater public concern than the single offender. Finally, given that arrest data are imprecise indicators of true offence rates (many delinquent offences go undetected and unprosecuted) the contrast between repeat offenders and non-offenders is particularly informative. Persons with more than one delinquent adjudication are clearly repeat offenders. Persons with no arrests may quite likely be infrequent offenders (single offenders) but are less likely to be repeat offenders. Therefore, the contrast between *no* delinquent adjudications and *repeat* delinquent adjudications is a fair measure of the presence or absence of repeat offending and is superior to comparisons of *no* delinquent adjudications and *any* delinquent adjudications.

Intelligence Scores

At 8 months of age, the members of the cohort had been administered the Bayley Scales of Mental and Motor Development. These tests are age-specific and structured with normative responses based on the largest and most diverse sampling of American children (Bayley, 1969).

At four years of age, each child was administered the Stanford-Binet Intelligence Scale, Form L-M (Terman and Merrill, 1960).

As part of the seven-year psychological assessment, the Wechsler Intelligence Scale for Children (WISC) was administered. The WISC (Wechsler, 1963) was developed as a downward extension of the adult intelligence test, and covers an age range from 6-0 to 16-11 years.

RESULTS

Table 1 represents the size of the cohort and the rates of delinquent offences by gender and race.

TABLE 1
Rates of Delinquent Offences By Sex and Race

		ONE		TWO OR MORE		ANY	
	N	#	%	#	%	#	%
MALE	1568	170	10.84	171	10.91	341	21.75
WHITE	1174	120	10.22	128	10.90	248	21.12
BLACK	394	50	12.69	43	10.91	93	23.60
FEMALE	1596	51	3.20	39	2.44	90	5.64
WHITE	1194	35	2.93	20	1.68	55	4.61
BLACK	402	16	3.98	19	4.73	35	8.71
TOTAL	3164	221	6.98	210	6.64	431	13.62

NUMBER OF DELINQUENT OFFENCES

Table 2 compares the mean scores for the non-delinquents and delinquents with two or more offences (repeat offenders). These data are computed for all cases, as well as for males, white and black subjects. At 8 months of age, no significant differences were found between non-offenders and repeat delinquents on the Bayley Scales of Mental and Motor Development.

TABLE 2
Comparison of Mean IQ Scores ––– Non-Offenders and Repeat Delinquents

	8 Months		4 Years		7 Years	
	Mental	Motor	S–B	VIQ	PIQ	FSIQ
ALL SUBJECTS						
NO OFFENCE	79.4	33.7	97.6	91.7	98.0	93.9
RPT DEL	80.1	34.0	93.4	88.6	93.4	90.0
p-value	n.s.	n.s.	.002	.002	.001	.001
MALES						
NO OFFENCE	79.3	33.6	95.8	92.4	97.6	93.9
RPT DEL	80.0	33.9	93.3	88.6	92.8	89.7
p-value	n.s.	n.s.	.073	.001	.001	.001
BLACKS						
NO OFFENCE	79.0	33.9	94.1	88.0	93.9	89.5
RPT DEL	80.0	34.3	90.5	83.4	89.2	84.8
p-value	n.s.	n.s.	.090	.008	.016	.012
WHITES						
NO OFFENCE	79.6	33.7	98.8	93.0	99.5	95.4
RPT DEL	80.2	33.9	94.9	90.9	95.3	92.4
p-value	n.s	n.s.	.015	.077	.002	.013

However, the intelligence test scores at age 4 show significant differences between those who later committed no offences and the delinquent sample. The average score for non-offenders (97.6) is higher than that for single offenders (see Figure 1) and those with two or more offences have the lowest IQ scores (93.4).

The results of the WISC scores at age 7 are consistent with the results at age 4. The Full Scale IQ scores range from 93.9 for the non-offenders to a low of 90.0 for repeat delinquents. The slop is monotonic for single and repeat offenders. The scores on the performance IQ scale on the WISC range from 98.0 for non-offenders to 93.4 for repeat delinquents. Verbal IQ scores also show comparable significant differences between delinquents and non-offenders.

The bar graph in Figure 1 shows the mean values for each of the offence categories on the Bayley, Stanford-Binet, and Wechsler Scales. As noted above, a trend emerges beginning at age 4 with the Stanford-Binet results and repeated at age 7 on the three summary scales of the Wechsler, showing approximately 1/3 standard deviation between the repeat delinquents and non-offenders, with single offenders falling midway between the two extremes. Differences between repeat delinquents and non-offenders are significant at the .002 level at age 4 and at close to the .001 level at age 7 on the WISC for Verbal, Performance and Full Scale IQ. No statistical analysis was performed on the single offenders, shown for contrast purposes only. It is also notable in this figure that the Performance score on the Wechsler is consistently higher than the Verbal, regardless of offence categories, by approximately 4 IQ points.

FIGURE. 1
Comparison of mean IQ scores at ages 8 months, 4 years and 7 years for
repeat and single delinquents and non-offenders.

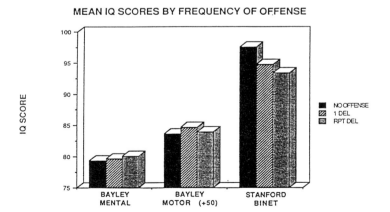

MEAN IQ SCORES BY FREQUENCY OF OFFENSE

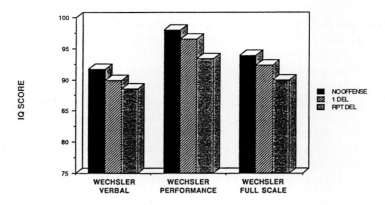

Figure 2 shows the sub-test scores on the Wechsler, again reflecting the trend in each offence group to score lower as a function of frequency of offence. The scores for the sub-tests that make up the Performance Scale are all higher than for the Verbal Scale sub-tests, for delinquents and non-offenders alike.

FIGURE. 2
Comparison of Wechsler IQ subtest scores at age 7 for repeat and single delinquents and non-offenders.

MEAN WECHSLER IQ SUBTEST SCORES (ALL SUBJECTS)

By Frequency of Offense

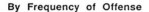

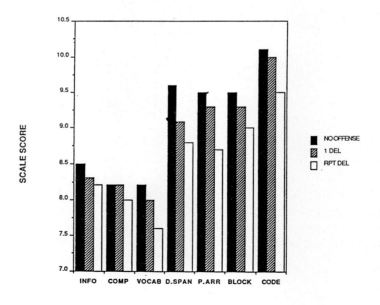

Figure 3, males only, shows the same pattern, with single or mild offenders scoring between non-offenders and repeat delinquents at age 7.

FIGURE 3
Comparison of mean IQ scores at ages 8 months, 4 years and 7 years for repeat and single delinquents and non-offenders, for males only.

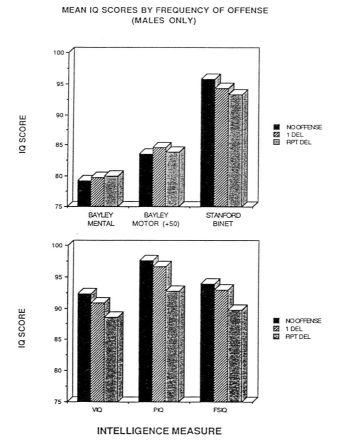

MEAN IQ SCORES BY FREQUENCY OF OFFENSE
(MALES ONLY)

INTELLIGENCE MEASURE

Figure 4 shows separate graphs for white and non-white subjects. Scores for blacks are generally lower, but the relationship between non-offenders and repeat delinquents remains consistent. Differences on the Stanford-Binet in the comparison of blacks alone do not reach significant level.

FIGURE. 4.
Comparison of mean IQ scores at ages 8 months, 4 years and 7 years
for repeat and single delinquents and non-offenders, for non-white
and white subjects.

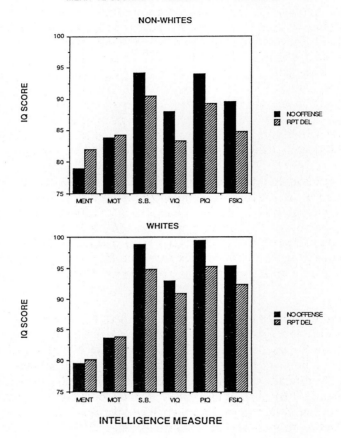

MEAN IQ SCORES BY FREQUENCY OF OFFENSE

DISCUSSION

Statistically significant differences occur between repeat delinquents and non-offenders on virtually all measures of intellectual capacity available for analysis at age 4 and age 7. Single offenders show signs of consistently higher intelligence scores at 4 and 7 years of age than repeat delinquents. An examination by race and gender reveals that the differences are consistent within race and for males alone, except for non-whites at age 4, where differences do not reach a statistical level of significance.

Juvenile offenders do not demonstrate a different set of intellectual strengths and weaknesses from non-offenders. In particular, we did not find that offenders' verbal scores were profoundly lower than their performance scores, as would have been predicted from much delinquency theory and from findings by Glueck and others (1950). In fact, for both the delinquents and non-offenders, verbal scores were consistently higher than performance scores. One of the best documented longitudinal studies, the Cambridge Study by Farrington and West (1981) and continued by Farrington (1986), consistently found, using four different types of analyses, that IQ at 8-10 years of age has a significant relationship to delinquency. Farrington identifies intelligence as related to school failure and shows a high correlation with troublesomeness. Another longitudinal study by Wolfgang (1972), involving 9945 boys for whom records existed dating from between their 10th and 18th birthdays, found lower IQ scores and fewer grades completed among chronic delinquents than non-chronic or single offenders. The present study supports the findings of these two longitudinal studies, although suggesting further that the relationship is identifiable as early as ages 4 and 7.

The relationship between intelligence and delinquency has important implications for the juvenile justice system. Psychologists and juvenile court judges have long grappled with perplexing questions about causes and controls of juvenile delinquency. The juvenile justice system, with its roots in 19th Century social-welfare philosophy, initially perceived its mission to be that of saving errant children. Following the notion of *parens patriae,* the court could assume a broadly discretionary role in an attempt to compensate for early impairments and deprivations.

During the 1960's, a changing philosophy of the role of the juvenile court developed. This new approach argued that it was neither good therapy nor judicial fairness to use the legal system to impose "treatment" without the procedural safeguards that are accorded adults in the criminal justice system. The first two cases from the juvenile court to reach the United States Supreme Court (Kent v. United States [1966]; In re Gault [1967]), were concerned about the cavalier manner in which children were treated in the name of *parens patriae.* Justice Fortas, reflecting this concern, observed in Kent (1966), "the child receives the worst of both worlds....he gets neither the protections accorded to adults nor the solicitous care and regenerative treatment postulated for children". In addition to the due process considerations, early signs of delinquency risk may point the way towards timely intervention and treatment.

P.D. Lipsitt (1969), attempting to reconcile the original philosophy of care and rehabilitation with the growing constitutional concerns for the civil liberties of children, concluded that, while due process was necessary, it was not sufficient to ensure effective intervention towards rehabilitation in the juvenile justice system. The impact of otherwise commendable practices of fairness and due process, now a routine condition of the juvenile justice system, may actually diminish the likelihood of implementing rehabilitative functions, the aim of the early juvenile court in the days of *parens patriae*. There must be more discriminating screening of cases appropriate for the juvenile court and resources for treatment of those selected for such processing. The findings of the present research strongly suggest opportunities for much earlier intervention.

Although an association between lower intelligence scores and subsequent delinquency has been demonstrated here, it is important to emphasize that the majority of low-IQ youngsters do not pursue delinquent careers. Further study is needed to determine what factors tend to buffer those children who may be vulnerable but do not pursue delinquent or criminal careers. A study to interview a sample of low-IQ subjects in the cohort, offenders and non-offenders, in order to determine what factors may have contributed to the avoidance of a delinquent outcome in spite of low IQ scores at an early age, is next in order.

These findings suggest that intervention at an early state for children who exhibit intellectual deficits may expand opportunities to avoid a hazardous course of development and, in particular, to escape an adolescent pathway to a delinquent career.

ACKNOWLEDGMENT

In carrying out this work, the Child Study Center of Brown University was aided by grants from the W.T. Grant Foundation, the March of Dimes Birth Defects Foundation, and Brown University.

REFERENCES

Bayley, N. (1969). *Manual for the Bayley Scales of Infant Development.* New York: The Psychological Corporation,.

Broman, S.H., Nichols, P.L., & Kennedy, W.A. (1975). *Preschool IQ: Prenatal and Early Developmental Correlates.* New York: Halstead Press.

Caplan, N.S. (1965). Intellectual Functioning. In H.C. Guay (Ed.) *Juvenile Delinquency.* Princeton: Van Nostrand Co., 100-138.

Farrington, D.P. & West, D.J. (1981). The Cambridge Study in Delinquent Behavior. In S.A. Mednick & A.E. Baert (Eds.) *Prospective Longitudinal Research.* Oxford: Oxford University Press.

Farrington, D.P. (1986) Stepping Stones to Adult Criminal Careers, In Olweus, D., Block, J. & Yarrow, M.R. (Eds.). *Development of Antisocial and Prosocial Behaviour: Research, Theories and Issues.* New York: Academic Press, Inc., 359-384.

Glueck, S. & Glueck, E.T. (1934). *One Thousand Juvenile Delinquents.* Cambridge: Harvard University Press.

Glueck, S. & Glueck, E.T. (1950). *Unraveling Juvenile Delinquency.* New York: Commonwealth Fund.

In re Gault 387, U.S. 1 (1967).

Kent v. United States, 383 U.S. 541.(1966).

Kvaraceus, W.C. (1945). *Juvenile Delinquency and the School.* New York: World Book.

Lipsitt, P.D. (1969). Due Process as a Gateway to Rehabilitation in the Juvenile Justice System. *Boston University Law Review, 49*, 62-78.

Merrill, M. (1947). *Problems of Child Delinquency.* Boston: Houghton Mifflin Co.

Nichols, P.L. & Chen, T.C. (1981). *Minimal Brain Dysfunction: A Prospective Study.* Hillsdale, New Jersey: Lawrence Erlbaum Associates.

Niswander, K.R. & Gordon, M. (1972). *The Women and their Pregnancies.* Washington, D.C.: U.S. Government Printing Office.

Terman, L. M. & Merrill, M.A. (1960). *Stanford-Binet Intelligence Scale.* Boston: Houghton Mifflin.

Wechsler, D. (1963). *Manual for the Wechsler Preschool and Primary Scale of Intelligence.* New York: Psychological Corporation.

Wilson, J.Q. & Herrnstein, R.J. (1985). *Crime and Human Behavior.* New York: Simon & Schuster.

Wolfgang, M., Figlio, R.M. & Sellin, T. (1972). *Delinquency in a Birth Cohort.* Chicago: University of Chicago Press.

Social Applications and Issues in Psychology
R.C. King and J.K. Collins (editors)
©*Elsevier Science Publishers B.V. (North-Holland), 1989*

THE EFFECTIVENESS OF THE EPQ AS A MEASURE OF DELINQUENCY IN AN AUSTRALIAN CONTEXT

C. J. Lennings*

The current research reports on a controlled study in which 50 school children, 25 children at risk (Welfare) and 25 delinquents (Committed by a court) were assessed with the EPQ. In addition two other tests, the Jesness and the Pd scale of the MMPI were administered to gauge the relative superiority of the EPQ. A cognitive assessment was also completed and treated as a covariate in the analysis. The Pd Scale was able to discriminate clearly between all three groups at high levels of significance. In addition the Pd scale did not seem affected by either age or IQ in terms of the effectiveness of the statistical analysis. Both of the other personality tests performed poorly. It is proposed that in future studies the Pd scale (with a T-score cut off at 80) would prove to be an effective screening instrument for high school populations where there is a requirement to select out "delinquent-prone" subjects.

A considerable amount of work has been done in the field of juvenile corrections on the predictors of delinquency. Several tests exist that purport to be useful measures of the likelihood to engage in delinquent or criminal acts. Such tests include the Jesness Inventory (Jesness, 1983; 1986), the Eysenck Personality Questionnaire (Eysenck & Eysenck, 1975) and the MMPI (especially the Pd scale of the MMPI) (Gynther et al, 1973). In addition these tests also purport to measure a wide range of other emotional and personality factors. Theoretically, a profile can be constructed that allows one to predict (i) the likelihood of delinquency, (ii) the degree to which personality and emotional factors play a role in the delinquent behaviour of the person and (iii) the likelihood of recidivism. In addition, several researchers have used the various scales as exit tests in order to determine responsiveness to therapy or residential programs (e.g., Habgood, 1980; Howard, 1986; Munson & Reeves, 1986).

The Eysenck Personality Questionnaire (EPQ) is a relatively short test (81 items), reputed to give reliable pictures of an individual's personality structure and an index of "delinquency" or criminality. This test, in both a Junior and Adult form provides, along with the "normal" scales of personality function, an additional scale of criminality - the "C" scale. This scale was initially constructed as a useful discriminator of the extent of criminality within already established criminal populations (Rush, 1985) rather than a diagnostic tool in its own right. The EPQ has considerable theoretical advantages over other tests in that it comes complete with a theory of personality functioning and a theory of criminality. Eysenck has proposed a theory, based on elevations of the Extroversion, Neuroticism and Psychoticism scales that suggest two profile types to fit criminals. The first, Primary Sociopathy proposes elevations on E and P scales but low scores on N whilst the second, Secondary Sociopathy, implies elevations across all three scales (Gray et al, 1983).

The EPQ however has come in for considerable criticism as a reliable indicator when applied to forensic groups (Emler, Reicher & Ross, 1987) although its basic factor structure within a general Australian population has in general been upheld (Campbell & Ross, 1984; Putnins, 1981).

McEwan (1983) produces evidence to contradict Eysenck's theory of criminality, based as it was on the theory of Extraversion and Neuroticism, and found not two, but four, profile patterns, at least two of which were in direct contradiction of Eysenck's theory. Similarly Beilby (1985) reviews a number of studies that throw doubt on Eysenck's theoretical proposition linking extraversion (assuming as it does low cortical arousal) and impulsivity - an essential ingredient in many theories of criminal behaviour.

Beilby (1985), in his study, assessed 298 male and female delinquents on either the EPQ Junior or Adult. This was an investigative study with the purpose of establishing some normative data for its use with a local delinquent population. No control group was used although Beilby did make use of comparison data from other studies. His study concluded that although there was some useful discriminatory power to the EPQ, in the main the EPQ was useful only as a component of other assessment techniques. Although in one sense this is true of all tests, the question remains as to whether the EPQ is useful in its own right as an indicator of delinquency and whether it can form the basis for predictions on the degree of delinquency and the likelihood of recidivism.

Rush (1985), in her New Zealand study of adult offenders and army volunteers, did suggest that with an older population the EPQ was able to provide such information. Within the New South Wales context the test most used in the prediction and research on delinquency is the Jesness Inventory. Gorzynski, (1977); Habgood, (1980) and Howard, (1986) used the Jesness test as either entry tests, or as measures on exit to assess change in functioning due to incarceration and/or treatment. However none of these studies used control groups, although both Howard and Habgood attempted to make use of data from other studies as a kind of statistical control.

Howard, (1986) conducted a major review of the Jesness and its use with a delinquent population. He used the Jesness as an entry-exit test for delinquents referred to a youth centre for counselling. From a review of both international and Australian studies Howard found that there was considerable instability in the scales of the Jesness in discriminating between delinquent and non-delinquent populations as well as predicting change with delinquent populations. In particular, the A-Social Index of the Jesness proved effective in only 60% of the studies.

The Minnesotta Multiphasic Personality Inventory (Hathaway & McKinley, 1970) is in general regarded as an accurate test that allows for a more independent estimate of personality disorder in varied population groups. Most studies tend to be supportive of its use, although not of the Jesness and the EPQ. Practical experience, however, mitigates against the MMPI. The test can be criticised for being too long, too American in its wording and oriented more towards obtaining clinical or symptom pictures of the person rather than looking at underlying personality traits. It has also been seen as outdated and requiring major revision (Steiner & Miller, 1986). Length, incidentally, is also an issue with the Jesness, which at only a quarter of the length of the MMPI nevertheless is still 155 items long.

Major claims have been made for the accuracy of the Psychopathic Deviate (Pd) sub-scale of the MMPI in discriminating between forensic populations and between forensic and other populations (Mayer, Bonta & Motiuk, 1985). Mayer's study involved comparing the ability of the Pd scale to discriminate among prisoners adaptating to supported accommodation on release, with tests based on the Pd scale, but, theoretically, possessing more discriminative power. Their study demonstrated that even after considerable development of alternative tests the Pd scale was generally the more accurate predictor.

To date no study has been found using the Pd Scale of the MMPI as a predictor of change within a New South Wales delinquent population. In addition to the clinical difficulties found with the above tests, factors such as Socio Economic Status (S.E.S.), intelligence, literacy level and sex have also to be considered.

Neither Howard nor Beilby found IQ to be an important variable with their subjects although one might have expected otherwise. Socio Economic Status was included as a variable in both Howard's and Beilby's studies and in both failed to prove significant as a discriminator between the various groups. SES will not be included in the current study.

There are similarities as well as substantial differences between each of the tests in their item content (Furnham, 1982; Howard, 1986). It is therefore the intent of this project to establish (i) the usefulness of the various scales as a measure of delinquency and (ii) the superiority, if any, of the scales. It is hypothesised that the EPQ will be at least as good as any of the other tests but, with the advantage of its relatively higher yield of information over the MMPI-Pd and brevity over the Jesness, will prove on cost-benefit grounds to be the best test.

In addition it is proposed to assess the degree of interaction that cognitive factors such as intelligence, age and reading ability will have on the subjects' performance on the tests.

METHOD

All three personality tests and Raven's Progressive Matrices were administered to three separate groups of male adolescents. Groups 1 and 2 were also administered a reading test. The first group consisted of juvenile offenders in a committal setting; the second group were children coming to the notice of the Department or private institutions, who may have presented as welfare or sub-cultural problems but who had not become involved in serious juvenile delinquency; and the third group were school children who had no history of Departmental or criminal involvement.

PROCEDURE

Subjects for Group 1 (Committal) were obtained in the course of professional work over a three month period at Yasmar. All subjects were committed, had several previous charges or were on a first but very serious charge and were functionally literate.

Subjects from Group 2 were obtained from a variety of sources. Some were first time offenders, referred by the Courts for a psychological assessment. These subjects did not subsequently receive a committal. Other subjects were obtained from Rosemount, a Catholic Church administered programme that provided living skills programmes to behaviourally disturbed children. These children had no prior history of committal although most had a prior history of police cautions and court appearances. Some subjects from a local Catholic High School had revealed, during information gathering for the control group, that they had either a past history of involvement with the law or a welfare history.

Group 3 subjects, the control group, were obtained from a local Catholic High School. This was a fee-charging high school and the pupils came, in general, from a higher socio-economic background although not invariably so. Teachers were asked to send along pupils from Years 8 to 12 and to select pupils from a cross-section of ability. Participation was voluntary, but as it was conducted during class time, the volunteer rate was high.

Subjects in Groups 1 and 2 were assessed on a reading test, the Schonnel Graded Reading Test and Raven's Progressive Matrices. It was not possible to obtain measures of reading ability for Group 3 from the school - which proved to weaken the design of the study. All subjects were then given the three questionnaires with the order randomised and asked to complete them within a specified time.

The groups were organised such that Groups 1 and 2 had equal numbers (25) and Group 3 was equal to this combined number. This was done to allow for the pooling of Groups 1 and 2 in a statistical analysis, if that should be warranted. Larger sample sizes would have been preferrable, however, the constraints imposed by data collection prevented this.

RESULTS

The Subjects

Table 1 reports IQ and reading scores for the three groups.

TABLE 1
Intelligence and Reading Scores for Sample.

Group [yrs]		Intelligence		Reading Level	
		Mean	S.D	Mean	S.D
Committal	(1)	104.04	12.25	11.36	1.84
Welfare	(2)	106.96	12.75	12.11	1.32
Control	(3)	110.86	12.02	n/available	

Age. There are no significant differences in the distribution of ages between the groups ($X^2 = 10.76$, d.f. 6 ; p=.09 n.s.) - as is expected given that age was carefully considered in selecting subjects for the study.

Intelligence. As Table 1 demonstrates the Control group is somewhat higher in intelligence than either the Welfare or Delinquent groups. An Anova was performed to determine whether there was any significant interaction betwen Group and Intelligence. Included in this Anova was the age variable. Although neither main effects for age (p≥. 063) or group (p≥ .065) proved significant in themselves the interaction effect for both age and group across Intelligence was significant (p≥. 02). Consequently it was decided to use both Age and Intelligence as covariates in further analyses to control for any effect they may have on the dependent variables.

Reading Ability Due to a failure to obtain reading levels for the High School subjects reading level could only be compared between the Committal and the Welfare group. A t-test was performed but no significant difference was obtained (t=1.47; d.f. 41; p≥ .148). As reading levels could not be obtained for Group 3 this variable was dropped from further analyses.

Table 2 shows the means and standard deviations for each of the dependent variables across all three groups.

TABLE 2
Means and Standard Deviations for Test Variables

Variables:	Committed Mean	S.D.	Welfare Mean	S.D.	Control Mean	S.D.	Total Mean	S.D.
EPQ: "N"	13.64	4.07	12.80	4.20	13.10	3.70	13.16	3.90
"E"	12.80	3.76	15.68	3.56	15.56	3.90	14.90	3.90
"P"	5.88	3.19	6.92	2.72	5.24	4.03	5.82	3.57
"L"	5.00	4.28	5.12	2.99	6.50	3.69	5.90	3.68
"C"	17.08	4.47	14.44	3.83	14.38	4.83	15.07	4.67
MMPI:Pd	80.64	14.78	72.76	9.06	62.20	10.83	69.45	13.85
Jesness								
"SM"	44.56	6.80	44.08	4.99	38.42	8.87	41.37	8.07
"VO"	62.00	11.34	62.20	11.17	57.16	10.30	57.85	11.67
"Imm"	58.88	11.86	58.56	7.97	61.42	9.38	60.07	9.74
"Aut"	64.00	10.79	64.04	9.15	56.80	10.09	60.41	10.98
"Al"	64.00	7.33	64.84	8.21	56.98	9.03	60.70	9.15
"MA"	60.52	13.26	58.08	12.99	53 10	10.48	56.20	12.12
"Wd"	57.28	11.38	54.8	8.53	50.72	10.98	53.39	10.82
"SA"	51.40	9.07	50.32	7.83	48.86	8.26	49.86	8.52
"Rep"	50.40	10.77	51.00	10.80	55.24	9.26	52.97	10.20
"Den"	40.00	9.16	40.88	9.12	47.42	10.22	44.06	10.18
Asocial Index	37.16	8.30	36.44	7.75	34.74	8.18	35.77	8.09

A considerable amount of data had been collected regarding the comparative standing of the current sample under study to previous studies. As this data is time consuming to relate and in general the sample under examination did not differ greatly from other studies (with the exception of EPQ data) no further discussion of this data is offered here. Detailed analyses are available from the author on request.

Four MANCOVA's were performed on the data. In each case Intelligence and Age were included as covariates. The first Mancova analysed the three criterion variables of the C scale (EPQ); the Pd scale from the MMPI and the Asocial Index from the Jesness across all three levels of group. In this analysis the covariates were not significant (F .98; d.f. 6; p≥ .437). However the overall Manova for the dependant variables was highly significant (p≥ .000). Univariate F tests revealed only the MMPI Pd scale as significant (F 19.28; d.f. 2; p≥ .000). However the C scale approached significance at p≥ .054. The Asocial Index had no effect at all (p≥ .240).

In the second Mancova all three groups were compared across all the test variables. This involved a large number of variables (17) and consequently there are considerable reservations held about the power of this analysis.

The covariates this time were significant (F 1.7; d.f. 34; p ≥ .01). An analysis of the correlation co-efficients revealed that Intelligence was the most important contributor to this effect (r=.93). The univariate F tests suggested that much of the effect of the covariates was due to the influences of the Immaturity, Value Orientation, Repression, Alienation and Social Maladjustment scales of the Jesness. The only scale in addition to the Jesness to show significance values was the Lie scale of the EPQ.

The overall Manova for this second analysis was highly significant (p≥ .000) with the uinvariate tests demonstrating a number of scales contributing to this. Table 3 shows the effects for all significant scales. At the .01 level or better the scales that demonstrate significance are the Pd scale of the MMPI followed by the Jesness subscales of Value Orientation, Social Maladjustment, Autism and Denial. At the .05 to .01 level the Extroversion scale of the EPQ achieves significance and the C scale again approaches significance at the .054 level. However, if one examines the means for the E scale one finds a condundrum. One would expect the means for the Committal group to be highest on this variable but in fact the results are reversed with the extroversion score for the committed group the lowest of the sample.

In the Dimension Reduction Analysis two roots are found. The first seems to be accounted for primarily by the MMPI Pd subscale whilst the second seems to be primarily accounted for by the E, P, N and C scales of the EPQ. This latter result does suggest there is some sort of association between these variables and delinquency, as predicted by Eysenck's theory.

TABLE 3
Manova results on Dependent Variables
Univariate F tests (p values only)

Scale		Manova 1 (3 gp X 3 var)	Manova 2 (3 gp X All Var)
"C" Scale		(.054)	(.054)
MMPI-Pd		.000	.000
Asocial Index			
EPQ	"N"	XXX	
	"E"	XXX	.011
	"P"	XXX	
	"L"	XXX	
Jesness	"SM"	XXX	.001
	"VO"	XXX	.001
	"Imm"	XXX	
	"Aut"	XXX	.015
	"Alien"	XXX	.000
	"MA"	XXX	
	"Wd"	XXX	
	"SA"	XXX	
	"Rep"	XXX	.023
	"Den"	XXX	.009

The last two Mancova's investigate the effect of collapsing the results for the Welfare and Committal groups, thus providing for two levels of the independent variable. Essentially the results are unchanged, even though the groups are now equal. Since there is little change in the results, and none that is central to the current set of hypotheses, there will no further discussion of these results. However this data is available from the author on request.

DISCUSSION

In summary, then, the Manovas suggest that the test with most discriminative power is the Pd scale of the MMPI. Little evidence for the usefulness of the EPQ "C" scale was obtained and, generally, the EPQ failed to live up to expectations. In particular the results for the Extroversion variable were generally in the direction opposite from that expected on the basis of Eysenck's theory. This provides a note of caution in attempting to generalise from test results to some general theory of criminality. It may be, when comparing the current sample with previous studies, that this is an unusal sample in that extroversion scores were lower than normally found with delinquent groups and, in fact, lower scores than normally found in the general population. The possibility that this reflects the combining of the ages was considered, but an analysis of the means for the subjects by ages showed that the highest extroversion scores were obtained by the fourteen and fifteen year olds. This suggests that the use of the Adult form with younger subjects did not act to "pull down" the relevant scales.

What is also of interest is the relatively poor showing of the Jesness, particularly the Asocial Index in acting to discriminate between the groups. This result calls into question the validity of this measure with identifying delinquent populations as opposed to assessing change within them.

In common with the other unpublished studies reported here, the interaction of intelligence with the test scores was not particularly significant, at least in regard to the main predictor variables. Generally, cognitive factors do not seem to be related to performance on the tests (with the exception of the Jesness) and, in line with the observation of Howard (1986), there may be little useful purpose in treating intelligence as a contributing variable to delinquency.

The above results are vulnerable to design considerations. A relatively small number of subjects was used and there may well be some criticism of the homogeneity of the make up of the Welfare group. In addition, there may be some criticism of having administered the one form of the EPQ to all ages. In this regard, however, other studies have used this procedure (McEwan, 1983) and found it to be satisfactory. In any case, it would be hoped that by controlling for age effects, the worst abuses of the single form would be obviated. There may well be some reservations about the power of the statistical analysis given the large number of variables to relatively few subjects. However, the first analysis reflected the general trend of the results, and satisfied the assumptions regarding the power of the technique.

A possiblity that this particular sample was an idiosyncratic one must be entertained, although, with the exception of the EPQ data the sample did seem reasonably consistent with other Australian studies. It would be appear that replication with larger samples would be necessary to resolve this question.

The primary aim of this study was to investigate the utility of the C scale of the EPQ as a good enough indicator of delinquency. It was not to enlist support or criticism for Eysenck's theory of criminality. The results of this study suggest that the EPQ is not as valid an indicator as would be hoped for, and that the Pd scale of the MMPI is the more useful indicator.

Even though there are some differences between the current population and other delinquent populations there are sufficient similarities to suggest that this study has some repercussions for the assessment of delinquency. It must be borne in mind that this study did not examine the usefulness of the Jesness or the EPQ as tests able to monitor change in delinquents. Studies that make use of these tests for that purpose may prove to be quite justified in doing so.

*ACKNOWLEDGEMENTS:

I would like to thank Rod Beilby, Alan Habgood and John Howard for their helpful discussions and access to their previous research. I would also like to thank Alan Taylor for his help with the statistical analysis. The research reported here, whilst completed with the knowledge of the Department of Family and Community Services, was not a Departmental project and the opinions expressed do not reflect the views or policies of the Department. In addition I would also like to thank the Principal, teachers and pupils of Christian Brothers, Lewisham and the staff and participants of the Rosemount programme.

Address for correspondence: "Yasmar", 185 Parramatta Rd., Haberfield, NSW 2045

REFERENCES

Beilby, R. (1985). Eysenck Personality Questionnaire: Findings in Court Referred Australian Adolescents. Unpublished Study. Department of Youth & Community Services.

Campbell, R. & Ross, M. (1984). An Australian Investigation of the Eysenck Personality Questionnaire. *Acer Bulletin for Psychologists, 34,* 22-24.

Emler, N.; Reicher, S. & Ross, A. (1987) The Social Context of Delinquent Conduct. *Journal of Psychology & Psychiatry, 28.,* 99-109

Eysenck, H. J. & Eysenck, S. B. (1975). *Manual for the Eysenck Personality Questionnaire. Hodder & Staughton.*

Gynther M. D; Altman H. & Warbin R. W.(1973). Behavioural Correlates for the Minnesota Multiphasic Personality Inventory 4-9, 9-4 Code Types. *Journal of Consulting and Clinical Psychology, 40 ,* 259-263

Habgood, A. (1980). An evaluation of Tallimba and Daruk Training Schools. Report for the Dep. of Youth & Comunity Services.

Howard, J. (1986). The Jesness Inventory. Unpublished Thesis Use of the Jesness Inventory - An Australian Study. Macquarie University.

Furnham, A. (1982). A Content Analysis of Four Personality Inventories. *Journal of Clinical Psychology, 38,* 818-824.

Gray, J. A.; Owen, S.; Davis, N. & Tsaltas, E. (1983). Psychological and Physiological Relations between Anxiety and Impulsivity. (p181-227) in Zuckerman, M. (Ed) *Biological Bases of Sensation Seeking, Impulsivity, and Anxiety.* L.E.A. New Jersey.

Hathaway, S. R. & McKinley, J. C. (1970). *The Minnesota Multiphasic Personality Inventory.* Psychological Corporation.

Jesness, C. (1983). *The Jesness Inventory.* Consulting Psychologists Press.

Mayer, B. A.; Bonta J. L. & Motiuk, L. L. (1985). The Pd Sub-scales: an empirical evaluation. *Journal of Clinical Psychology,* 41 780-788.

McEwan. A. W. (1983). Eysenck's theory of criminality and the personality types and offences of young delinquents. *Journal of Personality and Individual Differences ,* 4, 201-204

Munson, R. & Revers, M. P.(1986). Program effectiveness of a residential treatment centre for emotionally disturbed adolescent females as measured by exit personality tests. *Adolescence, 21,* 305-310

Putnins, A. (1981). *Summary Statistics for 179 students tested with Junior EPQ at Cambelltown High School.* South Australian Department for Community Welfare.

Rush. C. (1985). Predicting reconvictions using the Eysenck Personality Questionnaire. Paper presented at the First Joint Conference of the Australian and New Zealand Psychological Societies.

Steiner, D & Miller, H. R. (1986). Can a good short form of the MMPI ever be developed. *Journal of Clinical Psychology, 42 ,* 109-113

Social Applications and Issues in Psychology
R.C. King and J.K. Collins (editors)
©Elsevier Science Publishers B.V. (North-Holland), 1989

WELLBEING, CLOSE RELATIONSHIPS AND PSYCHOLOGICAL HEALTH

Gabrielle M. Maxwell, Ross A. Flett and Helen C. Colhoun

University of Otago, New Zealand

Recent New Zealand studies of wellbeing, self-esteem and close relationships are reviewed. The findings are similar to those of overseas studies and suggest the value of a concept of positive mental health which is defined by a sense of wellbeing, high self-esteem and effective personal relationships. These in turn reflect the presence of skills that enable persons to cope with the world in which they live; the working world, family life, friendship, leisure and community activities. The acquisition of social skills enhances psychological health variables. Unemployment, loneliness, depression and social anxiety are associated with a lack of health. The value of the analysis lies in providing a quantifiable concept of positive mental health which can be used for the assessment of social programmes and in suggesting social policy changes which may enhance the wellbeing of the community and prevent mental ill-health.

Conceptualizations of disease and mental ill-health or psychological abnormality have been well developed for many years and the principles which guide diagnosis are set out in detail and generally accepted. On the other hand, conceptualizations of physical and mental health have been poorly developed. There has been a lack of agreement on definitions and decisions on positive health status have tended to revolve around the absence of diagnosable disorder. The medical model of psychological health presents difficulties because psychological problems do not generally arise because of physical malfunction.

Criteria for health involving such concepts as maturity, creativity, self-actualization, independence and successful functioning in the social system (e.g. Coan, 1974; Jahoda, 1958) have also proved problematic in that they identify a relatively small and privileged portion of the population as "mature", "self-actualized", etc. Moreover, those identified may also show symptoms of neurotic disorder. Also, such definitions are inevitably value-laden and lack cross-cultural or cross-situational reliability.

The search for adequate definitions of positive psychological health have been further handicapped by the lack of adequate research on the "healthy"; i.e., those who are not identified as social problems. However, the last twenty years of social psychological research have been characterized by an increasing attention to the processes which enable successful functioning; in particular the development of social skills, parenting skills, work skills and stress management skills. Community psychologists have called for health promotion through the empowerment of individuals to take control of their own lives and change the nature of the world in which they live rather than be changed by a system that demands adaptation to its rules (Rappaport, 1976). The criteria for assessing validity of such preventive and promotion programmes becomes the enhancement of psychological and social wellbeing rather than the elimination of symptoms of ill health. The measurement of wellbeing thus becomes a primary goal and so too does the measurement of the two most important correlates of wellbeing; self-esteem and satisfaction with relationships.

The following review concentrates chiefly on recent unpublished findings of studies on the nature of subjective wellbeing and its relationship to other factors including socio-demographic factors, physical health, stressful life-events, self-esteem and satisfying interpersonal relationships. It proposes a method of conceptualizing and assessing psychological health and discusses the implications of such a conceptualization for social policy formation and evaluation.

RESEARCH REVIEW

Wellbeing

The last twenty years have seen the emergence of the concept of subjective wellbeing as a global self assessment of personal happiness which can serve as a central component in the measurement of quality of life (Andrews & Withey, 1976; Bradburn, 1969; Campbell, Converse & Rodgers, 1976; Diener, 1984).

In New Zealand, a series of studies was carried out or supervised by Richard Kammann between 1975 and 1983 which involved issues in the assessment and correlates of wellbeing. These studies led to the development of the Affectometer 2 (Kammann & Flett, 1983), a 40 item scale measuring subjective wellbeing defined in terms of a predominance of positive or good feelings and a complete and lasting satisfaction with life as a whole. This implies feelings of cheerfulness, energy, freedom, a sense of purpose and control and the feeling that life is meaningful.

The data (Kammann & Flett, 1986, Flett, 1986) confirm overseas findings that subjective wellbeing is not simply a product of current mood; nor can it be equated with social desirability. Both mood and social desirability correlate with wellbeing. But mood also correlates as highly with wellbeing a week earlier or a week later suggesting that current mood is a manifestation of wellbeing rather than a source of response bias.

Correlations between mood and social desirability tend to be about 0.30 in most studies. The relatively small size of the correlation coefficient makes it clear that subjective wellbeing cannot be equated with social desirability. Subjective wellbeing is correlated with depression, usually at about 0.70. However, the Affectometer 2 is unlike depression scales in that it effectively discriminates among the non-depressed and hence can be used to assess health as well as illness.

There is a clear link in both the New Zealand and overseas studies (Kammann & Flett, 1986), between physical health and psychological wellbeing. Although the presence of diagnosable complaints is rarely related to wellbeing, there are clear correlations between wellbeing and general ratings of physical health which signify a sense of bodily health and energy. In general, most major studies of wellbeing only find small associations between wellbeing and demographic indicators such as age, gender and socio-economic status (Diener, 1984) and these findings are similar in New Zealand (Kammann & Flett, 1986).

Wellbeing and social indicators

Social indicator research has often attempted to define geographical areas that differ in terms of affluence, privilege and services. Such studies have helped highlight issues of poverty and deprivation and have assisted in targeting services to those most in need. In 1985, the New Zealand Health Department used census information to classify geographical areas throughout New Zealand on the basis of a complex multivariate analysis. A subset of areas was identified as low or high on the criterion variables and described as "areas of misery" and "pockets of bliss". The indicators included such variables as income, education, socio-economic status, being employed, number of cars and race.

While such an approach is potentially useful in guiding the delivery of social services, there are problems in assuming an automatic relationship between social indicator scales based on census data and subjective wellbeing. Colhoun and Maxwell (1987) surveyed 193 people from two "areas of misery", two pockets of bliss" and three intermediate areas measuring social indicators, wellbeing, self-esteem, close relationships and physical health. The data showed that although the expected social indicator differences were replicated, there were no significant overall differences between the areas in subjective wellbeing or self-esteem. Nor were the areas differentiated in physical health.

These results demonstrate that social indicators do not necessarily predict human happiness. Geographical areas can be differentiated in terms of socio-economic factors. Some of these factors are linked to wellbeing and in this study they were linked to loneliness. But although areas may be rich or poor, they should not be referred to in terms of "bliss" or "misery" as such terms do not describe the feelings the people themselves express about their lives. Poverty can be degrading and can make people unhappy, but the people in areas low on social indicators are in need of employment opportunities and services rather than inaccurate labels that might further reduce the self-esteem of those who live there.

Wellbeing and Stressful life events

Many studies have failed to demonstrate a link between stressful life events and wellbeing. This is partly because they have selected events that observers believe will be negative without checking whether the person experiencing the event has found it so. It is also partly because in some studies there has been a tendency to assess the occurrence of an event without regard to its recency.

Major catastrophes, such as becoming a paraplegic, have not necessarily led to chronically lowered wellbeing, but there is certainly an initial impact (Brickman et al., 1978). There is substantial support for the negative effects of major changes in relationships, such as the breakup of a partnership, on wellbeing (Andrews & Withey, 1976, Campbell, Converse & Rodgers, 1976). There is also support for the impact of hassles in one's daily life (Delongis et al., 1987) and the effects of unemployment (Diener, 1984),

In New Zealand, Flett (1986) found that negative events perceived by the respondents as involving major failures, loss of social support and tense times, were related to wellbeing although the effects were not great. Maxwell & Robertson (1988) have demonstrated the impact of marital breakup on wellbeing in a sample of Family Court clients. They also report a link between wellbeing and the stress of life changes both in terms of the number of changes and their rated impact.

The effects of unemployment are usually to create a marked drop in wellbeing and even more substantial effects have been noted for the long term unemployed. Such findings have been replicated in New Zealand by Hesketh (1984) and Macky (1987).

Self-esteem

Self-esteem is one of the strongest predictors of wellbeing (Diener, 1984) and has often been regarded as its primary component. Furthermore self-esteem drops during periods of unhappiness. Although self-esteem is related to wellbeing, it is not identical. Correlations vary from 0.35 to 0.70 depending on the measures used.

Conceptually, self-esteem and wellbeing are both expressions of satisfaction with aspects of life. Self-esteem focuses on satisfaction with self and wellbeing reflects on overall life satisfaction. Thus wellbeing is affected by satisfaction with all aspects of life although satisfaction with oneself has usually been regarded as the most important component (Campbell, 1981).

Satisfaction with work has an impact on both wellbeing and self-esteem. Findings relating wellbeing and unemployment have already been discussed. Studies which include self-esteem measures find that it is lowered by lack of job satisfaction and by unemployment. In New Zealand, McIntosh (1985) reported that satisfaction with university work was important for self-esteem, particularly for male students. Macky (1987) compared employed and unemployed school leavers and found that the unemployed were more depressed and showed lower self-esteem. Hesketh (1984) studied unemployed adults and found that the longer people were unemployed, the more likely they were to be depressed; a consequence particularly true of the middle-aged. Unemployment was also linked to other negative life circumstances such as family problems and poor living conditions. Hesketh's work led her to conclude that not just unemployment, but the quality of working conditions, has a very important impact on wellbeing.

McIntosh's (1985) study examined a variety of sources of self-esteem and wellbeing in a sample of 105 university students. She demonstrated that the most important predictors of self-esteem were satisfaction with university work, body image, close relationships and the living environment and those in it. Body image and leisure activities were more important for females than males. However, if body image is seen as unimportant, satisfaction with body image is unrelated to self-esteem.

Wellbeing and close relationships

Effective social support is the other (with self-esteem) most important correlate of subjective wellbeing and has also been seen as an intrinsic part of psychological health. Social support has now been well established as important in buffering the effects of stressful life events (Brown & Harris, 1978). In studies of wellbeing, the quality and nature of interpersonal relationships emerges as the single most important predictor. Campbell, Converse and Rodgers (1976) conclude that it is "the intimate areas of primary relationships which have the most potent impact on general feelings of wellbeing enjoyed by members of the population".

There are several different aspects of interpersonal relationships that have been related to wellbeing (Diener, 1984). Married people are generally reported as happier. Satisfaction with one's love life has also been linked to wellbeing; so too is having a close confidant. Greater amounts of social contact are associated with increased wellbeing. George & Fillenbaum (1985) in their review of the factors that have proved important in the study of older people, suggest that wellbeing is related to all the three components that have been identified as comprising social support: the frequency of contact, the availability of emotional support and tangible assistance, and the perceived quality of relationships. The key role of satisfaction rather than amount of contact, is emphasized throughout the social support literature and focuses attention again on the subjective evaluation of life circumstances rather than their objective nature.

New Zealand studies again echo the overseas findings. Dixon (1981) confirms that married people tend to be happier than unmarried. Flett (1986) found small significant correlations between wellbeing and the total number of people in a person's network (r=.21) and the average closeness to all of them (r=.26). He found higher correlations between wellbeing and closeness to the five closest people (r=.41) and closeness to the closest person (r=.47). These results underline the importance of close personal relationships for wellbeing.

Studies of the correlates of loneliness show a similar pattern of association with close relationship variables. Maxwell and Coebergh (1986) found the best predictors of loneliness were satisfaction with close relationships r=.56; closeness to the closest person r = .46; number of people one feels close to r = .44; and amount of contact with people at work r =.28. These four variables in combination accounted for nearly half the variance in loneliness (r = .69). The two most important factors were close relationships and satisfaction with relationships. These data suggested that loneliness can be reconceptualised as dissatisfaction with one's relationships.

Accounts of events leading to loneliness confirm the above analysis. Maxwell and Coebergh (1986) reported that loneliness was most commonly an outcome of major life changes (including new jobs, new loves, travel and retirement), the loss of close relationships (through death, divorce, illness or moving) and isolating circumstances (spouse and family away, shift work, isolated living). All these events can be viewed as affecting close relationships or making them difficult to maintain. Three other common reasons also relate to the pattern of social relationships; namely, having unhappy close relationships, getting married or being at home with young children. Thus in at least 78% of the cases in the Maxwell and Coebergh (1986) study, the events which precipitated the loneliness periods in people's lives can be seen as those that have affected the pattern of their relationships with others.

It can be suggested that a wellness concept of satisfaction with relationships is preferable to the illness concept of loneliness and that, like the relationship between depression and wellbeing, a "satisfaction with relationships" scale allows for differentiation among the satisfied while "loneliness" scores tend to discriminate more strongly among the dissatisfied.

Colhoun and Maxwell (1985) carried out a study designed to examine the relationship among the variables of wellbeing, self-esteem, satisfaction with relationships and loneliness. They report a correlation of r = .59 between a "loneliness" score derived from a modified version of the UCLA Loneliness Scale and a scale designed to measure "satisfaction with relationships". Their study also confirms the link with wellbeing which correlated at r = .52 with "satisfaction with relationships" and r = -.52 with loneliness. Loneliness and self-esteem correlated at r = -.38, loneliness and depression, r = .52 and loneliness and social anxiety, r = .44. These results lend support to the thesis that satisfaction with relationships plays a crucial role in psychological wellbeing.

Summary and Discussion

The research reviewed here indicates that it is practicable to assess psychological health by measuring subjective wellbeing, self-esteem and satisfaction with relationships. The measures all fulfil appropriate criteria in that they are:

(i)   Independent. While these measures are correlated, they are not identical.

(ii)   Related to the individual's experience. They assess the psychological and social wellbeing of individuals as experienced by them rather than as rated by others.

(iii)   Global. They are all global measures relating to a broad and important aspect of an individual's experience rather than to being limited in time or to part of life.

(iv)   Reliable. They are able to be measured reliably and able to be used by most of the population.

(v)   Useful. They are useful in the sense of being sensitive to changes in life circumstances which alter the quality of life as it is experienced by the individual.

Debate about the relationship between the variables is possible and about whether there are other possible measures such as control over life. These issues deserve to be addressed but space precludes a discussion here.

CONSEQUENCES FOR SOCIAL POLICY

While we have been diligent in monitoring the economic performance of governments, social monitoring has often been overlooked. In part, the failure to assess the quality of life as it is experienced by people reflects the very real difficulty of measurement. Campbell (1981) observes that it is difficult for governments to act on a problem until they are able to count it. The most common panaceas for obvious social ills are programmes that can be counted in terms of money and numbers of projects dealt with or jobs created. Campbell suggests that governments "follows the principle that whatever the problem may be, the application of a particular amount of money will make it better. Governments have a more difficult time with such subjective states as alienation, job dissatisfaction, fear of crime, loneliness, resentment of discrimination, marital discord or other conditions which diminish the psychological quality of people's lives. They do not have a clear sense of how wide these problems are or a sure feeling of how to deal with them".

The development and acceptance of standard methods of measuring psychological health is an important step on the road to effective social monitoring. There are two ways in which the assessment of psychological health can be used in social policy planning: in identifying situations where people are at risk and in assessing the effectiveness of intervention programmes.

The identification of situations in which people are likely to be at risk is already an important achievement of wellbeing research and programmes designed to meet the needs of groups targeted by earlier work (Campbell et al., 1976) has led to successful new initiatives in developing programmes for health promotion and problem prevention. The results reported here suggest that quality of life surveys rather than social indicator studies based on census data, are more likely to be successful in identifying situations where people are at risk.

New Zealand wellbeing research has already targeted the unemployed (Hesketh, 1984; Macky, 1987) and those experiencing marital breakdown (Maxwell & Robertson, 1988). Self-esteem research has identified adolescent and young adult females with poor body images (McIntosh, 1985; Williams, 1981). The loneliness research of Maxwell & Coebergh (1986) identifies further targets.

A second major use of assessment of psychological health in policy planning is as a method of determining the effectiveness of programmes designed to promote health or prevent ill-health. In New Zealand, Raeburn (1986) has used wellbeing measures as a criterion of the effectiveness of his community health programmes and Colhoun (1988) has demonstrated the effectiveness of an individual social skills training programme in improving wellbeing, self-esteem and satisfaction with relationships.

Conclusions

The research reviewed here confirms that a definition of psychological health involving wellbeing, self-esteem and satisfaction with close personal relationships is one which is practicable. All three concepts are measurable.

Wellbeing and self-esteem can be regarded as criterion variables which are intimately affected by satisfactions with various aspects of life: satisfactions with personal relationships, the quality of the living environment, the quality of the working environment and for those people who regard it as important, satisfaction with body image. Such satisfactions are likely to be affected by the realism of aspirations and the skills which people have to cope with the environment in which they live. In particular social skills, the ability to manage stress, job skills, living skills and general education are all likely to be important factors. The combination of adequate social support, realistic aspirations and skills is likely to ensure that the adverse effects of stressful life events are minimized.

The direct implications of these findings for a social policy of mental health promotion are a focus on reducing unemployment, improving working conditions, and encouraging life styles that promote close personal relationships.

In addition the provision of training for life skills must be stressed and this implies the availability of job training programmes, social skills programmesm social support groups, community health services, and general educational services for both younger and older people.

The challenge of translating theoretical findings into applied policies and assessing the effectiveness of promotion and prevention interventions is one which can now be given greater conceptual and methodological clarity through a realistic and practicable definition of psychological health.

ACKNOWLEDGEMENTS

The research reported here has been supported by funds from the NZ Social Science Research Fund Committee, Medical Research Council of NZ, Alcohol Liquor Advisory Council and the Otago University Research Committee.

REFERENCES

Andrews, F.M. & Withey, S.B. (1976). *Social indicators of wellbeing.* New York, Plenum Press.

Bradburn, N.M. (1969). *Structure of psychological wellbeing.* Chicago: Aldine.

Brickman, P., Coates, D. & Janoff-Bulman, R. (1978). Lottery winners and accident victims: Is happiness relative? *Journal of Personality and Social Psychology. 36,* 8, 917-927.

Brown, G.W. & Harris, T. (1978). *Social origins of depression.* London, Tavistock.

Campbell, A., Converse, P.E. & Rodgers, W.L. (1976). *The quality of American life.* New York, Russell Sage Foundation.

Campbell, A. (1981). *The sense of wellbeing in America.* New York, McGraw Hill.

Coan, R. (1974). *The optimal personality.* New York, Columbia University Press.

Colhoun, H.C. (1988). Close relationships, psychological health and social skill. Unpublished PhD thesis, University of Otago, Dunedin.

Colhoun H.C. & Maxwell G.M. (1985). Social anxiety: Antecedents and consequences. Report to the New Zealand Medical Research Council.

Colhoun, H.C. & Maxwell, G.M. (1987). Social Indicators and Psychological Health. *Community Mental Health in New Zealand, 3,* 2, 63-79.

Delongis, A., Folkman, F.& Lazarus, R. (1988). The impact of daily stress on health and mood: psychological and social resources as mediators. *Journal of Social and Personality Psychology, 54,* 3, 486-495.

Diener, E. (1984). Subjective wellbeing. *Psychological Bulletin, 95,* 3, 514-575.

Flett, R. (1986). Subjective wellbeing: its measurement and correlates. Unpublished PhD thesis, University of Otago, Dunedin.

George, L.K. & Fillenbaum, G.G. (1985). OARS methodology; A decade of experience in geriatric assessment. *Journal of the American Geriatric Association. 33,* 9,607-615.

Hesketh, B. (1984). Attribution theory and unemployment: Kelley's covariation model, self-esteem and locus of control. *Journal of Vocational Behaviour, 24,* 1, 94-109.

Jahoda, M. (1958). *Current concepts of positive mental health.* New York, Basic Books.

Kammann, R. & Flett, R. (1983). Affectometer 2: A scale to measure current levels of general happiness. *Australian Journal of Psychology, 35,* 257-263.

Kammann, R. & Flett, R. (1986). *The structure and measurement of psychological wellbeing.* Social Science Research Fund Committee, Wellington.

McIntosh, G. (1985). Self-esteem and life satisfaction. Unpublished honours dissertation, Department of Psychology, University of Otago, Dunedin.

Macky, K.A. (1987). Psychological aspects of unemployment: A review of the New Zealand literature. *Community Mental Health in New Zealand, 3,* 2, 18-32.

Maxwell, G.M. & Coebergh, B. (1986). Patterns of loneliness in a New Zealand population. *Community Mental Health in New Zealand, 2,* 2, 48-61.

Maxwell, G.M. & Robertson, J. (1988). Wellbeing, self-esteem and closeness of relationships in separating couples. Paper presented at XXIVth International Congress of Psychology in Sydney.

Raeburn, J. (1986). Mental health promotion in the community: How to do it. *Community Mental Health in New Zealand, 2,* 1, 22-33.

Williams, L.R.T. (1981) New Zealand school pupil's attitudes to physical education. A report to the Department of Education. Wellington.

Social Applications and Issues in Psychology
R.C. King and J.K. Collins (editors)
©Elsevier Science Publishers B.V. (North-Holland), 1989

STUDENT LIFE STRESS IN THE FIRST YEAR OF TERTIARY COLLEGE

Margaret F. Robertson

Royal Melbourne Institute of Technology, Australia, and

Douglas Farnill

Rusden Campus, Victoria College

The paper investigates stressful life events, social support, psychological symptoms and aspects of life style reported by young first-year tertiary students. Respondents were 139 female and 67 male students aged between 18 and 21 years studying at R.M.I.T. and Victoria College during 1987. Instruments were the Tertiary Students Stressful Life Events Scale (Farnill & Robertson, 1988) and the Brief Symptom Inventory (Derogatis & Spencer, 1982). Students also responded to a life style questionnaire on matters such as body weight, dieting, smoking, sleeping patterns, and headaches. Frequency, average stress, and social support levels are reported for 46 potentially stressful events. Some events, experienced as highly stressful, were associated with only low social support. Possible interventions by student services are suggested. Stronger associations (median r = 0.37) were observed between average stress levels and psychological symptoms than between number of stressful events reported and psychological symptoms(median r = 0.15). This finding is related to the literature on subjective and objective indicators of stress. Among the other results reported were that few females recorded satisfaction with their body weight; most wanting to be lighter.Twenty-five per cent of students reported two or more headaches per week.

It is most important that we increase our understanding of the transitional developments and stresses that many students appear to experience in their first year of study. Reports on student attrition from North America (Tinto, 1975) and Australia (Power, Robertson & Beswick, 1986; Williams, 1982; Williams & Pepe, 1983) indicate very high rates, particularly in the first year of study. Power et al. (1986) were able to differentiate between categories of students who either: fail and repeat, fail and withdraw, change course, or pass and continue, in terms of socio-economic, motivational, academic-preparedness, course-commitment, financial and social-support variables. North American literature on adjustment to college (Baker, McNeil and Siryk, 1985) and student lifestyles (Wolf & Kissling, 1984; Wolf, Kissling & Burgess, 1986) suggests the importance of understanding changes in lifestyle and recommend interventions with students experiencing particular difficulties. Wolf and Kissling (1984) reported that over a seven-month period the lifestyle of freshman medical students displayed a decrease in physical activity, sleep, general health, leisure, recreational activities and low maintenance of a balanced diet.

In seeking to advance our understanding of students' experience of stressful events associated with entrance to tertiary education we designed an additive stressful life-events scale. Review of previous work with such scales revealed an extensive life-change stress literature, dating from the pioneering work of Holmes and Rahe (1967) who developed the Social Readjustment Rating Scale. In more recent years, researchers have challenged Holmes and Rahe's basic assumption that it is change *per se* rather than undesired changes that produce stress. Several workers have demonstrated the utility of differentiating positive from negative events (e.g., Johnson & Sarason, 1979). It is also argued that a particular category of event may have a different impact on one person relative to another (e.g., Linn, 1986; Newcomb, Huba & Bentler, 1981). Thus life-event scale developers now favour scoring by idiosyncratic ratings of disruption rather than by totalling events and weighting them by values derived from population means.

Several other issues have received attention. Hurst, Jenkins and Rose (1979) raised the issue of the time intervals covered by a respondent's recall of events, reporting that recall covering more than six months was unreliable. Newcomb, Huba and Bentler (1981) argued that life events should be clustered when scored, reporting in their study that stress was correlated over time only for corresponding types of events. Linn (1986) discussed the difficulties of comparison among studies, but argued the need to tailor the events to be included in a scale for relevance to the particular population under study.

Significant correlations have been consistently found between stressful events and psychological symptoms but, as Compas, Wagner, Slavin and Vannatta (1986) argue, the causal direction of this influence is not always clear because the relationship between events and symptoms is frequently reciprocal. Moreover, the subjective rating of the stressful impact of events may mean that the objective status of the events may be compromised. As Dohrenwend and Shrout (1985) have pointed out, this may result in confounded measurement because events may take on symptom-like quality when they cross the threshold from the mundane non event to the status of stressful event. For one individual, a given quality of family interaction may be viewed as merely a warm debate, but for another it may register as family conflict. Despite these problems, research has demonstrated relationships between stressful life events and academic adjustment, particularly in periods of transition. Periods of transition have received particular attention as times of vulnerability due to the unavailability of usual sources of social support (Felner, Farber & Primavera, 1983). The normative transitions of late adolescence associated with the adjustments to tertiary college life have been identified as giving rise to such vulnerability (Coelho, 1979). A recent prospective longitudinal study which examined life events, perceived social support and psychological symptoms in a group of older adolescents during the transition from high school to college, found that these variables were reciprocally related in patterns that changed over a period of six months (Compas et al., 1986). Specifically, the association of symptoms with prior life events was highest two weeks following college entry. The authors suggest that an 'at risk' group could be identified from the life-events scale before actual psychological distress was experienced. Another longitudinal study measured stressful life events in a group entering university and found significant negative associations between life change and academic performance for the academic grades of first and second year students but not for third year (Lloyd, Alexander, Rice & Greenfield, 1980).

Observations that individuals vary greatly in what they will define as a stressful event and that they report quite wide variations in stress for a given event has led to the search for situational moderators of individual response. Social support has been studied as such a moderator (e.g., Dohrenwend & Dohrenwend, 1978; Linn, 1986) Whether social attachments and supports act as environmental buffers protecting the individual, or whether their presence indexes the individual's coping adequacy is a theoretical point debated by Felner, Farber and Primavera (1983). Sarason, Sarason, Potter and Antoni (1985), in research with a group of naval academy students, found that among subjects with low levels of social support, the relationship between negative life events and illness was significantly stronger than for those enjoying high levels of support. The assessment of social support is also not without its measurement difficulties, but it seems that subject perceptions of support do have significant correspondence with actual interpersonal transactions (Vinokur, Schul & Caplan, 1987).

The developmental tasks and transitions of late adolescence have an extensive literature. Erikson's concept of identity formation as the major task of this life stage (Erikson, 1968) and Blos' construct of individuation or achievement of separateness from parents (Blos, 1962) have been influential. Separation from the family, or leaving home, is an important developmental task of late adolescence and early adulthood that can have strong influences upon adjustment to tertiary studies. Moore (1987) has shown that adolescents who construe physical separation from parents and home as emotional detachment appear to be at a disadvantage compared with those who are able to integrate autonomy with positive family relationships. Recent Australian reports highlight the particular difficulties of our students in transition to university or college. Simmonds (1987) argues that the achievement of separateness from parents is made more difficult by prolongation of financial dependence and extended residence in the parental home that tertiary study commonly entails. Clifton (1987) delineated 'first-year blues' in relation to study motivation among university students, linking the syndrome with the competitive preparation, assessment and selection processes for tertiary entrance that encourage highly-structured and teacher-directed school environments. In such environments, self regulation, intrinsic motivation and independent identity can be casualties in the striving for a tertiary place, resulting in the student being poorly prepared for the transition stresses of tertiary entry.

Against this background we decided to investigate tertiary-transition life events for students at two Melbourne colleges of advanced education, the Royal Melbourne Institute of Technology (RMIT) and Victoria College (VC). We investigated students' experience of stress and social support associated with the events and we examined the relationships between events, stress, and psychological symptoms. We also investigated some aspects of student lifestyle such as sleep, dieting, smoking, and experience of headaches.

METHOD

Subjects

Subjects were 139 female and 67 male students in their first year of tertiary study, aged between 18 and 21 years. One hundred and three of these were RMIT students surveyed in July 1987. A further 22 RMIT students, and 81 VC students were surveyed in mid October. Of the total student group, 125 were enrolled in medical laboratory sciences, engineering, information sciences, and media studies and 81 students were enrolled in psychology as part of education and applied science awards. Some of the students surveyed in July were retested in October and, because the differences were slight, all data reported in this paper are from the students' first exposure to the instruments regardless of the month. Due to some incompleteness of response, resulting in missing data, the effective group size varied between 206 and 196 students. Few sex differences were found and only sex differences relating to bodyweight and body image will be reported in this paper.

Material

(i) *Stressful life events.* The Tertiary Students Stressful Life Events Scale (TSSLES) designed by the authors, consists of 46 life events which we believe to be fairly comprehensive of major life events impinging upon students during the 12 months of their tertiary-transition year. Two thirds of the events would commonly be regarded as negative (e.g., "breaking up with a boyfriend or girlfriend"), with the remainder capable of being experienced as either positive or negative (e.g., "choosing tertiary course preferences"). Students indicate whether they have experienced the event within the past 6 months, 12 months or in both periods and they indicate the amount of stress associated with this event on a scale ranging from 0 for 'no stress at all' to 5 for 'extreme stress'. They are also requested to make a judgement of the amount of support they received from family and friends in dealing with the event from 0 for 'no support' to 5 for 'great support'. Abbreviated description of item content is shown in Table 1.

TABLE 1
Frequencies, means, and standard deviations of stress and support
levels for the 46 items of the TSSLES scale.

Item Content	% frequency	stress mean (s.d.)	support mean (s.d.)
1 Commencing tertiary study	94	2.6 (1.4)	3.2 (1.5)
2 Choosing tertiary course	93	2.4 (1.4)	3.3 (1.6)
3 Final secondary school exams	91	4.0 (1.0)	3.8 (1.4)
4 Leaving secondary school	87	1.5 (1.3)	2.7 (1.8)
5 Tertiary study workload	77	3.5 (1.3)	2.5 (1.6)
6 Tertiary study skills	70	2.7 (1.3)	2.3 (1.6)
7 Losing contact with friends	69	2.6 (1.3)	1.8 (1.6)
8 Failing test or assignment	63	3.5 (1.3)	2.4 (1.7)
9 Argument with parents	59	3.3 (1.4)	2.0 (1.5)
10 Family conflicts	50	3.5 (1.2)	2.1 (1.5)
11 Worry physical appearance	50	3.2 (1.3)	2.3 (1.6)
12 Breakup with boy/girl friend	42	3.6 (1.6)	2.5 (1.7)
13 Making new friends	41	2.6 (1.6)	2.3 (1.7)
14 New boy/girl friend	39	2.4 (1.8)	2.6 (1.8)
15 Finding a job	37	2.6 (1.4)	2.9 (1.7)
16 Not getting tertiary pref.	34	3.0 (1.7)	3.1 (1.8)
17 Worry about sexual matters	31	3.1 (1.6)	2.1 (2.0)
18 Family illness	29	3.7 (1.4)	3.2 (1.8)
19 Wanting a change of course	29	3.0 (1.4)	2.4 (1.9)
20 Buying a car	27	2.2 (1.6)	3.6 (1.6)
21 Moving out from family home	26	3.0 (1.6)	3.6 (1.7)
22 Trouble with lecturer	25	2.2 (1.7)	1.9 (1.9)
23 Rejected in new relationship	23	3.3 (1.6)	1.7 (1.6)
24 Moving to city from country	21	2.8 (1.9)	3.6 (1.8)
25 My serious illness or injury	20	3.5 (1.4)	3.7 (1.6)
26 Going into financial debt	19	2.8 (1.5)	1.8 (1.6)
27 Trouble with Austudy	18	2.8 (1.5)	2.9 (1.7)
28 Earning money for first time	18	2.0 (1.6)	2.7 (1.9)
29 Traffic accident	17	3.8 (1.3)	3.6 (1.3)
30 Hassles with accommodation	16	3.9 (1.1)	3.4 (1.7)
31 Death in the family	15	3.6 (1.8)	3.6 (1.7)
32 Change in religious beliefs	13	2.6 (1.5)	2.6 (1.9)
33 Serious illness of a friend	12	2.9 (1.6)	2.8 (1.7)
34 Death of a friend	12	3.5 (1.6)	2.9 (1.8)
35 Receiving academic warning	12	2.3 (2.0)	1.9 (1.8)
36 Losing a job	11	3.2 (1.7)	2.7 (2.0)
37 Changing my accommodation	10	3.7 (1.3)	3.6 (1.6)
38 Fear of insufficient money	9	3.6 (1.4)	3.3 (1.5)
39 Problems with police	8	3.6 (1.7)	2.2 (2.0)
40 My parents separation/divorce	5	3.3 (2.2)	1.2 (0.9)
41 Mine or partner's abortion	2	2.5 (2.9)	1.7 (2.4)
42 Getting married	2	0.0 (0.0)	1.3 (2.5)
43 Getting divorced or separating	2	1.2 (2.5)	0.8 (1.5)
44 Mine or partner's pregnancy	1	3.3 (2.9)	2.3 (2.5)
45 Mine or partner's childbirth	1	0.0 (0.0)	5.0 (0.0)
46 My parents' remarriage	1	0.0 (0.0)	0.0 (0.0)

(ii) *Psychological Symptoms.* The Brief Symptoms Inventory (BSI) of Derogatis and Spencer (1982) is a 53-item self report and was chosen because of the range of symptoms it assesses and its suitability for non-clinical populations. Respondents are asked to rate on a scale of 0 to 4 their experience of a symptom during the last seven days. The reliability and validity of the BSI scales have been well documented with North American populations. Australian norms and reliabilities are beginning to be established (Farnill & Robertson, 1988). The BSI provides 9 symptom dimensions and 3 global indices of distress.

(iii) *Student lifestyle.* Students completed a Student Lifestyle Inventory (LSI) which inquired about a wide range of issues including source of financial support, family details, accommodation, height, weight, eating habits, dieting, drinking, sleep, cigarette smoking, headaches, health and study habits. The data are too numerous to report fully here. We shall comment briefly upon weight and dieting, smoking, sleep and headaches.

RESULTS AND DISCUSSION

The mean stress and support levels for the items of the TSSLES are reported in Table 1. The items are listed from the most frequently experienced event during the previous 12 months down to the least frequent event.

It may be seen that 11 of the 46 items were reported by 50% or more of the students and 40 items were reported by 5% or more of the students, indicating that the TSSLES has succeeded in its relevance to this specific group. The standard deviations of stress reflect wide variability in the extent of stress associated with these life events. This wide inter-subject variability is also reflected in the fact that on 43 of the 46 items the widest extremes of rating from 'no stress' to 'maximum stress' were employed by students. This variability supports the decision to assess the subjective impact of stressful events rather than to rely upon the occurrence or not of the event. Events associated with the highest averages of stress were: final secondary school exams, hassles with accommodation, traffic accident, family illness, changing accommodation, breaking up with boy/girl friend, death in the family, fear of insufficient money to complete the course and problems with police. All of these variables achieved a mean rating of 3.6 or above on the stress scale. The mean number of stressful events reported by the total group was 14.3 (s.d.= 5.7) and the average stress for reported items was 2.9 (s.d.= 0.8).

Support levels also showed wide differences in level from item to item and, as indicated by the standard deviations, wide inter-subject variability. Items for which high support was reported were childbirth, final secondary school examinations, buying a car, moving from the family home, moving from the city to the country, traffic accident, death in the family, own serious illness or injury and changing accommodation. Low social support items included getting divorced or separated, parents' separation or divorce, rejection in new relationship, going into financial debt and losing contact with old friends. It is noted that the summary statistics for items of low frequency are probably not stable because they rest upon only a few cases.

It may be seen from Table 1 that some high-stress items are items for which high social support is also reported (final secondary exams, hassles with accommodation, traffic accident, death in the family, serious illness or injury, fear of insufficient money, changing accommodation). Peers and families are apparently mobilized to respond in the face of these events. Three items for which only relatively low stress levels are reported (buying a car, choosing tertiary course, own or partner's childbirth) are accompanied by high levels of social support . It is not clear whether the lower stress levels of these items are intrinsic to the event or are due in part to the ameliorative effects of high support. Other items attract ratings of moderate to high levels of stress conjointly with low levels of support. These include some reasonably frequent events (arguments with parents, losing contact with old friends and going into debt). High stress associated with low support is also reported for some less common events (serious illness of a friend, and parents' separation or divorce). Though infrequent, these events are no doubt very important to the individuals concerned. The appearance of high stress associated with low levels of support appears to invite interventions by student services, either to provide support or to engage in educational activities which increase the likelihood of support being mobilized during these events. Student Services at our two institutions do provide accommodation and financial aid services, but given the high stress levels reported we need to review the adequacy of our provision. Programmes on such topics as handling conflicts with parents, negotiating intimate and other relationships, dealing with death, particularly of age peers whose deaths are most likely to be accidental or suicidal, seem indicated. We are, of course, familiar with these problems through individual counselling with students, but the frequency of occurrence and the high associated stress levels suggest that there is a wider need that perhaps group programmes could address.

Table 2 shows the correlations between psychological symptoms as assessed by the B.S.I. and the total number of stressful events. Average stress levels are reported.

The 9 symptom scales of the BSI are named to correspond with the general constructs established in clinical psychiatry and psychology. The Global Index Scale is the total sum of item endorsements divided by the total number of items. The Positive Symptom Distress Index is the total sum of item endorsements divided by the number of items endorsed above a zero level. The Positive Stress Total is the total sum of item endorsements. There were no significant sex differences for any of the scales or indices. It may be seen that all correlations were positive as predicted and that most were statistically significant. It is interesting that consistently higher associations were obtained between the BSI scales and average stress than between the BSI and total events experienced. It appears that subjective judgements about the stressful impact of past events are more strongly associated with current psychological symptoms than with a simple totality of events. We acknowledge, of course, the issues of confounded measurement to which we previously referred and the expected strengthening of association where similar rating-scale methods have been used.

TABLE 2

Correlations between stressful events, average stress and BSI symptoms and indices for students at the end of their tertiary transition year.

	Total Events	Average Stress
Brief Symptom Inventory Scales:		
Somatization	.16 *	.40 ***
Obsessive-Compulsive	.22 ***	.36 ***
Interpersonal Sensitivity	.20 **	.40 ***
Depression	.12	.37 ***
Anxiety	.12 *	.39 ***
Hostility	.12 *	.31 ***
Phobic Anxiety	.15 *	.35 ***
Paranoid Ideation	.20 **	.30***
Psychoticism.	.12 *	.28 ***
BSI Global Indices:		
Global Severity Index	.19 **	.47 ***
Positive Symptom Distress Index	10	.37 ***
Positive Symptom Total	.24 **	.41 ***

Note: The number of subjects for whom data were complete was between
      196 and 206
* = p < .05,   ** = p < .01,   *** = p < .001   (one-tailed tests)

Consideration will now move to some of the results from the LSI. Students were asked to report their weight and height by reference to the height and weight chart of the Australian Nutrition Foundation. We coded each student as very underweight, underweight, healthy weight, overweight or very overweight. Results were very different for the sexes. For females, 28% were underweight or very underweight, 62% were healthy weight and 10% were overweight or very overweight. For males, 14 % were underweight or very underweight, 71% were healthy weight and 15% were overweight or very overweight. Students were also asked to state whether they would like to change their weight by up to 3 kg or over3 kg. Of the underweight or very underweight females, only 8% wanted to be heavier, 40% thought that they were about right and 51% wanted to be even lighter. Few females of healthy weight appeared to be satisfied, 89% wanting to be lighter and a majority of these wanting to be more than 3 kg lighter. All the overweight or very overweight females wanted to be lighter.

The males appeared in general to be much more satisfied with their body weight. Of the underweight males, 78% wanted to be heavier and 11% thought they were about right. Only 11% thought that they would like to be even lighter. Of the males at healthy weight, 42% were satisfied, 38% wanted to be heavier and 20% wanted to be lighter. Of the overweight males 67% wanted to be lighter, with the remainder evenly divided between being satisfied and wanting to be heavier.

It is clear that the body image of our females and the criteria of the Australian Nutrition Foundation are very out of kilter. In our total sample, 13% reported that they frequently or constantly diet to lose weight, with an additional 31% reporting that they occasionally diet. We do not have a breakdown of dieting by sex and weight category to report at this stage, but we observed instances where very underweight females described themselves as frequently dieting.

Other results from the LSI show a high incidence of headaches; 25% of respondents reporting a frequency of 2 or more headaches per week, 8% reporting a frequency of more than 4 headaches per week and 37% of the total group experiencing a headache within the last week. Ten percent of our subjects reported that they were currently experiencing a headache.

This report has raised issues regarding students' wellbeing and transition to college that warrant attention from student services and others concerned with students' successful adjustment to tertiary study.

CORRESPONDENCE

Student Services, Royal Melbourne Institute of Technology, LaTrobe Street, Melbourne, Victoria, Australia.

REFERENCES

Baker, R.W., McNeil, O.V. & Siryk, B. (1985). Expectations and reality in freshman adjustment to college. *Journal of Counseling Psychology, 32,* 94-103.

Blos, P. (1962). *On adolescence: a psychoanalytic interpretation.* New York: Free Press.

Clifton, L. (1987). Difficulties experienced in transition to University. *The Australian Counselling Psychologist, 3,* 74-81.

Coelho, G.V. (1979). Environmental stress and adolescent coping behavior:Key ecological factors in college student adaptation. In I.G. Sarason & C.D. Spielberger (Eds). *Stress and Anxiety* (vol 7) Washington, DC: Hemisphere Press.

Compas, B.E., Wagner, B.M., Slavin, L.A. & Vannatta, K. (1986). A prospective study of life events, social support, and psychological symptomatology during the transition from high school to college. *American Journal of Community Psychology, 14,* 241-257.

Derogatis, L.R. & Spencer, P.M. (1982). *The brief symptom inventory (BSI) Administration, Scoring & Procedures Manual.* John Hopkins University School of Medicine: U.S.A.

Dohrenwend,B.P. & Shrout, P.E. (1985). "Hassles" in the conceptualization and measurement of life stress variables. *American Psychologist, 40,*780-785.

Erikson, E.H. (1968). *Identity: youth and crisis.* New York: Norton.

Farnill, D. & Robertson, M.F. (1988) The Brief Symptom Inventory performance of young Australian tertiary students. Paper presented at the *XXIV International Congress of Psychology,* Sydney, Australia.

Felner, R.D., Farber, S. & Primavera, J. (1983). Transitions and stressful life events: A model for primary prevention. In R.D. Felner, L.A. Jason, J.N. Moritsugu & S.S. Farber (Eds.). *Preventive psychology: theory, research and practice* (199-215). New York: Pergamon.

Holmes, T.H. & Rahe, R.H. (1967). The social readjustment rating scale. *Journal of Psychosomatic Research, 11,* 213-218.

Johnson, J.H. & Sarason, I.G. (1979). Recent developments in research on life stress. In V. Hamilton & D.M. Warburton (Eds). *Human stress and cognition: an information processing approach.* London: Wiley.

Linn, M.W. (1986). Modifiers and perceived stress scale. *Journal of Consulting and Clinical Psychology, 54,* 507-513.

Lloyd, C., Alexander, A.A., Rice, D.G. & Greenfield, N.S. (1980). Life events as predictors of academic performance. *Journal of Human Stress, 6,* 15-25.

Moore, D. (1987). Parent-adolescent separation: the construction of adulthood by late adolescents. *Developmental Psychology, 23,* 298-307.

Newcomb, M.D., Huba, G.J. & Bentler, P.M. (1981). A multidimensional assessment of stressful life events among adolescents: derivation and correlates. *Journal of Health and Social Behavior, 22,* 400-415.

Power, C., Robertson, F. & Beswick, G. (1986). *Student withdrawal and attrition from higher education.* Working Paper Series No. 89. National Institute of Labour Studies Incorporated.

Sarason, I.G., Sarason, B.R., Potter, E.H. & Antoni, M.H. (1985). Life events, social support, and illness. *Psychosomatic Medicine, 47,* 156-163.

Simmonds, J. (1987). Psycholgical and developmental tasks of the tertiary adolescent: Theoretical background. *The Australian Counselling Psychologist, 3,* 66-73.

Tinto, V. (1975). Dropouts from higher education: A theoretical synthesis of recent research. *Review of Educational Research, 45,* 89-125.

Vinokur, A., Schul, Y. & Caplan, R.D. (1987) Determinants of perceived social support: Interpersonal transactions, personal outlook, and transient affective states. *Journal of Personality and Social Psychology, 53,* 1137-1145.

Williams, C. (1982). *The early experiences of students on Australian University Campuses.* Sydney: University of Sydney.

Williams, C. & Pepe, T. (1983). *The early experiences of students on Australian Colleges of Advanced Education Campuses.* Sydney: University of Sydney.

Wolf, T.M. & Kissling, G.E. (1984). Changes in life-style characteristics, health, and mood of freshman medical students. *Journal of Medical Education, 59,* 806-813.

Wolf, T.M., Kissling, G.E. & Burgess, L.A. (1987). Hassles and uplifts during the freshman year of medical school. *Psychological Reports, 60,* 85-86.

Social Applications and Issues in Psychology
R.C. King and J.K. Collins (editors)
©Elsevier Science Publishers B.V. (North-Holland), 1989

DEVELOPMENTS IN FRENCH PSYCHOLOGICAL RESEARCH IN POLAR ENVIRONMENTS

Jean Rivolier

University of Reims, France

Participation at the International Biomedical Expedition to the Antarctic (1981) in association with other disciplines to study stress in a group during a traverse is reported. Analysis of data collected during the winterings of the four French bases between 1983 and 1986 was concerned with the differential study of 3 tests of selection, the MIPG and the validity of RLCQ. All were correlated with the adaptation of the subjects. Cognitive and psychophysiological styles and coping processes of· people in polar stress .conditions (traverses and winterings) are discussed. It is suggested that our polar methodology may be applied to extended space flights.

French polar research has a long history (Rivolier, 1973, Rivolier et al., 1983) where human factors are concerned, particularly in relation to medicine, physiology and psychology. Two options have long been at the forefront of this research, i.e., the selection (Cazes et al., 1984; Rivolier, 1975) and the control of small isolated groups under unfamiliar and hostile conditions (Rivolier, 1975; Rivolier et al., 1982; Rivolier & Cazes, 1987b). At the same time, the topic of psychopathology has not been ignored (Bouvel, 1986; Rivolier, 1979).

In the beginning, the psychological studies resulted from a "need" in the field. Those currently in progress are less concerned with application to life in the Antarctic and more with specifics such as the identification of mental mechanisms, pathogeny of psychomatic states and specialised groupings of personnel for exceptional civil or military situations. In effect the Antarctic is a unique physical and social context for studies with international relevance. French polar research in psychology has become both psychobiological and psychosociological.

THE INTERNATIONAL BIOMEDICAL EXPEDITION TO THE ANTARCTIC (IBEA) IN 1980-1981

The IBEA in 1980-1981 (Rivolier et al., 1988) was a key element in recent French Antarctic research. As president of the human biology and medical group of SCAR (Scientific Committee on Antarctic Research), it was my responsibility to organise the research expedition and to involve the French in a strong scientific and logistic participation. It involved a study of twelve men (Argentineans,

Australians, English, French and New Zealanders). They were both researchers and subjects during an adjustment spell on the Antarctic plateau under predetermined stressful conditions. Base-line research was carried out in the laboratory of the Commonwealth Institute of Health in Sydney, before and after the polar stay. It necessitated physiological, psychophysiological, biological, biometeorological and psychological studies.

The French psychological group was closely associated with the New Zealand team directed by Professor Taylor. The research methods were those established in the past as appropriate for individuals and small groups and were developed as appropriate for the analysis of social, biological and psychophysiological data. This led to the adoption and study of the "holistic" concept of stress.

CURRENT STUDIES IN PROCESS

During the past five years the French have systematically collected data before the wintering-over departure and also in the field. At present, specific studies are being carried out on adaptative predictors from the results of selection tests. The purpose is to study their prognostic validity and to improve the selection procedures for candidates for polar wintering-over. The predictors include classical tools such as Cattell's 16 Personality Factor Test and the Rorschach psychodiagnostic test. They also include a new personality inventory devised by Bremond (1981) and essentially validated in the French Army Air Force. It consists of 101 questions for detecting potential difficulties in adaptation that are thought to arise from certain personality "tendencies". It requires self rating on four or five point scales, from the scoring of which readings can be obtained on ten factors. Nine of these factors are: activation capacity, depressive tendency, psychosomatisation, mental obscurity, antisocial aggression, sensitivity and susceptibility, tendency to isolation and introspection, emotional instability and histrionic personality. These ratings are supplemented with a scale that reflects the capacity for self evaluation.

Another inventory is given by observers at the end of the wintering-over stay (Rivolier et al., 1987a). It evaluates the adaptation of the subjects in terms of four variables: mental (mood, tonus, diverse psychological manifestations), social (relations with others and those in charge), physical (somatic manifestations, fatigue, sleeping problems, appetite problems), and functional or occupational (individual work, participation in collective work and housework).

The material collected between 1983 and 1986 comprises a total of 1020 files, half of which were from wintering-over subjects, and half from control subjects. Subjects will be differentiated into their respective subgroups (civil, military, technical and scientific) and then compared before appropriate publications are completed.

Another study in progress concerns the validity of Abraham's (1973) "Matrix on Intra- and Inter-Individual Processes in Groups" (MIPG). Experience suggests that the kind and quality of such interpersonal relations can be of crucial importance to small groups in unfamiliar and hostile conditions. Such was the case with one study of wintering-over personnel in Kerguelen Island (Bouvel, 1982; Bouvel et al., 1986) and with another of the summer participants on the IBEA. Briefly, the MIPG presents a series of behaviours and perceptions, of which eight related to the leader of the group. It requires subjects to rate themselves as they were, how they would like to be (ideal self), and how they think others see them (attributed self).

Another study has been concerned with the impact of life events on the adaptation of subjects living in isolated groups under long-term stressful conditions. Correlation between life events and illness behaviour was estabished by Holmes and Rahe (1967) and Rahe (1974). After some preliminary and inconclusive studies the French have carried out a study of the correlation between life changes that occurred at six monthly intervals over the two years preceding the Antarctic wintering-over, and the 55 item Recent Life Change Questionnaire (RLCQ) of Rahe (1968). Subjects were required to rank and scale those events according to perception of their importance.

Manifestations of maladaptability during the stay were taken from test data previously described, from the number of medical consultations made and from an overall evaluation of the stay. However, initial study of the data from 500 subjects has not shown significant correlations between the different events and any functional and psychosomatic manifestations. Currently, multi-variate analysis is in progress, and its results will be published in due course.

NEW APPROACHES

A fresh conceptual and methodological approach was made to explore cognitive, biological and psychophysiological components of Antarctic adaptation. It was based on two observations: Firstly, subjects under conditions of chronic difficulty respond either by regarding it as a challenge for them to overcome or as a situation that inevitably will defeat them. The former comprised competent subjects in the exceptional situations indicated, and the latter the pathological, psychosomatic group with symptoms of anxiety and depression (Rivolier, 1987). Secondly, subjects when stressed provide responses that are not only emotional and behavioural but also cognitive and biological (Ader, 1981; Bouvel, 1986; Cazes et al., 1984; Dantzer, 1984; Goetzl, 1985; Karli, 1987; Rivolier, 1989; Rivolier et al., 1988; Ursin et al., 1978; Vaernes et al., 1982; Vincent, 1986). Consequently plans were made to use the following neurological, psychophysiological and psychological procedures in future research:

(i) Cognition and psychophysiology.

Cognitive styles were coupled with classical measures for biofeedback (the most interesting of which appear to be those of skin conductance and muscular tension), in relation to dependence-independence using the embedded figures test; a spatial perception test of folded papers; a test of cognitive flexibility and the word-colour test for cognitive styles; the Bremond and Fourcade decision and risk taking questionnaire TD 9 (Bremond, 1981); an interpersonal distance measure (II) (Gilmour and Walkey, 1981); the Kagan matching familiar figure test; a flexibility/constraints measure; the D48 test of logical reasoning; the Helson reference level test; a study of vigilance; tests of simple attention, sustained attention and disturbed attention; a test of immediate memory and of numbers; and a study of neuromuscular responses.

(ii) Biological measures

Hormone doses. The elimination of catecholamines during the course of different tests is taken as an indicator of synchronic psychobiological responses of personality. Most often the level of these products is related to the level of different hormones that are common in studies of stress, such as cortisol, ACTH, growth hormone, prolactin, testosterone and insulin.

Immunity measures. Immunity depression in conditions of long term stress is determined by the levels of immunoglobulins (IgA, IgM, IgG), of special lymphocytes, of specific antigens and post vaccinations (in particular relating to vaccination for small pox and protein inflammation).

The French have used the same type of psychological research with mountain sports, expeditions in mountainous areas and with special military groups. For example it was used with the study "Des femmes pour un Pôle". In that study six women departed from Spitzbergen hauling their own sledges. On the way they carried out a series of glaciologic, oceanographic, physiologic and psychologic studies. The subjects were studied before, during and after the trip in terms of the procedures outlined above.

The same procedure was also used in the "IAGO" study on 22 men whose mission for two months was to study the catabatic winds on the Antarctic plateau. However, the main focus of French researchers was still with subjects wintering-over in four French stations in the southern islands and Adelie Land. It was a three year program of cognitive and psychophysiological examinations. Four hundred and fifty subjects provided interview and test data. A small group wintering-over in 1987-88 at Dumont d'Urville provided hormonal and immunological indicators. Again the data are of interest because they provide information for a chronobiological study. The results that currently are being scrutinised should be most instructive.

Finally, mention should be made of Project (Outer) Space Simulation (Rivolier, 1987a) that is still in a preliminary form. The French polar researchers were involved at the request of the ESA (European Space Agency). In the context of long term programs and of the study of human factors, they proposed different perspectives of space simulations in either the Arctic and/or the Antarctic. The project is in two phases. The first phase consists of the selection and the psychological preparation of a team for future long term sojourns in space (space station, lunar bases, voyage to Mars). It involves personnel of different nationality, sex, race, professions and ages. The second phase involves a full scale study at an isolated polar site, where living and activity conditions (with obvious exceptions of the weightlessness) would most simulate those of real space projects. There the manner of problem solving and adaptation would be studied, and the outcome should provide a guideline for the selection and preparation of individuals and groups for the space project proper. If the preliminary interest shown by NASA should flourish, and if the space-simulation project should take place in the Antarctic, it is conceivable the Working Group of Biology, Human and Medicine of SCAR would be able to coordinate the research.

CORRESPONDENCE

Jean Rivolier, professor, Laboratory of Applied Psychology, University of Reims, and Health Department of the French Polar Expeditions (EPF) and French Austral and Antarctic Territories (TAAF).

REFERENCES

Abraham, A. (1973). A model for exploring intra-and inter-individual processes in groups. *International Journal of Group Psychotherapy, 23* (1), 3-22.

Ader, R.E. (1981). *Psychoneuroimmunology.* New York : Academic Press.

Bouvel, B. (1982). Etude de validation du MIPG test sur un hivernage aux iles Kerguelen. Thèse de Médecine, Université de Reims.

Bouvel, B. (1986). A propos de quelques cas de pathologie mentale en hivernage polaire austral. Mémoire pour l'obtention du CES de psychiatrie, Université de Reims.

Bouvel, B. et al. (1986). Contrôle d'un groupe en hivernage à l'aide du MIPG. *XXIth International Congress of Applied Psychology,* Jérusalem, 13-18 july (in press).

Bremond, J. (1981). Sélection psychologique du personnel navigant. Un nouvel inventaire de personnalité, l'IP9. *Médecine et Armée,* 9, 889-896.

Cazes, G., and others (1984). Etudes des antécédents biographiques des sujets hivernant dans l'Antarctique. Application à la sélection. *Revue de Psychologie Appliquée, 34* (4), 291-304.

Dantzer, R. (1984). Psychobiologie des émotions. In J. Delacour, (Ed.). 110-143. *Neurobiologie des comportements.* Paris: Hermann.

Gilmour, D.A., & Walkey, F.H. (1981). Identifying violent offenders using a video measure of interpersonal distance. *Journal of Consulting and Clinical Psychology, 49* (2), 287-291.

Goetzl, E.J. (1985). Proceedings of a conference on neuromodulation of immunity and hypersensitivity. Florida, Coconut Grove, 12-14, November 1984. *Supplement to the Journal of Immunology*, 135.

Holmes, T.H., & Rahe, R.H. (1967). The social readjustment rating scale. *Journal of psychosomatic Research*, 11, 213-218.

Karli, P. (1987). *L'homme agressif.* Paris : Odile Jacob.

Rahe, R.H. (1968). Life change measurement as a predictor of illness. *Proceedings of the Royal Society of Medicine*, 61, 1124-1126.

Rahe, R.H. (1974). The pathway between subjects recent life change and their near future illness reports. Representative results and methodological issues. In B.S. Dohrenwend, & B.P. Dohrenwend (Eds). 73-86. *Stressful life events : their nature and effects.* New York: John Wiley.

Rivolier, J. (1973). Review of medical research performed in the French Antarctic territories. In O. Edholm & E.K.E. Gunderson (Eds).48-53. *Polar human biology.* London: Heinemann.

Rivolier, J. (1975). Sélection et adaptation psychologiques de sujets vivant en groupes isolés en hivernage dans l'Antarctique. *Pub. CNFRA*, 34.

Rivolier, J. (1979). Groupes isolés en environnements inhabituels et hostiles. Aspect psychoécologique. Thèse de Lettres et Sciences Humaines, Université Paris V - Sorbonne.

Rivolier, J. (1987a). A preliminary proposal for an international wintering in the Antarctic to study long term stress in group as a model of simulation to be applied to space. *Conference the human experience in Antarctica : Application to life in space.* California, Sunnyvale, 17-19 August, 1987 (in press)

Rivolier, J. (1987b). Stress en rapport avec l'environnement physique et social. *Colloque Space and Sea, Marseille,* 24-27 November 1987. *Pub ESA SP280,* 41-46.

Rivoier, J. (1989). *L'homme stressé.* Paris, PUF.

Rivolier, J., et al. (1982). Etude psychosociologique d'une expérimentation sur les effets physiologiques du froid. In R.W. Radomski et al. (Eds). 1-63. Aspects physiologiques, psychophysiologiques et ergonomiques de l'exposition de l'homme au froid hivernal arctique (Kool Stool II).Toronto. *Public Defense and Civil Institute of Environmental Medicine.*

Rivolier, J. et al. (1983). Summary of the French research in medicine and psychology conducted with Expeditions Polaires Françaises and Terres Australes et Antarctiques Françaises. Pub. TAAF ; complimentary references, 1984-1987.

Rivoier, J. et al. (1987a). Méthodologie d'étude d'un groupe en situation d'isolement et de stress. Applications possibles. *Colloque de médecine militaire, Val de Grâce,* 28-29 october.

Rivolier, J., & Cazes, G. (1987b). Sélection et préparation psychologique des sujets ayant à vivre et travailler en environnements inhabituels et hostiles. Colloque Space and Sea, Marseille, 24-27 November, 1987. *Pub. ESA SP 280,* 87-90.

Rivolier, J. et al. (Eds). (1988). *Man in the Antarctic.* London: Taylor and Francis.

Ursin, H., et al. (1978). *Psychobiology of stress. A study of coping men.* New York: Academic Press.

Vaernes, R.J. et al. (1982). Endocrine responses patterns and psychological correlates. *Journal of Psychosomatic Research,* 26(2), 123-131.

Vincent, J.D. (1986). *Biologie des passions.* Paris : Odile Jacob.

AUTHOR INDEX

COMMITTEES OF THE XXIV INTERNATIONAL CONGRESS OF PSYCHOLOGY

MANAGEMENT AND CONGRESS COMMITTEE

P. W. Sheehan, President
R. C. King, Chair
J. K. Collins, Director
H. P. Pfister, Secretary-General
B. J. Fallon, Treasurer
S. H. Lovibond, Director, Scientific Program
A. F. Bennett, Deputy Director, Scientific Program
K. M. McConkey, Secretary, Scientific Program
D. J. Kavanagh, Information Services
J. A. Antill, APS Treasurer
R. A. Cummins, APS Executive Officer
M. C. Knowles
L. Mann, APS President
D. McNicol, APS Vice-President
R. W. Russell, IUPsyS Liaison
G. V. Stanley, APS President-Elect
R. Taft
C. Williams

PREVIOUS MEMBERS:

J. A. Boughton; D. G. Cross; P. M. Lahy; D. M. Keats; D. Kiellerup; M. Macmillan; F. D. Naylor; P. G. Power; J. P. Young; I. K. Waterhouse

SCIENTIFIC PROGRAM COMMITTEE

S. H. Lovibond, Director,   A. F. Bennett, Deputy Director

Conveners:
N. W. Bond, Timetable
D. G. Cross, Young Psychologists' Program
J. A. Keats, Symposia
R H. Markham, Handbooks
P. W. Sheehan, Keynote/Invited Speakers
D. A. T. Siddle, Individual Papers
R. Taft, Satellite Program
D. Vickers, Publications
C. Williams, Workshops

APS Division of Professional Affairs Representatives:
R. Bradbury-Little;   D. P. Brunt

INTERNATIONAL UNION OF PSYCHOLOGICAL SCIENCE

Executive Committee 1984-1988

President   W. Holtzman (U.S.A.)
Vice Presidents   R. Diaz-Guerrero (Mexico)
                       B. Lomov (U.S.S.R.)
Secretary-General   K. Pawlik (F.R.G.)
Treasurer   D. Belanger (Canada)

H. Azuma (Japan)   F. Klix (G.D.R.)
G. de Montmollin (France)   M. Rozenzweig (U.S.A.)
M. O. A. Durojaiye (Nigeria) D. Sinha (India)
G. d'Ydewalle (Belgium)   R. Taft (Australia)
Q. Jing (China)   M. Takala (Finland)

Executive Committee (1988-1992)

President   M. Rosenzweig (U.S.A.)
Past President   W. Holtzman (U.S.A.)
Vice Presidents   H. Azuma (Japan)
                             M. Takala (Finland)
Secretary-General   K. Pawlik (F.R.G.)
Deputy Secretary-General   G. d'Ydewalle (Belgium)
Treasurer   D. Belanger (Canada)

R. Diaz-Guerrero (Mexico)   F. Klix (G.D.R.)
R. Gelman (U.S.A.   B. Lomov (U.S.S.R.)
T. Hogan (Canada)   L. Nilsson (Sweden)
Q. Jing (China)   P. Sheehan (Australia)
C. Kagitcibasi (Turkey)   D. Sinha (India)